THE BROKEN BIBLE

THE BROKEN BIBLE

PICKING UP THE EXTRATERRESTRIAL PIECES

Part I
The Old Testament

John E. Chitty

Writers Club Press
New York Lincoln Shanghai

THE BROKEN BIBLE
PICKING UP THE EXTRATERRESTRIAL PIECES

Writers Club Press
an imprint of iUniverse, Inc.

For information address:
iUniverse, Inc.
2021 Pine Lake Road, Suite 100
Lincoln, NE 68512
www.iuniverse.com

Previously published as
The Time of Our Visitation

(Front Cover Background Photo) "Trifid Nebula" Courtesy of NASA/Caltech/j. Rho et al. (Planet Earth Photo) Courtesy of NASA Apollo 17 mission. (Back Cover Background Photo) "Horsehead Nebula" Courtesy of "NASA, ESA, NOAO and the Hubble Heritage Team (STScI/AURA Acknowledgment: K. Noll (Hubble Heritage PI/STSeI), C.Luginbuhl (USNO), F. Hamilton (Hubble Heritage/STScI)".

ISBN: 0-595-22210-2

Printed in the United States of America

Contents

Numbers

Kings & Chronicles

Ezekiel

Isaiah & Jeremiah

Acknowledgements

My deepest thanks to Thomas R. Goldsworthy for his artistic talent in captivating the many collective drawings in this book. But above all, to my loving wife Elena for her years of enduring patience and understanding.

Foreword

As a youth, I became deeply involved in the controversy of UFOs and the probability that alien life existed on other worlds within our Universe. This extensive quest ultimately forced me into the related study of archeology.

The combined research into UFOs and archeology ultimately inspirited me to venture back into humankind's history as far as possible. This probe was essential if I was to find answers to the perplexing association between mankind's bygone chronicles and UFOs. Stepping back in time, it became unmistakable that mankind's true genesis and the mysterious UFO phenomena were profoundly shrouded within the Bible and all related scripture.

It is not my intention to dismantle, debase, or discredit the Bible, but rather to establish the probability that the Bible and its various scriptural derivatives may actually be ancient chronicles intentionally left behind by our founders (extraterrestrials) in a dedicated effort to assist mankind in comprehending its true origin, and ultimately reach the stars.

What you are about to examine is a serious detailed analysis of many historical texts from the Bible and other scriptures depicting physical entities utilizing flying machines and devices of extraterrestrial origin. Applying scripture, this book will expose the probability that these astonishing devices were used to create this world, as well as give birth to humanity.

This detailed chronicle will demand that you maintain an open mind as we analyze all the scriptural evidence. The data will ultimately reveal extraterrestrial entities who intentionally left behind scriptures detailing what is expected of mankind. Moreover, the data will disclose a physical **return** by these celestial entities that will scrutinizes those that have not complied with the documented demands.

Genesis

In realizing we are not alone in the Universe, I accepted the probability that numerous constellations were teeming with humanoid life. More importantly, as I will demonstrate from the written record, I discovered a chain of command governing at least twelve of these inhabited constellations.

This cosmic leader, or superior being is characteristically distinguished as Yahweh. (Elohim, YHVH, Yahveh, El, Adonai). Moreover, this extraordinary physical entity maintains authority over numerous inhabited worlds, as well as diverse craft, devices, machines, weapons and instruments of destruction at his command.

This phenomenal technology actually assisted me in resolving many of the believed miracles found within Scripture, including "**the Creation**" thesis. Over considerable time, my research ultimately revealed that the scriptural creation premise did not consist of the palpable construction of this Universe or its planetary constellations. Nor did the scriptural chronicles of the creation entail the construction of a single planet, including "Earth".

UFO Connection

Through my UFO research it became clear that if the reader was to comprehend the extraterrestrial implications of scripture and its creation thesis, I had no other choice but to disclose an astonishing device shrouded within the UFO enigma. Probing the nature of UFOs, I discovered that the occupants of these mysterious craft have been consistently using an extraordinary technological device. The application of this device has been witnessed time and time again in numerous UFO encounters, as well as exploited upon many individuals abducted by UFOs. Yet, more significantly, this miraculous device may in fact be the fundamental clue in resolving the creation theory found in Genesis.

Remarkably, these elusive entities have technologically mastered the physical manipulation of solid matter. Essentially, it would appear that these visitant beings have designed and fabricated a device fully capable of maneuvering solid objects from great distances without actual contact with the object.

The use of this unique device has been reported in numerous UFO abduction cases where individuals were bodily elevated by UFOs utilizing levitating beams of energy. Even the occupants of these prodigious craft have been observed as they were bodily elevated or lowered from a hovering craft with no strings attached.

Unmistakably, these are not isolated incidents, seeing how these matter maneuvering exploits have been reported numerous times. Here is a small selection of reports. Even if any one of these were considered to be questionable, they reinforce each other through the consistency of the reported events.

* * *

November 17, 1967 Alberta, Canada—A thirteen-year-old boy walking home from a friend's house encountered a silvery-grayish glowing object as big as a house. As the frightened boy began to run, he was bodily seized and elevated into the craft by an orange shaft/beam of light emanating from its lower mid-section. The boy was given a physical examination and lowered back down to the ground via the same beam. Published in, UFO Report April 1976

November 10, 1969 Quincy, ll.—An X-ray technician, along with his wife and son, were driving on State Highway 96 about 13 miles south of Quincy. Suddenly a red glowing object moved directly over their car. It raised the vehicle about a foot up off the paved highway. Published in, Sky Look, January 1970, May 1971/UFO Report March 1977

September 2 **1971** Tombos, Rio de Janeiro, Brazil—A man stopped his car to observe a UFO as it established a stationary position in front of him. Suddenly two bright beams of light shot from the craft, striking the car and forcing the door of the vehicle open. The two light beams began roaming the side of the car and focused on the driver's seat were they began pushing the man, forcing him from the car.

In desperation the terrified man grabbed the steering wheel, only to find that the beams of light began dragging him out of the car by his legs. Clawing at the ground, grabbing rocks and bushes, the man was extracted from the car and bodily floated into the awaiting craft where he was confronted by three gray beings in "jump suits". The last thing he remembered was the whine of a turbine as he opened his eyes and saw his car a few feet away. Published in Official UFO, Collector's Edition 1976

October 17 **1973**—A man reported that while driving his pickup truck, he exited the Loxley, Alabama, off ramp on interstate 10, where he was suddenly confronted by a huge UFO hovering directly over his truck. The massive object unexpectedly projected a beam of light down onto the truck, at which point the vehicle began rising up off of the paved road and was elevated into the craft where the driver was met by six strange-looking creatures.

The terrified witness remained in the craft for approximately thirty minutes while he was studied by the occupants. The Florida electrician and his truck were released unharmed on State Road 297, 50 miles east of Pensacola, 85 miles from where the bizarre abduction began. Published in, UFO Report, March 1977

February 25, 1999 Washington State—Three forestry workers planting seedling trees in the mountains witnessed a small, disc-shaped object traveling south as it entered into a valley to their north. The disc-shaped UFO appeared to wobble as it descended towards a herd of elk that the forest workers had been watching all morning.

Suddenly the Craft quickly positioned itself over one of the separated adult animals. The lone elk was lifted up off the ground by the disc-shaped craft. Although no visible method of support was observed, the forest workers claim the object began elevating the elk up to the disc-shaped object while ascending and accelerating up a clear-cut slope to the east.

The craft wobbled as it brushed tree tops and executed a 360-degree turn. It quickly ascended at a steep angle and disappeared from sight. Courtesy of National UFO Reporting Center (NUFORC) Peter B. Davenport, Director.

August 6 2002 Northumberland Pennsylvania—A Farmer reported a round object hovering near power lines on top of Montour Ridge. The object was observed moving a few hundred feet east, where it stopped and projected a beam of blue and white light to the ground.

The farmer claimed he saw a man suspended within the beam of light being pulled up head first into the hovering craft. The craft shuddered for a moment before quickly moving west and abruptly stopping prior to ascending straight up and disappearing. Two days later a 39-year-old Northumberland County man wearing only his underwear was found dead near Montour Ridge. Courtesy of National UFO Reporting Center (NUFORC) Peter B. Davenport, Director.

* * *

Seemingly, these evasive entities have devised a way to surgically manipulate solid matter without physical contact. They appear to possess artificial matter maneuvering devices harnessing the power to aerially levitate cars, trucks or even the human body. In fact, it would seem that these mysterious craft are fully capable of elevating and mobilizing a multitude of various objects to any given site while hanging in midair.

Quite naturally, super technology would dictate super structures, craft, weapons, and devices, indicating that these matter transporters could be as small as a hand-held device, or as large as a football stadium mounted on a mother ship.

The Creation and Matter Manipulation

The essential question would be, how do UFOs and their matter maneuvering devices fit into the scripturally accepted creation of this planet? This perplexing issue ultimately revealed that the planet Earth, and this entire Universe, existed **before** the creation actually took place.

> **3. There I saw the wooden receptacles out of which the winds became separated, the receptacle of hail, the receptacle of snow, the receptacle of the cloud, and the cloud itself, which continued <u>over the earth</u> <u>before</u> the creation of the world. CHAP. XLI. BOOK OF ENOCH**

How could the clouds, rain, hail and snow, existed "over" the Earth "before the creation of the world" occurred? Obviously, the planet Earth already existed, the creation was nothing more than a major modification, or face lift performed upon a pre-existing world.

1:1 In the beginning God created the heaven and the earth.

1:2 And the earth was without form, and void; and darkness [was] upon the face of the deep...

GENESIS

Naturally, the verses would entice one to believe that the planet Earth was created out of thin air. This assumption becomes even more credible when considering the version that God (Yahweh) created "Heaven" and "Earth". The word "Earth" is believed to be a direct reference to the planet Earth itself. In contrast, the word "Heaven" is considered to be a reference to the Universe, and/or an invisible realm.

However, the verses do not state that Yahweh/God created the waters of the deep. The waters ("the deep") already existed, indicating that the pre-existing waters/deep, were already on the pre-existing world.

EARTH—*The land surface of the world. The softer, friable part of land; Soil, especially productive soil. Soil or dry land, ground, dirt.*

HEAVEN—*The sky, the firmament*

FIRMAMENT—*The sky*

Instinctively we believe the earth to be the planet, and heaven to be an invisible realm or outer space beyond this world (the Universe). Yet, both words possess other definitions establishing an unprecedented narrative. The word 'heaven' defines the sky or firmament of this planet. The sky being the firmament, is actually the atmosphere or mass of air that encompasses this world. In essence, Yahweh created/altered this planet's atmosphere (sky/firmament/heaven), not the Universe. The word "Earth" implies land or dry ground, dirt. Hence, Yahweh created the dry land ("Earth") upon a pre-existing planet comprised of water. Remarkably, this conjecture is validated by the verses of Genesis.

1:8 And God called the firmament Heaven....

1:10 And God called the dry [land] Earth; and the gathering together of the waters called he Seas: and God saw that [it was] good.

GENESIS

Essentially, Yahweh created the sky or atmosphere (heaven) as well as "dry land/Earth" (continents), upon a pre-existing **aquatic** world. Yet, how could Yahweh and his universal forces perform such an incredible planetary feat?

This astonishing world altering maneuver began to disclose its genuine design by revealing the fact that the existing dry land "Earth" was without form and void.

> **FORM**—*The shape and structure of an object. The body or outward appearance, The mode in which a thing exists, shape.*
> **VOID**—*Not occupied; Unfilled. Completely lacking; Devoid. Ineffective; Useless. null.*

Obviously, insignificant land or dry ground (earth) existed upon the unaltered world. Yet, the diminutive land bodies displayed no basic "form" or defined shape, possibly indicating negligible land masses and enormous marshlands. The land was "void" suggesting that the insignificant unformed land masses, or marshlands (earth) that did exist at that time, were not occupied by many land dwelling life forms due to the planet's aquatic nature.

If in fact there were insignificant dry land bodies and massive marshlands then quite naturally the planet was an aquatic world consisting of mostly water "**The Deep**". It was this aquatic element that actually assisted me in resolving the issue as to how the creation was actually performed.

Gather Together the Waters

Surprisingly, the verses held nothing back in disclosing the global mutation. Yahweh and his universal host forcibly altered or manipulated the former seas and oceans (The Deep) of this planet, thus spawning the conversion of a pre-existing aquatic world. Verse 1:10 confirms that the waters of the planet were physically altered "**gathered together**" or forcibly refashioned.

> **4 He also divided the earth from the water, with which it is encompassed;...**
> **I. CLEMENT**
> **28...and with the word of his strength fixed the heaven, and founded the earth upon the waters;...**
> **I. HERMAS./VISION II. THE LOST BOOKS OF THE BIBLE**
> **6. Is not the whole sea, all its waters, and all its commotion, the work of him, the Most High; of him who has sealed up all its exertions, and girded it on every side with sand?**
> **CHAP. C. BOOK OF ENOCH**

Evidently, the massive oceans ("waters") of this planet played a major role in the transmutation of this previous aquatic world. Moreover, it would appear that this global conversion also created the prevailing sunlight that now exists upon the surface of this world today. That daylight surged into existence due to the forced mutation of the previous atmosphere (heaven/firmament/sky).

> **1:3 And God said, Let there be light: and there was light.**
>
> **1:4 And God saw the light, that [it was] good: and God divided the light from the darkness.**
>
> GENESIS

But How? How could these celestial entities have forcibly extracted, "**gathered together**" and stabilized a global body of water, and still maintained this planet's perfect perpetual balance? How was dry land/earth forced to appear on the surface of the planet were there was none before? How was the previous atmosphere altered (heaven) thus allowing the Sun (light) to radiate upon the newly exposed land?

Moon Alters Heaven and Earth

> **27. During the period of its fury he has established the sand against it, which continued unchanged for ever; and by this oath the abyss has been made strong; nor is it removable from its station for ever and ever.**
>
> CHAP. LXV III BOOK OF ENOCH
>
> **27…And thus I made the solid waters, that is to say, the bottomless. And I made a foundation of light around the water….**
>
> **28…The sea I gathered into one place, and I bound it with a yoke. And I said to the sea: Behold, I give you an eternal boundary. And you will not break through from your own waters. And so I fixed the solid structure and established it above the waters….**
>
> **30…and on the 7th, the lowest, [I placed] the MOON, and with the lowest stars I beautified the air below.** 2 ENOCH [J] (P)
>
> **2. I surveyed the stone which supports the corners of the earth.**
>
> **3. I also beheld the four winds, which bear up the earth, and the firmament of heaven.**
>
> CHAP. XVIII BOOK OF ENOCH

The mutation of this world was performed by the orbital installation of a Moon ("stone") around the planet. The evidence and obvious logic are overwhelming. The "yoke" or "solid structure" (Moon), established above the waters of this World, is the "stone" (Moon) that supports the creation (corners of the earth/dry land).

Remarkably, a simple encyclopedia validates the premise. Our scientists know that the gravitational pull of the Sun and Moon creates a massive aquatic bulge on the surface of the planet. This aquatic protrusion is in fact the waters of the planet that have been **"gathered together"** and are being pulled away from the surface of the planet. In essence, the lunar induced protrusion helps to keep the continents of the planet dry.

One needs only to examine the premise in reverse to expose the facts. One would only needs to reflect upon the detrimental impacts of our Moon being removed from its present orbit around this world. Those devastating repercussions would alter this entire planet back to its pre-existing aquatic state, being extremely deficient of dry land.

Evidently, this former aquatic world possessed no physical Moon as we know it today. The planet Earth was simply an isolated water world embracing only small segments of formless land masses and possibly vast marshlands scattered throughout its surface. If true, this aquatic factor would imply that the previous atmosphere (heaven/firmament) of the planet would have also been dissimilar from our present atmosphere.

By there being more water exposed on the surface of the Planet, the Sun would be thoroughly capable of generating more water vapor into the planet's atmosphere (**heaven**). Consequently, there would be perpetual rainfall, as well as horrendous storms on a global scale. The planet in this aquatic condition would maintain a relentless cloud coverage engulfing its surface.

1:2...and <u>darkness</u> [was] upon the face of <u>the deep</u>. GENESIS

The rays of sun would be unable to penetrate the atmosphere of the Planet, due to the overwhelming cloud formations within the firmament (atmosphere/sky/heaven). There would be no light (daylight) as we know it today.

The exposed small land masses and enormous marshlands that may have existed before the lunar alteration would be tropical in nature, much like the tropical rain forest of Brazil. The plant and animal life forms that may have existed on the surface of the former world would have been quite extraordinary.

If these world altering entities physically lodged a Moon into orbit around this type of aquatic world, the global repercussions would be incredible. The gravitational pull of the newly installed Moon would **"gather together"** and extract the massive oceans and seas away from the submerged land masses, thus forming dry land (earth). The larger the installed Moon, the greater the pull would be. The closer the Moon is orbitally established around the Planet, the greater the aquatic extraction would be.

Science and religion began to mesh together. These celestial entities selected just the right size planetoid satellite (Moon), and physically positioned it into the proper orbit to produce the perfect aquatic extraction to create the biosphere christened Earth (Dry Land).

By inaugurating a moon around the former aquatic world, they physically created or formed dry land masses (Earth/Continents), that did not exists before the lunar conversion was performed. Using the Moon to physically extract the oceans and seas away from the submerged land formations, they depleted the previous atmosphere of its perpetual water supply.

The lunar conversion had now left the aquatic planet with more solid land mass and reduced surface area of water, thereby globally reducing the area of water the Sun could physically evaporate into the atmosphere (firmament). The aquatic reduction depleted the amount of rainfall as well as reducing the cloud coverage of the planet. The Sun's rays could now penetrate the altered atmosphere and radiate the newly exposed dry land. Hence there was light.

> **1:6 And God said, Let there be a firmament in the midst of the waters, and let it divide the waters from the waters.**
> **1:7 And God made the firmament, and divided the waters which [were] under the firmament from the waters which [were] above the firmament: and it was so.**
> **1:8 And God called the firmament Heaven. And the evening and the morning were the second day.**
> **1:9 And God said, Let the waters under the heaven be gathered together unto one place, and let the dry [land] appear: and it was so.**
> **1:10 And God called the dry [land] Earth; and the gathering together of the waters called he Seas: and God saw that [it was] good.**
> **GENESIS**

Prior to the Lunar conversion, the "firmament" or highly humid atmosphere above (heaven/sky), was full of water vapor (rain), due to the Sun evaporating the enormous quantities of water covering the surface of the planet. Therefore, waters were above, within the firmament (atmosphere), as well as waters below the firmament, being the location of the massive oceans and seas.

The new lunar generated firmament would now insatiably divide and separate the waters of the atmosphere from the waters on the surface of the planet. Essentially, the conversion depleted the global cloud coverage due to reduced evaporation into the new atmosphere spawned by the lunar installation.

Jurassic Connection

Remarkably, there more here than just the rationalization of a lunar conversion imposed upon an aquatic world. Our home world Earth has been around for millions of years **before** the lunar metamorphosis ever took place. Today our scientists know that millions of years ago this planet was in fact an aquatic world consisting of an insignificant land mass, commonly known as "the age of fishes".

It's typically believed that the existing continents on the surface of this planet were formed by clashing plate tectonics, massive continental segmentation and/or volcanic magma oozing up from out of the planet's crust via global fault lines. However, as we have just discovered, this planet evolving assumption may not be the entire truth. Nor would be the deemed hypothesis of the sudden disappearance of the dinosaurs.

Today the most common theory is that, millions of years ago, a large asteroid or meteor struck this planet, spawning global devastation. This cosmic collision was believed to have transformed this planet into a frigid dying World due to enormous amounts of expelled soot, ash, and increased volcanic activity ascending into its atmosphere. The doomed atmosphere became so darkened by the horrendous event, that the sunlight was blotted out for years.

This event was believed to have caused the plant life on the surface of the Planet to die out, consequently exterminating the entire food chain, which eventually found its way to the rapid starvation, and ultimate demise of the dinosaurs.

However, we are now forced to face another possibility. The actual demise of the monstrous reptiles and their ecosystem may point an incriminating finger at the lunar conversion (creation) of this world. Moreover, this lunar perspective would reveal an astounding issue.

Extraterrestrial Intervention

Is it possible that this planet was physically claimed by extraterrestrial beings during the epoch in which it was inhabited by dinosaurs? Did they in fact remove or destroy the dinosaurs by way of the lunar conversion to establish accommodations for mankind?

The planet before the lunar transformation embraced only negligible land masses and vast marshlands. Due to the unaltered state of the atmosphere, the water-based planet at that time may have been extremely tropical in nature.

The highly aquatic environment of the planet before the lunar conversion may have actually dictated an extraordinarily savage form of evolution. Plant life would become aquatically bizarre, savage, and uncontrollable freaks of nature. The same savage nature would have ultimately evolved the aquatic and land-based animal life forms (Dinosaurs). This bizarre detail may not only explained the extinction of the dinosaurs, but the food chains that preserved their very existence.

Just like the theory of the asteroid or meteor that assaulted this planet decimating all plant and animal life, the lunar transmutation would yield similar effects. This lunar injection may have entailed devastating repercussions such as a possible pole shift capable of destroying every living thing on the surface of the former world.

Even if a catastrophic pole shift did not occur during the lunar conversion, by forcibly altering the planet, most of the plant and animal life forms would have been environmentally terminated due to lack of water.

The former cloudy and moisture laden atmosphere of the planet had been modified. The existing aquatic plant and animal life that were thriving under the previously cloudy atmosphere and abundant water supply would ultimately die out and/or be mutated. The water starved plants and animals, being saturated with the intense unfamiliar sunlight, would cease to exist, or transmogrify. The food chain would be utterly altered, consequently transmuting or destroying all life forms in the wake of the lunar metamorphoses. Naturally, it would take many generations for the recently converted planet and its mutated life forms to become stabilized within their new environment, which may account for this verse.

> **2:4 These [are] the generations of the heavens and of the earth when they were created, in the day that the LORD God made the earth and the heavens, GENESIS**

This timeless evolutionary balance is illustrated by the word "generations" suggesting that the "generations" spoken of in reference to the lunar creation may in fact delineate into millions of years.

A New World is Born

> Then you commanded that a ray of light be brought forth from your treasuries, so that your works might then appear." Again, on the second day, you created the spirit of the firmament, and commanded him to divide and separate the waters, that one part might move upward and the other part remain beneath. "On the third day you commanded the waters to be gathered together in the seventh part of the earth; six parts you dried up and kept so that some of them might be planted and cultivated and be of service before you....
>
> For immediately fruit came forth in endless abundance and of varied appeal to the taste; and flowers of inimitable color...
>
> 6:40-44 THE FOURTH BOOK OF EZRA (P)
>
> 1:11 And God said, Let the earth bring forth grass, the herb yielding seed, [and] the fruit tree yielding fruit after his kind, whose seed [is] in itself, upon the earth: and it was so.
>
> 1:12 And the earth brought forth grass, [and] herb yielding seed after his kind, and the tree yielding fruit, whose seed [was] in itself, after his kind: and God saw that [it was] good.
>
> 1:14 And God said, Let there be lights in the firmament of the heaven to divide the day from the night; and let them be for signs, and for seasons, and for days, and years:
>
> 1:15 And let them be for lights in the firmament of the heaven to give light upon the earth: and it was so.
>
> 1:25 And God made the beast of the earth after his kind, and cattle after their kind, and every thing that creepeth upon the earth after his kind: and God saw that [it was] good.
>
> GENESIS

A new and different world would now replace the old. Mutated life forms would now begin to spontaneously develop, multifaceted life based on the converted planet and its now sun permeated environment. The pre-existing plant and animal life would either be aquatically starved, or unable to biologically adjust fast enough to compensate for the rapid environmental change.

The new biosphere would now possess vast quantities of naked or barren land masses due to the extracted waters spawned by the lunar injection. The self seeding events spoken of in the verses would be a natural occurring condition on the surface of the void dry land masses (Earth) if exposed to direct sunlight. The verses themselves express the self-procreating methods by stating “yielding seed after his kind, whose **seed is in itself** upon the earth, **after his kind**”.

Essentially, Yahweh allowed nature to follow its own procedure after the lunar transmutation. Moreover, many specific plant and animal life forms were able to survive by weathering the altered environment. This would not include the dissimilar types of plant and animal life that naturally sprung up due to the dissimilar order of environment now imposed upon the transfigured planet. The same metamorphosis would also occur in reference to the light and darkness, or days and nights now established on the created biosphere.

Prior to the earthly creation, there may have been no day or night on the surface of this world as we know it today. The planet maintained a perpetual darkness or overcast environment due to the horrendous cloud coverage engulfing its surface. The lunar generated biosphere altered the overcast environment thus creating light, as well as darkness, hence the literal creation of day and night.

The tides established by the lunar induction, in contrast with the gravitational pull of the Sun, are contributing factors that produce the current perpetual state of rotation this planet maintains today. Essentially, the planet now generates an uninterrupted revolution that gives us our continuous twelve hour nights and days, which break down into weeks, months, years, or in essence time itself.

Matter Manipulation Connection

The ultimate question would be, just how was the lunar conversion physically performed? If the reader will recall, these mysterious entities have devised a matter manipulating device. Moreover, this device is capable of maneuvering solid matter at extensive distances. Seemingly, these devices are mounted on/or within the craft themselves, thus allowing the craft the ability to aerially elevate abducted victims, or to bodily hoist and/or lower the occupants from their hovering craft.

As mentioned before, super technology would naturally dictate super structures, craft, devices, and weapons. If these celestial entities have in fact constructed super starships of enormous dimensions, they could in all probability possess the same matter maneuvering device of enormous size mounted on the immense craft. Essentially, these mountainous space-bound craft possess the ability to physically manipulate solid matter of untold masses. In all probability, these beings may be navigating gargantuan craft fully capable of planetary manipulation on a mammoth scale.

These stellar beings may be quite proficient in not only locating a planetoid satellite (Moon) of their own choosing, but transporting the selected planetoid within the weightlessness of space. In fact, this astonishing satellite maneuver may be quite simple compared to their true stellar capabilities.

In essence, Yahweh utilized enormous craft and matter maneuvering devices to cosmically extract and transport a Moon of their own choosing to this barren aquatic world. Furthermore, it would appear that they physically positioned the selected planetoid (Moon) around this planet, in just the right orbit to acquire the proper aquatic extraction to create this biosphere Earth/Dry Land. Moreover, they bodily selected just the right size Moon to perform the converting task based on the size of the aquatic world to be altered. So just how many other planets have these universal beings created (altered/modified)?

Celestial Motive

This world altering premise would seem like a lot of cosmic strife without some type of long range motivation behind such a revolutionary creation. Why endeavor the mass manipulation of an entire world, unless there was some devised cosmic plan involving that planetary modification? Analyzing this extraterrestrial intervention from their possible perspective, it's quite reasonable to assume that they would have never arrived at this raw world, unless of course they were already exploring the Universe.

However, in the case of our home world, (Earth) it appears they came prepared to modify this pre-existing world before they actually arrived at the Planet to perform the alteration. This conjecture becomes even more credible if we consider that at the time of their arrival they were presently towing or transporting a specifically selected Moon to perform the physical creation of Earth (dry land). This would suggest that they had explored this solar system long before the creation actually took place.

Evidently, they returned at a later time to perform the Lunar modification on the most likely planet within this solar system suitable of being aquatically transformed into a biosphere. Moreover, they may have selected and transported a Moon from within the close proximity of this solar system to perform the corporal conversion (Creation). But why?

I soon realized that the solution to this puzzling issue may actually reside within our own history. Mankind, discovering that this Planet is not flat, struggled to expand his dominated territories upon its surface. The history of the United States is a good illustration of such global expansion. Mankind crossing the pond slowly moved further and further into the yet unexplored territorial United States. Pioneering his newly discovered land, mankind began marking the territories with his own kind. Hence we humans laid claim to those discovered regions by the very populations now residing within them.

The only way to truly prove one's mark or discovered territory would be to leave something behind, or place something on the discovered domain to physically identify, and confirm the discoveries and jurisdiction of the finder. In our case here in America, we ourselves, along with our industrial methods, are the proof of our discovered and dominated frontier.

In the case of these cosmic beings, the expansion of universal territories or frontiers could in all probability follow the same procedure, but on a cosmic scale. If these sovereign entities are exploring and marking their territories within the known Universe, they would need to physically lay claim to, or leave something behind to prove or identify the discovered and/or physically created worlds as theirs.

The lunar conversion of this world would not be enough to identify this planet as theirs. Obviously, there could be hundreds of thousands, if not millions of planets, much like this lunar created earth, naturally existing within the Universe. To truly mark their territory within this Constellation and Galaxy they would have to leave behind more than just an artificially converted world.

Unmistakably, mankind was not created for this manufactured biosphere, but rather the biosphere was created for mankind. Evidently, intelligent humanoid life already existed before the lunar transmutation was implemented, thus justifying the motivation behind the creation of a biosphere capable of sustaining human life. Put simply, these world altering entities are also humanoid in nature.

Laying Claim to the Creation

The only way to physically and acceptably expand their universal domain would be to leave behind something that would actually identify the discoverer and/or developer of that territory. To do so, they would have to leave behind, or mark their discovered and artificially created territory with one of their own kind, or a **facsimile thereof.** This colonizing premise may actually justify the cosmic logic behind the procreation of an Adam and Eve.

> **1:26 And God said, Let us make man in our image, after our likeness: and let them have dominion over the fish of the sea, and over the fowl of the air, and over the cattle, and over all the earth, and over every creeping thing that creepeth upon the earth.**
>
> **1:27 So God created man in his [own] image, in the image of God created he him; male and female created he them.**
>
> **1:28 And God blessed them, and God said unto them, Be fruitful, and multiply, and replenish the earth, and subdue it: and have dominion over the fish of the sea, and over the fowl of the air, and over every living thing that moveth upon the earth.**
>
> GENESIS

"Let **us** make man in **our image**". The question would be, who are "**us**" and "**our**"**?** Obviously the physical entities resembling us, considering we were created in their "likeness/image". Clearly, Yahweh (God) was not alone in his endeavors to pioneer and dominate this Universe. The optimum way to mark this planet as a part of their discovered universal domain would be to leave behind a reproduction or facsimile of the discoverers (creators).

This unquestionable mark would ultimately populate the entire planet with facsimiles of the discoverers which we are in the image thereof. Adam and Eve were therefore created as substantial marks to populate the fabricated biosphere.

The Hybridization of Man

Was mankind in fact a created byproduct of these alien beings confessing we were biologically formulated from their own physical nature (image)? The verses would even go so far as to imply that mankind is in the very image of God, (Yahweh), suggesting that Yahweh and his cosmic host are in fact physical men, or facsimiles thereof. However, this speculation would lead us to yet another perplexing issue.

Why create a human in the image of God? If these alien entities came to this world eons ago to create a biosphere, why not simply leave behind their own kind, to populate the transfigured world? Why genetically procreate a human in their image, if celestial humans ("us/our") already existed? The solution to this complex issue may actually reveal the fact that these celestial beings do not physically procreate.

After a thorough investigation, it became evident that these unique entities are immortal beings not requiring biological reproduction to preserve their species. This celibate detail might resolve the issue as to why create a man and woman. Obviously the converted world is in need of a proliferating population to lay claim to the planet.

Yet, this would suggest that Adam and Eve were not genetic conceptions deriving from just these alien beings alone. The contemporary homo sapiens may actually be a hybrid form of alien genetics combined with an unknown dissimilar gene. The question is, a crossbreed species between aliens beings and what?

The Missing Link

It's commonly believed that mankind ultimately evolved from the ape, or Neanderthal man, being nothing less than a highly-developed form of apes. This would suggest that an evolutionary stage of the primate or Neanderthal man may have actually been prevalent on the surface of this planet before and/or after the lunar conversion. Essentially, the ape, or Neanderthal man, was a natural evolutionary life form found on this planet prior to its discovery by these alien explorers. This would suggest that the ape and its evolutionary stages is an innate occurrence within the Universe and would naturally exist on numerous other worlds. Yet, the crude anthropoid species (apes) possibly found on life-sustaining planets within the Universe would biologically develop towards dissimilar evolutionary levels at various times. Some planets and their basic anthropoid life forms may have evolved millions of years before this planet was formed or even existed.

This might indicate that these celestial entities actually evolved from the same basic life forms as we humans have. In fact it's quite possible that they are nothing more than an extremely evolved anthropoid life form found on many planets throughout the Universe. Essentially, the various alien factors found within the Universe may actually be a variety of highly-developed life forms of what we humans are today, evolved anthropoids/apes.

This is not to say that the anthropoid species is the only type of universal life to evolve into an intelligent being. The Grays, and the numerous dissimilar entities frequently observed in many UFO encounters would indicate that there are many types of visiting beings. Quite naturally, hundreds of thousands of dissimilar life forms may be residing within the known Universe.

Nevertheless, the ape may in fact be our ancestors, as well as the forefathers of these planet transforming entities. Moreover, if these celestial beings are a highly evolved form of anthropoid, it would seem rather convenient to simply genetically crossbreed themselves with a lower form of their own existence. In doing so, they could procreate an underdeveloped species that would closely resemble that of their own kind.

As farfetched as it seemed, I began to consider the probability that these stellar entities arrived at this raw aquatic world, only to find the same unevolved anthropoid life forms already existing upon its surface. That pre-existing life form may have been the Neanderthal man or an evolutionary derivative thereof, the same life forms that these celestial individuals evolved from themselves.

These planetary architects may have genetically hybridized themselves with a lower form of themselves, consequently procreating a highly-developed form of Neanderthal man. In essence, they altered the evolutionary sequence of the Neanderthal, by genetically forcing it into an evolutionary leap.

Put simply, these alien entities may in fact be the genetic missing link between the Neanderthal man and contemporary Homo Sapiens. This hybridized humanoid creation would allow the populations of this planet to proliferate within the same genetic lines as the cosmic entities that artificially modified the Planet in the first place. This would biologically mark, and physically lay claim to the transformed world as their own, seeing how the augmented populations of the converted world will be inhabited by their own kind (in the image thereof).

Body Modifiers

Scripture would lead one to believe that this immense cosmic plan for the colonization of a new world was thwarted by a single Tree. Many would rather believe that the famed Trees of life and knowledge was nothing more than a symbolic reference to something other than genuine Trees. Yet, scripture establishes the fact that the Trees did actually exist on the surface of this modified world at one time.

> **2:9 And out of the ground made the LORD God to grow every tree that is pleasant to the sight, and good for food; the tree of life also in the midst of the garden, and the tree of knowledge of good and evil.**
>
> **2:16 And the LORD God commanded the man, saying, Of every tree of the garden thou mayest freely eat:**
> **2:17 But of the tree of the knowledge of good and evil, thou shalt not eat of it: for in the day that thou eatest thereof thou shalt surely die.**
> **GENESIS**

Each of the fruit bearing trees was not only being cultivated out of the newly established dry land, but actually possessed artificial body enhancing powers. Obviously the trees were authentic, considering their fruit could be bodily consumed. Furthermore, it would appear that Adam and Eve were only alive because they consumed the fruit from the tree of life. Evidently, there's more to this body sustaining fruit than meets the eye.

> **2…I passed along above the angel Zateel, and arrived at the garden of righteousness. In this garden I beheld, among other trees, some which were numerous and large, and which flourished there.**
> **3. Their fragrance was agreeable and powerful, and their appearance both varied and elegant. The tree of knowledge also was there, of which if any one eats, he becomes endowed with great wisdom.**
> **4. It was like a species of the tamarind tree, bearing fruit which resembled grapes extremely fine;… CHAP. XXXI. BOOK OF ENOCH**
> **16 "He further said to me, 'When thou hast taken them to thyself, give them to eat of the fruit of the Tree of Life, and give them to drink of the water of peace; and clothe them in a garment of light, and restored them to their former state of grace,.. CHAP. LX**
> **FORGOTTEN BOOKS OF EDEN**

Seemingly, these extraterrestrials had discovered or developed fruit trees with body-changing or regenerating powers. The body modifying functions found within the fruit can actually be observed in the verses.

Evidently, one of the fruit trees was highly effective in augmenting one's psychological aptitude (Tree of knowledge). This would suggest that the phenomenal fruit contains a powerful nectar of instantaneous genius. Another species (Tree of life) may have allowed cellular rejuvenation of the body.

Note, "restore them to their former state". What was their original biological state prior to eating the fruit? Clearly, the fruit of this life providing Tree had physically altered Adam's and Eve's biological functions in some way.

The same life-giving data can also be found in the verses of Genesis. Here the verses link this same life-sustaining fruit with their death. It would seem that the fruit of the Tree of life is self-explanatory. As long as they eat the fruit of this remarkable Tree they will live. However, if they stop eating the life bearing fruit they will "die".

By eating this miraculous fruit, they have become immortal beings immune to ageing death. Adam and Eve could have physically lived for hundreds, or perhaps thousands of years as long as they continued to consume the fruit of the Tree of life. Yet, there was a mandated stipulation pertaining to the phenomenal fruit (immortality). Those defied conditions ultimately led to the aging downfall of all mankind.

Evidently, these two immortal beings were to become the prototype parents and mentors of this transfigured world. Unfortunately, by dining on the fruit of the Tree of knowledge, Adam and Eve breached Yahweh's cosmic law. Consequently, Adam and Eve, as well their forthcoming posterity, were deprived of the fruit of the Tree of life. By the body rejuvenating fruit being withheld from Adam and Eve they began to grow old as we now all do. Hence, death was born due to the absence of the body reconstituting fruit.

> **3:2 And the woman said unto the serpent, We may eat of the fruit of the trees of the garden:**
> **3:3 But of the fruit of the tree which [is] in the midst of the garden, God hath said, Ye shall not eat of it, neither shall ye touch it, <u>lest ye die</u>.**
> **3:4 And the serpent said unto the woman, Ye shall not surely die:**
> **3:5 For God doth know that in the day ye eat thereof, then <u>your eyes shall be opened</u>, and <u>ye shall be as gods</u>, knowing good and evil.**
> **3:6 And when the woman saw that the tree [was] good for food, and that it [was] pleasant to the eyes, and a tree to be desired <u>to make [one] wise</u>, she took of the fruit thereof, and did eat, and gave also unto her husband with her; and he did eat.**

3:7 And the eyes of them both were opened, and they knew that they [were] naked; and they sewed fig leaves together, and made themselves aprons. GENESIS

Regrettably, this was a substantial price to pay for negligible knowledge. Then again, this scholarly fruit may cellularly contain an intellectual powerhouse. Obviously, this mind-altering fruit was capable of bestowing superior knowledge upon Adam and Eve. Moreover, this genius level possibly reached the intellectual heights of the celestial beings that partook of the same fruits ("Gods").

3:22 And the LORD God said, Behold, the man is become as one of us, to know good and evil: and now, lest he put forth his hand, and take also of the tree of life, and eat, and live for ever:
GENESIS

Here again the word "us" is used to identify the many physical beings residing within the same earthly settlement Adam and Eve had been forced to leave. Having consumed the fruit of the Tree of knowledge, Adam and Eve had artificially become as intellectually superior as their creators. Apparently this mind-altering event was not to be tolerated by Adam and Eve's stellar sires. To be as psychologically superior as their celestial creators, as well as possessing the power to live forever (immortality), would intellectually rank Adam and Eve on the same level as their extraterrestrial creators.

The Birth of Fallen Angels

Scripture readily establishes the fact that many of the descendants of Adam and Eve lived to be almost a thousand years of age. This longevity lasted only up and until the time of Noah's deluge. At that point in time, a new breed began encountering an ageing death. Seemingly, their dwindling immortality may have been directly related to the genetic residue of the fruit of the Tree of life which Adam and Eve consumed for many years.

3:5 "You have heard, my son Seth, that a Flood is coming and will wash the whole earth because of the daughters of Cain, your brother, who killed your brother Abel out of passion for your sister Lebuda, since sins has been created through your mother, Eve....

TESTAMENT OF ADAM (P)

> 24:5 And I saw, as it were, Adam, and Eve who was with him, and with them the crafty adversary and Cain, who had been led by the adversary to break the law,...
>
> APOCALYPSE OF ABRAHAM (P)
>
> 6 "Hear, O my son, hereafter there shall come a great destruction upon this earth on account of them; God will be angry with the world, and will destroy them with water.
>
> 7 "But I also know that thy children will not hearken to thee, and that they will go down from this mountain and hold intercourse with the children of Cain, and that they shall perish with them.
>
> CHAP.XVI
>
> 31 And when they looked at the daughters of Cain, at their beautiful figures, and at their hands and feet dyed with color, and tattooed in ornaments on their faces, the fire of sin was kindled in them.
>
> 32 Then Satan made them look most beautiful before the sons of Seth, as he also made the sons of Seth appear of the fairest in the eyes of the daughters of Cain, so that the daughters of Cain lusted after the sons of Seth like ravenous beasts, and the sons of Seth after the daughters of Cain, until they committed abomination with them. CHAP.XX
>
> FORGOTTEN BOOKS OF EDEN/ADAM AND EVE

Obviously, Cain, Abel, and Seth were not the only posterity of Adam and Eve. Notably, Eve bore one or more daughters that the boys may have lustfully killed over. Evidently the engendered human race derived from an incestuous households, a self seeding union stimulated by Satan and his host (The Adversary),

You will also discover that the impending flood of Noah is notably specified as a result of the daughters of Cain. This significant clue will assist us in comprehending just who Satan and his universal host may actually be (The Adversary).

Clearly, Cain and Seth fathered many daughters, suggesting that Cain and Seth maintained extremely long life spans to produce the numerous daughters submitted in Scripture. Seth alone lived to be nine hundred and twelve years of age, thus illustrating the biological overtones of the immortal fruit of the Tree of life eaten by Seth's parents, or Seth himself.

Unmistakably, Satan and his host were not invisible ghosts or spirits, but genuine bodily beings. Moreover, these universal entities not only misled and beguiled mankind into lusting after each other, but decided to literally take part, and physically join in the carnal lust themselves.

6:1 And it came to pass, when men began to multiply on the face of the earth, and daughters were born unto them,

6:2 That the sons of God saw the daughters of men that they [were] fair; and they took them wives of all which they chose.

6:3 And the LORD said, My spirit shall not always strive with man, for that he also [is] flesh: yet his days shall be an hundred and twenty years.

6:4 There were giants in the earth in those days; and also after that, when the sons of God came in unto the daughters of men, and they bare [children] to them, the same [became] mighty men which [were] of old, men of renown.

GENESIS

It would seem that from this point on, mankind was faced with short-lived lives spanning only one hundred and twenty years of age. Evidently, Adam and Eve, along with their offspring, maintained their fruitful longevity up until this period of time. This would lead one to assume that Yahweh and his host had removed all of the life-sustaining fruits from mankind's presence. In doing so, the life span of humans was greatly shortened by hundreds of years. In fact, it would appear that this life diminishing event involves an explicit objective.

The Sons of God

If the reader will closely examine the verses, you will discover an unknown third party involved with mankind and their daughters. That unknown third group was the "Sons of God." Clearly the Sons of God were genuine palpable men. It doesn't take a genius to realize that these extraterrestrial entities are not only physical in nature, but in the very image of mankind, thus justifying why the earthly women were charmed into sensual copulation.

Essentially, the Sons of God were exactly what their title implied, the physical extraterrestrial host of God, (Yahweh). Notably, these extraterrestrial entities indulged in sexual intercourse with the daughters of men, thus fathering genetic hybrids/giants.

Evidently, the same celestial entities (Sons of God) who transformed this world had physically intervened upon its surface and became intellectually and sexually involved with their own genetic creation. Furthermore, it appears unmistakable that there is a genetic dissimilarity between these lustful heavenly entities (Sons of God), and the downgraded homo sapiens (humans).

By intermixing their highly evolved and artificially altered state of existence with the genetically downgraded homo sapiens, the fathered brood could be extremely bizarre, if not downright freakish. The fusing of the two dissimilar genes could have actually spawn monstrous humanoids, titans that could physically take control of mortal men, as well as the entire Planet.

Seemingly, the body amplifying fruits were possibly removed from mankind's reach before the Sons of God copulated with the female issue of man. Or, the fruits were removed from mankind's table simply because the Sons of God indulged in sexual intercourse with the females of the Planet.

The Sons of God took wives for themselves (first), only to find that mankind had his life span or aging process immensely shortened (second). Essentially, the shortening of mankind's life may have been a deliberate retaliatory action against not only humans, but the Sons of God. This ageing castigation ultimately left the immortal Sons of God (Extraterrestrials) with mortal short-lived wives. Yet, this bizarre speculation does not answer the question as to, **who** are the Sons of God.

War In Heaven

To unravel this perplexing issue we need to journey back to the lunar conversion. This genesis data will allow us to examine the only scripture illustrating the Sons of God and their origin. This fascinating Scripture presents a cosmic point of view that not only deciphers who Yahweh (God) and his physical host are, but Satan and his host as well.

> **7 then the angels said unto Adam, "Thou didst hearken to Satan, and didst forsake the Word of God who created thee; and thou didst believe that Satan would fulfil all he had promised thee.**
> **8 "But now O Adam we will make known to thee, what came upon us through him, before his fall from heaven.**
> **9 "He gathered together his host, and deceived them, promising them to give a great kingdom, a divine nature; and other promises he made them.**
> **10 "His hosts believed that his word was true, so they yielded to him, and renounced the glory of God.**

11 "He then sent for us according to the orders in which we were to come under his command, and to hearken to his vain promise. But we would not, and we took not his advice.
12 "Then after he had fought with God, and had dealt forwardly with Him, he gathered together his host, and made war with us. And if it had not been for God's strength that was with us, we could not have prevailed against him to hurl him from heaven.
CHAP. LV. FORGOTTEN BOOKS OF EDEN/ADAM AND EVE
12:3 And there appeared another wonder in heaven; and behold a great red dragon, having seven heads and ten horns, and seven crowns upon his heads.
12:4 And his tail drew the third part of the stars of heaven, and did cast them to the earth:
12:7 And there was war in heaven: Michael and his angels fought against the dragon; and the dragon fought and his angels,
12:8 And prevailed not; neither was their place found any more in heaven.
12:9 And the great dragon was cast out, that old serpent, called the Devil, and Satan, which deceiveth the whole world: he was cast out into the earth, and his angels were cast out with him.
REVELATION
13 "But when he fell from among us, there was great joy in heaven, because of his going down from us. For had he continued in heaven, nothing would have remained in it.
14 "But God in His mercy, drove him from among us to this dark earth; for he had become darkness itself and a worker of unrighteousness.
CHAP. LV. FORGOTTEN BOOKS OF EDEN/ADAM AND EVE
1:6 And the angels which kept not their first estate, but left their own habitation, he hath reserved in everlasting chains under darkness unto the judgment of the great day. JUDE
3 And one from out the order of angels, having turned away with the order that was under him, conceived an impossible thought, to place his throne higher than the clouds above the earth, that he might become equal in rank to my power.
4 And I threw him out from the heights with his angels, and he was flying in the air continuously above the bottomless.
CHAP. XXIX FORGOTTEN BOOKS OF EDEN/SECRETS OF ENOCH

It is said that on the second day of the creation (Lunar conversion), an enormous celestial war was conducted in Heaven/The Universe. This rebellion was waged between the different extraterrestrial entities (angels) of the various constellations of this Universe (kingdom of Heaven). It's further believed that the size of the rebel legions of Satan numbered in the millions, while the forces of Yahweh were twice that number. The verses above give us a good perception of the motivation that marshaled those constellations and their inhabitants.

Outwardly, Satan and his host turned against God (Yahweh) in an effort to gain cosmic control, ranking himself and his benefactors above Yahweh's jurisdiction. Additionally, Satan and his disciples were unwilling to accept Yahweh's decision that mankind was to be placed above, or even ranked on the same level as those of the kingdom of Heaven. This obvious clue hinted to the probability that this stellar war took place within this solar system, if not around the recently converted planet (Earth).

Clearly, Satan maintained substantial control over many inhabited worlds, which ultimately magnified Satan into a powerful adversary capable of instigating a horrendous universal campaign. In close observation of the verses, we discover the actual size of the cosmic forces of Satan at the time of that rebellion.

The verses plainly substantiate the fact that it was a "third of the stars"(constellations) within this Universe (Heaven) that elected to follow the mutinous Satan in his stellar campaign. Essentially, the verses reveal the individual revolting star systems and inhabited constellations of the rebelling contenders. Moreover, this information allows us to identify Satan's constellation of origin.

Satan is paraphrased as the Dragon. Yet, more significantly, we are about to discover that Satan, the Dragon, is directly connected to the Constellation Draco (The Dragon). If you will closely observe the provided celestial charts of the Universe, you will discover in the Northern Celestial Pole, the Constellation Draco, a huge dragon shaped Constellation bearing an extensive **"tail"**.

The verses clearly indicate that the inhabited Constellation of Draco ("The Dragon") gained its power and rebel forces from its "tail". In essence, the tail of the Constellation of Draco is the actual location of not only the numerous inhabited worlds under Satan's command, but the significant worldly influences and power that drew a third of the stars (Constellations) and their physical inhabitants into this universal confrontation. Those constellations, and occupied worlds reside just below the tail of the Constellation of Draco.

Fallen Angels/Sons of God Cast into the Earth

These revolting angels **"kept not their first estate, but left their own habitation."** Obviously, these were the cosmic rebel forces that physically departed from their inhabited worlds within their various constellations, (orders in Heaven) to wage war in this enormous universal insurrection.

Satan's lost the celestial campaign. Not only did Satan and his supporters lose the stellar battle, the dark repercussions of their loss can be found in the same verses. These verses clearly in form us that the celestial rebels were not only cast out, or exiled from their home worlds and constellations (Heaven). They were literally cast "**into the earth**" inside this planet, hence cast into darkness (the Underworld). In essence, the fallen angels were incarcerated within the interior domains of this world (Earth).

Remarkably, the fallen angels were still allowed to "fly in the air continuously above the bottomless." The "bottomless" is not only a forthright reference to "the Underworld domains of this world," but to the great oceans and seas of this planet. Essentially, the exiled angels, imprisoned within (inside) the geothermal bowels of this world, were permitted to utilize their superior craft to travel within the atmosphere of this planet above the bottomless oceans and seas. Moreover, these astonishing verses may actually personify the modern UFO enigma.

The effort to dethrone Yahweh and his Universal jurisdiction was not the only cosmic blunder committed by the rebel angels. The fallen angels were previously distinguished as the Watchers/Sons of God. The watchful title given to these universal outlaws literally describes their responsibilities in reference to the lunar creation (Earth).

Initially, the Watchers were only to observe the progress of the recently converted world and its procreated population. The implication is that they were not allowed to interfere with earthly events. Nevertheless, Cain and Seth's beautiful female issue became too much of a sensuous enticement for the masculine male watchers (Sons of God) and their celestial duties.

> **In those days, when the children of man had multiplied, it happened that there were born unto them handsome and beautiful daughters. And the angels, the children of heaven, saw them and desired them; and they said to one another, "Come, let us choose wives for ourselves from among the daughters of man and beget us children."**

> **And Semyaz, being their leader, said unto them, "I fear that perhaps you will not consent that this deed should be done, and I alone will become (responsible) for this great sin." But they all responded to him, "Let us all swear an oath and bind everyone among us by a curse not to abandon this suggestion but do the deed." Then they all swore together and bound one another by (the curse). And they were altogether two hundred; and they descended into 'Ardos, which is the summit of Hermon. And they called the mount Armon, for they swore and bound one another by a curse. 6:1-6 I ENOCH**

The word "descended", would persuade one to consider that the virile Watchers were orbiting this planet, or possibly based on/or inside the recently installed Moon. This would be the perfect orbital post if one were keeping a watchful eye on the planet and its populations.

If in fact they were orbiting the planet, they would obviously need a physical craft or space station of some type. This substantial craft or station may have been enormous in size, considering it maintained living quarters, maintenance facilities, and possible space craft landing bays to support "two hundred" "descending" Watchers.

Notably, the two hundred watchers concluded among themselves to descend down to the surface of the planet. This decision was based on the fact that they knew they were not to intervene despite a prohibition to interfere with the population of the converted world. Unmistakably, they were more human than we have been led to believe.

The Fallen Angels Debase the Creation

Evidently the fallen angels' lust for the opposite sex blinded them in their cosmic responsibilities as Watchers. It was bad enough that the meddlesome angels became sexually and intellectually involved with their own split-gene humans. Yet, they took it further, and endeavored to influence the very evolutionary progress of humanity itself.

> **You see what Azaz'el has done; how he has taught all (form of) oppression upon the earth. And they revealed eternal secrets which are performed in heaven (and which) man learned. (Moreover) Semyaz, to whom you have given power to rule over his companions, co-operating, they went in unto the daughters of the people on earth; and they lay together with them-with**

those women-and defiled themselves, and revealed to them every (kind of) sin. 9:6-8

And they took wives unto themselves, and everyone (respectively) chose one woman for himself, and they began to go in unto them. And they taught them magical medicine, incantations, the cutting of roots, and taught them (about) plants.

7:1

And Azaz'el taught the people (the art of) making swords and knives, and shields, and breastplates; and he showed to their chosen ones bracelets, decorations, (shadowing of the eye) with antimony, ornamentation, the beautifying of the eyelids, all kinds of precious stones, and all coloring tinctures and alchemy. And there were many wicked ones and they committed adultery and erred, and all their conduct became corrupt. 8:1,2,

I ENOCH (P)

Because they walked in the stubbornness of their heart the Heavenly Watchers fell; they were caught because they did not keep the commandments of God. And their sons also fell who were tall as cedar trees and whose bodies were like mountains. The Exhortation

DEAD SEA SCROLLS/THE DAMASCUS RULE (CD)

The sensual angels/Watchers/Sons of God, (Elohim), having left their lofty station within the skies, began teaching humans about medicine, astrology, astronomy, body cosmetics, as well as weapons of war. Essentially the fallen angels/Sons of God betrayed the kingdom of heaven by teaching their celestial powers and culture to the human race.

The ancient Sumerian tablets corroborate this supposition. The Sumerian chronicles inform us that before the arrival of the shining or fiery Dragon-Serpent (Fallen Angels/Sons of God/Elohim/the shining ones), man did not know how to make beautiful clothes, durable shelters or weapons of war.

The Sumerian annals indicate that these alien teachers were "luminous beings", glowing entities that navigated through the sky in disc-shape craft of fire, strongly resembling the typical UFO report of today. These radiating individuals began teaching, and impregnating the human female population, and ultimately ruled humanity under the leadership of one individual.

In closely scrutinizing the verses, we unmask the plummeting chieftain angel characteristically referred to as Azaz'el, being just another title for Satan. Azazel was also alluded to as one of the Watchers who fell from heaven, as well as the chief of the Grigori (Watchers). He was a powerful angel boasting, "Why should a Son of Fire bow to a Son of Clay?" The Grigori or Watchers (Sons of God/Elohim) were the original titans, brawny humanoid males in contrast to their humble hybridized counterparts defined as mortal men/humans.

Giants Spawned by the Fallen Angels

The fallen angels began copulating with the female issue of the planet, spawning enormous offspring rivaling even their own mighty stature. Seemingly, the genetic mix ultimately fathered bizarre monstrous misfits. In fact "The Book of Enoch", as well as diverse scripture, would indicate that the hybridized behemoths were enormous beings of incredible dimensions. Obviously these towering giants created many worldly problems, considering they were now sharing a planet with what they considered to be nothing less than benighted dwarfs (mankind).

> **...they went in unto the daughters of the people on earth; and lay together with them-with those women-and defiled themselves, and revealed to them every (kind of) sin. As for the women they gave birth to giants to the degree that the whole earth was filled with blood and oppression....and those who have died will bring their suit up to the gate of heaven. Their groaning has ascended (into heaven), but they could not get out from before the face of the oppression that is being wrought on earth.**
>
> **9:7-10 And the women became pregnant and gave birth to great giants whose heights were three hundred cubits. These (giants) consumed the produce of all the people until the people detested feeding them. So the giants turned against (the people) in order to eat them. And they began to sin against birds, wild beasts, reptiles, and fish....**
>
> **7:2-5**
>
> **Then Michael, Surafel, and Gabriel observed carefully from the sky and they saw much blood being shed upon the earth, and all the oppression being wrought upon the earth. And they said to one another, "The earth, (from) her empty (foundation), has brought the cry of their voice unto the gates of heaven. And now, [O] holy ones of heaven, the souls of people are putting their case before you pleading, bring our judgment before the Most High.'"**
>
> **9:1-3**
>
> **I ENOCH (P)**

The fallen angels (Sons of God), and their goliath issue, began to multiply out of control, as they caused monumental disorder on the planet. I began to suspect that the Sons of God were not fully aware of the genetic repercussions produced by their interbreeding with mortal females. Yet, as extremely advanced as they were, it seems highly unlikely that they were unaware of the serious genetic error induced by proliferating with mortals. This might suggest that the Sons of God simply did not care.

The verses leave us with the conclusion that the rebel angels had taken complete control over the surface of the Planet. They began inflicting their brutal administration upon mortal man, as well as allowing their monstrous mutations to tyrannize and persecute the mortal humans to no end. Obviously the behemoths insatiably required enormous quantities of food due to their substantial size. Ultimately, mortal men became slaves not only to the fallen angels (Sons of God), but their huge offspring as well.

Evidently, the titans proliferated into great numbers that overwhelmed the existing food supply. Even the wildlife appears to have massively suffered in wake of the enormous need for food required by the giant hybrids. The verses would even go so far as to suggest that the ravenous giants began to suffer starvation, thus forcing them into cannibalism of their own slaves (mortal man).

Events on the surface of the Planet became extremely unstable, in light of the rebel angels and their gluttonous mutated seed. Evidently mortal men tried to challenge these superior beings and their dominating cannibalistic administration. Regrettably, the humans stood no chance against such advanced beings and their behemoth brood. Ultimately, the terrorized humans were left with only one alternative, comply or die, a death that placed the demised humans on the Goliath menu.

Periodic Visitation of the Creation

The fallen angels (Watchers) were originally left behind to keep watch, and assist the procreated humans when necessary. Yet, it seemed unmistakable that sooner or later someone would eventually "police the police". Inevitably, the Watchers would routinely be evaluated, or cosmically checked on by the very stellar confederation that left them behind from the Genesis.

The Watchers had now been "carefully observed", and scrutinized "from the sky". Evidently, Michael, Surafel and Gabriel had just arrived at this modified world, possibly indicating a substantial craft now orbiting the planet. From this orbital location, they could effortlessly observe ("observe carefully from the sky") everything that transpired on the surface of the planet.

Plainly, if Michael, Surafel and Gabriel had been here all along, there would be no need to physically observe. They would be fully aware of the detrimental chain of events from the very beginning of the Sons of God/fallen angels' original descent to the surface of the planet. Evidently, these observant angelic beings had unexpectedly arrived from some place other than this world.

Obviously, the official eyes in the sky did not like what they found. Mortal man, genetically fathered to be the prototype caretakers and universal marks laying claim to this world, had now become oppressed slaves of their very creators.

The lunar creation had become bastardized and totally out of hand. Clearly, the widespread tyranny justified the oppressed mortal prayers for outside help. Essentially, a resolution to ascertain the fate of everyone on the surface of the Planet, including the rebel angels was now in order. That judgment call is nowhere better illustrated than in "The Book of Enoch".

> 2. He was wholly engaged with the holy ones, and with the Watchers in his days.
>
> 5. Then the Lord said to me: Enoch, scribe of righteousness, go tell the Watchers of heaven, who have deserted the lofty sky, and their holy everlasting station, who have been polluted with women.
>
> 6. And have done as the sons of men do, by taking to themselves wives, and who have been greatly corrupted on the earth;
>
> 7. That on the earth they shall never obtain peace and remission of sin. For they shall not rejoice in their offspring; they shall behold the slaughter of their beloved; shall lament for the destruction of their sons...
>
> CHAP. XII. [SECT. III] BOOK OF ENOCH
>
> 1. Then Enoch, passing on, said to AZAZEL: Thou shalt not obtain peace. A great sentence is gone forth against thee. He shall bind thee;
>
> 3....on account of every act of blasphemy, tyranny, and sin which thou hast discovered to the children of men. CHAP. XIII.
>
> 1....Go say to the Watchers of heaven, who have sent thee to pray for them, You ought to pray for men, and not men for you.
>
> 2. Wherefore have you forsaken the lofty and holy heaven, which endures for ever, and have lain with women; have defiled yourselves with the daughters of men; have taken to yourselves wives; have acted like the sons of the earth, and have begotten an impious offspring?

3. You being spiritual, holy, and possessing a life which is eternal, have polluted yourselves with women; have begotten in carnal blood; have lusted in the blood of men; and have done as those who are flesh and blood do.
4. These however die and perish.
6. But you from the beginning were made spiritual, possessing a life which is eternal, and not subject to death for ever.
7. Therefore I made not wives for you, because, being spiritual, you dwelling is in heaven.

CHAP. XV. BOOK OF ENOCH

Enoch was involved with not only Yahweh and his physical host, but Satan and his mutinous flock (the Watchers) as well. Additionally, the verses reveal where the Watchers/Sons of God, (Satan and his host) were physically residing prior to their actual descent to the surface of the planet. That orbital detail is confirmed by the declaration of an "everlasting station" located in "the lofty sky" (heaven/outer space). Naturally the assertion "everlasting station" may be a direct testimony to the fallen angels' cosmic rank, or status within the kingdom of heaven.

However, given my analysis, it's clear we're dealing with physical entities. Therefore, a more likely interpretation is that the 'everlasting station' refers to an orbiting space vehicle.

> STATION—*a depot. An establishment equipped for observation and study.*

The word "station" is a directly related to the word "everlasting". Quite naturally, immortal beings would require a massive immortal, (everlasting) station/craft of operations from which to function. Notably, these stellar entities are not typical humans by our earthly standards.

Yet, the verses do authenticate the fact that these cosmic beings are physically immortal entities that possess a "life" (body). This concrete detail is substantiated by the fact that these celestial individuals performed sexual intercourse with carnal females.

Celestial Assessment and Retribution

Obviously a judgment call had now been ordained upon the immortal angels and their goliath offspring. Yet, the imposed judgment would suggest that two entirely dissimilar castigations are to be inflicted. Unmistakably, the Giants and mankind were to meet with slaughter and destruction. However, the fallen angels themselves (Watchers/Sons of God) were to be bodily bound: "he shall bind thee".

> 10:8 And the whole earth has been corrupted by Azazel's teaching of his (own) actions; and write upon him all sin.
> 10:9 And to Gabriel the Lord said, "Proceed against the bastards and the reprobates and against the children of adultery; and destroy the children of adultery and expel the children of the Watchers from among the people. And send them against one another (so that) they may be destroyed in the fight,...
> 10:12 And when they and all their children have battled with each other, and when they have seen the destruction of their beloved ones, bind them for seventy generations underneath the rocks of the ground until the day of their judgement and of their consummation, until the eternal judgement is concluded.
> 14:4...and judgment is passed upon you.
> 14:5 From now on you will not be able to ascend into heaven unto all eternity, but you shall remain inside the earth, imprisoned all the days of eternity.
> 14:6 Before that you will have seen the destruction of your beloved sons...
> 10:2...for the earth and everything will be destroyed. And the deluge is about to come upon all the earth; and all that is in it will be destroyed,
> 10:4 And secondly the lord said to Raphael, "Bind Azazel hand and foot (and) throw him into the darkness!" And he made a hole in the desert which was in Duda'el and cast him there;
> 10:5 he threw on top of him rugged and sharp rocks. And he covered his face in order that he may not see light;
> 67:1 In those days, the word of God came unto me, and said unto me, "Noah, your lot has come up before me-a lot without blame, a lot of true love.
> 67:2 At this time the angels are working with wood (making an ark) and when it is complete, I shall place my hand upon it and protect it and the seed of life shall arise from it; and a substitute (generation) will come so that the earth will not remain empty (without inhabitants).
> 67:4 And they shall imprison those angels who revealed oppression in that burning valley which my grandfather Enoch had formerly shown me in the West among the mountains of gold, silver, iron, bronze, and tin.

67:5 I also saw that valley in which there took place a great turbulence and the stirring of the waters.
67:6 Now, when all this took place, there was produced from that bronze and fire a smell of sulfur (which) blended with those waters.
67:7 This valley of the perversive angels shall (continue to) burn punitively underneath that ground;...
67:8 Those waters shall become in those days a poisonous drug of the body and a punishment of the spirit unto the kings, rulers, and exalted ones, and those who dwell on the earth; lust shall fill their souls so that their bodies shall be punished,...
67:9 In proportion to the great degree of the burning of their bodies will be the transmutation of their spirits forever and ever and ever...
67:10 So the judgment shall come upon them, because they believed in the debauchery of their bodies and deny the spirit of the Lord.

I ENOCH (P)

Here again we find "Azazel", marking Satan as the principal luminary and instigator of the insurgent angels, and their behemoth brood. Unmistakably, two entirely dissimilar events had occurred. The first episode was the psychological maneuver that compelled the giants to violently turn on each other. The second sequel was the imprisonment of the fallen angels within (inside) this planet

The verses do in fact clarify the detailed discipline to be inflicted upon the exiled angels. One of those imposed penalties was the actual loss of their physical right to space-travel, "ascend into heaven," beyond this planet. This would lead one to believe that a second set of Watchers may have stayed behind to ensure that the defiant Sons of God did not leave this world to inflict their tyrannical methods elsewhere.

Moreover, the fallen angels are to be bound ("bind them"). The genuine location of their bound incarceration can actually be found in the same verses. They are to be bound "underneath the rocks of the ground", they are to be "imprisoned" "inside the earth", "into the darkness", hidden from the light of the Sun. In essences, the mutinous angels were physically confined inside this planet where there are "burning valleys", and the "smell of Sulfur".

How could physical living entities possibly survive within the interior geothermal domains ("inside") of this world? Yet, therein lies the clue, seeing how the verses do not proclaim that the fallen angels are residing inside the magma of the planet, but rather "Burning Valleys".

The verses actually inform us that the unruly angels have been isolated within the interior domains, or subterranean "valleys" of this world, adjacent to volcanic magma, or Rivers of fire. This ardent underworld technicality actually elaborates upon the words "smell" and "Sulfur".

The word "smell" would outright suggest an atmosphere in which the odor of sulfur can be sensed. This would indicate a sulfur laden atmosphere located somewhere inside this Planet. That subterranean locality is housing an open space, hollow void, or regional "Valleys" for that Sulfur burdened atmosphere to exist.

In essence, we may be unraveling chronicled evidence of a genuine Underworld domain located inside this planet. This subterranean region may harbor enormous caverns ("Valleys") reeking with the odor/smell of sulfur, due to the ("Burning") rivers of volcanic magma running throughout them. These huge caverns could in all probability contain numerous underground springs or rivers of water merging with the magma and sulphurous atmosphere, thus producing a fiery Underworld hell.

This is not to say that the Planet is hollow. Yet, the crust of the Earth is enormously thick, an outer world husk viably honeycombed with colossal caverns that have been geothermically produced. Logically, if land masses, mountainous volcanoes and volcanic upheavals on the surface of the Planet were created by volcanic magma springing up out of the earths interior, then quite naturally huge hollow voids or caverns would be left behind inside the outer crust of the planet in absence of the now surfaced Magma. Essentially, these hollow voids or caverns could be as large as mountains.

The scriptural implication is that this planet genuinely possesses a concealed, but tangible Underworld domain. Furthermore, this subterranean empire may actually harbor fallen angels boasting technological superiority far beyond our wildest comprehension. Moreover, these highly advanced fallen angels are just waiting for the day that "the eternal judgment is concluded". This will unleash the rebel angels from their subterranean penitentiary to once again rule humanity.

Noah's Ark

Notably, the verses validate the fact that Noah was directly involved with events working up to the final demise of the surviving giants and mankind.

Moreover, there is a systematic sequence that actually provides us with the motivation behind the construction of Noah's Ark.

First, the giants and corrupt mankind were partly exterminated by self-decimation while their stellar forebears (fallen angels) were forced to watch. Second, the fallen angels were not killed, but rather incarcerated inside the subterranean domains of this world. Third, Noah was to build an Ark to escape the deluge designed to destroy the lingering debased populations of the Planet.

Yet, why liquidate the surface of the planet if the giants have largely been destroyed? Why devastate the surface of the planet if the fallen angels have been physically confined to the subterranean realms (inside) of this world? The answer is obvious.

> **6:5 And God saw that the wickedness of man [was] great in the earth, and [that] every imagination of the thoughts of his heart [was] only evil continually.**
> **6:6 And it repented the LORD that he had made man on the earth, and it grieved him at his heart.**
> **6:12 And God looked upon the earth, and, behold, it was corrupt; for all flesh had corrupted his way upon the earth.**
> **6:13 And God said unto Noah, The end of all flesh is come before me; for the earth is filled with violence through them; and, behold, I will destroy them with the earth.**
> **GENESIS**

The enduring demoralized humans, as well as the surviving giants still remained on the surface of the planet. The surviving populations would only need to proliferate, consequently spawning the very same corruption previously established by the fallen angels.

Clearly, Yahweh was prepared to start over with the colonization of the Planet. Noah and his pure lineage morally qualified for the new generation of mankind. Remarkably, the verses genuinely submit that it was Yahweh and his celestial host that constructed the Ark, and not Noah. This is quite believable, if we consider the immense size of the proposed Ark. This massive Ship/Ark actually reveals astonishing dimensions of four hundred feet long, seventy-five feet wide, and forty-five feet high.

If the Ark were being built by Noah, his three sons and their wives, it would have taken them their entire lifetime, along with a forest of cut and formed lumber. Not to mention the tools, levers, pulleys and the substantial man-power required to operate them.

As for the selected animals of the world allowed to survive the inundation, the same rationality may apply. Let's be realistic! It's highly improbable that Noah traveled the entire world to physically collect and transport every conceivable species of animal to the given location of the Ark.

Noah must have received some type of physical assistance from an unknown source. That global support may have come in the form of Yahweh and his cosmic host utilizing their numerous craft to gather, and physically transport [some] of the regional animals to Noah Ark.

Furthermore, I personally do not believe Noah shepherded two wild and uncontrollable lions, tigers, bears, elephants, or even rhinos, into the Ark. This zoological nightmare obviously required some type of mental manipulation inflicted upon the wild animals. This would suggest that Yahweh and his host were fully capable of mentally exploiting the wild animal psyche into a docile state manageable by humans.

Additionally, it's highly probable that in light of the impending inundation, Yahweh and his host substantially supplied arks, (ships/craft) of their own. This extraordinary speculation would suggest that Yahweh utilized many enormous craft to collect and orbitally store as many animals as they could until the deluge had ended.

It may have taken millions of years after the original lunar conversion (Creation) to substantially evolve the now existing animal population. It would take too long to restart the animal evolution all over again. Therefore, they had to be saved if they were to be replanted to replenish the planet.

> **3:5 Likewise <u>the watchers</u> departed from nature's order; the Lord pronounced <u>a curse on them at the flood</u>. On <u>their account</u> he ordered that the earth be without dweller or produce.**
>
> TESTAMENTS OF THE TWELVE PATRIARCHS (P)
>
> **4:10 and the angel said to me, "Rightly you ask me. When God made the flood upon the earth, he drowned every firstling, and <u>he destroyed 104 thousand giants</u>, and the water rose above the highest mountains 20 cubits above the mountains, and the waters entered into the garden, bringing out one shoot from the vine as God withdrew the waters.**
>
> **4:11 And there was dry land, and Noah went out from the ark**
>
> 3 BARUCH/SLAVONIC

70:22…For the devil became ruler for the third time. The first was before paradise; the second time was in paradise; the third time was after paradise,<and> continuing right up to the Flood. 2 ENOCH [J] (P)
6:13 And God said unto Noah, The end of all flesh is come before me; for the earth is filled with violence through them; and, behold, I will destroy them with the earth.
6:17 And, behold, I, even I, do bring a flood of waters upon the earth, to destroy all flesh, wherein [is] the breath of life, from under heaven; [and] every thing that [is] in the earth shall die.
7:4 For yet seven days, and I will cause it to rain upon the earth forty days and forty nights; and every living substance that I have made will I destroy from off the face of the earth
GENESIS

Yahweh will "destroy them with the Earth". Essentially, Yahweh utilized something that already exists on the planet to destroy the Earth/land. Yet, the word "flood" lacks' substantial detail in describing what was physically implemented in the earthly inundation. Just how did the flood actually occur?

The Flood of Noah

Is it literally possible for unremitting rainfall to totally submerge this entire planet above its own mountain tops? I think not! In fact, I would go so far as to state, it's naturally impossible. I submit that nature itself will assist us in validating the fact that rains alone could not have generated the great flood of Noah.

To better comprehend this earth submerging development we need to analyze how nature generates rain. Water on the surface of the planet is evaporated into the Earth's atmosphere, thus forming enormous rain clouds. The greater the evaporation the more abundant the rainfall. Without water evaporation there would be no rain. Therefore, the question should be, where did the clouds get their substantial evaporated water supply to create rain? Obviously, "evaporation" holds the key to the forty day and night inundation of Noah.

However, there is a major difference between rain and the deluge of Noah. Rain does not occur where there is no water to begin with. Clouds do not produce water vapor or rain on their own. If they did, this entire planet would be completely submerged underwater today.

It's the enormous oceans, seas, lakes and rivers of this world that feed the clouds. If there were no oceans, seas, rivers, or lakes there would be no rain. If it continuously rained for forty days and nights, all that would physically occur is the constant recycling of preexisting water reservoirs on the surface of the planet. There would be no surplus of water added to the already existing water supplies that are either located on the surface of the planet, or in the atmosphere.

Eventually, the overwhelming inundation would run back to the oceans, seas, lakes and rivers of the planet from whence they came. In doing so, the waters would once again be evaporated into the atmosphere, accordingly generating rain all over again. Simply put, water seeks its own level.

This is not to say there would be no massive flooding induced by the tremendous deluge. Yet, the inundating rains would only establish burdensome volumes of water storming the land masses of the planet in a furious torrent to seek out and find the oceans, seas, lakes, and rivers of the world. (its own level/water table)

Naturally, the massive moving torrents of water would literally cut new earthly ravines, gorges, and rivers into the huge land masses. Nevertheless, the inundating waters would **not** cover the continental land masses of this planet above its mountain tops.

Obviously, the water table of the planet establishes a discrepancy in the inundation of Noah. Yet, the solution to this perplexing issue has already been resolved by not only the verses above, but also earlier in the chapter of Genesis. In closely scrutinizing Noah's chronicles, we discover that more than just a global inundation was used to destroy the surface of the Planet.

> **7:11 In the six hundredth year of Noah's life, in the second month, the seventeenth day of the month, the same day were all the fountains of the great deep broken up, and the windows of heaven were opened.**
>
> **7:12 And the rain was upon the earth forty days and forty nights.**
>
> GENESIS

We now have an additional incident that was used to perform the aquatic destruction of the planet. The verses even give us the sequence in which each episode transpired. In fact, it was the first primary aquatic event that produced the repercussions of the second.

Clearly, the inundating rains did not develop until **after** "all the fountains of the great deep were broken up". This was precisely "the same time" when the windows of heaven (sky) opened up generating forty days and nights of rain.

Reverse Lunar Conversion

Plainly, "the fountains of the great deep" identify all the great oceans, seas, lakes and rivers of this planet. These great deeps actually dominate the underground rivers, springs and/or fountains of the world. Yet, how does one literally break up all the great oceans, seas, lakes and rivers (Deeps) of an entire planet to constitute rain? Surprisingly, we have already analyzed, and systematically organized the prevailing aquatic events.

The verses are actually informing us that a reverse Lunar Conversion had occurred. Therefore if we examine the lunar conversion of the planet in reverse, we simultaneously satisfy the inquiry as to how the aquatic inundation of Noah came about.

Before the lunar transmutation occurred, the planet consisted of negligible land masses and enormous swamps and marshlands. Naturally, with most of the surface being submerged underwater, the atmosphere of the planet at that time was entirely different from today's sun-permeated world. By more water occupying the surface of the planet, more consistent aquatic evaporation would logically take place within the atmosphere, consequently spawning horrendous storms and rainfall on a global scale.

By establishing a Moon around the aquatic world, all the waters on the surface of the planet would be "gathered together" due to the gravitational pull of the newly installed Moon. Hence the global aquatic reservoirs (Oceans/Seas) of the planet would be pulled away from the negligible land bodies, thus exposing the submerged land masses.

Consequently, the surface of the planet would now possess more land mass with considerably less water mass, which in turn physically transfigured the atmosphere of the planet. The once rainy and heavy overcast skies of the world now became constrained, due to the decreased aquatic territories exposed to the heat of the Sun.

In essence, to bring about the flood of Noah, the kingdom of heaven extracted the Lunar Satellite (Moon) from around the planet. Simply put, they reverted the planet back to its original aquatically engulfed condition which constantly generates rain.

> **9....Go for I have ask the Lord of spirits respecting this perturbation of the earth; who replied, On account of their impiety have their innumerable judgments been consummated before me. <u>Respecting the moon have they inquired</u>, and they have known that the earth will perish with those**

who dwell upon it, and that to these there will be no place of refuge for ever. CHAP. LXIV. [SECT. XI.]

1. After this he showed me the angels of punishment, who were prepared to come, and to open all the mighty waters under the earth:

2. That they may be for judgment, and for the destruction of all those who remain and dwell upon the earth. CHAP. LXV. THE BOOK OF ENOCH

He threw clouds together and hid the brightly gleaming disk. Having covered the moon, together with the stars, and the crown of heaven all around, he thundered loudly, a terror to mortals, sending out hurricanes. All the storm winds were gathered together and all the springs of waters were released as the great cataracts were opened from heaven, and from the recesses of the earth and the endless abyss measureless waters appeared and the entire immense earth was covered.

THE SIBYLLINE ORACLES
Book 1 217-224

Those still remaining on the surface of the planet, including the prevailing giants, were well aware of the fact that the Moon would play a major roll in their conclusive demise. This was the very justification behind their respective inquiry about the Moon.

Essentially, these celestial entities were once again "prepared" to employ their matter maneuvering devices to remove the gleaming disk shaped Moon out of its orbit from around the planet. The Moon was hidden from everyone on the surface of the planet due to the cloud engulfing state it globally created.

Moreover, the Moon was physically removed from its existing orbit to be isolated further out into outer space (heaven). This lunar withdrawal ultimately gave the extracted Moon the physical appearance of just another star. In doing so, the **inner** and **outer** waters of the world were physically released to submerge the continental land masses on the surface of the planet.

Accordingly, the atmosphere of the planet was thrown into massive global upheavals. Water vapor would now fill the atmosphere of the planet generating horrendous rainfall, storms, and hurricanes on a worldwide scale. The overcast conditions would create utter darkness upon the surface of the planet. The oceans and seas of the world would now seek a new water level/table, (measure), thus engulfing the entire planet with water.

...the great loud thundering God will reduce the depths of the sea to other measures, having defined it around the land with harbors and rough shores. SIBYLLINE ORACLES Book 1 321-333

34:3 And that is why I shall bring down the flood onto the earth, and I shall destroy everything, and the earth itself will collapse in great darkness. 2 ENOCH [J] (P)

54:7 And in those days, the punishment of the Lord of the Spirits shall be carried out, and they shall open all the storerooms of water in the heavens above, in addition to the fountains of water which are on earth.

54:8 And all the waters shall be united with (all) other waters....

1 ENOCH (P)

Global Repercussions

In light of the obscured data concealed within, it's essential that we scrutinize additional verses pertaining to Noah's lunar recall. The removal of the Moon from its orbit around this planet would produce considerably more submerging damage than just horrendous rains, storms, or hurricanes. Obviously the former verses are lacking consequential details in deciphering the full repercussions of such a tremendous lunar event.

70:7 All the earth will change its order, and every fruit and every herb will change their time, for they will anticipate the time of destruction. And all the nations will change on the earth, and all my desire.

70:8 And then I, I shall command the bottomless. It will come out and rush out over the earth, and the storages of the waters of heaven will rush <from above> onto the earth in a great substance in accordance with the first substance.

70:9 And the whole constitution of the earth will perish, and all the earth will quake,...

2 ENOCH [A] (P)

1. In those days Noah saw that the earth became inclined, and that destruction approached.

3. And Noah cried with a bitter voice, Hear me; hear me; hear me: three times. And he said, Tell me what is transacting upon earth; for the earth labours, and is violently shaken.

6. A commandment has gone forth from the Lord against those who dwell on the earth, that they may be destroyed; for they know every secret of the angels, every oppressive and secret power of the devils,...

CHAP. LXIV. [SECT. XI.] BOOK OF ENOCH

> **67:11 And these waters will undergo change in those days; for (on the one hand) when those angels are being punished by these waters, the temperatures of those fountains of water will be altered (and become hot), but (on the other hand) when the angels get out, those waters of the fountains shall be transformed and become cold. 1 ENOCH (P)**

Outwardly, the verses sum up the undeniable repercussions of an event that had not yet been revealed. Notably, the entire planet had radically experienced a horrifying aquatic transformation. Moreover, this submerging punishment appears to have literally altered time itself.

The planets' previous days, weeks, months, and years "order" no longer exist. All vegetation in wake of the lunar recall had their normal growing seasons altered. The lunar established continents on the surface of the planet were physically transfigured or rearranged. The entire "constitution" of the planet appears to have been physically reorganized.

Seemingly, the entire planet had been literally moved or turned in some way by the violent cascading waters. In fact, the planet appears to have actually performed a pole shift in Noah's obvious presence. Noah genuinely observed the dawning of the "incline" (pole shift) of the planet as it unbridled death and destruction upon all its remaining surface dwellers.

> *Inclined—to deviate from the horizontal or vertical; slant. To lower or bend the head or body, as in a nod or bow. To cause to lean, slant, or slope.*

It's no wonder "all the nations on earth" (land masses/continents) were transfigured or globally reestablished. It's no marvel that the entire "constitution" of the planet has been physically altered.

> *Constitution—the basic law of an organized body, physical composition or structure, makeup, construction, design, formation.*

It's not surprising that the planet began to labor and violently shake. That which was previously above water before the lunar withdraw appears to have been repositioned and submerged below the oceans and seas of this world today. The continental re-configuration and/or relocation, was due to the planet being tipped or shifted from its normal axes.

As to just how much of a shift the planet may have executed is unclear. What is known to us today as the polar ice caps could conceivably be the true location of the dry continental land masses of this planet prior to the lunar extraction and inundation of Noah.

What used to be the frigid ice caps of the world would now be shifted to warmer locations on the surface of the planet. The warmer oceans and seas of the previous world would now be shifted to colder location, reasonably forming new ice caps as the old ones melted.

This displacing factor may actually resolve the last set of verses, specifying that the incarcerated angels will be allowed out of their subterranean brig after the global shift had concluded. This would indicate that the global waters were entirely dissimilar on the surface and interior of the planet than when the insurgent angels were first imprisoned.

Atlantis Connection

In thoroughly analyzing these Earth altering developments, I was forced into an interesting probability. There may be a link between Noah's lunar deluge and the noted legend of the lost continent of Atlantis/Mu. This myth coincides with all the Earth transforming events examined up to this point.

It is said that at the dawning of time a super civilization existed on the surface of this planet. This highly advanced culture employed the use of various crystals to produce imposing power sources, and technological advances. This super race of beings was alleged to posses incredible flying machines, weapons and devices far beyond the intellectual scope of modern technology today.

The very birth of this super race, as well as its final demise, would fit quite convincingly into the chapters of Genesis. The Atlantean race was alleged to have originated from the stars. Their super civilization ultimately inflicted tyrannizing control over the surface of the planet, as they interbreed, and enslaved its inhabitants.

The Atlantean people alleged that they were foretold of an impending aquatic cataclysm that would destroy the world they dominated. They knew the predicted earthly catastrophe would cause massive earthquakes, geothermal upheavals, and tidal waves before the coming of a new ice age, fathered by the gradual shifting of the poles of this planet.

The Atlanteans were well aware of their impending global cataclysm before it occurred, as did the mutinous angels and their titan descendants. This would lead one to believe that the fallen angels may in fact have been the Atlanteans who established their rebellious regime on the surface of the planet prior to the lunar inundation/pole shift of Noah.

It has been submitted that this technologically superior race flourished on a continent that ultimately sank into the sea. Yet, if the Atlanteans were in fact the fallen angels, their precious continent did not sink into the oceans, but rather the oceans of the world swallowed them alive via the lunar extraction of Noah.

The continent of Atlantis may in reality be what we now distinguish as the North or South Pole. Then again, the continent of Atlantis could in all probability be in any number of various global locations under the concealing oceans of the Atlantic or Pacific.

Naturally, the aquatic location would depend on the degree or type of pole shift, as well as the newly established location of the reinstalled Moon in contrast to the shift. Essentially, the new lunar orientation would establish land masses where there were non before, as well as submerge old land masses that previously existed.

Lunar Reinstatement

> **8:1 And God remembered Noah, and every living thing, and all the cattle that [was] with him in the ark: and God made a wind to pass over the earth, and the waters asswaged;**
> **8:2 The fountains also of the deep and the windows of heaven were stopped, and the rain from heaven was restrained;**
> **8:5 And the waters decreased continually until the tenth month: in the tenth [month], on the first [day] of the month, were the tops of the mountains seen.**
> **8:3 And the waters returned from off the earth continually: and after the end of the hundred and fifty days the waters were abated.** GENESIS

The end of the lunar destruction signifies the beginning of the lunar reinstatement. The waters were "asswaged" (asswage—subsided/decreased), insinuating that the waters deviated erratically from their course. Clearly, an outside influence was utilized to manipulate the waters. That outside influence caused, or "made a wind to pass over the Earth" and "stop" all the fountains of the deep.

The verses actually give us the systematic order of events. That orderly procedure began by withdrawing ("asswaged"/gather together) the oceans and seas (fountains of the deep) from around the planet, followed by the "windows of heaven" or "rain from heaven" being "restrained".

By installing the Moon around the planet for a second time, the lunar metamorphosis would occur a second time. The atmosphere (wind) of the planet would now forcibly be "made" to change, as would be the entire face of the planet.

The atmosphere of the planet would now become aquatically starved due to the extraction of the oceans and seas away from the submerged land masses, consequently forcing the atmosphere into horrendous convulsions. Moreover, the forced displacement of the massive bodies of water on the planet surface would actually create winds as the planet was being converted.

Considering the enormous convulsions the planet may have endured when faced with a possible pole shift, the moon manipulated waters would have taken ample time to fully reestablish themselves around the surface of the planet. This obvious detail is validated by the wording "the waters decreased continually", "the waters returned from off the earth continually", "the waters were abated".

This receding factor would indicate one of two possibilities: Either, the massive bodies of water on the surface of the planet were slowly withdrawn from the submerged land masses as the Moon was gradually inaugurated into its present orbit. Or the Moon was rapidly affixed into its permanent orbit, where it required considerable time to extract the global bodies of water away from the submerged land masses. Either way, there may have been survivors.

Survivors Populate a New World

It's important to remember that the planet was not entirely an aquatic world before the primary lunar transfiguration occurred. As mentioned before, the planet may have harbored inferior land masses and enormous marshlands. Those negligible land bodies may have been protruding mountain ranges, or earthly plateaus jutting up out of the submerged planet.

If in fact the lunar constrained oceans and seas were physically released, it would stand to reason that many protruding land masses were not totally affected to the point of killing off all the prevailing inhabitancy.

This speculation would propose that many dissimilar roots of mankind could have survived the second lunar metamorphosis. Those weathering roots could have proliferated into entire nations, possibly accounting for the many diverse empires that appear to have originated from out of nowhere.

If the grand plan was for the lunar induced flood to totally eradicate the evil spawned by the insurgent angels, it would appear that the lunar objective had failed. If in fact, there were survivors other than Noah and his family, they would have undoubtedly been the residues of the giants or debased mankind. This would imply that the evil of the fallen angels still genetically exists.

Obviously the surviving few branched out and began new earthly empires of their own. Furthermore it's significant to remember that the fallen angels were periodically released from their subterranean prison **after** the lunar inundation of Noah was concluded. Moreover, we are about to discover that their covert activity on the surface of the planet will ultimately unravel the mystic gods of Egypt and Babylon.

The Destruction of Sodom and Gomorrah

Sodom and Gomorrah also appear to be a perverted remnant of Noah's lunar inundation. Notably, these demoralized populations seem to have been contaminated by the behavioral characteristics of their fallen angels' ancestry. Evil begets evil, which may elaborate upon the ill will festered within the city walls of Sodom and Gomorrah.

> **18:1 And the LORD appeared unto him in the plains of Mamre: and he sat in the tent door in the heat of the day;**
> **18:2 And he lift up his eyes and looked, and, lo, three men stood by him: and when he saw [them], he ran to meet them from the tent door, and bowed himself toward the ground,**
> **18:4 Let a little water, I pray you, be fetched, and wash your feet, and rest yourselves under the tree:**
> **18:6 And Abraham hastened into the tent unto Sarah, and said, Make ready quickly three measures of fine meal, knead [it], and make cakes upon the hearth.**
> **18:7 And Abraham ran unto the herd, and fetched a calf tender and good, and gave [it] unto a young man; and he hasted to dress it.**
> **18:8 And he took butter, and milk, and the calf which he had dressed, and set [it] before them; and he stood by them under the tree, and they did eat.**
> **GENESIS**

For the first time in our scriptural analysis, it would appear that Yahweh (the Lord) and his stellar disciples have now made their physical presence known. As we shall discover, Yahweh is known to incessantly employ his superior host to interact with humans on the surface of the planet.

Here again, it becomes clear that Yahweh and his universal host possess physical bodies that consume food, and require personal hygiene (wash their feet). The same palpable evidence found within the city walls of Sodom and Gomorrah.

> 19:1 And there came two angels to Sodom at even; and Lot sat in the gate of Sodom: and Lot seeing [them] rose up to meet them; and he bowed himself with his face toward the ground;
>
> 19:2 And he said, Behold now, my lords, turn in, I pray you, into your servant's house, and tarry all night, and wash your feet, and ye shall rise up early, and go on your ways. And they said, Nay; but we will abide in the street all night.
>
> 19:3 And he pressed upon them greatly; and they turned in unto him, and entered into his house; and he made them a feast, and did bake unleavened bread, and they did eat.
>
> 19:4 But before they lay down, the men of the city, [even] the men of Sodom, compassed the house round, both old and young, all the people from every quarter:
>
> 19:5 And they called unto Lot, and said unto him, Where [are] the men which came in to thee this night? bring them out unto us, that we may know them.
>
> 19:6 And Lot went out at the door unto them, and shut the door after him,
>
> 19:7 And said, I pray you, brethren, do not so wickedly.
>
> 19:8 Behold now, I have two daughters which have not known man; let me, I pray you, bring them out unto you, and do ye to them as [is] good in your eyes: only unto these men do nothing; for therefore came they under the shadow of my roof.
>
> 19:9 And they said, Stand back. And they said [again], This one [fellow] came in to sojourn, and he will needs be a judge: now will we deal worse with thee, than with them. And they pressed sore upon the man, [even] Lot, and came near to break the door.
>
> 19:10 But the men put forth their hand, and pulled Lot into the house to them, and shut to the door.
>
> 19:11 And they smote the men that [were] at the door of the house with blindness, both small and great: so that they wearied themselves to find the door.
>
> GENESIS

Clearly the "two angels" were physical "men". This corporal detail is substantiated by the fact that Lot, and the entire city physically observed them. Additionally, they consumed food, and could have their feet washed. Moreover, If it had not been for the two angels (men), Lot's door would not have detained such an aggressive mob, which brings us to the how of the matter.

Just how did the two men/angels genuinely stop the assaulting crowd? Obviously, the two men/angels smote the crowd outside the door with blindness. Yet, the word "smote" would suggest a blunt contradiction in reference to the two angels/men.

> **SMOTE**—*To inflict a heavy blow on, with or as if with the hand, a tool, or a weapon. To drive or strike (a weapon, for example) To deal a blow with or as if with the hand or a hand-held weapon.*

The verses would suggest that the two men/angels utilized a weapon, and possibly a hand-held weapon, to assault the crowd. However, when closely scrutinizing the verses we discover that the two angels/men pulled Lot back into the house, at which point they shut the door with everyone inside the house, including the two angels/men. From this concealed location the two men then smote the mob.

How could the two men/angels strike any crowd with a hand-held weapon, or any weapon for that matter, if they were concealed inside the house? The verses would sway one to assume that the two men/angels were not alone in their city calling. Not only did the two men appear to be receiving assistance from another location, but the unknown location looms to be outside the door of Lot's home.

Tower of Babel and Sodom and Gomorrah Link

Given the violent nature of the cities and their unruly populations, it's highly unlikely that the two men entered the cities completely alone and unsupervised. This would propose that the two men/angels were under constant surveillance.

Then again, the device itself may shed some feasible light on the blinding blow inflicted upon the crowd. The verses would imply that the crowd was struck with blindness. However, the word blindness harbors numerous meanings, most of which do not imply the lack of visual sight.

BLINDNESS—*Unable or unwilling to perceive or understand. Drunk. Independent of human control. Difficult to comprehend.*

This detail should sound quite familiar considering the definition is a befitting interpretation of what may have been inflicted upon the builders of the Tower of Babel. This entire population was suddenly struck (smote) with stupidity to the point of babbling at each other.

11:7 Go to, let us go down, and there confound their language, that they may not understand one another's speech.
GENESIS

Ancient mankind being extremely captivated by these physical godlike beings ("us"), began constructing a heaven-bound edifice to reach the stars. Yet, the essential factor to be questioned would be, just how was the verbal confounding of the language of possibly thousands of people performed simultaneously?

CONFOUND—*To cause to become confused or perplexed. To fail to distinguish; mix up. To frustrate.*

It would seem that Yahweh and his host had mentally tampered with, or crippled the speech patterns of everyone involved in the construction of the Tower. We are even informed as to the manner in which the speech patterns were vocally impaired. This obvious clue derives from the word babel, hence the Tower of Babel.

BABEL—*A confusion of sounds or voices. A scene of noise and confusion. Clamor, pandemonium, tumult, commotion of a great crowd. Agitation of the mind or emotions.*

BABBLE—*To utter a meaningless confusion of words or sounds. To talk foolishly To make a continuous low, murmuring sound, To utter rapidly and indistinctly. To blurt out impulsively; Inarticulate or meaningless talk or sounds.*

As we continue to move through Scripture, we will consistently encounter the remarkable ability of Yahweh and his host to manipulate the mind not only of humans, but the animal kingdom as well. The same type of psychological manipulation frequently reported within the modern UFO phenomena.

The mental disruption appears to have caused the workers of the Tower to verbally babble, or speak gibberish resulting in utterance chaos. Essentially, it would seem that some type of mass psychological intervention was inflicted upon the entire population.

Moreover, it would seem that the vocal disruption points an accusing finger at the brain as the culprit. The brain's main source of behavior patterns derives from electrical impulses that trigger the operation of most all functions of the body including speech.

This might suggest that the babbling incident at the Tower of Babel could have feasibly been executed by an unobserved electro-magnetic field (EMF), pulsed microwave irradiation, or some unknown disrupting fields of energy originating from a concealed craft hovering in the sky. ("let us go down") These types of unseen energy fields would induce a cerebral breakdown, as the disrupting energy mentally twisted many body functions of the brain, including vision and speech patterns.

Undoubtably, a mental disruption of this magnitude would induce a crowd of any size to disperse and scatter in as many directions as possible. Essentially, the psychological manipulation at the Tower of Babel and at Lot's home are possibly one and the same. This would suggest that the blinding incident at Lot's home may not have entailed eyesight alone, but a psychological blindness as well.

Furthermore, the blinding episode may have been executed by the two angels while inside Lot's home. Both men may have actually possessed handheld devices capable of mentally disrupting (blinding) the crowd outside Lot's home while they remained inside.

However, I'm more inclined to believe that both men did in fact come prepared to be confronted by the debased inhabitants of both cities. This would argue that the two men/angels were possibly under constant surveillance by a concealed craft.

That hidden craft and its watchful eyes were possibly prepared to impose death upon anyone who endeavored to harm the two angels. In fact, this observant lofty party may have been the very method of transportation utilized by the two angels to arrive at Sodom and Gomorrah in the first place.

As with the three men who escorted Lord Yahweh ("him"?) to the camp of Abraham, the two men/angels at Sodom and Gomorrah must have procured some type of tangible transportation other than just walking to the city sites from out of nowhere. Essentially, the two men at Lot's home may have been physically transported near the site of Sodom and Gomorrah by the same craft that had a hand in the psychological blindness at Lot's home.

This might imply that a concealed craft could have flooded the area outside Lot's home with some type of unknown energy fields, consequently they caused everyone within the wave induced area to become mentally crippled and/or blind, hence "*they wearied themselves to find the door*".

> **19:12 And the men said unto Lot, Hast thou here any besides? son in law, and thy sons, and thy daughters, and whatsoever thou hast in the city, bring [them] out of this place:**
> **19:13 For we will destroy this place, because the cry of them is waxen great before the face of the LORD; and the LORD hath sent us to destroy it.**
> **19:15 And when the morning arose, then the angels hastened Lot, saying, Arise, take thy wife, and thy two daughters, which are here; lest thou be consumed in the iniquity of the city.**
> **19:16 And while he lingered, the men laid hold upon his hand, and upon the hand of his wife, and upon the hand of his two daughters; the LORD being merciful unto him: and they brought him forth, and set him without the city.**
> **19:17 And it came to pass, when they had brought them forth abroad, that he said, Escape for thy life; look not behind thee, neither stay thou in all the plain; escape to the mountain, lest thou be consumed.**
> **GENESIS**

Examining the Delivered Weapon

There are some interesting particulars seated within these verses. The verses would not only suggest a specific time frame, but a determined safe distance from the cities as well. Evidently, the two angels/men, possibly fearing for their own lives, do not want to be caught in the immediate area at the time of the destruction.

One might conclude that someone/something was coming to inflict mass destruction. Evidently, the inbound destruction was to arrive at the location of the condemned cities at a given time, possibly justifying why the two men took matters into their own hands.

Note verse 19:16 Lot and his family were "lingering". Obviously, this punctual detail forced the two men/angels to waste no time in physically removing the family. The verses actually go so far as to suggest that the two men had literally and physically taken the hands of the entire family, and pulled them out of the house.

Not only did the two men forcibly remove the family from their own home, they escorted them outside the city. In fact, the verses would lead one to believe that these two men did much more than just walked Lot's family outside the city walls. This revealing factor is disclosed in the declaration: "brought them forth", "set", and "abroad".

> SET—*To put in a specified place. To move toward the shore. To disappear below the horizon. To elevate; raise. To land (an aircraft).*
>
> ABROAD—*Out of one's own country. In a foreign country or countries. Away from one's home covering a large area; widely.*

These definitions literally assist us in resolving the statement "brought them forth". This removed location would propose a distance of many miles. The verses and their defined words would entice one to consider the probability that the two angels brought Lot and his family outside of the city to an awaiting craft.

This anticipated conveyance was utilized to "set" (transport) the entire family "abroad" at a safe distance. Obviously, rapid transportation (craft), would be required if the family and the angels were to quickly establish a vast distance between the cities and themselves. This possibly justified the two angels hasty time frame and expeditious removal of Lot's family from the city.

Just how many miles would be considered a safe distance? In close observation of the verses, it would seem that Lot's family was only transported to the outer fringes of what might be considered a kill zone. Yet, Lot and his family were still not out of danger until they entered into the mountains.

This might suggest that Lot and his family were literally transported directly to the edge of the mountain range for that very reason. This would allow Lot and his Family to shield themselves within the mountains to escape the repercussions of the weapon. Obviously, the weapon in question required an extensive distance if one wishes to abide within a safe zone. In fact, the powerful device actually appears to resemble one of the assorted nuclear devices mankind possesses today.

> **19:24 Then the LORD rained upon Sodom and upon Gomorrah brimstone and fire from the LORD out of heaven;**
>
> **19:25 And he overthrew those cities, and all the plain, and all the inhabitants of the cities, and that which grew upon the ground.**
>
> **19:26 But his wife looked back from behind him, and she became a pillar of salt.**
>
> **19:27 And Abraham gat up early in the morning to the place where he stood before the LORD:**

19:28 And he looked toward Sodom and Gomorrah, and toward all the land of the plain, and beheld, and, lo, the smoke of the country went up as the smoke of a furnace. GENESIS

2:6 And turning the cities of Sodom and Gomorrah into ashes condemned [them] with an overthrow, making [them] an ensample unto those that after should live ungodly; II PETER

29:23 [And that] the whole land thereof [is] brimstone, and salt, [and] burning, [that] it is not sown, nor beareth, nor any grass groweth therein, like the overthrow of Sodom, and Gomorrah,... DEUTERONOMY

Obviously, the weapon originated from out of the sky (heaven/outer space). The weapon harnessed enough destructive power to burn up not only the two cities, but the surrounding region as well. At first glance, one might envision a massive super laser weapon was implemented to generate the enormous destruction in just a matter of moments. This possible star wars technology would be consistent with the location from whence the fire (laser) in the sky derived.

However, the weapon in question may not have been the utilization of laser technology, but rather an unknown nuclear device. This speculation becomes even more credible when we take into account the geographical repercussions defined within the verses.

The verses actually suggest that a nuclear blast may have been employed to hurl smoke and ash soaring up into the atmosphere "as the smoke of a furnace". The word "furnace" would imply an extensive column of smoke created by the destruction, the same repercussion fathered by a nuclear detonation.

The immense power of the weapon left the countryside a burned up wasteland unfit to cultivate any plant life for many years. The nuclear blast was so powerful Lot and his family had to flee for many miles to escape the horrendous repercussions. Once again, this justified the angels' vital task to rapidly transport Lot and his family to the mountains to shield them from the blast, blinding light, and horrendous heat.

Flesh to Salt

Remarkably, the verses submit that the weapon transformed Lot's wife into a pillar of salt. This incredible chronicle would beg the question as to the true nature of the weapon. A query based on, which came first, the chicken or the egg?

The Dead Sea is believed to be the true location of what was once Sodom and Gomorrah. The entire area of the Dead Sea consists of huge rock salt, salt pits, mines, and saline deposits. The Dead Sea is so saline saturated, that a swimmer becomes totally buoyant in its waters. This salt permeated site is so acidic that the atmosphere above the Dead Sea actually diverts birds away from crossing over it.

The question is, was this colossal salt shaker the previous home of Sodom and Gomorrah, before the destruction of the cities, or after? Is it possible the device employed to destroy Sodom and Gomorrah chemically and/or anatomically transformed all living and non living objects within the inflicted area into salt, including Lot's wife?

> **2:9 Therefore [as] I live, saith the LORD of hosts, the God of Israel, Surely Moab shall be as Sodom, and the children of Ammon as Gomorrah, [even] the breeding of nettles, and saltpits, and a perpetual desolation:...**
> **ZEPHANIAH**

The word "breeding" would suggest that the weapon physically transformed the entire area into salt. Yet, therein lies another probability. It would seem quite conceivable that the salt pits, and mines within the area of the Dead Sea already existed below the surface of the planet before the destruction of Sodom and Gomorrah actually occurred. If an atomic device was used it would have literally blown up the salt pits hurling enormous salt residue high in the sky as well as all over the entire area, consequently "breeding" "saltpits".

This speculation would suggest that the weapon used to destroy Sodom and Gomorrah could have explosively actuated the salt mines within the underground area. The salt deposits may have become radically air born while destroying Sodom and Gomorrah, thus bodily inflicting Lot's wife with heated saline residues while she lingered behind the others to watch. (?)

Exodus

The defiant angels, even though confined to their Underworld ambiance, still maintained dynamic control on the surface of the planet. Evidently, the second shrouded corruption of humanity reared its ugly head following Noah's lunar deluge. Essentially, the Fallen Angels were still allowed to interact with events on the surface of the planet even though chained to this world. This transitory arrest marked the fallen angels as gods of the underworld.

I began to unravel evidence that the remnants of humanity accounted for not only the dawning empires of Egypt and Babylon, but their idolized underworld gods as well. Remarkably, the empire of Egypt acquired most, if not all of its extraordinary culture and powerful dominion from the contemptuous angels *(gods of the Underworld)*.

The Egyptian empire was not only governed by this covert regime of rebel angels but idolized their subterranean gods and considered them to be directly responsible for their powerful sovereign authority. Moreover, these subterranean entities were once again covertly controlling every significant nation on the surface of the planet. Consequently, the kingdom of heaven was once again faced with the mutinous angels stealthily inflicting their authoritarian will upon oblivious humanity.

Israel Slips into Egypt

The house of Noah ultimately flourished into the twelve diversified tribes of Israel, and found themselves coexisting with the Egyptians in the land of Goshen. Yet, the relocation of the twelve tribes of Israel into Egypt appears to have been a shrouded and deliberate act by Yahweh to infiltrate the powerful Egyptian empire.

Yahweh had devised a cosmic plan that required his people to coexist with the very population he previously tried to keep them isolated from. This timely strategy can be confirmed by Joseph, being the first of the Trojan horse infiltrators.

Joseph was well aware of Yahweh's plan for him to enter into Egypt, even though it appeared as if his brothers sold him into bondage. Truly Joseph's unobtrusive tactic into Egypt saved many from starvation, including Yahweh's own people. Yet, it would appear that Joseph's delicate entrance into Egypt may have harbored significantly more motivation than just mere sustenance for the body.

The subtle infiltration of the Hebrews into Egypt may have been the ulterior plan from the beginning. The stellar design would go completely unnoticed by the Egyptians, as well as their underworld gods (Fallen Angels). Once Joseph got his foot in the door, Yahweh was able to seasonably augment Joseph's power within the Egyptian empire, ultimately permitting the obscured infiltration of the entire twelve tribes. But why?

Egypt's subterranean gods were nothing more than masquerading rebel angels manipulating Egypt's sovereign authority. Clearly, Yahweh had planed to utilize the nation of Israel to humiliate and disgrace, not only the Egyptian populace, but their extraterrestrial underworld leaders as well. Essentially, Yahweh's intervention would allow the kingdom of heaven to destroy the authority of the defiant angels for a second time, starting with the Egyptian empire

> **12:12…and against all the gods of Egypt I will execute judgment: I [am] the LORD.**
>
> **EXODUS**

Yahweh's cosmic design was to augment his people into a powerful nation fully capable of destroying the other nations, as well as dethroning the covert administration of the fallen angels' now spread throughout the surrounding nations.

Seemingly, the oblivious, yet superstitious nations were being developed and augmented by the many diverse rebel angels stealthily operating from their subterranean domain. This allowed the insurgent angels the concealed freedom to come and go as they pleased under the guise of gods. The covert dismantling of the empire of Egypt was merely the beginning of Yahweh's efforts to dislodge and destroy the clandestine control that the mutinous angel maintained over the many nations.

The insurgent angels/other gods, unaware of Yahweh's planed reprisal, welcomed the twelve tribes of Israel into Egypt with open arms. Clearly, it would be to the advantage of the rebel angels to allow Yahweh's chosen people to betray, or turn their back on the kingdom of heaven, by coexisting with the Egyptians and their underworld gods.

The Fallen Angels' believed they had not only won over Yahweh's selected populace, but struck a severe blow at the kingdom of heaven in doing so. Or at least that was how the fraudulent act was to appear from the beginning. Moreover, the obscure fallen angels' control over Yahweh's choice people literally warranted their slavery.

The Hebrews' were greatly loved by Yahweh during that epoch of their bondage. Consequently the fallen angels (Gods of the Underworld) deliberately instigated the Hebrew slavery as a cheap retaliatory shot at the kingdom of heaven. In doing so, they savored their cosmic revenge by disgracing Yahweh's enslaved populace.

The Egyptians and the surrounding nations worshiped their mysterious gods unaware of their subterranean, or 'fallen angel' affiliation. Essentially, Egypt as well as the surrounding nations, superstitiously adhered to the directives of their underworld gods. Simply put, the rebel angels imposed the authority upon the ancient pharaohs of Egypt to enslave Yahweh's select people.

Yahweh Returns

Evidently, Yahweh and his host had left the planet, thus permitting the Hebrews to multiply into a full-blown population to be reckoned with. This disappearing act by Yahweh and his host appears to have been the stellar strategy from the beginning. Yahweh knew he would ultimately return to the planet at a later time, at which point Egypt and the surrounding nations would ultimately be dismantled while liberating his augmented nation of Israel.

> **50:24 And Joseph said unto his brethren, I die: and God will surely visit you, and bring you out of this land unto the land which he sware to Abraham, to Isaac, and to Jacob.**
> **50:25 And Joseph took an oath of the children of Israel, saying, God will surely visit you, and ye shall carry up my bones from hence. GENESIS**

13:19 And Moses took the bones of Joseph with him: for he had straitly sworn the children of Israel, saying, God will surely visit you; and ye shall carry up my bones away hence with you.

EXODUS

Obviously, Yahweh and his host were not on the planet during the period of his people's bondage. There would be no reason for Yahweh to return to "visit" his people if he was already there. One has to go somewhere to return and "visit". This would imply that Yahweh and his host had left this planet to return to the kingdom of heaven (the Universe). That celestial departure presumably took place prior to Joseph's reign and death in Egypt.

12:40 Now the sojourning of the children of Israel, who dwelt in Egypt, [was] four hundred and thirty years.

12:41 And it came to pass at the end of the four hundred and thirty years, even the selfsame day it came to pass, that all the hosts of the LORD went out from the land of Egypt.

EXODUS

Seemingly, Yahweh and/or his host perform periodic visitations to this planet. Evidently, Yahweh had now returned to the planet to reclaim his elected populace, a chosen lineage that was not to become slaves to the surviving cultures now dominated by their forefathers (Fallen Angels/other gods).

The Miracles of Moses'

Water to Blood

Quite naturally, the Egyptians having enslaved the Hebrew people for some four hundred years, would be quite reluctant in giving up their toiling servants. Nor would they be willing to give up their laborious slaves to a god they have known nothing about for over four hundred years.

7:4 But Pharaoh shall not hearken unto you, that I may lay my hand upon Egypt, and bring forth mine armies, [and] my people the children of Israel, out of the land of Egypt by great judgments.

7:19 And the LORD spake unto Moses, Say unto Aaron, Take thy rod, and stretch out thine hand upon the waters of Egypt, upon their streams, upon their rivers, and upon their ponds, and upon all their pools of water, that they may become blood; and [that] there may be blood throughout all the land of Egypt, both in [vessels of] wood, and in [vessels of] stone.

7:21 And the fish that [was] in the river died; and the river stank, and the Egyptians could not drink of the water of the river; and there was blood throughout all the land of Egypt.
7:24 And all the Egyptians digged round about the river for water to drink; for they could not drink of the water of the river. EXODUS

The word "blood" actually harbors many definitions most of which do not pertain to red blood cells of the human body

__Blood__—gore, Act of taking a life. Murder, foul play, homicide, killing, manslaughter.

The word "blood" embraces numerous meanings, one of which would suggest death or massive carnage. Examining the verses from this perspective, a totally dissimilar narrative emerged. Essentially, the verses established the fact that Yahweh and his celestial host literally transformed the waters within the surrounding area into death (blood). Put simply, Yahweh and his host had literally poisoned the surrounding water supplies.

The word "blood" may actually depict the color the waters turned in the process of poisoning them. Evidently, Yahweh and his host injected or induced some type of poison, chemical, or molecular debasement into the exposed rivers, streams, ponds, and wells.

Consequently, they contaminated all of the local water supplies within the immediate area, while at the same time altering the color of the opened waters into a deep red pigment. Then again, the poisoned waters may have displayed no color variation at all, other than the death (Blood) they contained.

The scriptural implication is that only the bodies of water subjected to the open air/sky were effected. This technicality can be further substantiated by the fact that the Egyptians were able to dig new wells around the various rivers and streams to obtain clean drinking water. Essentially, the aerially exposed water supplies were poisoned from a source up above. The aquatic contamination may have derived from an aerial object or craft that stealthily tainted all the local water supplies exposed to the open sky (from above).

The Frogs

Quite naturally, an ecological catastrophe of this magnitude would appear to be nothing short of a miracle to the populace of that era. However, considering the local water supplies may have been physically altered or tainted by some unobserved craft from above, the thought of any miracle is lost. Furthermore, by fully comprehending the primary aquatic contamination, we can resolve the other miracles

> **8:2 And if thou refuse to let [them] go, behold, I will smite all thy borders with frogs:**
> **8:3 And the river shall bring forth frogs abundantly, which shall go up and come into thine house, and into thy bedchamber, and upon thy bed, and into the house of thy servants, and upon thy people, and into thine ovens, and into thy kneading troughs:**
> **8:4 And the frogs shall come up both on thee, and upon thy people, and upon all thy servants.**
> **8:5 And the LORD spake unto Moses, Say unto Aaron, Stretch forth thine hand with thy rod over the streams, over the rivers, and over the ponds, and cause frogs to come up upon the land of Egypt.**
> **8:6 And Aaron stretched out his hand over the waters of Egypt; and the frogs came up, and covered the land of Egypt.**
> **8:8 Then Pharaoh called for Moses and Aaron, and said, Entreat the LORD, that he may take away the frogs from me, and from my people; and I will let the people go, that they may do sacrifice unto the LORD.**
> EXODUS

Obviously, the second miracle, or aquatic episode was spawned by the first. It would only stand to reason that the frogs would leave their aquatic environment in light of its poisoned condition. Clearly, all the local water supplies have become death (blood) to all aquatic life within the immediate area. The frogs were able to massively leave the contaminated area, whereas the fish were not as lucky.

Naturally, the frogs would retreat from their aquatic habitat in search of any source of refuge, or untainted water supply to survive. This would logically justify the frogs' strange behavior and unnatural appearance. Yet, it appears that the frogs were not as fortunate as they believed, considering they had already been infected with the poisoned waters they were obviously fleeing from. Essentially, the frogs found themselves faced with the same bloody/deadly fate as the fish.

> **8:8 Then Pharaoh called for Moses and Aaron, and said, Entreat the LORD, that he may take away the frogs from me, and from my people; and I will let the people go, that they may do sacrifice unto the LORD.**
> **8:13 And the LORD did according to the word of Moses; and the frogs died out of the houses, out of the villages, and out of the fields.**

8:14 And they gathered them together upon heaps: and the land stank.
EXODUS

The episode with the frogs would naturally appear to have derived from divine intervention to those unaware of the aquatic repercussions of the first event. Quite naturally, all the frogs would die out around the same time, seeing how they were all contaminated at the same time. Clearly, a preplanned domino effect had taken place in the forecasted plagues. Moreover, the aquatic repercussions or chain reactions were already accounted for by Yahweh and his host, before the events occurred, hence the prediction.

The Lice and Flies

This aquatic induced domino effect had just begun, seeing how we are about to examine a third and forth sequence of events fathered by the first two. Note what had transpired with the carcasses of the dead frogs. The frogs were gathered together into large piles, or heaps located all around the contaminated area. Furthermore, the piles or heaps of dead frogs were decomposing, hence causing the entire area ("land") to emit a strong offensive odor.

Now that the frogs had died out, the pharaoh overturns his decision to let Yahweh's people go. This allowed Moses to predict the forthcoming castigation, a forecasted miracle that would have occurred without any prior prediction at all.

8:15 But when Pharaoh saw that there was respite, he hardened his heart, and hearkened not unto them; as the LORD had said.
8:16 And the LORD said unto Moses, Say unto Aaron, Stretch out thy rod, and smite the dust of the land, that it may become lice throughout all the land of Egypt.
8:17 And they did so; for Aaron stretched out his hand with his rod, and smote the dust of the earth, and it became lice in man, and in beast; all the dust of the land became lice throughout all the land of Egypt.
8:20 And the LORD said unto Moses, Rise up early in the morning, and stand before Pharaoh; lo, he cometh forth to the water; and say unto him, Thus saith the LORD, Let my people go, that they may serve me.
8:21 Else, if thou wilt not let my people go, behold, I will send swarms [of flies] upon thee, and upon thy servants, and upon thy people, and into thy houses: and the houses of the Egyptians shall be full of swarms [of flies], and also the ground whereon they [are].

8:22 And I will sever in that day the land of Goshen, in which my people dwell, that no swarms [of flies] shall be there; to the end thou mayest know that I [am] the LORD in the midst of the earth.
8:24 And the LORD did so; and there came a grievous swarm [of flies] into the house of Pharaoh, and [into] his servants' houses, and into all the land of Egypt: the land was corrupted by reason of the swarm [of flies].
8:29 And Moses said, Behold, I go out from thee, and I will entreat the LORD that the swarms [of flies] may depart from Pharaoh, from his servants, and from his people, tomorrow: but let not Pharaoh deal deceitfully any more in not letting the people go to sacrifice to the LORD.
8:30 And Moses went out from Pharaoh, and entreated the LORD.
8:31 And the LORD did according to the word of Moses; and he removed the swarms [of flies] from Pharaoh, from his servants, and from his people; there remained not one.
EXODUS

Yahweh has now plagued the contaminated area with lice. Yet, in scrutinizing the chain of events, we discover it was not Yahweh that directly caused the plague of lice. Rather, it was the first aquatic incident that has now produced the third and fourth swarming conditions.

It was the poisoned water supplies that spawned the lice dilemma. If you will research the insect in question, you will find lice to be tiny insects that suck the blood of small animals. These types of animal and plant parasites survive on even the smallest of animals including birds.

Let's stop a moment to review. Yahweh and his host first poisoned the water supplies within the local area, consequently causing the death of the fish. In doing so, Yahweh constituted a domino effect which biologically affected the entire ecosystem of every living thing within, or around the polluted waters, including plant life. Quite naturally, wildlife such as birds and small animals including frogs would withdraw from the toxic area.

Many of the residing birds and smaller creatures within the aquatically contaminated area may have become sick, or simply died out just as the fish and frogs did. The parasites subsisting on the plants, birds and smaller animals would no longer be able to survive on the tainted blood, or sap of the animals and plants. Therefore, the tiny parasites were forced to find another host, or untainted food supply if they were to survive. The only close and immediate un-tainted food supply within the contaminated area would be the Egyptians (humans) and their land based environment.

The very same domino effect, or natural repercussion generated the flies. The flies were a direct result of the dead frogs, and possibly many other dead animals that may have succumbed to the deadly tainted waters. By gathering together the dead frogs into many piles or heaps around the local area, the Egyptians would have unknowingly created numerous hatcheries for the massive breeding of flies.

Flies customarily lay their eggs in soft masses of decaying plant or animal material. One fly can lay as many as two hundred and fifty eggs at one time, depending on the species. Those eggs can hatch within 8 to 30 hours. With possibly hundreds of piles of decaying dead frogs lying everywhere within the contaminated area, the preexisting fly population would have a virtual procreating field day.

The decaying frogs could have produced millions of flies all of which would be brought to life at approximately the same time, as well as in the same vicinity. Furthermore, all the flies would have died out, or ultimately left the area at approximately the same time.

The Livestock and Boils

Obviously, Yahweh and his host were well aware of the natural repercussions long before they ever occurred, hence allowing Moses to predict the events before they actually transpired. Yet, the same natural eco-impacts would have taken place whether the Egyptians had been advised or not.

> **9:3 Behold, the hand of the LORD is upon thy cattle which [is] in the field, upon the horses, upon the asses, upon the camels, upon the oxen, and upon the sheep: [there shall be] a very grievous murrain.**
>
> **9:4 And the LORD shall sever between the cattle of Israel and the cattle of Egypt: and there shall nothing die of all [that is] the children's of Israel.**
>
> **9:5 And the LORD appointed a set time, saying, To morrow the LORD shall do this thing in the land.**
>
> **9:6 And the LORD did that thing on the morrow, and all the cattle of Egypt died: but of the cattle of the children of Israel died not one.**
>
> **9:8 And the LORD said unto Moses and unto Aaron, Take to you handfuls of ashes of the furnace, and let Moses sprinkle it toward the heaven in the sight of Pharaoh.**

> **9:9 And it shall become small dust in all the land of Egypt, and shall be a boil breaking forth [with] blains upon man, and upon beast, throughout all the land of Egypt.**
> **9:10 And they took ashes of the furnace, and stood before Pharaoh; and Moses sprinkled it up toward heaven; and it became a boil breaking forth [with] blains upon man, and upon beast.**
> **9:11 And the magicians could not stand before Moses because of the boils; for the boil was upon the magicians, and upon all the Egyptians.**
> **EXODUS**

Let's keep in mind that Yahweh and his host utilize numerous craft boasting unimaginable capabilities. Those craft will be examined in extreme detail when we enter the book of Ezekiel. Essentially, Yahweh and his host could have aerially performed the slaughter of the livestock. That aerial butchery may have been simplified by the fact that the livestock of the Egyptians were presumably isolated from the livestock of the Hebrews, thus logically identifying which animals to kill.

However, therein lies another probability. If we take into account the fact that only the Egyptian livestock died, and not the animals of the Israelites, then the slaying of the Egyptian livestock may once again be rooted in the aquatic chain reaction now set into motion. Obviously, only the Egyptian water supplies were poisoned, a contaminant that ultimately found its way into the drinking water of the Egyptian livestock, consequently leading up to their toxic demise.

The massive demise of Egyptian livestock appears to have been calculated, "set time". This might imply that Yahweh and his host were not only aware of the fact that the Egyptian livestock were drinking the contaminated water. They were even proficient in calculating how long it would take for the livestock to succumb to the tainted drink, as predicted.

As for the "boils" inflicted upon the Egyptians and their livestock, it would appear that the aquatic repercussions of the first plague had once again claimed responsibility for the second. The frogs were gathered together into piles or heaps being the perfect breeding ground for flies. The legions of flies hatching from the masses of contaminated dead decomposing frogs swarmed the Egyptian empire as did the lice.

Flies and lice are principal carriers of disease. Flies are among one of the most dangerous pests known to man. When a fly bites or touches any object, it leaves behind many germs. Even the stiff hairs on a fly's body and legs carry many diseases and germs that brush off on anything the insect touches. This would not even include the bacterium and contaminants imposed upon the bodies of the Flies from the decaying contaminated bodies of the dead frogs.

Most boils are caused by a type of Staphylococcal bacteria. The bacteria can enter an oil gland, sweat gland, hair follicle or small shallow wound. They ultimately multiply and grow in the skin tissues and give off poisons. This might suggest that the massive hordes of flies aerially trafficked germs and/or diseases to not only the Egyptians but their livestock as well. That swarming condition was totally isolated from the Hebrews.

This speculative explanation might also account for the parasitic repercussions inflicted by the lice. The lice were infected by the tainted blood of the small animals they were at one time thriving upon. The lice were now forced to administer and biologically traffic their tainted blood with the blood of the Egyptians and their livestock. Essentially, the isolated Egyptians and their livestock could have been infected with many different types of germs, bacteria, or diseases from the Lice.

However, there may exist another infectious probability. The epidemic death of the Egyptian livestock may have actually been responsible for the infectious Staphylococcal bacteria or boils on the bodies of the Egyptians. The contaminated parasites, whether it was lice or any other parasitic insect, were subsisting on the livestock of the Egyptians.

This might suggest that the Egyptian livestock died from the tainted parasites. When the livestock perished the parasites were forced to find another host. The closest living host within the area would be the Egyptians. Hence, the parasites transferred and inflicted a type of Staphylococcal bacteria upon the Egyptians.

Clearly, Yahweh and his host were well aware of the impending ramifications due to the aquatic chain reaction set into motion by polluting the water supplies. By Moses predicting the ensuing repercussions before they actually occurred, the Egyptians would have believed the miraculous sequels to be nothing short of divine intervention.

The Fiery Hail

Up to this point, no one has been seriously harmed. However, Yahweh is now prepared to take even greater and more spectacular measures, subsequently punishing the Egyptians to no end. The proceeding manipulation of nature would truly leave one at a loss for words when trying to comprehension how such an atmospheric event could have been performed, much less technologically executed.

> **9:18 Behold, to morrow about this time I will cause it to rain a very grievous hail, such as hath not been in Egypt since the foundation thereof even until now.**
> **9:19 Send therefore now, [and] gather thy cattle, and all that thou hast in the field; [for upon] every man and beast which shall be found in the field, and shall not be brought home, the hail shall come down upon them, and they shall die.**
> **9:22 And the LORD said unto Moses, Stretch forth thine hand toward heaven, that there may be hail in all the land of Egypt, upon man, and upon beast, and upon every herb of the field, throughout the land of Egypt.**
> **9:23 And Moses stretched forth his rod toward heaven: and the LORD sent thunder and hail, and the fire ran along upon the ground; and the LORD rained hail upon the land of Egypt.**
> **9:24 So there was hail, and fire mingled with the hail, very grievous, such as there was none like it in all the land of Egypt since it became a nation.**
> **9:25 And the hail smote throughout all the land of Egypt all that [was] in the field, both man and beast; and the hail smote every herb of the field, and brake every tree of the field.**
> **9:26 Only in the land of Goshen, where the children of Israel [were], was there no hail.**
> EXODUS

Hail is a common occurrence throughout nature, yet how was it possible for hail to become "mingled" with fire, or vice versa? How did the hail storm develop when and where Yahweh wanted it to form? To truly grasp this unique manipulation of nature, we need to examine how hail it actually formed.

Hailstones generally display an onion like structure embodying a number of layers, or fused shells of ice. Hailstones form in much the same way as sleet does. Small ice crystals or snowflakes contact super cold water drops still in a liquid state at temperatures below freezing. When the ice particles strike the super cooled water drops, the water flows over the ice and instantly freezes. This perpetual process continues until the hailstone falls out of the region of the atmosphere containing the super cooled water. It may then be caught in an updraft and carried back up into the super cooled water region were it contin-

ues to grow larger. This relentless ice making process pers[…]
can no longer support the weight of the hailstones. Sub[…]
formed hailstones fall to earth.

This natural explanation of forming hailstones may actually hold the key to comprehending how fire was physically entrapped within the hailstones. Our scientists today hope to find a way to break up hailstorms by cloud seeding, or some similar process to lessen the damage to crops and property.

Atmospheric cloud seeding by mankind today is not as farfetched as it may seem. Yet, to a more advanced system, such as the kingdom of heaven, it may be a commonplace applied science to be utilized upon numerous planets in the manipulation of their many diverse atmospheres.

Essentially, it would appear that Yahweh and his celestial host may have actually seeded the clouds with an unknown chemical, or liquid element. That chemical, or liquid element, was able to unite with the forming hail as it developed. Furthermore, it would appear that a spontaneously combustible chemical was used.

This is not an uncommon chemical reaction, in light of the fact that mankind today produces chemicals, liquid elements and compounds that respond in the same manner. The reactions from these types of chemicals are labeled as spontaneous combustion. Spontaneous combustion is burning produced without the application of a flame and the rapid union of oxygen with any substance. Combustion occurs, for example, when chlorine burns in hydrogen gas, or in the spontaneous burning of any substance in chlorine, such as brake fluid.

Here again, we have no earthly perception of the truly evolved intellectual or technological capabilities that Yahweh and his universal host may retain. Chemically seeding the clouds may have been an elementary matter for Yahweh and his host. Particularly when we consider that these universal beings may actually possess the power of matter transfer/teleportation/manipulation.

If in fact Yahweh and his host seeded the clouds with some type of spontaneously combustible chemicals or liquid elements with the forming hail, it would have had to be temperature sensitive. This would justify the employment of developing hail to not only fuse the element to the growing hailstones, but literally transport the unstable chemical or liquid element to the surface of the planet in a stable medium such as ice.

As long as the chemical element remained united within the frozen hail, it would maintain its spontaneous stability. As long as the hailstones stayed within the colder regions of the atmosphere, no chemical reaction would take place.

However, when the hailstones fell to the warm ground they began to melt. The melting hail released and mixed the chemical elements into the warm atmosphere and oxygen, which in turn caused the spontaneous combustion. Consequently, the fiery liquid element was mixed with water as it ran along the ground from the melting hailstones. In essence, the chemical reaction took place exactly how the verses delineated it. **"there was hail, and fire mingled with the hail, and the fire ran along upon the ground".**

Weather Manipulation

In thoroughly analyzing the verses, we discover that the hailstones were so large that they may have killed not only livestock within the inflicted area, but humans as well. Yet, more significant would be the geographical objective that the storm targeted.

Obviously, Yahweh and his host are masterful in manipulating weather conditions on the surface of this planet. Yet, how was it possible for Yahweh and his host to physically generate, as well as manipulate, such a tremendous hailstorm within the preplanned given location?

As bizarre as it may seem, by analyzing the probable propulsion systems of these craft we can surmise their methods of manipulating weather. Just like the modern UFO phenomenon, Yahweh's unique stellar craft appear to be electro-magnetic machines. The craft appear to be propelled by a manipulated electro-magnetic field that luminously glow and engulf the entire craft.

Moreover, it would appear that this radiating electro-magnetic field or flux is being employed to utilize the planet's magnetic fields as a method of propulsion for the craft. This electromagnetic exploitation may account for the many diverse enveloping colors frequently reported by numerous witnesses observing these extraordinary machines (UFOs).

By manipulating the dissimilar electro-magnetic fields around the craft, the magnetic flux or energy shield changes colors/spectrums while at the same time utilizing the magnetic fields of the planet to push or repel the craft. Simply put, like magnetic poles repel each other, where unlike magnetic poles attract each other.

Quite naturally, one might inquire as to what this electromagnetic detail would have to do with artificially manipulated weather conditions? Yet, this electromagnetic factor would imply that Yahweh and his host are fully capable of manipulating enormous magnetic fields of unknown proportions and/or degrees.

The weather patterns of this world are actually generated by temperature variations within the atmosphere. These temperature fluctuations produce low and high fronts, which are nothing more than organized warm and cold fronts pushing each other around. The unlike fronts develop storm systems due to the clashing engagements of the two dissimilar fronts. Yet, the dominant factor of temperature variations actually derives from the Sun. Without the heat of the Sun there would be no global temperature variations or massive water evaporation (storms/rain).

However, the primary question should be, what genuinely governs the heat of the Sun as it assaults the surface of this world? Or, in different words, what controls the tremendous heat of the Sun from burning up this planet? The Sun produces what is referred to as the "solar wind". This rushing heat wave generates temperatures reaching a million degrees, and fully capable of incinerating this planet.

The radiation belts of this planet protect us from the Sun's tremendous heat. Without the radiation belts to filter out the intense heat of the Sun, the surface of this world would become a dying cinder. By combining all of the data together, we discover what may be an astonishing solution to what might have been a bewildering issue.

The radiation belts of this planet not only protect us from the searing heat of the Sun, they also govern our weather patterns. More significantly, however, would be the fact that the radiation belts of this planet are also commonly distinguished as the "magneto-sphere/magneto-pause". The "magneto-pause" is a boundary between the planet and outer space dominated by the Earth's magnetic field.

> MAG~NE~TO~SPHERE [MAGNETO-SPHERE] *that region surrounding a planet in which the planet's magnetic field is stronger than the interplanetary field:*

Essentially, this planet and its consistent battle against the horrendous heat of the Sun is being filtered and controlled by its magnetic fields/magnetosphere (radiation belts). If in fact Yahweh and his stellar host are genuinely capable of creating and manipulating massive magnetic fields around their craft, they may also be fully capable of manipulating the very magneto-sphere (radiation belts/magnetic fields') of this planet.

In doing so, they could literally control and manipulate the diverse temperature variations of the planet's atmosphere at strategic locations. By magnifying, or de-magnifying the magnetic fields (radiation belts) of the planet they could decrease or increase the amount of heat in the upper atmosphere. They could conceivably create or dissipate massive water evaporation within the atmosphere of the planet at any given location, consequently terminating or organizing rain.

By magnetically manipulating, or punching holes in the magneto-sphere, they could govern the heat of the Sun as it strikes the Planet. They could create storms, or even stop storms from forming by manipulating cold/low fronts and hot/high fronts.

However, in order to pull off a global event of this magnitude, it would require a massive craft, or craft and devices, capable of manipulating enormous areas of the magneto-sphere/radiation belts. Possibly, the same gargantuan craft and magnetic/matter manipulation utilized to bodily propel a Moon into orbit around this world eons ago.

The Locust

Note what the generated hailstorm inflicted upon the immediate area. The hailstorm destroyed an extensive area of farm land, as well as the encompassing "fields" and "trees". In fact, the geographical devastation actually renders the solution to the next plague.

> **9:31 And the flax and the barley was smitten: for the barley [was] in the ear, and the flax [was] bolled.**
> **9:32 But the wheat and the rie were not smitten: for they [were] not grown up.**
> **10:4 Else, if thou refuse to let my people go, behold, to morrow will I bring the locusts into thy coast:**
> **10:5 And they shall cover the face of the earth, that one cannot be able to see the earth: and they shall <u>eat the residue</u> of that which is escaped, which remaineth unto you from the hail, and shall eat every tree which groweth for you out of the field:**

10:12 And the LORD said unto Moses, Stretch out thine hand over the land of Egypt for the locusts, that they may come up upon the land of Egypt, and eat every herb of the land, [even] all that the hail hath left.
10:13 And Moses stretched forth his rod over the land of Egypt, and the LORD brought an east wind upon the land all that day, and all [that] night; [and] when it was morning, the east wind brought the locusts.
10:14 And the locusts went up over all the land of Egypt, and rested in all the coasts of Egypt: very grievous [were they]; before them there were no such locusts as they, neither after them shall be such.
10:15 For they covered the face of the whole earth, so that the land was darkened; and they did eat every herb of the land, and all the fruit of the trees which the hail had left: and there remained not any green thing in the trees, or in the herbs of the field, through all the land of Egypt.
10:6 And they shall fill thy houses, and the houses of all thy servants, and the houses of all the Egyptians;…
EXODUS

It's not uncommon for locusts to be found in this section of the world. Since ancient times, locusts have been destroying crops and lush "green" fields in nearly all continents, except for the extremely colder regions of the planet. Locusts travel in large swarms and settle on green fields like a blanket as they ravenously eat "**green**" leaves and stalks.

The verses would suggest that an "east wind" brought by Yahweh was responsible for the swarming Locusts. By the time you have finished this chapter, you will come to realize that the word "wind" may in fact be a direct testimonial to the matter-maneuvering devices of these astounding extraterrestrial machines. Essentially, Yahweh and celestial craft may have actually employed their matter maneuvering devices to physically force the Locusts to swarm.

However, therein lies another probability. The predicted arrival of the locusts' at that particular location and time would appear to have originated from divine intervention. Yet, here again, the preceding sequence was developed by a chain reaction created from the first event. Surveying the verses, we are enlightened to the fact that the locusts will eat the **"residue"**, or what remains of the green plant life left behind by the pulverizing hail.

Obviously, the hailstorm destroyed the crops of the fields, trees, scrubs, and most all "green" plant life within the storm inflicted area. The destructive hailstorm left in its wake a countryside devastated with smitten plant life now withering and drying up as it lies lifeless upon the earth.

By realizing locusts only thrive off of living green plant life, we are awakened to the fact that the food supply of all the locusts within the storm inflicted area has just been destroyed. Consequently, the locusts were compelled to find a new living green food supply. In essence, the locusts were forced to swarm in order to find what remained, or the "residue" of the last living green plant life within the hail pounded area.

We also need to keep in mind that the hailstorm may have been seeded with a spontaneously combustible chemical or liquid element that united with the developing hail. This would suggest that wherever the seeded hail crashed to the ground, it not only scorched the abiding plant life, but a residue of the chemical or liquid element would be present, thus leaving a bad taste in the mouth of the locusts.

This speculation might account for the time frame ("to morrow") given in the verses. Evidently, Yahweh and his host knew it would not take but a single day for the locusts to radically respond to the seeded hailstorm. Especially, if Yahweh and his host were to utilized their matter maneuvering devices ("wind") to motivate the swarm. Furthermore, the swarming locusts were not the only repercussion spawned by the tainted hail.

The Mysterious Thick Darkness

> **10:20 But the LORD hardened Pharaoh's heart, so that he would not let the children of Israel go.**
> **10:21 And the LORD said unto Moses, Stretch out thine hand toward heaven, that there may be darkness over the land of Egypt, even darkness [which] may be felt.**
> **10:22 And Moses stretched forth his hand toward heaven; and there was a thick darkness in all the land of Egypt three days:**
> **10:23 They saw not one another, neither rose any from his place for three days: but all the children of Israel had light in their dwellings. EXODUS**

This perplexing issue would leave one totally bewildered as to what manner of darkness could be considered thick, so thick it could physically be "felt". Moreover, the darkness was so profuse the populace was forced to remain within their homes.

Obviously, the dark phenomenon only developed within the Egyptian municipality and not in the camp of Israel. Or perhaps, I should say, this extraordinary episode transpired only where the induced Hailstorm had occurred. Furthermore, the cloudy incident transpired immediately after the hailstorm.

This gloomy event is not an uncommon occurrence in nature. However, the incident, even though common, may have been magnified to a much higher degree by Yahweh and his host. What ingredient in nature would appropriately fit the depicted phenomenon? What fundamental element would produce darkness and yet be localized only within the Egyptian metropolis? What manner of darkness would allow the human body to feel it?

The solution to this murky issue may actually reside in what is distinguished as Fog. If fog is thick or dense enough, it can actually be "felt" as it engulfs the human body. It's no marvel the populace of the Egyptian metropolis stayed indoors, considering the fog may have been so thick they could not see two feet in front of their own face, hence the Egyptians "saw not one another". Yet, the fog described in the verses appears to had been artificially amplified beyond its typical nature. But how?

Fog is actually a cloud formed so low that it settles near the ground, or the surface of bodies of water. Fog forms in much the same manner as a cloud appears around a steaming kettle. The moisture in the warm air coming from the steaming kettle condenses by forming small water drops when it strikes the cooler air.

Fog frequently occurs when relatively warm moist air passes over a colder surface, such as a cold ocean current, or an area covered by ice or snow (hail). Obviously, the main ingredients for fog are cold, heat, moisture, or water and temperature variations of the atmosphere which distinctly interact upon each other. Clearly, all the factors required to constitute fog can be found in the verses.

The frozen hail storm only occurred within the municipality of the Egyptians. Moreover, the frozen hailstorm actually produced heat (fire). The fog or darkness only occurred after the fiery hailstorm had concluded. This would suggest that the frozen hail and the induced heat created by the fire within the frozen hail were all the elements required within the preexisting atmosphere to create fog. Essentially, the melting frozen hail and fire generated a moist frigid atmospheric medium that merged with the heated air masses after the storm terminated, consequently producing dense fog.

Furthermore, Yahweh and his host may have manipulated the magnetosphere of the planet to produce isolated atmospheric conditions, to produce the hailstorm. Consequently, Yahweh and his host may have actually produced a heated atmosphere within the immediate area of the frozen hail. In doing so, they established the perfect conditions between the frozen hail and the heated atmosphere, to produce extremely dense fog.

However, we will discover that the "**darkness**" found within the fog may not be a testimonial to the obscuring fog alone. In fact, we will discover that another unknown element was utilized to darken the prevailing fog during the daylight hours. Moreover, we shall ascertain that this eclipsing element genuinely originated from the sky/heaven/outer space.

The Passover

The artificially induced events plagued upon the Egyptians now appear to be aimed at a more calamitous design. Up to this point, no one has been seriously hurt. However, Yahweh and his host are now prepared to inflict a detrimental rampage of death, being the celestial objective from the genesis.

Evidently, Yahweh and his host were just toying with the Egyptians prior to mobilizing their final plan of action. Seemingly, the ultimate objective was to destroy the Egyptian empire, as well as humiliate their underworld gods (Fallen Angels). In doing so, the celestial strategy was to kill as many Egyptians following the directives of their underworld gods as possible. Yet, it would appear that Yahweh and his host calculatedly planned to drag out the suffering of the Egyptians prior to their climactic demise.

> **11:4 And Moses said, Thus saith the LORD, About midnight will I go out into the midst of Egypt:**
>
> **11:5 And all the firstborn in the land of Egypt shall die, from the firstborn of Pharaoh that sitteth upon his throne, even unto the firstborn of the maidservant that [is] behind the mill; and all the firstborn of beasts.**
>
> **11:6 And there shall be a great cry throughout all the land of Egypt, such as there was none like it, nor shall be like it any more.**
>
> **11:7 But against any of the children of Israel shall not a dog move his tongue, against man or beast: that ye may know how that the LORD doth put a difference between the Egyptians and Israel.**
>
> **12:12 For I will pass through the land of Egypt this night, and will smite all the firstborn in the land of Egypt, both man and beast; and against all the gods of Egypt I will execute judgment: I [am] the LORD.**

12:13 And the blood shall be to you for a token upon the houses where ye [are]: and when I see the blood, I will pass over you, and the plague shall not be upon you to destroy [you], when I smite the land of Egypt.
12:21 Then Moses called for all the elders of Israel, and said unto them, Draw out and take you a lamb according to your families, and kill the passover.
12:22 And ye shall take a bunch of hyssop, and dip [it] in the blood that [is] in the basin, and strike the lintel and the two side posts with the blood that [is] in the basin; and none of you shall go out at the door of his house until the morning.
12:23 For the LORD will pass through to smite the Egyptians; and when he seeth the blood upon the lintel, and on the two side posts, the LORD will pass over the door, and will not suffer the destroyer to come in unto your houses to smite [you].
12:29 And it came to pass, that at midnight the LORD smote all the firstborn in the land of Egypt, from the firstborn of Pharaoh that sat on his throne unto the firstborn of the captive that [was] in the dungeon; and all the firstborn of cattle.
12:30 And Pharaoh rose up in the night, he, and all his servants, and all the Egyptians; and there was a great cry in Egypt; for [there was] not a house where [there was] not one dead.
EXODUS

Egypt had suffered a great physical loss due to the death of their future legacy. Yet, the true sufferers of Egypt's massacred posterity was not so much the Egyptians, but rather their Underworld gods (Fallen Angels), being the true leaders of Egypt. That judgment call exterminated the insurgent angels' future administrators of Egypt, by slaying its firstborn.

The Hebrews were informed to paint the lintel and the two side posts of their homes if they wished to escape Yahweh's deadly binge. This remarkable declaration actually implies that Yahweh and his host were unable to visually distinguish who was who. The verses genuinely establish the fact that we are dealing with bodily entities possessing palpable eyes in need of physical sight to perform tangible acts.

The Hebrews had to paint, or mark their houses, so Yahweh and his host would be able to physically distinguish by visual sight his people from the Egyptians. This substantial detail is further clarified by the assertion "and when I **see** the blood/when he **seeth** the blood".

Yahweh and his host are not only physical in nature, but are obviously observing the evolving events from up above. This would justify the location of the painted blood on the lintels of the Hebrew dwellings.

By the blood being painted on the protruding lintel and side posts of the homes, Yahweh and his host would be able to physically see the marked houses from above. Consequently, the firstborn slaughter will also derive from the sky, an aerial assault substantiated by the phrase "**pass over the door**".

Obviously, something (craft) will "pass over the door" of the dwellings as they physically look for the marked or unmarked homes. This would suggest that numerous concealed craft were employed to covertly carry out the first-born massacre.

Israel Leaves Egypt Following a Cloud

Inasmuch as all the firstborn children of the Egyptians have now been massively and mysteriously slaughtered, fear would run rampant throughout the Egyptian empire. The Egyptians would not only let the populace of Israel go, but insist on their exodus from Egypt.

Nevertheless, Yahweh and his host are not through dealing with the Egyptians or their underworld gods/fallen angels. In fact, Yahweh and his host are now prepared to substantially escalate the true definition of the word "death" by destroying most of the population of Egypt that forcibly governs it. Essentially, this will leave Egypt's underworld gods lacking one of their covertly governed estates on the surface of the planet.

Thus far, we have scrutinized an extensive body of data alluding to the possible existence of stellar craft that may be physically involved in ancient events found within Scripture. However, as of yet, we have not assembled any substantial details to produce tangible evidence of an authentic craft. This missing detail was due to the fact that Yahweh and his host kept their physical appearance concealed from mankind up to this point in Scripture.

However, Yahweh had now returned to this planet to free his selected populace. In doing so, Yahweh and his host will have no other choice but to physically show themselves if they are to execute the severing of Israel from Egypt. This placed Yahweh in an extremely sensitive position, seeing how they must now become physically involved. Consequently, Yahweh and his party will be forced to expose their genuine mode of conveyance.

12:51 And it came to pass the selfsame day, [that] the LORD did bring the children of Israel out of the land of Egypt by their armies.
13:21 And the LORD went before them by day in a pillar of a cloud, to lead them the way; and by night in a pillar of fire, to give them light; to go by day and night:
13:22 He took not away the pillar of the cloud by day, nor the pillar of fire by night, [from] before the people.
14:1 And the LORD spake unto Moses, saying,
14:2 Speak unto the children of Israel, that they turn and encamp before Pihahiroth, between Migdol and the sea, over against Baalzephon: before it shall ye encamp by the sea.
14:3 For Pharaoh will say of the children of Israel, They [are] entangled in the land, the wilderness hath shut them in.
14:4 And I will harden Pharaoh's heart, that he shall follow after them; and I will be honoured upon Pharaoh, and upon all his host; that the Egyptians may know that I [am] the LORD. And they did so.
14:8 And the LORD hardened the heart of Pharaoh king of Egypt, and he pursued after the children of Israel: and the children of Israel went out with an high hand.

EXODUS

Are we to believe God (Yahweh) is just a cloud? Are we to also embrace the belief that this massive moving populace is simply following a lone cloud that advances and stops at will? Obviously, this well defined cloud is maintaining an intelligently navigated direction of movement, contrary to the other clouds in the sky, not to mention the mysterious fiery elements concealed within.

Yet, how does a common cloud become a pillar of fire only during the darkness of night? These are but trivial technicalities considering our study does not concern the cloud, nor its pillar like fiery attributes. Alternatively, we are more concerned with what lurks within (inside) the cloud.

24:1…"He mounted a cherub and flew."
24:2 He has the chariots of wind, as it is written, "He soared on the wings of the wind."
24:3 He has the chariots of swift cloud, as it is written, "See! The Lord comes riding a swift cloud."
24:4 He has the chariots of clouds, as it is written, "I am coming to you in a dense cloud."

APPENDIX TO 3 ENOCH (P)

Note the verses use the word "chariots" implying more than one. The word "mounted" would suggest that Yahweh had to bodily mount, get on, or into a material object identified as a chariot/cherub. Moreover, the tangible objects ("chariots") boast flight capabilities ("flew"), as if the "wind" itself maintained the source of power for the chariots to fly.

Yet, more notably would be the statement "I come to you in a dense cloud". The key word would be ("in"), implying that Yahweh is inside the dense cloud, and not the cloud itself. In essence, the cloud is not the chariots, nor are the chariots the cloud, but rather the chariots are inside the cloud.

From this moment on, we will constantly be confronted with this mysterious cloud and the solid chariots concealed within. This remarkable cloud will be quite unyielding in revealing its true inner form until we enter the book of Ezekiel.

At that time, we will discover that this enigmatic cloud is actually concealing inside its shrouding body not only one metallic craft, but **five** metallic craft (chariots), all of which wield miraculous powers, and modern UFO characteristics.

The Cloud Splits Up

Yahweh's cloud shrouded craft/chariots not only piloted his extracted populace out of Egypt, but aerially navigated them directly into a preplanned location for a specific reason. Evidently, the charted destination for Yahweh's people to camp, and the final chase scene by the Egyptian army was to coincide at the same time and place. Clearly, Yahweh had deliberately led the Israelites into an obvious dead end, thus allowing for a flawless ambush by the Egyptians.

> **14:3 For Pharaoh will say of the children of Israel, They [are] entangled in the land, the wilderness hath shut them in.**
> **14:4 And I will harden Pharaoh's heart, that he shall follow after them; and I will be honoured upon Pharaoh, and upon all his host; that the Egyptians may know that I [am] the LORD. And they did so.**
> **14:9 But the Egyptians pursued after them, all the horses [and] chariots of Pharaoh, and his horsemen, and his army, and overtook them encamping by the sea, beside Pihahiroth, before Baalzephon.**

14:10 And when Pharaoh drew nigh, the children of Israel lifted up their eyes, and, behold, the Egyptians marched after them; and they were sore afraid: and the children of Israel cried out unto the LORD.
14:19 And the angel of God, which went before the camp of Israel, removed and went behind them; and the pillar of the cloud went from before their face, and stood behind them:
14:20 And it came between the camp of the Egyptians and the camp of Israel; and it was a cloud and darkness [to them], but it gave light by night [to these]: so that the one came not near the other all the night.
EXODUS

Unmistakably, the Hebrews were intentionally entrapped. Yet, this obvious snare would seem to have been the stellar plan from the outset. Outwardly, the ambush was not designed for the populace of Israel, but rather the Egyptians. Clearly, the geographical lure was deliberately devised by Yahweh and his host to misled the Egyptians into the ploy.

The Egyptian arrival prompted the mysterious cloud masking the five craft/chariots to execute a complex maneuver. The craft have now aerially relocated themselves between the two encampments. Obviously, the maneuver would ensure that the Egyptian's army could not attack the Hebrews during the night.

However, look at the verses again. Clearly, there were two entirely different aerial maneuvers taking place. At first glance, one might assume that the cloud enveloped craft/chariots simply relocated themselves from the front of the Hebrew encampment to the rear of the camp. Yet, why would the verse repeat itself?

Remarkably, the verse did not repeat itself, but rather describes two entirely separate acts of aerial navigation. First, the verse informs us that "the angel of God, that went before the camp of Israel, removed and went behind them". The verse then turns right around and declares that "and the pillar of the cloud went from before their face, and stood behind them;".

Naturally, one would assume the verse is depicting both maneuvers as one and the same event. Yet, the word "removed", and the word "and" would bring to light another conceivable narrative. The word "and" would suggest two separate actions, where the word "removed" would insinuate the act of a secondary event.

The "angel of God" had now "removed" himself from the cloud of God. In essence, the cloud shrouded craft formation split into two dissimilar objects.

Both of the separated objects maneuvered themselves from the front of the Hebrew encampment to establish two dissimilar locations behind the camp.

Clearly, if both objects were to move to the same location behind the camp, it would be quite unnecessary to split up (removed) to perform the aerial relocation. The very word "removed" would actually indicate the disjoining of the craft/chariots. Essentially, the angel of God (not God) "removed" himself from the cloud (craft/chariot formation) of God. This would imply that the angel of God was inside the same cloud (craft formation) before he removed himself.

The enveloping cloud conceals a total of five separate craft/chariots (craft formation). Evidently one or more of the craft dislodged (removed) themselves from the total five craft formation. In doing so they independently repositioned themselves behind the camp of the Israelites.

This was a logical "divide and conquer" maneuver considering the size of the indignant Egyptian army now at the back door of the Hebrews. Consequently, any surprise attack by the Egyptians during the night has now been eliminated. However, as we are about to discover, this strategic "divide and conquer" technique may have been deliberately performed for an exceeding more calamitous objective.

The Dividing of the Red Sea

One would think that in light of all the miraculous and devastating events imposed upon the Egyptians, that they would simply throw in the towel and return home. Clearly, the subterranean gods of the Egyptians (Fallen Angels) were unable to intervene, or save their Egyptian populace from the havoc being inflicted by Yahweh and his host.

> **14:21 And Moses stretched out his hand over the sea; and the LORD caused the sea to go [back] by a strong east wind all that night, and made the sea dry [land], and the waters were divided.**
>
> **14:22 And the children of Israel went into the midst of the sea upon the dry [ground]: and the waters [were] a wall unto them on their right hand, and on their left.**
>
> **14:23 And the Egyptians pursued, and went in after them to the midst of the sea, [even] all Pharaoh's horses, his chariots, and his horsemen.**
>
> **14:24 And it came to pass, that in the morning watch the LORD looked unto the host of the Egyptians through the pillar of fire and of the cloud, and troubled the host of the Egyptians,**

14:25 And took off their chariot wheels, that they drave them heavily: so that the Egyptians said, Let us flee from the face of Israel; for the LORD fighteth for them against the Egyptians.
14:26 And the LORD said unto Moses, Stretch out thine hand over the sea, that the waters may come again upon the Egyptians, upon their chariots, and upon their horsemen.
14:27 And Moses stretched forth his hand over the sea, and the sea returned to his strength when the morning appeared; and the Egyptians fled against it; and the LORD overthrew the Egyptians in the midst of the sea.
14:28 And the waters returned, and covered the chariots, and the horsemen, [and] all the host of Pharaoh that came into the sea after them; there remained not so much as one of them.
14:29 But the children of Israel walked upon dry [land] in the midst of the sea; and the waters [were] a <u>wall</u> unto them on their right hand, and on their left.
EXODUS

Evidently, the Egyptians were visually capable of distinguishing that Yahweh and his chariots/craft were physically fighting for the Hebrews. This is a remarkable declaration considering the affirmation would confirm the fact that the Egyptians could substantially observe that whatever was inside the cloud, was responsible for the aquatic events now taking place. Obviously, the physical presence of something very real was spotted inside the cloud.

By now, the reader should be well versed in how the Red Sea was actually divided, as well as how the fissured body of water maintained its severed position for an extended period of time. Taking into account the fantastic events we have analyzed up to this point, it should come as no astonishment that Yahweh and his host had once again utilized their matter maneuvering devices to wedge apart and timely maintain the division of the Red Sea.

Essentially, this was the same matter maneuvering devices' utilized to mobilize a Moon into orbit around this planet on two separate occasions. In essence, the applied severing and maintained separation of this massive body of water could be considered child's play by these cosmic entities.

In thoroughly examining the verses, it would appear that an unseen force or translucent energy field is producing what is alluded to as a "wall". Seemingly there is an unseen force between the void of the separation, and the waters being held back. (force field/matter manipulation) That invisible force has cause the outer surface of the supported waters to appear as if they were smooth walls.

The probability does exist that a mammoth craft could have technologically mastered the matter maneuvering operation from a planetary orbit, possibly justifying the enormity of the act. If true, the concealed craft would have had to maintain a sequenced orbit matching that of the planet's rotation (stationary orbit) to stabilize the fields of force utilized to perform the aquatic maneuver.

However, I'm more inclined to believe that the craft implementing the matter maneuvering apparatus originated from the immediate area, thus justifying the constant state of precise aquatic control over the manipulated body of water. This technicality became even more apparent when I took into account the fact that the waters of the Red Sea began and maintained their separation throughout the night. This suggested a time frame consistent with the ever present cloud/craft.

As we shall discover, the matter maneuvering devices on board each of the craft possess enormous power, in contrast to the negligible size of the total five craft/chariot formation. This might suggest that the trivial size of the craft formation justified the logic behind the aquatic feat taking place at the narrowest site along the Red Sea. Essentially, there was less water be bodily mobilized to perform the aquatic maneuver. This consequently permitted the smaller craft (craft formation) the mass and ability to performed the procedure.

Remarkably, the aquatic feat may actually resolve the issue as to why the five craft formation (Cloud) separated ("removed") into two dissimilar objects positioning themselves at two totally different aerial locations. In essence, it would appear that the aerially separated craft performed a twofold maneuver. True, their detached and relocated positions between the Egyptians and the Israelites would prevent a pitch black assault. Yet the "divide and conquer" maneuver may have been genuinely orchestrated to perform the physical severing of the Red Sea.

This would allow each of the secluded craft to work together as they jointly manipulated and maintained two completely different fields of energy (Force Fields/Matter manipulation) at two entirely dissimilar aquatic locations. Essentially, each of the separated objects (Craft) maintained their own individual wall of water from their two separate locations.

However, therein lies an enigmatic issue shrouded within the verses and their purposed explanation of the aquatic separation. The verses would have us believe that the waters of the Red Sea were divided so the Israelites could walk upon "dry land". Yet, there exists a profound unsolved consequence in this assertion, considering this walk upon dry land is actually taking place at a depth well below the existing water table.

If in fact the waters were wedged apart by two indiscernible fields of force, the dry ground on which the Israelites were to walk upon would be profusely boiling up with water. Water seeks its own level. The ground under the feet of the Israelites would not only be muddy, but a deluge of surging waters forcing itself up out of the ground in a relentless effort to seek its own level/water table.

At first glance, the verses would entice one to consider that the winds created by Yahweh were responsible for drying up the exposed depths of the Red Sea. Yet, with the perception of what we have just discovered, there is no amount of wind (evaporation), that could outrun the massive amounts of water trying to spring forth from the exposed sea floor. With this revealing comprehension, we are left with two other possibilities not found within the verses, both of which entail the same invisible fields of force at work.

The first speculation would suggest that the invisible fields of energy producing the walls of force were capable of being driven down far below the sea floor. By isolating this area of the Red Sea far below the depths of the existing water table, the water table within the exposed area might have been modified or altered.

This might suggest that the lingering water within the open area of the separation may have started to seep back down through the sea floor. In essence, the existing water table within the exposed void may have been forcibly blockaded to a level far below its previous existence. In embracing the first probability we obtain the second. If in fact these powerful fields of energy were able to be forced down through the sea floor, the probability exists that a third field of force may have been employed to dry up the exposed sea floor.

This third force field may have been literally placed horizontally inside the exposed sea floor. Moreover, the third field of force may have been placed below the exposed sea floor, where it was joined with the other two fields on both sides. Essentially, the boxed in area would not only dry up, but stay dry.

Evidently, the invisible spectacle was timely fabricated before the crossing of the Israelites took place. Moreover, the manipulated fields must have been structured in such a way as not to harm anyone within the field induced areas.

This might resolve the issue as to why it took all night to perform the phenomenal aquatic sequence prior to the actual crossing.

Matter Manipulation with Surgical Precision

It's significant to keep an open mind regarding the astonishing powers employed by these elite universal entities. We genuinely have no idea as to what degree of technology these stellar beings may have timely acquired. The matter exploiting devices effortlessly utilized by these celestial beings may harness incredible capabilities far beyond anything we understand. Obviously, these stellar entities are fully capable of manipulating their powerful fields of force (force field/matter manipulation) with astonishing surgical precision as expressed in verse 14:25

Note verse 14:24 Yahweh physically looked through not only the pillar of fire, but the cloud. Plainly, Yahweh was not the pillar of fire, nor was he the cloud. Alternatively, Yahweh was peering through his fiery chariot (craft) shrouded by the cloud. In essence, the cloud is obscuring the view of the glowing craft/chariots inside the cloud.

In carefully surveying the same verse, we discover Yahweh's surgical manipulation of matter. Yahweh looked out of his fiery craft through the cloud and "troubled the host of the Egyptians". Yet, verse, 14:25, establishes how Yahweh substantially troubled the Egyptians. This revealing verse actually recounts how Yahweh and his Chariots/Craft surgically maneuvered their matter navigating devices (force fields), to extract the wheels off the Egyptian chariots while they were chasing after the Israelites.

Obviously, the Egyptians visually observed Yahweh and his crafts as they performed the wheel extracting procedure. This revealing detail can be established by the Egyptians declaring that Yahweh was fighting for the Israelites.

Seemingly the surgical maneuver was deliberately designed to humiliate and/or entrap the Egyptians prior to their final demise. That conclusive blow was inflicted by Yahweh abruptly shutting down their matter maneuvering devices maintaining the severed Red Sea. The aquatic repercussions of this are self-explanatory.

The Maneuvering Wind

One would think that with all the matter maneuvering exploits taking place, the obscured fields or beams of forces would leave behind some tangible remnant, or evidence of the fields of energy in operation. One would assume that someone, if not all the spectators involved in these incredible events, would be able to visually perceive something to suggest that blurred fields, rays, or beams of energy were being maneuvered. Someone must have seen something obscure but not quite invisible, something vague or undefined, but yet quite real. And indeed this does appear to be the case.

> 15:3 The LORD [is] a man of war: the LORD [is] his name.
> 15:5 The depths have covered them: they sank into the bottom as a stone.
> 15:6 Thy right hand, O LORD, is become glorious in power: thy right hand, O LORD, hath dashed in pieces the enemy.
> 15:8 And with the blast of thy nostrils the waters were gathered together, the floods stood upright as an heap, [and] the depths were congealed in the heart of the sea.
> 15:10 Thou didst blow with thy wind, the sea covered them: they sank as lead in the mighty waters.
> 15:12 Thou stretchedst out thy right hand, the earth swallowed them.
>
> EXODUS
>
> 23:1...How many winds blow from under the wings of the cherubim? From there the hovering wind blows, as it is written, "God's wind hovered over the water."
> 23:2 From there the strong wind blows, as it is written, "The Lord drove back the sea with a strong easterly wind all night."
> 23:6 From there the wind of earthquake blows, as it is written, "Afterwards the wind of earthquake, but the Lord was not in the earthquake."
> 23:7 From there the wind of YAHWEH blows, as it is written, "He carried me away by the wind of the Lord and set me down."
> 23:16...All these winds blow only beneath the wings of the cherubim, as it is written, "He mounted a cherrub and flew, and soared on the wings of the wind,"
>
> APPENDIX TO 3 ENOCH (P)

These verses not only give us a substantial description of the fields of force in operation. They actually establish the fact that the Hebrew populace was able to visually observe the force fields, as well as the physical device utilized to maneuver them.

The verses depict a song the Hebrew congregation sang after Yahweh destroyed the Egyptians. Obviously, the Israelites described the severing fields of force as a "blast" of Yahweh's nostrils, or a "wind" As we are about to discover, this declaration validates the fact that the Israelites could indeed vaguely see something quite tangible (wind/blast), being utilized to divide the Red Sea. That obscured wind or blast originated from Yahweh's cloud (craft/nostrils).

The word "wind" does in fact define the invisible forces of a storm, hurricane, or tornado. Quite naturally, this would lead one to believe that Yahweh utilized the very wind itself to maneuver and maintain the severed sea. However, the physical separation of the Red Sea would in actuality generate winds, due to atmospheric displacement produced by the enormous artificial partition of this massive body of water. Obviously, the "wind" or "blast" coming from Yahweh's nostrils (cloud/chariots) is no ordinary wind.

It would appear that the Hebrews were recounting what they saw the best way they knew how. The Israelites, lacking our level of science and technology, were describing what they observed in reference to what they comprehend based on their uneducated existence. The unschooled Israelites would naturally delineate or associate ambiguous events by correlating those incidents with their everyday conditions. Hence the credited wind may genuinely be an allegorical depiction.

The Israelites were unable to intellectually grasp the obscure, but not quite invisible fields of force being utilized. Hence, they allegorically delineated their observation to something they did understand and/or could compare to (the wind). The Israelites, fully aware of the immense power and force of the wind, equated the obscure fields of force to the wind, considering both forces are transparent but yet powerful. However, in this case, the powerful winds (force fields) were emanating from Yahweh's cloud engulfed craft/chariots.

To summarize, "Cherubim" is the plural term for "cherub/chariot hence identifying the five chariots/craft Yahweh mounted to fly. Moreover, the "winds" of the chariots/craft were responsible for their flight capabilities. This would lead one to believe that the power, or energy (wind) generated by the propulsion system of the craft, as well as the energized power (wind) of their matter maneuvering devices, may actually be interconnected.

It was the "wind" (fields of force) of Yahweh's chariots that "hovered" over, and drove back (divided) the Red Sea. It was the "wind" (force fields) of Yahweh's chariots that produced earthquakes. It was the "wind" (force field) of Yahweh's chariots that "carried me away" and "set me down". The very same manipulative fields of force mirrored in the modern UFO mystery.

Remarkably, the modern UFO enigma elaborates upon these mysterious entities ability to exploit solid matter by implementing fields of force. Not only do they employ the prodigious power to navigate solid matter at will, they appear to possess the ability to maneuver these astounding fields of force with surgical precision. In fact, their matter jockeying devices are so precise they are fully capable of lifting a human body up off the ground as they levitate the individual into their "hovering" craft/chariots.

The verses above indicate the same processes. Obviously, an individual was literally picked up from off the ground and aerially transported to some undisclosed location. That person was then gently set back down on the ground, all of which was attributed to the wind (force fields) of the chariots (craft). Essentially, the massive cleaving of the Red Sea was but a negligible feat compared to what these phenomenal craft/chariots and their devices are fully capable of doing.

Yahweh's "Hand" At Work

The "wind" symbolizes the invisible fields of force emanating from *underneath* the chariots, as stated in the verses. Yet, it is the prior set of verses [Exodus 15:3-12,] that actually reveals the applied device and its visual description even though allegorically obscured underneath the cloud shrouded chariots/craft.

Seeing how we have yet to examine the book of Ezekiel, the reader will not easily acknowledge the allegorically depicted device at just a glance. The book of Ezekiel will immensely elaborate upon Yahwehs' five craft hidden within the cloud, as well as the names of each of his four escorts (men) piloting them.

Moreover, the book of Ezekiel will detail the shape, size and propulsion systems of the five craft, as well as the location of their weapons and devices mounted "**underneath**" each of the craft. Those weapons and devices have now been physically revealed in verses 15:3-12. Yet, without the precepts of the book of Ezekiel, the devices are not recognized for what they actually are, but rather what they allegorically appear to resemble.

Verse 15:3-12 not only establishes the fact that the power of the wind (force fields), was emanating from the device underneath the chariots/craft, but the visual shape of the device (weapon) as well. Clearly the applied powers of the maneuvering fields of force (wind) were attributed to the "right hand of God". Notably, Yahweh "stretched" out his right hand, and the earth swallowed them.

Indeed, one might assume the verse is symbolically referring to Yahweh destroying the Egyptians by his own hand. Yet, the word "stretched" would indicate a totally dissimilar story. Evidently the observant Hebrews could see a solid hand-shaped object emanate ("stretch") from out of the cloud to destroy the Egyptians with a wind (force fields).

Obviously, the Israelites personally witnessed the stretching out of the hand prior to the destruction. This bizarre device or hand shaped appliance will continue to establish its obvious presence throughout scripture. However, it will be the book of Ezekiel that will confirm the fact that this substantial device is not only located underneath each of the craft (Cherubim/chariots). But is in fact in the bodily shape of a hand.

The hand-shaped device appears to be mounted on a telescopic arm, or mechanism capable of not only moving in any direction from underneath the craft/chariots, but masterful when "stretching" in and out of the craft via its telescopic appendage. Furthermore, we shall discover that this hand-shaped appliance possesses more than just one weapon revealing finger like characteristics (finger of God).

Manna From Heaven

As we venture further and further into Scripture, it will become evident that Yahweh and his cloud concealed craft are but a trivial drop in the bucket as far as the numerous aerial machines under Yahweh's cosmic command. Seemingly, Yahweh's five personal craft are not intergalactic vehicles, given their negligible size. Obviously, craft of this seemingly trivial measure would require a parent ship to harbor and sustain their short-run maintenance. That mother ship, as we shall discover, is so enormous that it possesses all the facilities required to produce bread or provision, enough to feed six hundred thousand people.

In essence, this massive craft arrived at this planet totally prepared to intercede and feed its Hebrew population. That cosmic nutrition came in the form of Manna (bread) which appears to be nothing more than a fabricated wafer easy to pack and store. (See Exodus 16:31 Num,11:7) Simply put, the nutrition Bread (Manna) could easily be dispensed from the sky by the many possible smaller craft of the kingdom of heaven.

Here again, if one will observe the verses in reference to this lofty event, one will discover that the manna (bread) falling from the sky took place only under the cover of darkness. Seemingly, the kingdom of heaven, and their many possible craft were deliberately concealing themselves from the prying eyes of mankind. However, we're about to discover that the numerous craft of the kingdom of heaven were utilized to destroy the global control that the fallen angels/other gods maintained over the surrounding nations.

Yahweh Marshals Israel For War

In order for Yahweh to mold Israel into a powerful war machine he led his people to a private location, (Mount Sinai) where he began his organization and disciplining of the twelve armies of Israel. That secure towering site permitted Yahweh to hold private meetings with Moses.

> **19:3 And Moses went up unto God, and the LORD called unto him out of the mountain, saying, Thus shalt thou say to the house of Jacob, and tell the children of Israel;**
>
> **19:4 Ye have seen what I did unto the Egyptians, and [how] I bare you on eagles' wings, and brought you unto myself.**
>
> **19:12 And thou shalt set bounds unto the people round about, saying, Take heed to yourselves, [that ye] go [not] up into the mount, or touch the border of it: whosoever toucheth the mount shall be surely put to death:**
>
> **19:21 And the LORD said unto Moses, Go down, charge the people, lest they break through unto the LORD to gaze, and many of them perish.**
>
> EXODUS

Although considerable data is missing, the verses actually disclose precisely how Moses was able to physically ascend to the top of Mount Sinai. Those absent factors would substantiate that the "eagle wings" spoken of in the verses are in fact tangible flying machines (Craft) referred to as Eagles.

> **24:11 He has the chariots of eagles, as it is written, "I carried you on eagles' wings." They are not eagles but fly like eagles.**
>
> **24:14 He has the chariots of clouds, as it is written, "He makes the clouds his chariots."**
>
> APPENDIX TO 3 ENOCH (P)

It's not uncommon for even contemporary man to christen, and insignia their aircrafts after birds, or flying insects. Quite naturally the various types of craft and their aerial functions would correspond to the given name, or portrayed drawing found on the craft. This seemingly universal factor would suggest that Yahweh sent a craft/chariot, designated as the Eagle, to pick Moses up and "fly" him to the top of Mount Sinai.

Moreover, the verses establish the deadly deterrent that anyone trying to climb or even come near the mountain will be killed without question. Quite an interesting detail, considering the verse would authenticate the fact that Yahweh and his host were not invisible ghosts or spirits. This would logically justify their intentional security tactics to conceal their physical presence and craft from inquisitive eyes. That security measure was enforced with the pledge of death to anyone who may jeopardize their safeguarded base of operations.

This was a logical and powerful strategic procedure, considering the mystery and fear of the unknown would not only maintain their ambiguous control over the superstitious populace, but also insure that their protected base of operations would not be breached.

Moses having now returned from Yahweh's mountain, possessed the ten commandments, as well as elaborate building instructions. Yet, more significant would be the mandated declaration that there is only one God (Yahweh), being the first of the ten commandments.

This bold proclamation placed Yahweh and his host in a militant situation, seeing how they must now substantially validate that charge by physically displaying incredible powers aimed at dismantling the encompassing nations covertly controlled by the **other gods**. Those other gods, as we shall discover, were nothing more than disguised rebel angels, stealthily manipulating the surface dwellers of the ancient world.

Obviously the twelve tribes of Israel were not seasoned warriors capable of such mass destruction on their own. Consequently, Yahweh and his host, along with their powerful craft and weapons will physically fight for the Israelites as they moved from kingdom to kingdom, in a relentless rampage of death and destruction.

> **22:20 He that sacrificeth unto [any] god, save unto the LORD only, he shall be utterly destroyed.**
>
> **23:13 And in all [things] that I have said unto you be circumspect: and make no mention of the name of <u>other gods</u>, neither let it be heard out of thy mouth.**
>
> **33:2 And I will send an angel before thee; and <u>I will drive out</u> the Canaanite, the Amorite, and the Hittite, and the Perizzite, the Hivite, and the Jebusite:**

34:11 Observe thou that which I command thee this day: behold, I drive out before thee the Amorite, and the Canaanite, and the Hittite, and the Perizzite, and the Hivite, and the Jebusite.
34:13 But ye shall destroy their altars, break their images, and cut down their groves:
34:14 For thou shalt worship no other god: for the LORD, whose name [is] Jealous, [is] a jealous God:
23:24 Thou shalt not bow down to their gods, nor serve them, nor do after their works: but thou shalt utterly overthrow them, and quite break down their images.
23:28 And I will send hornets before thee, which shall drive out the Hivite, the Canaanite, and the Hittite, from before thee.
23:30 By little and little I will drive them out from before thee, until thou be increased, and inherit the land.
EXODUS

The other gods/rebel angels were not only covertly debasing the superstitious nations, but maneuvering the beguiled populations into their clandestine objectives. Accordingly Yahweh had the task of utterly destroy everyone and/or everything that could be implemented as a worshiping tool, altar, or image designed to pay homage to the insurgent angels/other gods.

It's no surprise Yahweh demanded the dissociation of his chosen populace from the dissimilar nations, considering their mutinous angels' administration, and the global disorder they had consistently created on this mutated world. It's no wonder Yahweh clearly warned his own people about the horrifying retribution against anyone who may choose to side with them.

Clearly, the assemblage of Israel was not going to be alone in their purging rampage seeing how Yahweh and his host, along with their phenomenal craft, traveled with the Israelites from nation to nation, to personally help the Hebrews destroy the encompassing nations. Moreover, if you will closely review the verses, you will actually discover the individual craft to be employed against the numerous nations to be eradicated.

"I will send hornets before thee, which shall drive out the Hivite, the Canaanite, and the Hittite from before thee".

Are we to believe that Yahweh sent a swarm of bugs to drive out the surrounding nations? Are we to simply embrace the idea that swarms of hornets were bodily wielded to attack and drive out the populations of thousands dwelling within each ancient empire? This stinging declaration would not only challenge one's common intellect, but nature itself.

Quite naturally, the kingdom of heaven possesses many assorted types of aircrafts/spacecrafts, to be utilized for many dissimilar aerial operations. Each of the various craft were given the title and insignia of different symbolic characters such as animals, birds, or insects, thus corresponding to the function and/or operation of the craft. Essentially, this allegorical reality may also apply to the "hornets".

Yahweh reaching each nation or empire to be destroyed would send in his destructive craft symbolically identified as Hornets. You will also note the word Hornet is pluralized denoting more than one (Hornets). This would indicate that many such craft were used to destroy each empire or nation.Notably, mankind today symbolically identifies its most destructive craft and/or aircrafts in the same manner.

One such awesome attack craft boasting immense stinging power was the aircraft carrier USS Hornet. This floating arsenal inflicted enormous destruction before it was ultimately sunk. Another such craft wreaking extraordinary devastation, and still in operation to this very day, is the Mc Donnell Douglas F-18A Hornet. This powerful aircraft possesses an aerial arsenal of incredible devastation, not to mention its aerial range, thus earning its stinging symbolic title "Hornet".

As if this allegorical example was not startling enough, the campaign tactics illustrated in the verses are in fact the unequivocal match to the war tactics utilized by our military today. Our modern military forces journey to destinations of preplanned destruction on aircraft carriers (USS Hornet). Upon their arrival, they send in jet aircraft (F-18 Hornets) to wreak as much destruction as possible before unleashing the infantry.

Naturally, the aerial assaults are designed to massively destroy the enemy and its hardware before the foot soldiers enter the devastated combat zone. This would consequently eliminate the number of casualties during the final assault. The very same military strategy is given in the verses.

However, when addressing Yahweh's celestial machines of the kingdom of heaven, we may be witnessing craft of unimaginable destructive power. As we shall discover, these cosmic hornets harness laser weapons capable of unleashing incredible destructive power. This is not to mention their astonishing ability to physically manipulate enormous objects of solid matter at will.

Yahweh's Migratory Base of Operations

If Yahweh is to discipline and impose supreme authority over his newly established armies and the encompassing nations, it will require his personal attention to dictate control. This would justify the logic behind Yahweh and his host personally coexisting with the Israelites as they move from empire to empire.

Moses having received many decrees from Yahweh, also received instructions on how to build an immaculate tent. The tent allowed Yahweh and his host to dwell with the Hebrews while seeking out each empire to be destroyed. This flawless command post/residence permitted Yahweh to dictate and maintain absolute authority. Moreover, this immaculate base of operation could be packed up and moved, as the armies of Israel journeyed from nation to nation, inflicting their devastating rampage of death and destruction.

> 25:8 And let them make me a sanctuary; that I may dwell among them.
> 25:9 According to all that I show thee, [after] the pattern of the tabernacle, and the pattern of all the instruments thereof, even so shall ye make [it].
> 29:45 And I will dwell among the children of Israel, and will be their God.
> 38:9 And he made the court: on the south side southward the hangings of the court [were of] fine twined linen, an hundred cubits:
> 38:11 And for the north side [the hangings were] an hundred cubits, their pillars [were] twenty, and their sockets of brass twenty; the hooks of the pillars and their fillets [of] silver.
> 38:12 And for the west side [were] hangings of fifty cubits, their pillars ten, and their sockets ten; the hooks of the pillars and their fillets [of] silver.
> 38:13 And for the east side eastward fifty cubits.
> 33:7 And Moses took the tabernacle, and pitched it without the camp, afar off from the camp, and called it the Tabernacle of the congregation....
> 33:9 And it came to pass, as Moses entered into the tabernacle, the cloudy pillar descended, and stood [at] the door of the tabernacle, and [the LORD] talked with Moses.
> 33:10 And all the people saw the cloudy pillar stand [at] the tabernacle door: and all the people rose up and worshipped, every man [in] his tent door.
> 40:33 And he reared up the court round about the tabernacle and the altar, and set up the hanging of the court gate. So Moses finished the work.

40:34 Then a cloud covered the tent of the congregation, and the glory of the LORD filled the tabernacle.
40:35 And Moses was not able to enter into the tent of the congregation, because the cloud abode thereon, and the glory of the LORD filled the tabernacle.
40:36 And when the cloud was taken up from over the tabernacle, the children of Israel went onward in all their journeys:
40:37 But if the cloud were not taken up, then they journeyed not till the day that it was taken up.
40:38 For the cloud of the LORD [was] upon the tabernacle by day, and fire was on it by night, in the sight of all the house of Israel, throughout all their journeys.
EXODUS
24:6 He has the chariots of twice ten thousand, as it is written, "The chariots of God are twice ten thousand, thousands of angels."
24:7 He has the chariots of the tent, as it is written, "The Lord showed himself in the tent, in a pillar of cloud."
24:8 He has the chariots of the tent of meetings, as it is written, "The Lord addressed Moses from the tent of meeting."
APPENDIX TO 3 ENOCH (P)

A good question at this point would be, why would invisible entities need a tent to reside or "dwell in"? Obviously, we are not dealing with invisible specters, but rather genuine physical beings requiring a life-sustaining shelter if they are to journey and coexist ("dwell") with the Israelites.

This portable base of operations/tent would allocate a safe harbor for Yahweh and his host to work with the Israelites without being observed. This would imply that, if indeed there was an orbiting parent ship, Yahweh and his host were utilizing this tent as a ground base of operations.

Scripture would lead one to believe that the tent and tabernacle were designed to be an elegant structure befitting a king. This all-inclusive tent was composed of fine linen woven together with gold, silver, and brass, furniture, cooking facilities, lighting facilities and private quarters, as well as a private room for worship by the Israelites.(See Exodus chapters 25&26)

Remarkably, the measurements given in the verses render a possible clue to the actual size of Yahweh's cloud engulfed craft/chariot formation. Moreover, in thoroughly inspecting the last set of verses, we discover that there is no guess work as to what actually lurks within this mysterious cloud. Clearly, the enveloping cloud is genuinely concealing chariots (craft), implying more than one.

The court of the tent and tabernacle are approximately one hundred cubits by fifty cubits. A cubit is the ancient unit of length based on the length of the forearm, or approximately eighteen inches. This would imply that the court of the tent is rectangular in shape. The rectangular courtyard measures one hundred and fifty feet on the north and south sides, by seventy-five feet on the east and west sides.

These measurements would not actually give us the exact dimensions and shape of the tent and tabernacle. Yet, they would give us a general idea as to the size of the tent, considering the tent that surrounds the tabernacle would have to be smaller than the dimensions of the court in which it resides, as expressed within the verses.

The verses greatly elaborate upon the fact that the cloud obscuring the craft formation appears to routinely land "stand/stood" at the front door of the Tent. This would suggest that the craft formation lurking within the cloud is no larger than the inner court in which it stood/landed. Evidently, the craft formation, "standing" at the door of the tabernacle/tent, is located between the east court wall and the tabernacle (tent) front door.

Naturally, this would not give us a true measurement as to the actual size of the craft formation, considering we have no idea as to how large the tent may be, in reference to the court. That missing detail would actually give us the distance between the tent and the east court wall.

Another obvious dilemma exists in the fact that the tent may not be in the center of the court. This would suggest that the tent and tabernacle were not proportionate to the size of the court. The Tent and tabernacle may actually be located further down within the rectangular court. This would allow for a much larger area between the front of the tent/tabernacle and the east court wall. This would also leave considerably more room for the cloud shrouded craft to land, ("stand/stood") as well as revealing the possible size of the craft formation.

The measured width of the court is only seventy-five feet. This might suggest that the east court wall may be approximately the same distance from the front door of the tent/tabernacle. Essentially, the craft formation could not be any larger than seventy-five feet wide, or it would not fit inside the court walls, much less stand at the door of the Tent. In fact, the craft formation would have to be less than seventy-five feet in diameter, or it would be touching the sides of the outer court walls, thus exposing it to possible intruders. Obviously, this was a highly safeguarded area in which even Moses was not allowed to enter at certain times.

Evidently, the craft formation would have to be approximately sixty feet or less in diameter. This would allow the craft the ability to not only fit inside the seventy five-foot court, but also give the chariot formation sufficient room between the tent and the east court wall. In essence, the allocated landing pad would permit the craft formation to descend and land inside the court walls, as well as maintain additional room on every side of the craft formation, and still be concealed by the court walls.

Obviously, the cloud routinely covered the tent by hovering above it, or simply landed at the front door. Interestingly, this time frame also coincides with Yahweh and his host filling the tabernacle. When the cloud hovered or landed in front of the tent, Yahweh and his host were inside ("filled the tabernacle"), consequently Moses was not allowed to enter the tent.

As long as the craft formation remained (landed) within the court, or hovered over the tent, the encampment was to maintain its present location. Yet, when Yahweh was prepared to relocate to the next destination, the craft formation would leave the tent, thus heralding the obvious sign to move on. This informed the congregation to take down the tent, pack it up, and transport it to the next location for Yahweh and his host to dwell inside once again.

Essentially, Yahweh's cloud shrouded craft and their mysterious pilots had now taken up short-term residence inside this large immaculate tent. Wherever the tent went, the craft formation (cloud) went. Or perhaps I should say wherever the craft formation went, the tent went. (See Numbers 9:16,-19, 21/10:11, 34-36)

Yahweh and His Host Setup Control Factors To Be Fed

Yahweh and his host had now established a secure command center and migratory foundation for residence within the congregation. Essentially, they could now begin to mobilize the twelve armies of Israel towards the nations to be exterminated. However, if Yahweh and his host were to accompany the Israelites in their migration, there remained a paramount issue yet to be resolved within the Hebrew ranks.

In realizing that Yahweh and his host are in reality highly evolved physical beings, we arrive at the obvious conclusion that they did in fact require bodily substance. Simply put, Yahweh and his host will require food as they progress across the wilderness with the Israelites.

Notably, this consuming detail was previously accounted for in the complex construction of this stately tent. As mentioned before, this extraordinary tent was built with living quarters, furniture, lighting facilities, cooking facilities, as well as cooking utensils to be used in the preparation of food for Yahweh and his host.

Furthermore, the altar constructed for the tent and tabernacle appears to have been fabricated for a more elaborate reason than just simple animal sacrifices. The design and size of the altar, along with its brass web like cooking surface, speaks for itself. Obviously, this elaborate grill, measuring seven and a half feet square, was designed for cooking large quantities of meat.

> 27:1 And thou shalt make an altar [of] shittim wood, five cubits long, and five cubits broad; the altar shall be foursquare: and the height thereof [shall be] three cubits.
>
> 27:4 And thou shalt make for it a grate of network [of] brass; and upon the net shalt thou make four brazen rings in the four corners thereof.
>
> 29:23 And one loaf of bread, and one cake of oiled bread, and one wafer out of the basket of the unleavened bread that [is] before the LORD:
>
> 29:24 And thou shalt put all in the hands of Aaron, and in the hands of his sons; and shalt wave them [for] a wave offering before the LORD.
>
> 29:25 And thou shalt receive them of their hands, and burn [them] upon the altar for a burnt offering, <u>for a sweet savour before the LORD: it [is] an offering made by fire unto the LORD</u>.
>
> 29:38 Now this [is that] which thou shalt offer upon the altar; <u>two lambs of the first year day by day continually.</u>
>
> 29:39 The one lamb thou shalt offer <u>in the morning</u>; and the other lamb thou shalt offer <u>at even:</u>
>
> 29:40 And with the one lamb a tenth deal of flour mingled with the fourth part of an hin of beaten oil; and <u>the fourth part of an hin of wine [for] a drink offering</u>.
>
> 29:41 And the other lamb thou shalt offer <u>at even</u>, and shalt do thereto according to the meat offering of <u>the morning</u>, and according to <u>the drink offering</u> thereof, for a sweet savour, an offering made by fire unto the LORD.

29:42 [This shall be] a continual burnt offering throughout your generations [at] the door of the tabernacle of the congregation before the LORD: where I will meet you, to speak there unto thee.
EXODUS
2:13 And every oblation of thy meat offering shalt thou season with salt; neither shalt thou suffer the salt of the covenant of thy God to be lacking from thy meat offering: with all thine offerings thou shalt offer salt.
2:14 And if thou offer a meat offering of thy firstfruits unto the LORD, thou shalt offer for the meat offering of thy firstfruits green ears of corn dried by the fire, [even] corn beaten out of full ears.
2:15 And thou shalt put oil upon it, and lay frankincense thereon: it [is] a meat offering.
2:16 And the priest shall burn the memorial of it, [part] of the beaten corn thereof, and [part] of the oil thereof, with all the frankincense thereof: [it is] an offering made by fire unto the LORD.
LEVITICUS

Clearly the cooked provisions were being prepared for, and were bodily consumed by, Yahweh and his host. Obviously, we are not examining transparent entities lacking the ability to devour physical sustenance. Evidently, Yahweh and his host not only require food, but it appears as if they love to eat. Not only did they delight in consuming food, the verses substantiate the distinct likes and dislikes of the various provision they preferred.

Yahweh and his four escorts in particular required a set menu of lamb twice a day, which they obviously savored. Quite naturally, one does not eat meat alone, hence Yahweh required bread with each meal, as well as corn, if available. As with any meal, salt was always on the table, in fact, Yahweh demanded that salt be served with every meal.

Naturally, when dining one requires something to drink, especially when thirst inducing salt is involved with the meal. In this particular case, the preferred drink of choice for Yahweh was wine. In fact, Yahweh demanded the fourth part of a "hin" of wine with each meal. The word "hin" is the ancient Hebrew unit of liquid measure equivalent to a gallon and a half. Hence, Yahweh required over a quart of wine with each meal.

Evidently, Aaron and his sons were allowed to share in the numerous meat offerings made to Yahweh. This was a notable concession considering Aaron and his sons maintained the loyal preparation of Yahweh's food. This was an enormous task, considering Yahweh demanded extreme cleanliness, insisting that anyone within his immediate presence or preparing his food maintain impeccable hygiene and housekeeping, or face death as a consequence in the lack thereof.

The provisions offered to Yahweh and his hosts were directly associated with the burnt sacrifices. Essentially, the foods provided to Yahweh and his host appear to have been an organized method for the Israelites to be forgiven of their less than perfect demeanor (Sins). Yet, this food swap was in fact a great teaching tool, as well as establishing an endless food supply for Yahweh and his host.

This powerful tool not only organized, but maintained the legislation and/or decrees put forth by Yahweh. Those ordinances and precepts could not be forgotten, seeing how a physical act (animal sacrifice) was perpetually performed to be released from the given transgressions.

Yahweh's Painful Display of Noncompliance

At this phase of our scriptural analysis, Yahweh is now prepared to unveil a truly frightening weapon. For the first time in these writings we are now prepared to examine the high-tech laser technology used by the Kingdom of heaven.

This radiating power of inconceivable destruction will further substantiate the fact that Yahweh will not tolerate any insubordination, whether it be a meat offering, or anything else. Moreover, this fiery show of power was but the beginning of Yahweh's confirmation of blazing death to be inflicted upon anyone not conforming to his administrative doctrines.

> **9:23…and the glory of the LORD appeared unto all the people.**
> **9:24 <u>And there came a fire out from before the LORD, and consumed</u> upon the altar the burnt offering and the fat: [which] when all the people saw, they shouted, and fell on their faces.**
> **10:1 And Nadab and Abihu, the sons of Aaron, took either of them his censer, and put fire therein, and put incense thereon, and offered strange fire before the LORD, which he commanded them not.**
> **10:2 And <u>there went out fire from the LORD, and devoured them</u>, and they died before the LORD.**
> **10:3 Then Moses said unto Aaron, This [is it] that the LORD spake, saying, I will be sanctified in them that come nigh me, and before all the people I will be glorified. <u>And Aaron held his peace.</u>**

10:4 And Moses called Mishael and Elzaphan, the sons of Uzziel the uncle of Aaron, and said unto them, Come near, carry your brethren from before the sanctuary out of the camp.
10:5 So they went near, and carried them in their coats out of the camp; as Moses had said.
10:6 And Moses said unto Aaron, and unto Eleazar and unto Ithamar, his sons, Uncover not your heads, neither rend your clothes; lest ye die, and lest wrath come upon all the people: but let your brethren, the whole house of Israel, bewail the burning which the LORD hath kindled.
10:8 And the LORD spake unto Aaron, saying,
10:9 Do not drink wine nor strong drink, thou, nor thy sons with thee, when ye go into the tabernacle of the congregation, lest ye die: [it shall be] a statute for ever throughout your generations:
LEVITICUS

Aaron, and his sons were assigned the responsible job of "high priests" to Yahweh's tent. Those duties involved the domestic charge of Yahweh's tent inside and out, as well as preparing food for Yahweh and his essential host. Additionally, the committals required that Aaron and his sons maintain complete obedience and cleanliness throughout all ceremonial or religious formalities.

One such religious right was the burning of incense in hallowed censers. Evidently, Aaron's sons were playing with the sanctified censers by burning something other than what was allowed in the censers. Obviously, this was rude display of disrespect towards Yahweh's ordained laws, particularly since the disobedient act was performed right before the Lord.

Clearly Aaron, the boys' father, was extremely disturbed about the entire incident, considering both his sons were killed. Yet, Aaron had no other choice but to control his anger, "held his peace", or bring death upon all the congregation. If there was any mourning to be done, the congregation outside Yahweh's court walls would have to do it.

In closely scrutinizing the verses, we discover that the two boys may have been intoxicated prior to enacting their fatal blunder. This lethal detail is validated by Yahweh's conversation with Aaron, enlightening him to the fact that no one is to drink wine or strong drink when entering the tabernacle. This would suggest that both of Aaron's sons may have not only been drinking, but may have been drunk. This might possibly explain the boy's lack of respect with the Holy Censers.

Here again, many will be unwilling to believe that a laser weapon may have been used in this fiery event at all. Yet, the verses make no mistake about it. Yahweh obviously employs something other than himself to perform the two deaths.

As with most scripture, Yahweh did not simply cause the two boys to suddenly vanish into thin air. There is no 'puff-puff' within these verses. Yahweh plainly employed an artificial device of some type to ardently destroy or "devour" the bodies of the two boys, as well as the meat offerings consumed on the altar.

That device is described as being a mechanism capable of discharging a disintegrating beam of fire at a great distance with remarkable accuracy. The same definition is given to describe advance laser technology. Clearly the device discharging the laser produced a streaming fiery beam which flowed from Yahweh's cloud shrouded craft formation.

This blazing detail can be confirmed by the affirmation "And there went out fire from the Lord". The verses even elaborate on the type of ardent effects the laser (fire) inflicted upon the physical bodies of the two men. Evidently the bodies of the two men were physically "devoured/consumed" by the laser. This would suggest that the laser molecularly incinerated (devoured/consumed) the flesh of the two men.

However, Aaron's sons were not completely destroyed/devoured. The two men were only partly, or substantially, burned up/incinerated (devoured). This might suggest that most or a large part of their bodies may have been missing (devoured). Essentially, it would appear that the residual human remains had to be wrapped in coats and carried outside the camp to be buried. Obviously, the two bodies could have been totally incinerated (devoured/consumed), if Yahweh wanted to finish the job. This might imply that Yahweh deliberately left human remains as a visual reminder rendering the obvious repercussions for the non-conformist.

A weapon of this magnitude could forcibly impose unequivocal authority over not only a nation, but an entire world. This revealing detail will be greatly elaborated upon when this miraculous weapon of fire is utilized to bring about the Revelation of this world. At that time, this planet killing weapon will reveal its true title known as the "**Sword of God**".

Moreover, we are about to discover that this powerful weapon is actually incorporated within the telescopic Arm that supports the "Hand of God". That hand-shaped device is attached to an arm like contrivance mounted on the undercarriage of each of these phenomenal craft/chariots.

Numbers

Yahweh's established control factors maintained law and order within the camp. Moreover, those imposed mandates were enforced by death if necessary. This shocking reality was demonstrated by Yahweh utilizing his powerful laser (fire) weapon to incinerate Aaron's two insubordinate sons. Clearly, Yahweh's' vigorous control factors were directly aimed at organizing a compliant mobile army of destruction compelled to advance into war.

> **1:1 And the LORD spake unto Moses in the wilderness of Sinai, in the tabernacle of the congregation, on the first [day] of the second month, in the second year after they were come out of the land of Egypt, saying,**
> **1:2 Take ye the sum of all the congregation of the children of Israel, after their families, by the house of their fathers, with the number of [their] names, every male by their polls;**
> **1:3 From twenty years old and upward, all that are able to go forth to <u>war</u> in Israel: thou and Aaron shall number them by their <u>armies</u>.** NUMBERS

From the very moment Yahweh led his people out of Egypt, he referred to them as his "armies". Yahweh was now prepared to make that declaration a reality by physically marshaling the congregation of Israel into a massive migrant war machine designed to destroy the surrounding nations and their other gods/rebel angels.

Yahweh Organizes His Armies

As with any military encampment positioned behind enemy lines, a strategic command post is unquestionably essential. That militant command post was in fact the tent Yahweh and his escorts were residing in. Moreover, Yahweh and his host were extremely decisive to ensure that their tent, as well as themselves was out of harm's way while mobilizing the Hebrew armies from nation to nation. This intense security measure became quite impressive when analyzing how Yahweh bodily organized and positioned the twelve armies of Israel around his personal tent.

> **2:1 And the LORD spake unto Moses and unto Aaron, saying,**
>
> **2:2 Every man of the children of Israel shall pitch by his own standard, with the ensign of their father's house: far off about the tabernacle of the congregation shall they pitch.**
>
> **2:3 And on the east side toward the rising of the sun shall they of the standard of the camp of Judah pitch throughout their armies:**
>
> **2:5 And those that do pitch next unto him [shall be] the tribe of Issachar:...**
>
> **2:7 [Then] the tribe of Zebulun:...**
>
> **2:10 On the south side [shall be] the standard of the camp of Reuben according to their armies:...**
>
> **2:12 And those which pitch by him [shall be] the tribe of Simeon:...**
>
> **2:14 Then the tribe of Gad:...**
>
> **2:18 On the west side [shall be] the standard of the camp of Ephraim according to their armies:...**
>
> **2:20 And by him [shall be] the tribe of Manasseh:...**
>
> **2:22 Then the tribe of Benjamin:**
>
> **2:25 The standard of the camp of Dan [shall be] on the north side by their armies:...**
>
> **2:27 And those that encamp by him [shall be] the tribe of Asher:...**
>
> **2:29 Then the tribe of Naphtali:...** NUMBERS

The twelve armies of Israel not only established their camps "far off" from Yahweh's personal tent, but completely encompassed it. Three of the armies were positioned on the East side, three on the South side, three on the West side, and three on the North side. This security measure would logically shield Yahweh and his host from any outward threat.

As if this external human shield was not sanctuary enough. Yahweh required that his security measures be taken yet a step further by bodily utilizing the Levites. The tribes of the Levites were created by Yahweh to be an elite force required to work directly under the leadership of not only Yahweh, but Moses and Aaron.

The Levites were intentionally separated from the twelve tribes of Israel to function as Yahweh's transportation and reconstruction unit for his personal tent and its essential items. Yet, more significantly, they were a secondary bodily shield of protection against any outside intruders. To form this elite inner shield within the outer shield, Yahweh segmented the Levite tribes into three separate units under the guidance of three diverse families and their leaders.

> **3:14 And the LORD spake unto Moses in the wilderness of Sinai, saying,**
>
> **3:15 Number the children of Levi after the house of their fathers, by their families: every male from a month old and upward shalt thou number them.**
>
> **3:16 And Moses numbered them according to the word of the LORD, as he was commanded.**
>
> **3:17 And these were the sons of Levi by their names; Gershon, and Kohath, and Merari.**
>
> **3:23 The families of the Gershonites shall pitch behind the tabernacle westward.**
>
> **3:29 The families of the sons of Kohath shall pitch on the side of the tabernacle southward.**
>
> **3:35 And the chief of the house of the father of the families of Merari [was] Zuriel the son of Abihail: [these] shall pitch on the side of the tabernacle northward.**
>
> **3:38 But those that encamp before the tabernacle toward the east, [even] before the tabernacle of the congregation eastward, [shall be] Moses, and Aaron and his sons, keeping the charge of the sanctuary for the charge of the children of Israel; and the stranger that cometh nigh shall be put to death.**
>
> **3:39 All that were numbered of the Levites, which Moses and Aaron numbered at the commandment of the LORD, throughout their families, all the males from a month old and upward, [were] twenty and two thousand.**
>
> NUMBERS

Essentially, the entire congregation was transformed into two dissimilar military forces purposely designed to physically protect Yahweh and his host. The outer perimeter completely encompassed Yahweh's tent at a "far off" distance. While the closer inner perimeter was comprised of three segmented tribes, twenty-two thousand strong.

These three large tribes partly surrounded Yahweh's tent on three sides, leaving only the East side of the inner perimeter open. This breach in the human shield allowed only Moses, Aaron and his remaining sons the right to safeguard the only entrance into Yahweh's open court exposed to the East.

It doesn't take much gray matter deduction to realize that Yahweh and his escorts were cautious physical beings requiring a double human shield to safeguard themselves against any outside attack upon their lives. That aggressive and/or violent outside influence could originate from any number of nations and/or populations that Yahweh and his host were now prepared to destroy. Moreover, Yahweh's security tactics further isolated any and all undesirables from their highly organized camp.

> **5:1 And the LORD spake unto Moses, saying,**
> **5:2 Command the children of Israel, that they put out of the camp every leper, and every one that hath an issue, and whosoever is defiled by the dead:**
> **5:3 Both male and female shall ye put out, without the camp shall ye put them; that they defile not their camps, in the midst whereof I dwell.**
> **5:4 And the children of Israel did so, and put them out without the camp:**
> NUMBERS

Clearly, Yahweh demanded extreme cleanliness to guard themselves against anyone who came close to them, or prepared their food. Anyone with an open sore, wound, or possessing a potential contagious disease was removed from the camp.

However, scrutinizing this quarantine issue from another perspective, we discover that the contagious and possible infectious undesirables were not removed (put out of the camp) from the population of the camp. Alternatively, they were removed from Yahweh and his host who physically lived in the camp.

Obviously, Yahweh and his host were well aware of the possibility that they themselves, as well as their demanded food supply, could potentially contract many body threatening diseases transmitted by the dirty or diseased Israelites.

This sterile perception would lead one to believe that Yahweh, and his party were physically walking around within the camp, consequently subjecting themselves to close bodily contact with the Hebrews. This revealing speculation became all to real when examining the word "walking". Quite naturally, a ghost or invisible spirit would not require the bodily function of walking, considering there would be no physical body to function (walk).

> **23:12 Thou shalt have a place also without the camp, whither thou shalt go forth abroad:**

> **23:13 And thou shalt have a paddle upon thy weapon; and it shall be, when thou wilt ease thyself abroad, thou shalt dig therewith, and shalt turn back and cover that which cometh from thee:**
> **23:14 For the LORD thy God walketh in the midst of thy camp, to deliver thee, and to give up thine enemies before thee; therefore shall thy camp be holy: that he see no unclean thing in thee, and turn away from thee.**
> DEUTERONOMY

I seriously doubt an invisible entity would worry about stepping in the body waste of a human. The sanitary motive genuinely speaks for itself. Clearly, Yahweh and his escorts did not want to bodily step in the human waste of anyone within the camp, a camp they were physically walking in the midst thereof.

Hunger in the Congregation, Quenched by Fire

As with any military force of this size, it's a given, that conflicting issues will ultimately fester within the ranks. Obviously, an army of this magnitude and constant mobility would greatly heighten the potential problem factors, especially considering the significant number of women and children involved.

We also need to take into account the fact that a migrant force of this size would require an enormous amount of provisions (food) to maintain its existence. The congregations' provisions (food) were not only deficient, but provoked the **outer** congregation into excessive disorder.

The livestock of the congregation were primarily used for meat sacrifices to Yahweh and his host, leaving only small portions designated to Moses, Aaron and his sons, along with the Levites (the inter-perimeter).

Seemingly, the twelve tribes or outer perimeters of the Yahweh's bodily shield were only allowed to partake of small portions of the meat (livestock). Needless too say, the outer perimeter or congregation grew weary of eating just manna (bread). Ultimately, the meatless diet pressured the **outer** congregation to revolt, thus kindling Yahwehs' raging anger.

> **11:1 And [when] the people complained, it displeased the LORD: and the LORD heard [it]; and his anger was kindled; and the fire of the LORD burnt among them, and consumed [them that were] in the uttermost parts of the camp.**
> **11:2 And the people cried unto Moses; and when Moses prayed unto the LORD, the fire was quenched.**

> 11:3 And he called the name of the place Taberah: because the fire of the LORD burnt among them.
> 11:4 And the mixed multitude that [was] among them fell a lusting: and the children of Israel also wept again, and said, Who shall give us flesh to eat?
> 11:10 Then Moses heard the people weep throughout their families, every man in the door of his tent: and the anger of the LORD was kindled greatly; Moses also was displeased.
> NUMBERS

The verses would entice one to believe that Yahweh only opened fire upon the twelve tribes of his outer shield of defense. Notably, Yahweh did nothing to Moses, Aaron and his sons, or the Levites, being Yahweh's elite inner shield. However, let's keep in mind, the Levites, as well as Moses, Aaron and his sons, were allowed to partake in the meat offerings given to Yahweh and his host. Essentially, they had no logical reason to express any grief as far as meat was concerned.

In thoroughly analyzing this retaliatory move by Yahweh, it seems clear that the weapon or laser technology being employed possessed inconceivable destructive power. The twelve armies or outer-perimeter of Israel was camping around Yahweh's tent "far off".

Yahweh and his five craft formation (chariots), positioned within the center of the congregation and hovering just above his tent opened fire on the congregation in numerous directions. The powerful laser devices beamed outward incinerating ("devouring") hundreds of men, women and children within the outer congregation.

As with the half-incinerated son's of Aaron, the outer congregation may have suffered hundreds, if not thousands, of half incinerated (consumed) corpses now lifelessly lying everywhere throughout the camp. Seemingly the mass human carnage was performed in a matter of moments, not to mention the destruction inflicted upon the camp itself.

Moses was able to ultimately calm Yahweh fiery plague. Yet this was not to be the end of Yahweh's aimed inferno. If Yahweh was to stop the outer congregations lust for flesh he had to furnish some form of meaty provisions. Yet, it's quite interesting to note that the meat Yahweh delivered did not derive from the congregation. Here again the livestock of the congregation were too only be used for the meat offerings given to Yahweh and his host, along with the Levites, Moses, Aaron, and his sons.

11:31 And there went forth a wind from the LORD, and brought quails from the sea, and let [them] fall by the camp, as it were a day's journey on this side, and as it were a day's journey on the other side, round about the camp, and as it were two cubits [high] upon the face of the earth.
11:32 And the people stood up all that day, and all [that] night, and all the next day, and they gathered the quails: he that gathered least gathered ten homers: and they spread [them] all abroad for themselves round about the camp.
11:33 And while the flesh [was] yet between their teeth, ere it was chewed, the wrath of the LORD was kindled against the people, and the LORD smote the people with a very great plague.
11:34 And he called the name of that place Kibrothhattaavah: because there they buried the people that lusted.
NUMBERS

The wind flowed from Yahweh (cloud), once again indicating that Yahweh's craft formation was responsible for the generated wind. Evidently, Yahweh and his host utilized their matter maneuvering devices (Wind) to bring thousands of quails from the sea shores, towards the congregation.

In fact, it would appear that Yahweh employed their matter navigating devices to forcibly collect and aerially cage thousands of quails and physically transported them ("brought") to the camp of the congregation. Upon reaching the congregation, the craft matter maneuvering devices were shut down, allowing the quails to "fall" to the ground, as so stated in verse 11:31, "and let them fall by the camp".

Obviously, a feeding frenzy began to escalate within the outer camp of the meat starved armies. Here again, the Israelites lust for flesh touch off Yahweh's ardent anger. That fiery indignation ultimately motivated Yahweh into employing ("kindling") his laser weapons to incinerate possibly hundreds of men, women and children within the **outer** congregation. The verses would even sway one to believe that many of the victims were only partly incinerated leaving fragmentary remains to be buried.

Evidently, before Yahweh and his newly organized armies could begin their war exploits, they had many personal problems to work out. Many of those issues could only to be worked out by death, thus elaborating upon our next fiery outcome.

Mutiny in the Congregation

Unmistakably, Yahweh and his host highly favored the Levites, Moses, Aaron and his sons above the twelve armies of Israel. This perception became even more conclusive when realizing that Yahweh and his host allowed the Levites, along with Moses, Aaron and his sons to partake of the meat offerings given each day. This placed these men and their families in not only a principal rank of authority, but even allowed them to reside adjacent to Yahweh's tent. That favoritism further strengthened the Levites' authority over the twelve outer tribes of Israel.

The Levites belief in their superiority over the twelve outer armies of Israel ultimately found the Levites trying to place themselves even above the jurisdiction of Moses and Aaron. In their efforts to do so, the Levites were smitten with the repercussions of what might befall anyone insubordinate within Yahweh's established ranks.

> 16:2 And they rose up before Moses, with certain of the children of Israel, two hundred and fifty princes of the assembly, famous in the congregation, men of renown:
>
> 16:3 And they gathered themselves together against Moses and against Aaron, and said unto them, [Ye take] too much upon you, seeing all the congregation [are] holy, every one of them, and the LORD [is] among them: wherefore then lift ye up yourselves above the congregation of the LORD?
>
> 16:7 And put fire therein, and put incense in them before the LORD to morrow: and it shall be [that] the man whom the LORD doth choose, he [shall be] holy: [ye take] too much upon you, ye sons of Levi.
>
> 16:9 [Seemeth it but] a small thing unto you, that the God of Israel hath separated you from the congregation of Israel, to bring you near to himself to do the service of the tabernacle of the LORD, and to stand before the congregation to minister unto them?
>
> 16:10 And he hath brought thee near [to him], and all thy brethren the sons of Levi with thee: and seek ye the priesthood also?
>
> 16:26 And he spake unto the congregation, saying, Depart, I pray you, from the tents of these wicked men, and touch nothing of theirs, lest ye be consumed in all their sins.

16:27 So they gat up from the tabernacle of Korah, Dathan, and Abiram, on every side: and Dathan and Abiram came out, and stood in the door of their tents, and their wives, and their sons, and their little children.
16:31 And it came to pass, as he had made an end of speaking all these words, that the ground clave asunder that [was] under them:
16:32 And the earth opened her mouth, and swallowed them up, and their houses, and all the men that [appertained] unto Korah, and all [their] goods.
16:33 They, and all that [appertained] to them, went down alive into the pit, and the earth closed upon them: and they perished from among the congregation.
16:34 And all Israel that [were] round about them fled at the cry of them: for they said, Lest the earth swallow us up [also].
16:35 And there came out a fire from the LORD, and consumed the two hundred and fifty men that offered incense.
NUMBERS

Unmistakably, Yahweh will not tolerate any betrayal or insurrection against his established officers. Evidently, the three Levite leaders along with the two hundred and fifty Levite dignitaries considered themselves to be just as influential or Holy as Moses and Aaron. Obviously, they were wrong.

As we are discovering, Yahweh is not a physical being to be angered or trifled with, in light of the fiery (consuming/devouring) consequences. Notably, Yahweh and his host had once again called upon the application of their matter maneuvering devices to render the demise of the Levite families. This detail is plainly revealed by the word "clave". The word "clave" is a direct reference to the word "cleave", defined as split apart.

Evidently, Yahweh utilized their matter maneuvering devices to literally split apart ("clave asunder") the very ground under the feet of the Levite families. Consequently the earth opened its mouth swallowing the insurgent heads of the Levites along with their tents and families. As if this abyssal demise was not vicious enough, Yahweh applied his matter maneuvering device to forcibly navigate the ground/dirt back into the severed chasm he created.

In light of what took place at the Red Sea and numerous other matter manipulating exploits, this demonstration of matter shifting force should come as no surprise to anyone reading this analysis. Obviously, if these incredible matter maneuvering contrivances possess the manipulative power to split apart (clave/cleave) an entire channel of water (Red Sea), and maintain its severed position for hours. Then quite naturally wedging apart (clave/cleave) the very ground itself was child's play for Yahweh and his powerful craft. It's no marvel that everyone standing close by, or witnessing this horrifying event began to run in sheer panic and fear for their own lives.

However, as the verses so ardently indicate, Yahweh was not through dealing with the rebelling Levites. Yahweh and his host had now opened fire, utilizing their powerful laser weapons, against the two hundred and fifty men standing in front of his tent. Essentially, Yahweh burn up or consumed (incinerating) all two hundred and fifty men in a matter of moments.

One might assume that this monumental exhibition of authoritarian leadership would be the end of the matter, considering the grotesque human carnage. Yet, this was not to be the case.

> **16:41 But on the morrow all the congregation of the children of Israel murmured against Moses and against Aaron, saying, Ye have killed the people of the LORD.**
>
> **16:42 And it came to pass, when the congregation was gathered against Moses and against Aaron, that they looked toward the tabernacle of the congregation: and, behold, the cloud covered it, and the glory of the LORD appeared.**
>
> **16:43 And Moses and Aaron came before the tabernacle of the congregation.**
>
> **16:44 And the LORD spake unto Moses, saying,**
>
> **16:45 Get you up from among this congregation, that I may consume them as in a moment. And they fell upon their faces.**
>
> **16:46 And Moses said unto Aaron, Take a censer, and put fire therein from off the altar, and put on incense, and go quickly unto the congregation, and make an atonement for them: for there is wrath gone out from the LORD; the plague is begun.**
>
> **16:47 And Aaron took as Moses commanded, and ran into the midst of the congregation; and, behold, the plague was begun among the people: and he put on incense, and made an atonement for the people.**
>
> **16:48 And he stood between the dead and the living; and the plague was stayed.**

16:49 Now they that died in the plague were fourteen thousand and seven hundred, beside them that died about the matter of Korah.
NUMBERS

Unmistakably, the killing of the Levite dignitaries and the two hundred men had induced a major riot within the entire congregation. Remarkably, the congregation blamed Moses and Aaron for the demise of the Levites and their families. This allegation appears to be valid, seeing how Moses deliberately designed the death of the Levites by having them offer incense before the Lord. However, it was not Moses or even Aaron that wreaked the actual slaughter, but rather Yahweh.

Seemingly, the congregation had now personally turned on Moses and Aaron. However, this time the Levites were not alone in their revolt, considering the entire congregation of six hundred thousand strong ("all the congregation") had now joined in. Regrettably, the insurrection infuriated Yahweh and his host into wreaking monumental slaughter among the entire congregation.

In noting verse 16:42, you will discover **two** entirely different objects now positioned above the Tabernacle. The verse states that the cloud covered the tabernacle (tent). The verse then turns right around and states that the glory of the Lord appeared. Obviously, the glory of the Lord was not the cloud, nor was the cloud the glory of the Lord.

As mentioned before, it is the cloud that conceals the craft formation within. That craft formation was now visually referred to as the glory of the Lord. Evidently, the entire congregation could visually observe the craft formation/glory of the Lord inside the cloud.

Moses, in his efforts to persuade Yahweh from killing many within the congregation, proved many times to be quite effective in saving numerous lives in the past. However, in this particular instance, Moses was unable to stop Yahweh from venting his fiery anger against the entire congregation of Israel, for "the plague is begun".

The method of death rendered in the plague can actually be found in verse 16:45 ("that I may consume them in a moment."). Every time the words "consume" "kindled" or "devour" are used in the verses, Yahweh was utilizing his high-tech laser weapons. The verses are actually identifying exactly what Yahweh's craft and their actuated laser systems were physically inflicting upon the congregation. (consume/devour/burn up).

Obviously, Aaron's efforts to stop Yahweh's fiery anger were too late, considering fourteen thousand seven hundred people, including women and children, had been bodily incinerated (consumed/devoured) by Yahweh's laser weapons in just a matter of moments.

This might suggest that all five craft/chariots within the formation (cloud) opened fire in as many directions. Consequently, each craft could simultaneously wreak unimaginable fiery death and destruction at five dissimilar locations within the encompassing congregation. The death toll would be incredible to say the least. Not to mention the numerous injured or maimed individuals now in need of immediate medical attention.

Yahweh Begins His Migratory War Campaign

With proven massive death and destruction of this magnitude, there is no doubt that law and order would now be restored within the congregation. Essentially, everyone left within the remaining congregation was faced with the terrifying realization that they either comply or die.

> **17:12 And the children of Israel spake unto Moses, saying, Behold, we die, we perish, we all perish.**
>
> **17:13 Whosoever cometh any thing near unto the tabernacle of the LORD shall die: shall we be consumed with dying?** NUMBERS

This compliance directive was an absolute must, if the armies of Israel were to work together as a military force to be reckoned with. The congregation couldn't proceed into battle if they were constantly clashing among themselves. With this proven authority Yahweh and the remaining congregation could now begin their binge of death and destruction aimed at the surroundings nations and their other gods.

> **13:32 And they brought up an evil report of the land which they had searched unto the children of Israel, saying, The land, through which we have gone to search it, [is] a land that eateth up the inhabitants thereof; and all the people that we saw in it [are] men of a great stature.**
>
> **13:33 And there we saw the giants, the sons of Anak, [which come] of the giants: and we were in our own sight as grasshoppers, and so we were in their sight.** NUMBERS
>
> **2:10 The Emims dwelt therein in times past, a people great, and many, and tall, as the Anakims;**

2:11 Which also were accounted giants, as the Anakims; but the Moabites call them Emims.
2:20 (That also was accounted a land of giants: giants dwelt therein in old time; and the Ammonites call them Zamzummims;
2:21 A people great, and many, and tall, as the Anakims; but the LORD destroyed them before them; and they succeeded them, and dwelt in their stead:
3:11 For only Og king of Bashan remained of the remnant of giants; behold, his bedstead [was] a bedstead of iron; [is] it not in Rabbath of the children of Ammon? nine cubits [was] the length thereof, and four cubits the breadth of it, after the cubit of a man.
3:13 And the rest of Gilead, and all Bashan, [being] the kingdom of Og, gave I unto the half tribe of Manasseh; all the region of Argob, with all Bashan, which was called the land of giants.
DEUTERONOMY

Also see Joshua 12:4, 13:12, 15:8, 17:15, 18:16.

Closely observing the verses, we discover that the giants originated from "Old times", "in time past", "giants of giants". The verses actually expose these giants as the ancestors of the giants before the flood of Noah.

Evidently many of the goliath hybrids survived the lunar deluge of Noah. Not only did they survive, they outwardly flourished into dissimilar nations of many mixed breeds (hybrids). These revealing verses may genuinely resolve just who or what was the reported giant found in the legend of David and Goliath/Giant (See 1 Samuel 17:).

One factor certain, Yahweh and his stellar host had returned to the planet to cleanse its genetically mixed populace. This would consequently reestablish Yahweh's chosen seed as the dominant culture upon a world that had obviously forgotten who it belongs to. Moreover, Yahweh was prepared to administer this global purging with his own chosen people now prepared to exterminate giants or any other surviving culture.

Clearly, the primitive weapons of the ancient nations were unable to stand against the armies of Israel. This rude awakening came in the form of high-tech laser weapons and phenomenal matter maneuvering devices that devastated any and everything in their path. Obviously, Yahweh's incredible craft and weapons physically inflicted the primary war confrontations for Israel. This allowed the armies of Israel to launch their offensive strikes behind Yahweh's destructive weaponry, hence ravaging what remained.

21:3 And the LORD hearkened to the voice of Israel, and delivered up the Canaanites; and they utterly destroyed them and their cities: and he called the name of the place Hormah.
21:28 For there is a fire gone out of Heshbon, a flame from the city of Sihon: it hath consumed Ar of Moab, [and] the lords of the high places of Arnon.
21:34 And the LORD said unto Moses, Fear him not: for I have delivered him into thy hand, and all his people, and his land; and thou shalt do to him as thou didst unto Sihon king of the Amorites, which dwelt at Heshbon.
21:35 So they smote him, and his sons, and all his people, until there was none left him alive:...
NUMBERS
1:28 Whither shall we go up? our brethren have discouraged our heart, saying, The people [is] greater and taller than we; the cities [are] great and walled up to heaven; and moreover we have seen the sons of the Anakims there.
1:29 Then I said unto you, Dread not, neither be afraid of them.
1:30 The LORD your God which goeth before you, he shall fight for you, according to all that he did for you in Egypt before your eyes;
2:33 And the LORD our God delivered him before us; and we smote him, and his sons, and all his people.
2:34 And we took all his cities at that time, and utterly destroyed the men, and the women, and the little ones, of every city, we left none to remain:
2:35 Only the cattle we took for a prey unto ourselves, and the spoil of the cities which we took.
2:36 From Aroer, which [is] by the brink of the river of Arnon, and [from] the city that [is] by the river, even unto Gilead, there was not one city too strong for us: the LORD our God delivered all unto us:
3:1 Then we turned, and went up the way to Bashan: and Og the king of Bashan came out against us, he and all his people, to battle at Edrei.
3:2 And the LORD said unto me, Fear him not: for I will deliver him, and all his people, and his land, into thy hand; and thou shalt do unto him as thou didst unto Sihon king of the Amorites, which dwelt at Heshbon.
3:3 So the LORD our God delivered into our hands Og also, the king of Bashan, and all his people: and we smote him until none was left to him remaining.

3:4 And we took all his cities at that time, there was not a city which we took not from them, threescore cities, all the region of Argob, the kingdom of Og in Bashan.
3:5 All these cities [were] fenced with high walls, gates, and bars; beside unwalled towns a great many.
3:6 And we utterly destroyed them, as we did unto Sihon king of Heshbon, utterly destroying the men, women, and children, of every city.
7:2 And when the LORD thy God shall deliver them before thee; thou shalt smite them, [and] utterly destroy them; thou shalt make no covenant with them, nor show mercy unto them:
DEUTERONOMY

There was no army too large, or no wall too high, that the twelve armies of Israel could not totally destroy. It does not take a genius to realize that Yahweh and his host, along with their numerous craft ("hornets") were advancing before the armies of Israel as they approached each city to be destroyed.

Unmistakably, Yahweh and his astonishing craft/chariots were utilizing their powerful weapons to exterminate each and every city. This was an effortless matter, considering their highly advanced laser weapons could burn up entire cities and populations in a matter of moments.

Moreover, Yahweh's craft could activate their matter maneuvering devices to literally thrust down the massive towering walls on top of their own populations. Yahweh's craft could kill thousands in just moments, at which point the twelve armies of Israel would launch their ground-based offensive, killing everyone remaining within the crushed and burning cities. There would be no stopping them, they could now move from city to city, and empire to empire with the same devastating results.

Yahweh and his newly established armies were destroying and taking over every city and empire within the middle east region. Ultimately they established a permanent stronghold within the immediate geographical locations of their supervised path. That conducted avenue was an eastward direction aimed at a focused site across the river Jordan.

33:50 And the LORD spake unto Moses in the plains of Moab by Jordan [near] Jericho, saying,
33:51 Speak unto the children of Israel, and say unto them, When ye are passed over Jordan into the land of Canaan;

33:52 Then ye shall drive out all the inhabitants of the land from before you, and destroy all their pictures, and destroy all their molten images, and quite pluck down all their high places:
33:53 And ye shall dispossess [the inhabitants] of the land, and dwell therein: for I have given you the land to possess it.
32:21 And will go all of you armed over Jordan before the LORD, until he hath driven out his enemies from before him,
32:27 But thy servants will pass over, every man armed for war, before the LORD to battle, as my lord saith.
NUMBERS
9:3 Understand therefore this day, that the LORD thy God [is] he which goeth over before thee; [as] a consuming fire he shall destroy them, and he shall bring them down before thy face: so shalt thou drive them out, and destroy them quickly, as the LORD hath said unto thee.
9:4 Speak not thou in thine heart, after that the LORD thy God hath cast them out from before thee, saying, For my righteousness the LORD hath brought me in to possess this land: but for the wickedness of these nations the LORD doth drive them out from before thee.
31:3 The LORD thy God, he will go over before thee, [and] he will destroy these nations from before thee, and thou shalt possess them: [and] Joshua, he shall go over before thee, as the LORD hath said.
31:4 And the LORD shall do unto them as he did to Sihon and to Og, kings of the Amorites, and unto the land of them, whom he destroyed.
3:21 And I commanded Joshua at that time, saying, Thine eyes have seen all that the LORD your God hath done unto these two kings: so shall the LORD do unto all the kingdoms whither thou passest.
3:22 Ye shall not fear them: for the LORD your God he shall fight for you.
DEUTERONOMY

Yahweh's organized campaign of genocide ultimately marched right out of Numbers, headlong into the chapters of Deuteronomy. The book of Deuteronomy fills our senses with the unquestionable demise of hundreds of thousands, and the monumental eradication of enormous towering cities in which they lived.

The verses hold nothing back in their explicit clarification of how Yahweh, along with his many powerful craft, proceeded before the armies of Israel as a consuming fire (laser technology) of death and destruction. The verses even validate the reality that the armies of Israel were quite aware of the fact that

Yahweh (God) and his host, was physically engaged in destroying the cities and empires for the armies of Israel ("for the LORD your God he shall fight for you").

The Hand Of God

Many verses within Deuteronomy actually establish the fact that the armies of Israel could visually see how and what was being utilized to inflict this incredible devastation. Not only did they physically observe the weapons or devices, they clearly recognized the fact that the weapons were actually being fired or discharged.

Quite naturally, this would lead one to speculate upon the veracity of the verses. If such weapons or devices were present within Scripture, where were they? There should be numerous verses illustrating the weapons employed to destroy (consume/burn up) the cities. And indeed there is.

> 4:34 Or hath God assayed to go [and] take him a nation from the midst of [another] nation, by temptations, by signs, and by wonders, and by war, and by a mighty hand, and by a stretched out arm, and by great terrors,...
> 5:15 And remember that thou wast a servant in the land of Egypt, and [that] the LORD thy God brought thee out thence through a mighty hand and by a stretched out arm:...
> 7:19 The great temptations which thine eyes saw, and the signs, and the wonders, and the mighty hand, and the stretched out arm, whereby the LORD thy God brought thee out: so shall the LORD thy God do unto all the people of whom thou art afraid.
> 9:29 Yet they [are] thy people and thine inheritance, which thou broughtest out by thy mighty power and by thy stretched out arm.
> 11:2 And know ye this day: for [I speak] not with your children which have not known, and which have not seen the chastisement of the LORD your God, his greatness, his mighty hand, and his stretched out arm,
> 26:8 And the LORD brought us forth out of Egypt with a mighty hand, and with an outstretched arm, and with great terribleness, and with signs, and with wonders:
> 33:2 And he said, The Lord came from Si'nai, and rose up from Se'ir unto them; he shined forth from mount Pa'ran, and he came with ten thousands of saints: from his right hand went a fiery law for them.
> DEUTERONOMY

If the reader will recall, we have already examined the device found within these verses. However, it's essential to thoroughly scrutinize these verses if we are to accurately comprehend the same apparatus found within the book of Ezekiel.

In order to truly grasp all the informative verses, it's significant that we analyze the last verse first. In doing so, we discover a word that actually helps us to decipher all the previous verses. It's the last verse that identifies the physical power established within the "**Hand**".

Note the statement "stretched out arm." The very word "arm" would suggest something quite physical in nature. However, we are not concerned with the word "arm" at this time, but rather the assertion "stretched". In defining the word "stretched" we discover some very interesting facts.

> **STRETCHED**—*to hold out or reach out; extend, to cause (the body or limbs) to reach out to full length, a given space, distance, to cause to reach or extend farther, to become stretched or be capable of being stretched to greater size, become extended without breaking.*

The very word "stretched" would inform us of the act of physical movement, implying an "in" and "out" application. Obviously, the congregation verbally applied the word "stretched" to indicate that they were actually able to see the "in" and "out" maneuver of the arm.

If the reader will recall, we found this same "stretched out arm" in the chapter of Exodus. Yahweh used his stretched out arm [and] hand device to divide the Red Sea. Furthermore, it became evident that this "stretched out arm" was originating from underneath Yahweh's five craft/chariots concealed inside the cloud.

Here again, the Israelite spectators were describing what they saw the best way they knew how. Hence, they allegorically identified the object the best way their ancient intellect could interpret the apparatus. In essence, the physical device resembled an extended "arm" (appendage) and" hand" (open fist) shaped mechanism when observed from a distance.

Upon entering the book of Ezekiel, we will discover that Yahweh's craft formation possesses not only one such arm and hand shaped device, but <u>four</u> such devices on each and every craft. Each of the craft supporting the hand shaped devices are mounted on what appears to be a telescopic arm (appendage) capable of extending/stretching in and out of the craft for quite some distance. The telescopic arm was quite proficient in being maneuvered from side to side, or up and down. Hence, the armies of Israel allegorically portrayed Yahweh's awesome weapon as the "stretched out arm, and hand of God".

Clearly, the arm and hand-shaped device was held totally responsible for all the mass destruction being inflicted by Yahweh and his craft. Furthermore, we will discover that these incredible arm and hand shaped devices control numerous perfunctory fingers adept in matter manipulation, as well as enormous fire power (Laser technology), as stated in the last verse.

Notably, there is a distinct dissimilarity between the actual arm and the hand. The verses would even go so far as to suggest that they are two entirely different objects, even though they appear to be coupled or linked together. This would entice one to speculate that the hand shaped apparatus is in fact detachable from its telescopic arm. Yet, this same observation may be a testimony to the fact that these arm and hand fashioned devices are capable of operating independently of each other.

The mechanical arm is either flexible, or capable of extending out of the craft with a telescopic (**stretching**) type of maneuver, as well as bending or flexing in a multitude of directions. Then again, the flexible telescopic arm, could be hinged to the craft by a ball or knuckle type of apparatus allowing the arm to move in any direction necessary (up/down/around/side to side).

At the end of the resilient arm would be the hand-fashioned device (weapon), joined to the arm by yet another type of mechanical ball or knuckle mechanism. This would consequently allow the flexible mechanical arm and knuckled hand the ability to maneuver in opposite direction of each other. If the arm was to swing down and to the left, the hand shaped device knuckled to the arm could actually swing up and to the right without ever moving the arm. The possible combinations of various directions would be endless.

However, therein lies another probability. The entire mechanical arm and hand shaped apparatus may be a totally solid malleable unit. This might imply that there are no mechanical swivels, balls, or knuckles attaching the hand to the arm, or the arm to the body of the craft. In essence, the entire mechanism is a completely pliable unit.

This would presuppose that the hand-shaped device is just as flexible as the telescopic arm, even though they appear to be one and the same mechanism. The resilient mechanical arm could effortlessly extend out of the craft and bend or flex in any direction deemed by the pilot. While, at the same time, the hand-shaped device may be extremely flexible at the location of its streamlined attachment to the arm. This would allow the hand to bend or flex in any direction contrary to the resilient mechanical arm. Here again, the entire arm and hand-assembled device would boast the power of an endless focus in any direction.

Evidently, the pliable arm and hand shaped appliances working together could be directed or aimed in any direction the pilot wanted. This resilient appliance becomes even more frightening when we realize that each craft controlled four such devices. Each of the multifaceted devices is fully capable of moving in any direction, as well as logically functioning cooperatively as a team (matter manipulation).

Each, if not all of the craft utilizing their arm and hand appliances could actually elevate objects of truly phenomenal dimensions. By maneuvering the numerous arm and hand shaped apparatus of each craft, they could forcibly oppose objects from many dissimilar sides. Essentially, the craft boast the ability to elevate, twist or turn solid objects of astonishing dimensions while suspended in midair. Essentially, the craft could perform numerous matter maneuver feats together and/or laser fire in a spherical configuration simultaneously.

Israel Crosses the River Jordan

This awesome array of craft and hand-shaped weapons was now prepared to cross the river Jordan, where they will kill, pillage and burn everyone and everything in their path as they advanced eastward in a deadly rampage designed to show no mercy to anyone.

A good question at this point would be, how did the massive armies of Israel cross this large river? In contrast to crossing the Red Sea, the crossing of the River Jordan was much easier, considering the river Jordan is much smaller than the Red Sea. Yet, more significantly the river Jordan is flowing one way.

> **3:13 And it shall come to pass, as soon as the soles of the feet of the priests that bear the ark of the LORD, the Lord of all the earth, shall rest in the waters of Jordan, [that] the waters of Jordan shall be cut off [from] the waters that come down from above; and they shall stand upon an heap.**
>
> **3:15 And as they that bare the ark were come unto Jordan, and the feet of the priests that bare the ark were dipped in the brim of the water, (for Jordan over-floweth all his banks all the time of harvest,)**

3:16 That the waters which came down from above stood [and] rose up upon an heap very far from the city Adam, that [is] beside Zaretan: and those that came down toward the sea of the plain, [even] the salt sea, failed, [and] were cut off: and the people passed over right against Jericho.
3:17 And the priests that bare the ark of the covenant of the LORD stood firm on dry ground in the midst of Jordan, and all the Israelites passed over on dry ground, until all the people were passed clean over Jordan.
4:18 And it came to pass, when the priests that bare the ark of the covenant of the LORD were come up out of the midst of Jordan, [and] the soles of the priests' feet were lifted up unto the dry land, that the waters of Jordan returned unto their place, and flowed over all his banks, as [they did] before.
4:19 And the people came up out of Jordan on the tenth [day] of the first month, and encamped in Gilgal, in the east border of Jericho.
4:23 For the LORD your God dried up the waters of Jordan from before you, until ye were passed over, as the LORD your God did to the Red sea, which he dried up from before us, until we were gone over:
JOSHUA

Yahweh's craft/chariot formation had now come to "rest" (hovering) in, or just above the river Jordan. Clearly, the location of the dammed up area was far upstream. This remote location upstream allowed the armies of Israel and the priests bearing the ark to cross the dried up Jordan downstream.

Obviously, Yahweh's craft formation had established a secure position upstream, where they utilized their matter maneuvering devices (stretched out arms and hands) to create an invisible field of force against the oncoming river. Consequently, the rushing waters of the river Jordan came face to face with an invisible dam forcing the waters to rise.

The verses would lead one to believe that the damming up of the river Jordan was in fact witnessed by the armies of Israel. This revealing detail can be corroborated by the word "heap" found within the verses. Essentially, the dammed up waters were actually observed as they began to heap up or rise.

Evidently, the rising of the river Jordan was observed from a flank position as the Israelites crossed over. This would imply that the Israelites were actually observing the waters of the river rise or "stand upon a heap" upstream while they were crossing downstream. Yet, the real issue would be how. How were the rushing waters of the river Jordan able to heap or rise up to the point, that even the witnesses standing quite some distance downstream were able to observe the rising?

If in fact Yahweh used some type of solid structure or object to dam up the River Jordan there is no way the Israelites downstream could have visually observed the waters of the River rise or "stand upon an heap" on the opposite side. Obviously, the Israelites downstream would not be able to physically see through any solid object or obstruction damming up the river Jordan. Therefore, the Israelites would have never known if the waters were rising (heaping up) or not.

Clearly, the armies of Israel downstream were actually able to see right through the object or structure damming up the river. Evidently, whatever was causing the river Jordan to be dammed up was transparent or invisible.

This incredible conjecture becomes even more credible when scrutinizing the word "stand". The word "stand" would imply that the Israelites were actually able to observe the very face of the dammed up river as it began to "stand", or "heap" up. Hence the testimony "stand upon an heap". Moreover, this would confirm the location of Yahweh's craft formation upstream (resting in) hovering just above the river Jordan where the invisible barrier (dam/force field) was in operation.

The verses indicate that there were more rivers or streams than just the river Jordan to be dammed up. This might suggest that the craft formation split up, and established different aerial positions over each stream or tributary feeding into the river Jordan. This would permit each of the craft the ability to dam up all water inlets feeding into the river Jordan.

However, considering there is no mention of another craft, therein lies another probability. Each craft possesses four arm and hand constructed devices. Each of the craft is proficient in aiming and implementing all four arm and hand shaped devices in any number of directions.

Seeing how we have no idea as to the full power, efficiency, or distance that the apparatus can be effectively utilized. It's conceivable that perhaps Yahweh's craft formation could have maintained their yoked together position over the river Jordan.

The craft formation as a combined unit could have dammed up the river Jordan from a great distance. Furthermore, they could have dammed up any other tributary within the immediate area without splitting up the craft formation. This would possibly warrant Yahweh's given location over the river Jordan.

This speculation becomes even more convincing when considering the probability that the total five craft formation embodies twenty resilient and powerful arm and hand devices, all of which possess the same matter maneuvering powers. Each of the devices could be aimed or focused in twenty dissimilar directions, as well as being utilized to work in unison or in opposition of each other.

Needless to say, Yahweh and his escort craft shut down their matter maneuvering (force field) devices after the Israelites crossed over the River Jordan. Consequently, the invisibly restrained waters of the river Jordan and its tributaries continued their perpetual journey.

Yahweh Destroys Jericho

Yahweh's armies, having now entered the land of Canaan, established their first encampment around what might be considered a paramount city of great significance. This massive city was to ultimately reflect the terrifying destruction yet to be unleashed upon the numerous cities within the land of Canaan.

Moreover, the annihilation of the city of Jericho was to be a grievous message of destruction sent to the other gods. That painful notice would display the awesome power of the one true god, in which the other gods (Fallen Angels) would be powerless to stop.

The city of Jericho appears to be a deliberate first stop at what was considered to be a well-fortified city. This citadel metropolis bragged of its massive high walls that could withstand any onslaught by any outside aggressors. Obviously, this was the very justification behind Yahweh choosing Jericho as his first major target marked for extinction. This would clearly notify the other empires that their burdensome high walls will not protect them from Yahweh's powerful craft and armies.

> **6:1 Now Jericho was straitly shut up because of the children of Israel: none went out, and none came in.**
>
> **6:2 And the LORD said unto Joshua, See, I have given into thine hand Jericho, and the king thereof, [and] the mighty men of valour.**
>
> **6:3 And ye shall compass the city, all [ye] men of war, [and] go round about the city once. Thus shalt thou do six days.**
>
> **6:4 And seven priests shall bear before the ark seven trumpets of rams' horns: and the seventh day ye shall compass the city seven times, and the priests shall blow with the trumpets.**

6:5 And it shall come to pass, that when they make a long [blast] with the ram's horn, [and] when ye hear the sound of the trumpet, all the people shall shout with a great shout; and the wall of the city shall fall down flat, and the people shall ascend up every man straight before him.
6:10 And Joshua had commanded the people, saying, Ye shall not shout, nor make any noise with your voice, neither shall [any] word proceed out of your mouth, until the day I bid you shout; then shall ye shout.
6:15 And it came to pass on the seventh day, that they rose early about the dawning of the day, and compassed the city after the same manner seven times: only on that day they compassed the city seven times.
6:16 And it came to pass at the seventh time, when the priests blew with the trumpets, Joshua said unto the people, Shout; for the LORD hath given you the city.
6:20 So the people shouted when [the priests] blew with the trumpets: and it came to pass, when the people heard the sound of the trumpet, and the people shouted with a great shout, that the wall fell down flat, so that the people went up into the city, every man straight before him, and they took the city.
6:21 And they utterly destroyed all that [was] in the city, both man and woman, young and old, and ox, and sheep, and ass, with the edge of the sword.
JOSHUA

Are we to believe that the massive walls of Jericho simply fell down because the armies of Israel hollered and screamed at them? I think not! Note, a systematic procedure was performed prior to the walls falling down. Yahweh had his armies marched once around the city, six times for six days, with the seventh day consisting of seven complete cycles around the city. Obviously, the number seven played a major roll in the destruction of the city of Jericho. Yet, why would the number seven possess such great significance in destroying this city?

In recalling the Genesis, it was a third of the inhabited stars (constellations) that chose to revolt against Yahweh. This third of the stars and their populations lost the cosmic campaign and was cast into the bottomless abyss (the Underworld) of this planet. Essentially, these subterranean fallen angels/other gods were once again covertly exploiting the other nations, including Jericho.

We shall continue to discover that this third of the stars actually accounted for four constellations out of a total of twelve systems (constellations) under

Yahweh's jurisdiction. This would leave eight star systems unaffected. However, this would not be an accurate account, considering the fact that the fallen angels maintained some degree of control over this very planet and the stellar system (constellation) in which it exists.

Essentially, the cosmic cold war continues dues to the fallen angel's control over this planet. When we include the star system (constellation Sagittarius) that mankind and the Planet Earth now reside in, we end up with a total of five constellations under the fallen angels' control.

Deducting five rebelling systems from twelve leaves' us with the holy number **seven.** The number seven is referred to as a holy number simply because the number corresponds to the inhabited star systems (constellations) that did **not** rebel against Yahweh. Essentially, these seven star systems are still holy within the ranks of the kingdom of heaven (the Universe).

The verses would suggest that the given amount of times (seven total days) and the number of cycles (seven) the armies of Israel marched around the city of Jericho were symbolic in reference to the holy number of star systems and their inhabitancy.

Those seven total star systems and their inhabitants are still waging a cold war against the remaining five disloyal star systems and their fallen angel leaders (The Underworld). In essence, the city of Jericho was under the control of the other gods/fallen angels and had to be destroyed.

We will continue to discover that the holy number seven is consistently used as a cosmic reminder to the fallen angels of their universal insurrection.

This physical reminder was to be constantly imposed upon the other gods/fallen angels, and every city or empire that they control. This was the motivation behind the armies of Israel marching around the city of Jericho seven, upon seven times, moments before its climactic demise. Yet, how was this enormous towering city genuinely destroyed?

Let be realistic! If six hundred thousand people yelled at the massive walls of this city, they would have ultimately lost their voice in a feeble attempt to dislodge the massive stones embodied within the walls of Jericho. Obviously, another source of devastation was inflicted upon the great walls.

Seemingly, Yahweh and his host deliberately set up this show of physical strength to establish a powerful reputation for the twelve armies of Israel. This notoriety would ultimately strike fear into the hearts of all the inhabitancy of the land of Canaan. Clearly, news of the massive destruction of Jericho would spread like wild fire. The astonishing reports, or psychological warfare would create the belief that the mighty armies of Israel merely yelled at the towering walls of Jericho causing them to fall down flat.

Quite naturally, this inconceivable event would be looked at as nothing short of a miracle. This marvel of destruction would genuinely display the awesome power of the armies of Israel. Yet, it was not the vocal power of the armies of Israel that inflicted this devastating blow. It was Yahweh and his host that performed this mammoth maneuver. In doing so he deliberately transferred this enormous show of power upon the twelve armies of Israel.

It would appear that Yahweh and his host had purposely designed and timed the screaming and yelling of the armies of the Israel with the destruction of the city walls. It was Yahweh that instructed Joshua to perform the number seven count down. This vocally orchestrated countdown made it quite easy to time the operation of Yahweh's invisible matter maneuvering (force field) devices with the shouting and yelling of the twelve armies.

Essentially, Yahweh and his numerous craft utilized their unseen force fields (matter manipulation) against the massive walls of Jericho, thus knocking them down "flat". This astounding show of power was just the beginning of Yahweh and Joshua's reign of terror within the land of Canaan.

Yahweh and Israel Take Control of Canaan

> **10:40 So Joshua smote all the country of the hills, and of the south, and of the vale, and of the springs, and all their kings: he left none remaining, but utterly destroyed all that breathed, as the LORD God of Israel commanded.**
>
> **10:41 And Joshua smote them from Kadeshbarnea even unto Gaza, and all the country of Goshen, even unto Gibeon.**
>
> **10:42 And all these kings and their land did Joshua take at one time, because the LORD God of Israel fought for Israel.**
>
> **11:6 And the LORD said unto Joshua, Be not afraid because of them: for to morrow about this time will I deliver them up all slain before Israel: thou shalt hock their horses, and burn their chariots with fire.**
>
> **11:8 And the LORD delivered them into the hand of Israel, who smote them, and chased them unto great Zidon, and unto Misrephothmaim, and unto the valley of Mizpeh eastward; and they smote them, until they left them none remaining.**

11:11 And they smote all the souls that [were] therein with the edge of the sword, utterly destroying [them]: there was not any left to breathe: and he burnt Hazor with fire.
11:12 And all the cities of those kings, and all the kings of them, did Joshua take, and smote them with the edge of the sword, [and] he utterly destroyed them, as Moses the servant of the LORD commanded.
11:14 And all the spoil of these cities, and the cattle, the children of Israel took for a prey unto themselves; but every man they smote with the edge of the sword, until they had destroyed them, neither left they any to breathe.
11:17 [Even] from the mount Halak, that goeth up to Seir, even unto Baalgad in the valley of Lebanon under mount Hermon: and all their kings he took, and smote them, and slew them.
11:19 There was not a city that made peace with the children of Israel, save the Hivites the inhabitants of Gibeon: all [other] they took in battle.
11:20 For it was of the LORD to harden their hearts, that they should come against Israel in battle, that he might destroy them utterly, [and] that they might have no favour, but that he might destroy them, as the LORD commanded Moses.
24:12 And I sent the hornet before you, which drave them out from before you, [even] the two kings of the Amorites; [but] not with thy sword, nor with thy bow.
24:14 Now therefore fear the LORD, and serve him in sincerity and in truth: and put away the gods which your fathers served on the other side of the flood, and in Egypt; and serve ye the LORD.
24:15 And if it seem evil unto you to serve the LORD, choose you this day whom ye will serve; whether the gods which your fathers served that [were] on the other side of the flood, or the gods of the Amorites, in whose land ye dwell: but as for me and my house, we will serve the LORD.
JOSHUA

Joshua and his armies wreaked a devastating path of death and destruction within the land of Canaan. Yet, the verses clarify the fact that it was not just Joshua and the twelve armies of Israel that enacted this reign of terror. Rather, it was Yahweh and his host that preformed this nonstop genocide of the surrounding nations and their fallen angels/other god's administration. Without Yahweh and his highly superior craft (hornets) and weaponry, Joshua and the twelve armies of Israel would have been vanquished long before.

Notably, Yahweh went so far as to deliberately instigate many of the war campaigns that took place. (See verse 11:2) This might suggest that Yahweh mentally manipulated the numerous Kings to incite war. In doing so Yahweh could intentionally draw out their adversary to utterly destroy them. Yet, more significant would be the motive as to why. Without a doubt, an accusing finger is being pointed directly at the fallen angels, notifying us that the fallen angels were not only alive and well, but still in control.

Evidently, the fathers of Israel did in fact serve the gods on the other side of the flood. Essentially, this is a direct reference to the controlling gods before Noah's lunar inundation actually occurred. As we have already discovered, the fallen angels dominated the inhabitancy of this planet prior to the lunar deluge of Noah.

Moreover, The fallen angels were incarcerated inside this planet before the lunar inundation was performed. This was obviously a preservation Yahweh may have wished he had never done, considering the fallen angels were once again in control of the surface of the planet. Not only were they in control of the planet, but the benighted populations were now worshiping them as gods.

> **"put away the gods which your fathers served on the other side of the flood, and in Egypt", "choose you this day whom ye will serve; whether the gods which your fathers served that [were] on the other side of the flood".**

Note the wording "put away the gods" and "whom ye will serve". How does one put away a god that does not exist? How does one serve gods that do not exist? Notably, the gods of Egypt have now been brought into the equation. This would once again imply that the underworld gods of Egypt were also from the other side of the flood. Simply put, the "other gods" being worshiped by the ancient world were nothing more than fallen angels. (Gods of the Underworld)

Furthermore, we will discover that this subterranean domain (Underworld) consists of massive caverns containing entire cities that harbor astonishing technology. Additionally, we will substantiate the fact that these elusive beings (Fallen Angels) were capable of coming up out of the very ground itself (the underworld), to enforce their clandestine control. Moreover, this enigmatic puzzle will ultimately reveal the numerous gateways to the underworld.

32:17 They sacrificed unto devils, not to God; to gods whom they knew not, to new [gods that] came newly up, whom your fathers feared not.

DEUTERONOMY

Kings & Chronicles

Yahweh and his host continued their migratory rampage of death and destruction throughout many of the chapters of the Old Testament. Eventually, Yahweh inflicted enormous destruction of all the surrounding nations, allowing Israel supreme control over all the territories within the region.

Ultimately, the twelve tribes became divided throughout the various territories in a direct effort to maintain jurisdiction over the nations they subjugated. In doing so, the twelve tribes were so well dispersed, that Yahweh began to lose control over what was previously a singular congregation of six hundred thousand.

It would take numerous books to totally elaborate upon the many exploits of Yahweh and his twelve tribes. However, we are more concerned with substantiating the actual existence of Yahweh's astounding craft, weapons, devices and the palpable personnel operating them.

Moreover, it's significant for us to quickly examine all the physical aspects of Yahweh's technology if we are unravel the book of Ezekiel. This will require that we examine a large number of verses in a short order of time. One of those significant details would be the understanding that Yahweh's Craft were not always referred to as a "cloud".

The Craft Of the Kingdom of Heaven

> **23:19 Behold, a whirlwind of the LORD is gone forth in fury, even a grievous whirlwind: it shall fall grievously upon the head of the wicked.**
>
> JEREMIAH

As we are about to discover, Yahweh's cloud was many times alluded to as a "whirlwind". Seemingly, the word "cloud" referred to Yahweh's craft formation while in a stationary or very slow moving state. While on the other hand, the "whirlwind" appears to be the same craft formation in an extremely active state of operation.

As long as the craft formation stays within a fixed, or slow-moving maneuver, the camouflaging cloud would do the same. Yet, if the craft formation begins to accelerate, the shrouding cloud would respond accordingly. Essentially, the cloaking cloud would convert into what was cited to be an agitated whirlwind encircling the craft formation.

Simply put, the propulsion system of the craft appears to be responsible for creating the dissimilar cloud or storm criteria (atomospheric distortion) skirting the formation. One factor remains certain, whether it was a mysterious cloud, or whirlwind, both shrouding conditions were concealing genuine solid objects.

> 104:3 Who layeth the beams of his chambers in the waters: who maketh the clouds his chariot: who walketh upon the wings of the wind:
> PSALMS
>
> 26:9 He holdeth back the face of his throne, [and] spreadeth his cloud upon it.
>
> 38:1 Then the LORD answered Job out of the whirlwind,... JOB
>
> 19:11 And he said, Go forth, and stand upon the mount before the LORD. And, behold, the LORD passed by, and a great and strong wind rent the mountains, and brake in pieces the rocks before the LORD; [but] the LORD [was] not in the wind: and after the wind an earthquake; [but] the LORD [was] not in the earthquake: KINGS I
>
> 2:1 And it came to pass, when the LORD would take up Elijah into heaven by a whirlwind, that Elijah went with Elisha from Gilgal.
>
> 2:11 And it came to pass, as they still went on, and talked, that, behold, [there appeared] a chariot of fire, and horses of fire, and parted them both asunder; and Elijah went up by a whirlwind into heaven.
>
> 2:12 And Elisha saw [it], and he cried, My father, my father, the chariot of Israel, and the horsemen thereof. And he saw him no more: and he took hold of his own clothes, and rent them in two pieces.
>
> "When Enoch had talked to the people, The Lord sent out darkness onto the earth and there was darkness and it covered those men standing with Enoch up on to the highest heaven where the Lord is; and he received him, and placed him before his face and the darkness went off from the earth and light came again." SECRETS OF ENOCH LXVII.

It's significant to remember that we are examining primitive mankind compelled to acclimate extraterrestrial intervention of the highest form. To imply that ancient humans were uneducated in applied science and technology, would be a gross understatement. As with the modern UFO phenomena, ancient humans were at a loss for words when trying to physically decipher and/or describe the many craft, and devices they observed or heard while in operation.

Verse (104:3) establishes the probability that the craft/chariots could actually immerse themselves in large bodies of water, (seas, oceans, lakes) a common UFO trait even today. Furthermore, the craft appear to be quite tangible considering they can produce physical after shocks by their very passing. This might suggest a highly dynamic propulsion system and/or atmospheric displacement due to something solid rapidly passing through the atmosphere.

Yahweh's witnessed craft (chariots) obviously transported physical beings ("horsemen") from one place to another, as did the chariots of old. The only dissimilarities would be the fact that these unparalleled chariots could fly, not to mention their fiery attributes, hence fiery flying chariots.

Obviously, Yahweh and his host had once again utilized their matter maneuvering device to physically retrieve the body of Elijah. Note the phrase "parted them both asunder", as if Elijah was literally snatched up off the ground while standing next to Elisha.

Clearly, the craft did not land to personally collect Elijah, but rather picked up the body of Elijah while passing overhead. This typical UFO procedure would once again confirm the fact that these cosmic beings' possess the ability to manipulate solid matter (force fields) with surgical precision.

Evidence of a Parent Ship

Evidently, Enoch was also bodily removed from the surface of the planet. In fact, we now possess evidence of two entirely different men (Elijah and Enoch) who were literally taken up into outer space (the Universe/kingdom of heaven) **alive**.

It's extremely significant to remember this detail, considering these same two men later returned to this planet the same way they left. Moreover, their return will ultimately allow them to assist in bringing about the foretold Revelation yet to come. However, more significant was the method by which Enoch was removed from the surface of the planet.

Obviously, Elijah was transported into outer space by a small craft (a fiery chariot). In fact it appears evident that a large number of these smaller craft were circulating the ancient skies of the biblical era. Yet, the primary question would be, where did they come from? Seemingly, these bantam craft are far too small for intergalactic or universal space travel. This might suggest that a mother ship was orbiting this world during the time the smaller craft made their presents known on the surface of the planet.

Ultimately, we will discover that this parent ship was capable of sustaining hundreds if not thousands of craft, as well as the men that piloted them. This obvious detail returns us to Enoch's last verse pertaining to his removal from the surface of the planet. The verse indicates that prior to Enoch removal from this world, darkness fell upon the planet.

That darkness only covered the area where Enoch and other men were standing. Yet, the mysterious darkness only lasted long enough for Enoch to be retrieved from the surface of the planet. Once Enoch was removed from the planet, the darkness left, indicating that the darkness had something to do with Enoch's retrieval.

I seriously doubt a lunar eclipse took place at the exact same time and place that Enoch was removed from the surface of the planet? What we may have here, is a possible starship eclipse. This would imply the mother ship would have to be enormous in order to cast such a massive shadow.

Moreover, this eclipsing maneuver may have also had a hand in the darkness that could be felt in the Exodus chronicles. Essentially, the darkness during the daylight hours of the fog may have been an enormous orbiting mother ship that strategically eclipsed the location.

Speculation, yes! Yet, I forewarn the reader, by the time you have finished these writings you will come to understand the true nature of this as of yet unseen **Starship**. Furthermore, we will discover that this cosmic **Starship** is so colossal it could indeed eclipse this planet on the same scale as that of our own moon.

Unmistakably, these extraordinary craft possess awesome firepower, as flaunted by the small craft we have surveyed up to this point. Seemingly, any weapons or devices embodied within the minute craft may also be incorporated within the mother ship. Furthermore, the weapons or devices mounted within the mother ship would quite naturally match the enormous size and power of the parent ship.

1:9 Then the king sent unto him a captain of fifty with his fifty. And he went up to him: and, behold, he sat on the top of an hill. And he spake unto him, Thou man of God, the king hath said, Come down.
1:10 And Elijah answered and said to the captain of fifty, If I [be] a man of God, then let fire come down from heaven, and consume thee and thy fifty. And there came down fire from heaven, and consumed him and his fifty.
1:11 Again also he sent unto him another captain of fifty with his fifty. And he answered and said unto him, O man of God, thus hath the king said, Come down quickly.
1:12 And Elijah answered and said unto them, If I [be] a man of God, let fire come down from heaven, and consume thee and thy fifty. And the fire of God came down from heaven, and consumed him and his fifty.
KINGS II
30:33 For Tophet [is] ordained of old; yea, for the king it is prepared; he hath made [it] deep [and] large: the pile thereof [is] fire and much wood; the breath of the LORD, like a stream of brimstone, doth kindle it.
ISAIAH
97:3 A fire goeth before him, and burneth up his enemies round about.
21:8 Thine hand shall find out all thine enemies: thy right hand shall find out those that hate thee.
50:3 Our God shall come, and shall not keep silence: a fire shall devour before him, and it shall be very tempestuous round about him.
68:17 The chariots of God [are] twenty thousand, [even] thousands of angels: the Lord [is] among them, [as in] Sinai, in the holy [place].
18:8 There went up a smoke out of his nostrils, and fire out of his mouth devoured: coals were kindled by it.
18:10 And he rode upon a cherub, and did fly: yea, he did fly upon the wings of the wind.
18:11 He made darkness his secret place; his pavilion round about him [were] dark waters [and] thick clouds of the skies.
18:12 At the brightness [that was] before him his thick clouds passed, hail [stones] and coals of fire.
18:13 The LORD also thundered in the heavens, and the Highest gave his voice; hail [stones] and coals of fire.
18:14 Yea, he sent out his arrows, and scattered them; and he shot out lightnings, and discomfited them.

77:19 Thy way [is] <u>in the sea, and thy path in the great waters</u>, and thy footsteps are not known.
144:6 Cast forth lightning, and scatter them: <u>shoot out thine arrows</u>, and destroy them.
144:7 Send thine <u>hand</u> from above;... PSALMS

(See II Samuel 22:8-16)

Once again, we find evidence of a possible mother ship intervening with events taking place on the surface of the planet. Furthermore, it would appear that Yahweh commands thousands of smaller craft' and pilots. Yet, where did such an immense force come from, and how did the ancient populace know of their existence?

Seemingly, this massive legion of craft (chariots) and pilots (angels) were mooring their craft, <u>inside</u> an enormous mother ship while orbiting the planet. Furthermore, the mother ship was so large, it could house and maintain thousands of craft and pilots, as well as the crew members maintaining the parent ship.

Here again, the craft consistency remains the same. Whether it was the mother ship, or the smaller craft, they all appear to support high-tech laser weapons. In fact it would appear that Yahweh's laser technology is the primary weapon of choice when it comes to inflicting massive death and destruction. If one will earnestly examine the verses, you will discover two possible locations in which the laser weapons were being discharged.

Thus far, we have only scrutinized the smaller craft and their extraordinary laser weapons in operation. Yet, now the destructive laser fire appears to be originating from a different location, "fell", "come down from heaven," "came down from heaven". In all the verses using this particular statement, the cloud or craft formation was nowhere to be found.

Clearly, the smaller craft lurking within the clouds high in the sky, could have been responsible for the fire (laser) that fell from heaven. Yet, in the verses there is no reference to the cloud (Craft) firing the device. If in fact there was no observable cloud or craft involved, what fired the laser from heaven?

What we may be analyzing here is an ancient analogy of star wars' technology. This would imply a science that would not only allow one to observe the surface of the planet under a microscope, but also permit pinpoint accuracy for high tech laser weapons orbiting the planet (heaven)

Taking into account the strong probability that a mother ship was required to support the legions of smaller craft on the surface of the planet, it becomes quite feasible that an orbiting parent ship could take aim and fire a laser weapon onto the surface of the planet.

In doing so, they could surgically strike any target from hundreds of miles up in outer space. Hence, "fire came down from heaven". Moreover, this fiery (laser) weapon was so powerful, it was proficient in surgically incinerating ("consumed/devour") fifty men and horses on two separate occasions.

Weapons of the Kingdom of Heaven

Evidently, the ancient witnesses were able of physically see the defined laser beam coming from out of the sky or craft. This obvious account can be found in verse 30:33 of Isaiah. Here the laser beam is described as "a stream of brimstone".

The words "stream" and "brimstone" is quite self-explanatory, seeing how the word "stream" defines a steady flow as if in a stream, or to give forth a continuous stream of light rays or beams. Moreover, the verse is quite specific as to just what those streams of light rays or beams were.

Here again the definition is self-explanatory, seeing how the word "brimstone" is a direct reference to the word "fire". In essence, the "stream of brimstone" was a continuous stream or beam of fire, which is the precise definition of a laser beam.

Obviously, the marksmanship of the angels (men) piloting the small craft, or even the mother ship, was extremely proficient in targeting their laser weapons on small objectives from great distances. Yet, this skillful aim might be due to the versatility of the weapon and/or devices being utilized. Essentially, the greatly feared hand-shaped device was once again held accountable for the destructive fire power (laser) unleashed by this phenomenal weapon.

In closer examination of the verses, we discover **three** other possible weapons we have yet to examine. At first glance, one might easily pass right over the allegorical weapons. ["Coals of fire", "arrows", and "lightning"] (See Psalms 97:4,/18:12,13,14,/77:18,/144:6). Moreover, we will discover that these same types of weapons were employed by the fallen angels, as well as Leviathan.

41:19 Out of his mouth go burning lamps, [and] sparks of fire leap out.

41:20 Out of his nostrils goeth smoke, as [out] of a seething pot or caldron.

41:21 His breath kindleth coals, and a flame goeth out of his mouth. JOB

What sort of weapon could create "coals of fire", (burning lamps), "arrows" that discomfit and destroy, "lightning" (leaping sparks of fire) that could be aimed and shot out/cast forth in any direction. Clearly, we are examining high tech weaponry, technology at its highest form.

Evidently, the coals of fire/burning lamps were propelled or discharged by some undetermined source incorporated within the craft. This fiery detail is easily detected by the words "passed" and "out of his mouth go".

This might suggest that the coals of fire or burning lamps were aimed and fired projectiles that detonated upon impact. In fact one might consider that the glowing coals/lamps of fire were possibly being discharged from a cannon type device, mounted on or within the craft themselves.

Evidently, the "arrows" were greatly feared weapon in light of the devastation they could inflict. Here again, the arrows appear to be fired or discharged from the craft. Yet, in this case we are not examining a mortar or cannon type device, but rather a sophisticated high tech missile (arrow) possessing enormous destructive power.

Remarkably, these same destructive weapons can actually be found within our own modern military arsenals. Many of our military aircraft, ships, tanks, and transports possess and utilize cannons and/or guns of diverse gauges and powers, as well as missile launchers.

However, what you won't find in our military arsenal is the technological ability to harness, direct, and fire bolts of lightning. The key words exposing this extraordinary weapon would be "shot" and "cast forth." Evidently, these electrifying bolts of energy could be aimed and fired towards their intended target.

Notably, we have already analyzed this electrifying weapon and may not even be aware of it. If the reader will recall, each of the craft appears to be an enormous electrostatic generator. This is to say that each of the craft is capable of producing massive amounts of static electricity to create the glowing electromagnetic fields that engulf the craft. The electromagnetic fields allow the craft flight capabilities, due to the maneuvered magnetic fields around the craft in contrast to the magnetic fields of the planet.

Taking into account the probability that these craft are fully capable of creating far more static energy than required for flight, it becomes clear that the over abundant energy would seek a means of discharging itself. In essence the overcharged craft could discharge in the same manner as natural lighting. The closer the craft is to the ground during such a electrifying amassment the more frequent the discharges from the craft would be.

We also need to take into account the probability that these unique craft are capable of manipulating the static flux of the engulfing energy fields encompassing the craft. Quite naturally, this would be necessary to manipulate the magnetic fields of this world at any given location on the surface of the planet. Essentially, each and every geographical location would constitute a different global magnetic circumstance.

This would submit that the craft were capable of creating a substantially stronger electromagnetic field on one side of the craft, than that of the other side. This would logically naturalize (hover) or substantially propel the craft in any direction based on the manipulated electromagnetic fields around the craft in contrast to the earths' magnetic fields, and/or location on the planet.

By overcharging the electromagnetic fields on the dissimilar sides of the craft they could produce bolts of lightning (massive static charges) on any side of the craft that the pilot so desires. Essentially, the craft could feasiblely pursue an individual, while at the same time discharging what would appear to be bolts' of lightning onto the surface of the ground.

Evidently, these craft are capable of incredible feats and firepower, as expressed within the many verses we have examined. Yet, more astounding would be the realization that Yahweh's extraordinary craft were skillful in submersing and traveling underwater, a typical UFO characteristic. (Psalms 18:11/77:19) In fact, an entire book could be written on the subject of UFOs entering or departing from large bodies of water.

Incredibly, these aquatic UFOs have been identified by their glowing attributes as they were observed traveling underwater. It's extremely important for the reader to remember this aquatic detail, seeing how this underwater factor will ultimately reveal the major gateways to the Underworld domains of this planet.

Matter Manipulation

In completing the verses above, we find Yahweh's ever present weapon of choice. Yet, it should come as no surprise that Yahweh's principal tool and/or weapon was in fact their matter maneuvering (force field) devices (the Hand).

13:3 And he gave a sign the same day, saying, This [is] the sign which the LORD hath spoken; Behold, the altar shall be rent, and the ashes that [are] upon it shall be poured out.

13:4 And it came to pass, when king Jeroboam heard the saying of the man of God, which had cried against the altar in Bethel, that <u>he put forth his hand</u> from the altar, saying, Lay hold on him. And his hand, which he put forth against him, <u>dried up, so that he could not pull it in again to him.</u>

13:5 The altar also was rent, and the ashes poured out from the altar, according to the sign which the man of God had given by the word of the LORD.

13:6 And the king answered and said unto the man of God, Entreat now the face of the LORD thy God, and pray for me, that my hand may be restored me again. And the man of God besought the LORD, and the king's hand was restored him again, and became as [it was] before.

20:29 And they pitched one over against the other <u>seven days</u>. And [so] it was, that in the <u>seventh day</u> the battle was joined: and the children of Israel slew of the Syrians an hundred thousand footmen in one day.

20:30 But the rest fled to Aphek, into the city;<u> and [there] a wall fell upon twenty and seven thousand of the men [that were] left</u>....

I KINGS

2:8 And Elijah took his mantle, and wrapped [it] together, and <u>smote the waters</u>, <u>and they were divided</u> hither and thither, so that they two went over on dry ground.

2:11 And it came to pass, as they still went on, and talked, that, behold, [there appeared] a chariot of fire, and horses of fire, and parted them both asunder; and Elijah went up by a whirlwind into heaven.

2:12 And Elisha saw [it], and he cried, My father, my father, the chariot of Israel, <u>and the horsemen thereof</u>. And he saw him no more: and he took hold of his own clothes, and rent them in two pieces.

2:13 He took up also the mantle of Elijah that fell from him, and went back, and stood by the bank of Jordan;

2:14 And he took the mantle of Elijah that fell from him, and smote the waters, and said, Where [is] the LORD God of Elijah? and when he also had smitten the waters, they parted hither and thither: and Elisha went over.

II KINGS

3:16 Shadrach, Meshach, and Abednego, answered and said to the king, O Nebuchadnezzar, we [are] not careful to answer thee in this matter.

3:17 If it be [so], our God whom we serve is able to deliver us from the burning fiery furnace, and he will deliver [us] out of thine hand, O king.

3:18 But if not, be it known unto thee, O king, that we will not serve thy gods, nor worship the golden image which thou hast set up.

3:19 Then was Nebuchadnezzar full of fury, and the form of his visage was changed against Shadrach, Meshach, and Abednego: [therefore] he spake, and commanded that they should heat the furnace one seven times more than it was wont to be heated.

3:20 And he commanded the most mighty men that [were] in his army to bind Shadrach, Meshach, and Abednego, [and] to cast [them] into the burning fiery furnace.

3:21 Then these men were bound in their coats, their hosen, and their hats, and their [other] garments, and were cast into the midst of the burning fiery furnace.

3:22 Therefore because the king's commandment was urgent, and the furnace exceeding hot, the flame of the fire slew those men that took up Shadrach, Meshach, and Abednego.

3:23 And these three men, Shadrach, Meshach, and Abednego, fell down bound into the midst of the burning fiery furnace.

3:24 Then Nebuchadnezzar the king was astonied, and rose up in haste, [and] spake, and said unto his counsellors, Did not we cast three men bound into the midst of the fire? They answered and said unto the king, True, O king.

3:25 He answered and said, Lo, I see four men loose, walking in the midst of the fire, and they have no hurt; and the form of the fourth is like the Son of God.

3:26 Then Nebuchadnezzar came near to the mouth of the burning fiery furnace, [and] spake, and said, Shadrach, Meshach, and Abednego, ye servants of the most high God, come forth, and come [hither]. Then Shadrach, Meshach, and Abednego, came forth of the midst of the fire.

> **3:27 And the princes, governors, and captains, and the king's counsellors, being gathered together, saw these men, upon whose bodies the fire had no power, nor was an hair of their head singed, neither were their coats changed, nor the smell of fire had passed on them.**
> DANIEL

One might ask the supreme question as to what would matter manipulation (force fields) have to do with the events expressed within these verses. Yet, we are about to discover that all of these ancient events were direct repercussions of Yahweh and his host covertly employing their matter maneuvering devices.

The Kings Arm and Hand

One might assume that the only matter maneuvering feat depicted within verses (13:3-6) was the renting (tearing apart) of the altar. Yet, this would completely disavow the obvious incident involving the arm and hand of the King. Obviously, a mysterious deformity was inflicted upon the King, paralyzing his arm and hand.

The King raised ("put forth") and began to shake his arm, hand or fist, ordering the people to take hold of the Prophet. In doing so, the king's arm and hand suddenly became fixed, or forcibly immobilized in its upright position. In this vertical position the Kings arm and hand became deformed, or took on the appearance of being "dried up". Essentially, the King was unable to move or even pull his arm and hand back to his body.

The words "**dried up**" exposes a major clue as to what may have actually transpired with the arm and hand of the King. Instead of looking at the words "dried up" as a possible deformity mysteriously inflicted upon the King, we should consider the words "dried up" as an outer body manifestation or repercussion, directly associated with the forced immobility of the king's arm and hand. Quite naturally, this explanation sounds confusing, until one incorporates matter manipulation with surgical precision.

Clearly, Yahweh and his hosts, along with their craft were in the immediate area, which would explain how the altar was rent (torn apart). At the same time, Yahweh's craft applied their matter maneuvering devices to physically seize the king's raised arm and hand.

The accurately manipulated fields of force (pressure) exerted around the king's arm and hand produced an outer body disfigurement, thus causing his arm and hand **to appear** as if it were dried up or wrinkled. This powerful invisible force not only made the king's arm and hand **appear** dried up, but physically captured and forced it to stay were it was, until the manipulated fields of force were shut down.

The Falling Wall

I KINGS 20:28-30. Would leave one totally mystified as to how a solid wall could simply fall on 27,000 men all at one time. (?) It doesn't take much deduction to realize that the verses are depicting more than just an insignificant wall that may have been pushed down by the armies of Israel. This factor becomes even more credible when we realize that the armies of Israel were not even involved in the event.

The wall killed 27,000 men in a single blow, submitting that the wall was not only very high and long, but massive. If one will read I Kings 20: you will discover that once again Yahweh and his host were present at the battle, as well as the great wall that fell.

Evidently, the Syrian armies retreated into the city of Aphek to hide behind its great walls. The massive walls were so large that they could actually hide 27,000 men. At which point, Yahweh and his craft employed their matter maneuvering (force field) devices to literally thrust down the huge walls of Aphek, on top of all 27,000 men This was the same type of maneuver performed on the massive walls of Jericho, including the time frame.

The walls of Jericho were not knocked down until the armies of Israel consecrated the number "seven" by marching around the city of Jericho "seven" times, for "seven" days. Once again we find the Holy number **seven** is being deliberately wielded to draw attention to not only the battle, but the destruction of the city walls of Aphek.

Obviously, this was once again a focused blow aimed towards the other gods/fallen angels and the inhabitancy under their covert control In essence, the fallen angels regulated the Syrians, as well as the city of Aphek.

The Jordan Crossing

In Kings II, we discover an unusual circumstance alluding to Elijah and Elisha crossing of the River Jordan. The factor in question would be the "mantle" used by both Elijah and Elisha to cross the river. Are we to believe that both Elijah and Elisha forced the great River Jordan to be divided by simply striking the shore with their cloak? I think not!

Clearly, there is a missing detail involving the enchanted robe (mantle). Why was a robe even necessary? What would a simply mantle/robe have to do with physically dividing an enormous body of running waters? The solution to this puzzling issue may actually reside in the sky.

Throughout the numerous scriptures we have examined, it has become all too clear that these elusive craft were lurking or concealing themselves inside natural cloud formations. Moreover, it would appear that the craft were capable of artificially producing cloud like conditions around their craft too hid while they maneuvered or hovered high in the sky (heaven).

This would suggest that both Elijah and Elisha were possibly being kept under continuous surveillance by a cloud enveloped craft positioned high in the sky above them. In fully scrutinizing the verses, it becomes unmistakable that there was indeed a craft present during this dividing of the River Jordan. This can be determined by the fact that a craft (**chariot**) removed Elijah from the surface of the planet at the same time the river Jordan was divided both times.

By combining all the information together we arrive at a feasible explanation for the "mantle". Obviously, Elijah and Elisha were constantly being watched by the occupants of a craft concealed somewhere in the sky above them. The wrapped together mantle used to strike the waters of the river Jordan was nothing more than a **visual signal** that could be seen from the air (sky) by the awaiting craft.

This apparently preplanned optical beacon was used to notify the observing craft and its pilots that Elijah was now ready to cross the river Jordan. After physically seeing the signal from above, the craft utilized their force field devices to divide the river. Furthermore, this same visual signal was used by Elisha when he was ready to return to the other side of the river.

Here again, these visual details would clearly indicate that we are not scrutinizing invisible ghosts or spirits. Rather, the verses are informing us of a very real and physical presence, physical craft and pilots in need of tangible signs to make physical decisions.

The Fiery Furnace

The verses of Daniel contain what might be considered a matter maneuvering feat of epic proportions. This incredible stunt establishes the true power and flexible maneuverability of these remarkable unseen fields of force.

As we can see, Daniel's <u>three</u> colleagues were not in the least distressed about being thrown into a fiery furnace. Obviously, the three men were either very brave, or very reckless to be talking to a King in this daring manner.

What we have here are three men who already knew what was going to take place before it actually occurred. This would suggest that they had been previously instructed, or specifically informed of what appears to be a preplanned event by Yahweh. The three men already knew they would be cast into the furnace, as well as being advised that they would not be harmed while **inside** the furnace. This might suggest that all three men even knew **how** they would be saved from the consuming heat of the furnace.

However, where was Daniel? Throughout chapter 3 of the Book of Daniel, his three closest companions were faced with certain death in the Babylonian inferno. Yet, Daniel was nowhere to be found. Chapter three establishes the fact that all the nations under Babylonian rule would be required to worship the same image created by King Nebuchadnezzar, or be cast into the furnace. No matter where Daniel was located within the Babylonian Empire, he too would be faced with the same problem. So why was Daniel not involved in this preplanned display of power, seeing how this is the Book of Daniel?

To truly unravel this death defying feat, we must closely scrutinize the verses to establish what may have actually transpired before, during and after the time the three men were thrown into the furnace. To begin with, the three men were tied and bound before being led to the mouth of the furnace by the Babylonian guards. Furthermore, it's quite evident that **all** of the men were standing **together** at the mouth of the furnace.

Next, we need to try and verify the basic type, or shape of furnace in question. This crucial detail can be found in verse 22, where we find the words "**took up**". This would suggest that the mighty men or guards clutching the three men had to climb steps of some kind to get up to the top of the furnace. This obvious impression becomes even more credible when considering verse 23, Note the words **"fell down/into"** insinuating the three men fell down into the furnace from above.

Seemingly, we have a very massive furnace, possibly surrounded by a large stone structure with steps leading up to the top or **mouth** of the furnace. Evidently the furnace had a large opening or aperture located at the **top**, where the victims were bodily thrown into its fiery orifice. Furthermore, it would appear that the furnace was not only located **outside**, but the mouth of the furnace appears to be exposed to the open sky above.

It is imperative that we keep track of the turn of events taking place. First, the guards took the three bound men up to the mouth of the furnace, where they cast them into the blazing pit. This was precisely the same time that fire surged out of the furnace killing the guards. The King watching the order of events, was now astonished to see that there were <u>four</u> men in the furnace instead of **three**. In realizing that the men were not being incinerated, the King had no other choice but to have them come up out of the furnace.

The enigmatic question would be **how**? How is it possible that **four** men who were placed directly inside a blazing inferno were not even remotely touched by the tremendous heat of the fire, or even the **smell** of fire (smoke)?

Let's keep in mind that this entire blazing event was deliberately designed by Yahweh and his host. This would suggest that Yahweh and his craft were in the immediate area to carry out the pre-designed plan. Yet, how was Yahweh and his concealed craft capable of pulling off such an incredible feat?

What type of power could keep a man from being burned to a cinder while trapped inside a burning inferno? What type of force could block out even the odor and smoke from a blazing pit? What sort of power is capable of performing such feats, and still remain invisible to the naked eye?

It was the same invisible force that severed apart an entire sea. The same force skillful in damming up an entire river. The same invisible force capable of knocking down mammoth city walls. The same force and precision used too evaluate a human body. An invisible field of force so precise that even a human arm shaking its fist can be stopped dead in its midair indignation.

Here again, it would appear that Yahweh and his unique craft were utilizing their force field devices in this invisible incident. This time it appears that Yahweh and his craft were implementing their invisible fields of force to physically protect the three men who were cast into the furnace. This would also resolve the issue as to how the Babylonian guards were burned to death. In fact, the Catholic version of this remarkable incident literally confirms the procedure used to kill the guards.

> **Three Holy Children 1:26. But the angel of the Lord came down into the oven…and smote the flames of the fire out of the oven;**
> **Three Holy Children 1:27….so that the fire touched them not at all, neither hurt nor troubled them.**

We have already determined that the top of the furnace is exposed to the open sky. This would allow Yahweh and his concealed craft, the ability to maneuver their fields of force inside the furnace from above.

Note verse 1:26, the angel "**came down**", which would suggest that someone physically saw the man (angel) descend into the furnace from above. In essence, a physical man was lowered down into the furnace from out of the sky. Evidently the angel (man) "**smote**" the flames of the fire out of the furnace/oven" possibly explaining the death of the Babylonian guards who pushed the three men into the furnace. Or did he?

First, we need to query the question as to how the man/angel got into the furnace? Apparently, Yahweh and his concealed craft utilized their matter maneuvering devices to transport the angel (man), from a hovering craft above, down into the blazing furnace at approximately the same time the three men were cast in.

If in fact this was the case, the angel and force fields entered the furnace just before the three men were cast in. In doing so, the flames and heat would have been forced "**smote**"out of the furnace, in order to make room for the controlled fields that were now thrust inside.

In essence, the force fields forced the flames and the tremendous heat out of the bottom of the furnace, up to the top of the furnace where the guards were standing, thereby burning up the Babylonian guards. Admittedly, we are examining precision timing and surgical manipulation of these elusive fields of force.

However, in thoroughly examining this extraordinary event, we may be scrutinizing more than just one field of force (device) in operation. We may actually be witnessing many different fields or devices working together to perform the fiery stunt.

If one will recall, Yahweh's five craft (craft formation) contains four matter maneuvering devices (Hands) underneath **each** craft. All of the devices were proficient in operating independently of each other, as well as being quite masterful when operating together.

This would suggest that part of Yahweh's isolated fields of force could be utilized as a possible floor which the four men could stand on while in the furnace. The invisible floor would not only stop any heat or flames from reaching the four men, but also suppress any smoke or odor from coming into contact with the bodies of the men while in the furnace.

Yahweh's craft formation could have simultaneously encased the three men inside an invisible shield of force as they fell into the furnace, or instantly established an invisible inter-chamber within the furnace. This would allow the mouth of the inter-chamber to be open, which the three men fell into. Hence, the mass displacement of the invisible fields encompassing the men, or the suddenly created inter-chamber consequently forced the heat and flames out and up to the mouth of the furnace where the Babylonian guards were standing.

This conjecture becomes even more likely when we realize the possible size of the furnace. Evidently, the furnace was so large that four men could actually "**walk**" around inside the furnace, as expressed in verse 3:25. Obviously, there was not only enough room to manipulate the force fields around the three men heaved into the furnace, but **inside** the furnace as well.

Notably, the three men were no longer bound, but "**loose**", which brings our attention to the mysterious forth man (angel). Are we to believe that the three bound men who were hurled into the furnace were able to untie themselves? Or was the fourth man (angel) responsible for uniting all three?

If so, we are obviously not questioning some type of invisible spirit or ghost, but rather a very real physical being (man), protected by the same fields of force used to safeguard the other three men. Seemingly, this fourth man may have been maneuvered down inside the furnace to help and comfort the other three men. This would be an obvious probability considering the fiery position, they have now been forced to endure.

This detail would bring us back to Daniel. There is no mention of Daniel throughout the entire chapter describing this blazing event. Moreover, this is the **only** chapter in the Book of Daniel in which Daniel himself is **missing.**

Why would Yahweh want to put on this incredible show of power without including Daniel, especially when we consider that the three men were Daniel's closest companions? Or is it possible we are witnessing Daniel's physical presence within these very verses and are not even aware of it? What better person to comfort and reassure Daniel's companions than Daniel himself?

The forth man in question may in fact be Daniel. This would imply that Daniel was also in on this pre-designed plan against Babylon and their ruling gods (Satan and the Fallen Angels/other gods). However, this may not be the case at all, considering the King should have recognized Daniel, as well as a few other probable factors.

Note the King acknowledged that the other **man** (angel) had the "form" or appearance of "the Son of God". This would lead one to believe that the king has physically seen the Sons of God before. The assertion would also indicate that there was a clear distinction between this man and the other three. Seemingly, the fourth man's dissimilar appearance may be a simple implication to his unorthodox attire, being contrary to that of the other three

However, let's stop for a moment and reevaluate this entire event. Evidently, there exists another probability resolving how the King was able to recognize this fourth man (angel) as one of the Sons of God.

It was not my intention to go into the **"Shining Ones"** at this time, considering we will be analyzing the subject in great detail when we enter the New Testament. Nevertheless, I will briefly touch on the subject, considering the topic will explain what may have happened in this blazing furnace.

It would appear that these extraterrestrial entities possess the ability to endow the human body with immortality.(eternal life) This artificial body modification would enable one to live for thousands, or possibly hundreds of thousands of years.

As we shall discover, this ageless longevity appears to be achieved through technology, consumption of body altering sustenances, applying something to the body, or the unification of all three. (Body Modifiers) Moreover, this unique gift of immortality is in some way directly linked to these cosmic beings ability to bodily shine or glow, hence the analogy **"The Shining Ones"**.

In simple terms, these extraterrestrial entities (angels) have been reported to glow or radiate a type of light or energy that surrounds their body. One might get the distinct impression that these stellar beings have discovered or synthetically produced a way to amplify, or greatly heighten, what is known as the human aura. This glowing factor may be just another interpretation of what is commonly known as the **soul**. This might suggest that the elusive soul and aura are one and the same, and can be artificially magnified.

Furthermore, this speculation may elaborate upon the many ancient drawings and painting depicting these elusive beings (angels) with what is known as a **halo**. The halo often associated with saints or angels may be nothing more than a symbolic representation of the individual glowing or radiating. (**Shining**).

It's traditionally believed that this can only be an angel, frequently misinterpreted as an invisible spirit or ghost (glowing being). Nevertheless, we are about to discover that these glowing entities are indeed tangible beings capable of bestowing the same glowing attributes to earthly humans while still alive.

> 34:28 And he was there with the LORD forty days and forty nights; he did neither eat bread, nor drink water. And he wrote upon the tables the words of the covenant, the ten commandments.,
> 34:29 And it came to pass, when Moses came down from mount Sinai with the two tables of testimony in Moses' hand, when he came down from the mount, that Moses wist not that the skin of his face shone while he talked with him.
> 34:30 And when Aaron and all the children of Israel saw Moses, behold, the skin of his face shone; and they were afraid to come nigh him.
> 34:33 And [till] Moses had done speaking with them, he put a veil on his face.
> 34:34 But when Moses went in before the LORD to speak with him, he took the veil off, until he came out....
> 34:35 And the children of Israel saw the face of Moses, that the skin of Moses' face shone: and Moses put the veil upon his face again, until he went in to speak with him.
> EXODUS
>
> 6 I turned his flesh to fiery torches and all the bones of his body to coals of light. I made the appearance of his eyes like the appearance of lightning, and the light of his eyes like "light unfailing." I caused his face to shine like the brilliant light of the sun,...
>
> 48C APPENDIX TO 3 ENOCH
>
> 8 And the Lord said to Michael: 'Go and take Enoch from out his earthly garments and anoint him with my sweet ointment, and put him into the garment of my glory.'
> 9 And Michael did thus, as the Lord told him. He anointed me, and dressed me, and the appearance of that ointment is more than the great light, and his ointment is like sweet dew, and its smell mild, shining like the sun's ray, and I looked at myself, and was like one of his glorious ones.
>
> CHAP. XXII.

> **2 Enoch answered to his son Methosalam and said: 'Hear, child, from the time when the Lord anointed me with the ointment of his glory, there has been no food in me, and my soul remembers not earthly enjoyment, neither do I want anything earthly.' CHAP. LVI.**
>
> **SECRETS OF ENOCH**

Evidently, the artificially induced effects radiating from Moses's body eventually wore off. Yet, more importantly would be how Moses acquired his frightening glowing attributes. Obviously Moses and Enoch applied the same ointment on their bodies.

In essence, this powerful ointment caused both the bodies of Enoch and Moses to glow just like the celestial beings that partake of the same ointment. This would once again establish the fact that the beings using the radiating ointment were indeed "flesh" and "bones" of a physical "body". (**The Shining Ones**) Yet, more importantly would be the body altering powers that the ointment contains.

Evidently, Moses and Enoch did not require food for an extended period of time after applying the ointment. (Forty days) The artificially induced glow appears to be the outer repercussion of the ointment after being placed on the body. Moreover, if one will closely examine the verses, you will discover that the ointment bodily endows one with more than just one artificial power.

However, at this time, we are only interested in the one power pertaining to the fiery events taking place in the Babylonian furnace. Evidently, at one time Adam and Eve possessed the same glowing attributes. Yet, this gift of light (glow) was ultimately taken from Adam and Eve due to their transgression within the Garden.

> **"And on thee, O Adam, while in My garden and obedient to Me, did that bright light rest also.**
>
> **"But when I heard of thy transgression, I deprived thee of that bright light.... XIII 6, 7**
>
> **Then Adam said to Eve, see this fire of which we have a portion in us: which formerly yielded to us, but no longer does so, now that we have transgressed the limit of creation, and changed our condition, and our nature is altered. but the fire is not changed in its, nor altered from its creation. Therefore has it now power over us; and when we come near it, it scorches our flesh." XLIV FORGOTTEN BOOKS OF EDEN**

Seemingly, the ointment generated Adam and Eves bright nature. ("bright light") In fact, the ointment appears to have produced an outer glowing shield of protection for their bodies. The concealed power of this glowing body armor becomes even more evident when we realize the nature of Adam and Eve conversation.

Obviously, Adam and Eve formerly had a portion in them ("a portion in us") a portion "which **formerly** yielded to us". A portion of what? Adam and Eve had a portion of **fire** (ointment/bright light/glow) inside their bodies that protected them.

Evidently, Adam and Eve had come into contact with the flames of a genuine fire, only to discover that for the first time in their mortal existence, fire would "**scorch**" their now exposed bodies. However, before, when they were immortal and indulged in the ointment, the fire was unable to penetrate their outer glowing shield (bright light) thus protecting their bodies. If true, we now have a feasible explanation of what took place in the Babylonian furnace.

Here again, we return to Daniel. It's quite possible Daniel was in fact the fourth man in the furnace. Daniel could have been given the same ointment as Moses and Enoch, thus protecting his body while in the furnace. This may also resolve the issue as to why the King was not able to identify the fourth man as Daniel, considering Daniel's face and entire body may have been brightly glowing. In fact, this might answer the question as to why the King recognized the fourth man as one of the Sons of God, seeing how **all** the Sons of God were given the same body modifiers, and could be readily recognized by their bodily glow (halo?).

The forth man in question, whether he was Daniel or just one of Yahweh's men (angels), appears to have been inside the furnace **prior** to the three men being cast in. This would indicate that the forth man was standing in the furnace **waiting** for the three men to be pushed in.

However, this assumption would leave one bewildered as to how he was able to breathe while inside this blazing pit, seeing how all the oxygen within the furnace would be consumed. Moreover, how did the three men breathe or even be saved from the tremendous heat and flames of the Furnace once pushed in?

This mysterious detail would confirm the fact that the angel (fourth man) was placed inside the furnace for a very significant reason. This essential factor would suggest that Yahweh was not capable of protecting the three men unless the angel/man was inside the furnace. In essence, Yahweh and his craft were not even involved in this incident, other than placing the fourth man inside the furnace.

Yahweh and his superior craft did not use their matter maneuvering devices to create a protective shield around the three men. However, this does not imply that an invisible field of force (matter manipulation) was not utilized to protect all four men.

Naturally, this conjecture sounds quite confusing, considering the only possible explanation of how the three men were saved would now be placed squarely on the shoulders of the fourth man (angel). Evidently, the fourth man performed the matter maneuvering feat **alone**.

> **Three Holy Children 1:26. But the angel of the Lord came down into the oven…and smote the flames of the fire out of the oven;**
>
> **Three Holy Children 1:27….so that the fire touched them not at all, neither hurt nor troubled them.**

It was in fact the forth man that forced (**smote**) the flames and heat **out** of the furnace. Yet, how was just a single man capable of not only forcing the flames, heat and smoke out of the furnace, but also creating a safe zone within the furnace so all four men could survive?

Obviously, Yahweh's small craft command **small**, but powerful matter maneuvering devices that were incorporated into their craft. (Hand shaped devices) Furthermore, it would stand to reason that the mother ship would also maintain the same type of weapons and/or devices, but on a grander scale. As mentioned before, super technology would naturally dictate super craft, weapons and devices.

This intriguing issue can actually be resolved by understanding our own military arsenal. The bigger the ship, the bigger the gun. However, I bring your attention to the fact that a cannon can actually be held within the very palm of a man's hand. The smaller the vessel, the smaller the weapon or device.

We humans possess weapons of massive size and destruction. However, we also maintain **hand-held weapons** (guns/rocket launchers…) of less power and destruction. The fundamental conclusion to all this data is to establish the fact that as surely as the kingdom of heaven possesses craft and weapons of incredible size and destruction, they also possess a celestial arsenal containing **hand-held** weapons and devices of the same powers, but on a smaller scale.

The point being that the fourth man (angel) in the furnace may have actually utilized such a hand-held device to create a controlled miniature force field in (**inside**) the furnace. Moreover, the hand-held device may have created a large void within the furnace at the very moment that the three men were pushed in.

The void created by the hand-held device produced a force field cavity complete with a floor. This would leave the force field at the top of the furnace open, allowing the three men to not only fall into the open cavity, but also insure that all four men were able to breathe while in the furnace.

The created cavity formed in the furnace altered and displaced the open space within the furnace, thus forcing the flames and heat up to the top of the furnace killing the guards. "**smote** the flames of the fire **out** of the oven"

The Kingdom of Heavens' Source of Power

It would appear that Yahweh's craft and weapons maintain a consistency in not only their diversified applications, but their very power source as well. This would suggest that the power source providing the craft's flight capability, may also be directly linked to their matter maneuvering devices and laser technology.

Seemingly, their main source of power derives from what appears to be a highly advanced form of electromagnetic energy. Essentially, these phenomenal craft, weapons and devices all appear to be designed to function by utilizing this electromagnetic premiss. In fact it would appear that this entire Universe down to the smallest atom is held together and made operational due to the same electromagnetic forces at work.

The craft themselves appear to be able to defy the laws of gravity, where in all probability, the craft may in fact be utilizing the laws of gravity to perpetuate their flight capabilities. The craft seemingly utilize electromagnetic energy to create an outer magnetic field that manipulates the magnetic field of this planet, thus allowing the craft atmospheric mobility.

Their matter maneuvering techniques also appear to be the utilization of condensed or concentrated beams of electromagnetic energy that can be aimed or directed to maneuver solid objects of dissimilar or like magnetic fields. This would permit the electromagnetic device the ability to maneuver solid objects of various masses, based on the magnetic and/or molecular structure of the object in contrast to the navigated fields of magnetic energy imposed upon them.

Remarkably, this would even include the human body, seeing how the human body is nothing more that a mass of molecular matter, consisting of molecules and atoms held together by their magnetic structure. That magnetic structure can be manipulated or physically moved if encountered by another extremely strong outside electromagnetic influence. This is much like the hair of one's body standing on end when exposed to an extremely strong electromagnetic field (charge).

Essentially, the physical manipulation of their craft, massive volumes of water, or even the human body may be nothing more than the manipulation and/or utilization of the magnetic fields of the objects being different than that of the powerful magnetic fields being imposed upon them. As mentioned before, opposite poles (fields) of magnetism attract each other, whereas poles of the same field repel each other.

By manipulating the different power levels and different poles of their created electromagnetic fields (beams/rays), they could push, pull, twist, turn and literally pick up objects of astonishing dimensions. This would even include objects that are much larger than the craft itself, seeing how the craft may be acting as nothing more than a powerful fulcrum between the magnetic forces of the planet and the object being manipulated.

If the craft were utilizing the magnetic fields of the planet to stay aloft, the planetary magnetic fields of force exerted upon the craft would be incredible to say the least. Essentially, the craft could become totally unmovable regardless of the navigated outside influences (Matter Manipulation). This would imply that the fulcrum craft could maneuver objects many times its size and weight in contrast to its fixed magnetic position.

In essence, a craft the size of a bus could literally pick up an aircraft carrier, and still maintain its stationary magnetic integrity in the sky. Nor would the tremendous weight of the carrier affect the structural integrity of the craft, seeing how the craft is located **inside** the created fulcrum, (magnetic flux) not on the outside.

This would imply that all the pressure involved in maneuvering enormous weights (mass/matter) would be exerted on the created field of electromagnetic flux (fulcrum) encasing the craft, in contrast to that of the magnetic fields of the planet manipulating the craft/magnetic flux.

These same conclusions may also account for their laser technology. Their applied laser science may be nothing more than a directed beam consisting of the very same energy source that powers the craft. The outer electromagnetic fields engulfing the craft appear to be so powerful, it creates an intense bright glow or fiery field.

The fiery field engulfing the craft may be quite deadly to anyone or anything coming into contact with it. This might be due to the fact that its powerful electromagnetic field creates a rapid disruption of any matter consisting of a magnetic field or molecular elements. This would essentially imply most all matter. Any physical body or matter coming into contact with the field would appear as if it had been burned up, or magnetically dismantled in a fiery display.

It's quite feasible that these universal beings have devised a way to condense, control and direct this same powerful electromagnetic energy into a fine fiery beam. (**Laser**) If the beam was to strike an object it would magnetically break down its mass in a fiery display depending on the type of matter or element it struck.

This might suggest that the powerful electromagnetic beam (laser) is destroying the magnetic fields of the atoms that make up and hold the matter together. This would cause the matter to appear as if it were being burned up in its rapid magnetic displacement, thus disintegrating the matter and/or altering the remaining matter into a different form such as ashes.

The electromagnetic transmutation of matter may also hold the key to matter teleportation. These celestial beings may be capable of electromagnetically breaking down human matter, transforming that matter into a highly agitated beam of fiery elements.

The beam or ray of discomposed matter (atoms), could be incorporated into a laser beam, which can be aimed and fired at inconceivable distances, only to be recaptured and electromagnetically reconstructed back into its original magnetic composition.

> **They raised me up into a certain place, where there was the appearance of a burning fire; and when they pleased they assumed the likeness of men. Chapter XVII. BOOK OF ENOCH**
>
> **13:19 So Manoah took a kid with a meat offering, and offered [it] upon a rock unto the LORD: and [the angel] did wonderously; and Manoah and his wife looked on.**
>
> **13:20 For it came to pass, when the flame went up toward heaven from off the altar, that the angel of the LORD ascended in the flame of the altar. And Manoah and his wife looked on [it], and fell on their faces to the ground.**
>
> **JUDGES**

Whether matter manipulation or teleportation, the fiery beam/ray always appears to play a major role in the maneuver. Again this is pure speculation, yet it's crucial that we put nothing past these extraordinary cosmic beings and their phenomenal craft and devices.

Mental Manipulation

Thus far, we have only examined the remarkable craft, weapons and devices illustrating the extremely high level of technology that these unique beings have clearly developed. In realizing their quantum leaps in applied science and technology, one would assume that these elite being would have also developed the ability to manipulate, alter and master the very brain itself.

> 1:17 As for these four children, God gave them knowledge and skill in all learning and wisdom: and Daniel had understanding in all visions and dreams.
> DANIEL
> 7:13 When I say, My bed shall comfort me, my couch shall ease my complaint;
> 7:14 Then thou scarest me with dreams, and terrifiest me through visions:
> 33:15 In a dream, in a vision of the night, when deep sleep falleth upon men, in slumberings upon the bed;
> 33:16 Then he openeth the ears of men, and sealeth their instruction JOB
> 10:6 And the spirit of the LORD will come upon thee, and thou shalt prophesy with them, and shalt be turned into another man.
> 16:13 Then Samuel took the horn of oil, and anointed him in the midst of his brethren: and the spirit of the LORD came upon David from that day forward....
> 16:14 But the spirit of the LORD departed from Saul, and an evil spirit from the LORD troubled him.
> I SAMUEL
> 6:18 And when they came down to him, Elisha prayed unto the LORD, and said, Smite this people, I pray thee, with blindness. And he smote them with blindness according to the word of Elisha.
> 6:19 And Elisha said unto them, This [is] not the way, neither [is] this the city: follow me, and I will bring you to the man whom ye seek. But he led them to Samaria.
> 6:20 And it came to pass, when they were come into Samaria, that Elisha said, LORD, open the eyes of these [men], that they may see. And the

LORD opened their eyes, and they saw; and, behold, [they were] in the midst of Samaria.
II KINGS
13:24 And when he was gone, a lion met him by the way, and slew him: and his carcase was cast in the way, and the ass stood by it, the lion also stood by the carcase.
13:25 And, behold, men passed by, and saw the carcase cast in the way, and the lion standing by the carcase: and they came and told [it] in the city where the old prophet dwelt.
13:28 And he went and found his carcase cast in the way, and the ass and the lion standing by the carcase: the lion had not eaten the carcase, nor torn the ass.
20:36 Then said he unto him, Because thou hast not obeyed the voice of the LORD, behold, as soon as thou art departed from me, a lion shall slay thee. And as soon as he was departed from him, a lion found him, and slew him.
I KINGS
6:16 Then the king commanded, and they brought Daniel, and cast [him] into the den of lions. [Now] the king spake and said unto Daniel, Thy God whom thou servest continually, he will deliver thee.
6:19 Then the king arose very early in the morning, and went in haste unto the den of lions.
6:20 And when he came to the den, he cried with a lamentable voice unto Daniel: [and] the king spake and said to Daniel, O Daniel, servant of the living God, is thy God, whom thou servest continually, able to deliver thee from the lions?
6:22 My God hath sent his angel, and hath shut the lions' mouths, that they have not hurt me: forasmuch as before him innocency was found in me;... DANIEL
2:23 And he went up from thence unto Bethel: and as he was going up by the way, there came forth little children out of the city, and mocked him, and said unto him, Go up, thou bald head; go up, thou bald head.
2:24 And he turned back, and looked on them, and cursed them in the name of the LORD. And there came forth two she bears out of the wood, and tare forty and two children of them.
II KINGS

The **four children** expressed within the first verse of Daniel represent Daniel and the same three men who were cast into the furnace. This would once again suggest that Daniel was in fact the fourth man in the furnace. Furthermore, the verses actually inform us how the three men were aware of the fiery event long before the incident actually took place. Evidently, Daniel was given the informative instructions, which he related to the other three men.

If you will read the book of Daniel, you will discover that most of the chapters deal with dreams and visions. You will also discover that those dreams, and visions may be nothing more than mind manipulation and/or infiltration. This would suggest a covert source of programmed and exploited brain wave activity, or mental telepathy.

This mental tampering appears to not only take place during one's sleep, but while mindfully awake as well. Yet, the experience is assumed to be vivid dream or vision by the individual. Obviously, the subject is well aware of the directed mental intervention taking place, seeing how the intercession is being directly attributed toYahweh.

UFO Connection

It doesn't take a rocket scientist to realize that all the events within the verses are a direct implication to some type of mental telepathy or highly advanced telepathic power capable of interceding with the psychological function of the human brain.

Evidently, Yahweh and his host could mentally converse with the subject without vocalizing. The verses would even have us believe that Yahweh could mentally instill knowledge or wisdom to the subject by way of psychologically mediating and programming the brain of the individual. The very same type of telepathic overtones are found within the UFO phenomenon.

It's significant for the reader to keep in mind that mental tampering and UFOs go hand in hand. Throughout the chronology of the UFO phenomenon, mental mediation plays a major role when humans are involved in extreme close encounters. This would also include many UFO abductees where amnesia of their frightening experience was deliberately induced.

In analyzing reports alluding to UFO abductees, it becomes apparent that the pilots of these elusive craft appear to maintain some type of mental or technological control which leaves the abductees with a loss of memory as to what genuinely took place before during and after the alarming encounter. In many cases, the abducted victims simply believe they suffered an ominous dream, much like the artificially induced dreams and visions found within the verses.

Many witnesses claim that these evasive UFO pilots were capable of communicating with them by mental telepathy. Essentially, the occupants of these craft appear to be quite capable of telepathically inducing thought transfer, or scanning one's mind.

Later we will discover that this unique ability to create and/or control dreams, visions, or even generate thought transfer, is a significant power consistently used by these stellar beings to manipulate and direct human affairs on the surface of this planet.

In analyzing the UFO phenomenon, it appears quite evident that the populations of this planet are under constant surveillance, and have been for quite some time. This might suggest that these cosmic guardians are psychologically controlling the industrial growth and regulating the intellectual evolution of this planet, including our advances in technology and science.

Remarkably, this covert psychological infiltration is being carried out right under the very noses of the humans being inflicted. Obviously, this cerebral manipulation could be utilized as a demoralizing tool or even a weapon. Wars cannot only be started, but won or lost by simply mentally implanting dreams or visions. (mental manipulation) Even the most famous inventions of the world may be nothing more than a pre-designed mental infiltration (dreams/visions) carried out by an anonymous third party with its own covert agenda in mind.

Great men of the world have proclaimed that they have seen a vision or had a dream that told them what to do or gave them the idea for remarkable inventions. Even Thomas Edison claimed that the very concept for his electric light bulb came from a dream. Obviously, we have no idea as to the intellectual or technological capabilities maintained by these stellar beings. Nor, as of yet, have we established their ultimate goal as far as their extraterrestrial intervention with mankind is concerned.

Soul Communication

A close examination of the verses substantiates the main source or power employed by Yahweh to perform what appears to be telepathic communication.

This exceptional mental intervention was being performed by what the verses describe as **"The Spirit** of The Lord". Once the spirit was installed, they "**turn into another man"**, possessing great knowledge and wisdom.

From this point on, we will be examining a large body of scripture alluding to the "Spirit of the Lord". We will also discover that the word "spirit" implies more than just a ghost or supernatural being. This is not to say that there is no such thing as a ghost or non-physical entity. However, it's important to realize that the word "spirit" contains many meanings alluding to various intellectual aspects of the human brain.

> **Spirit**—*The part of a human being associated with the mind, will, and feelings. A person as characterized by a stated quality. The actual though unstated sense or significance of something. To impart courage, animation, or determination to; inspirit.*

Clearly, Yahweh imposing his will (spirit) upon mankind, had intervened with the will (spirit) of the subject in question. However, by the time you have finished this book you will come to realize that these celestial beings have gone far beyond simple ESP, telepathy or brain to brain intercommunication. In fact, it would appear that these extraordinary beings have discovered and mastered the very principles of life and death itself, a quantum evolutionary leap that permits them to intercede with, and manipulate, the very **soul** itself.

Essentially, these beings did **not** discover or evolve into psychic entities capable of mind to mind communications (mental telepathy). Rather, they have discovered and mastered what appears to **operate** the brain, being nothing less than the phantom soul (Spirit). In essence, these celestial beings may be highly skilled in **soul** telepathy.

When we enter the New Testament, we will go into extreme detail about this soul to soul communication. Moreover, we will discover that this soul to soul contact directly involves what is known as the Holy Ghost, which may in fact be the mysterious "**Spirit** of the Lord."

Leading The Blind

After thoroughly scrutinizing the verses above, it would appear that much more than soul or telepathic mediation is taking place. The verses would suggest that an outside influence was technologically (artificially) induced by Yahweh and his host. Furthermore, this technological intervention appears quite capable of psychologically maneuvering the brains of humans, as well as of animals.

In surveying these few verses, we find that Elisha appears to be **leading** a small army of **blind men.** In order to fully fathom what is genuinely taking place, one may need to browse Kings II chapter 6. In doing so, you will discover that the King of Syria was determined to kill Elisha because he informed the King of Israel of their war plans. The Syrian King, intending to kill Elisha, sent a small army to surround the city of Dothan were Elisha lived.

Obviously, the army knew were the city was as well as who Elisha was. Elisha seeing that the city was surrounded asked Yahweh to inflict the army with blindness. Yet, in closely examining the verses, we discover that the Syrians were not stricken with optical blindness, but rather psychological blindness.

This entire army was standing right in front of the very man that they were seeking and didn't even know it. Elisha even tells the men they were at the wrong city if they wanted to find Elisha, even though they were facing the very city and man they were pursuing.

Elisha proceeds to advise the blind army that he would <u>lead</u> them to the right city if they would **follow him.** How does one <u>lead</u> an entire army of blind men? How does an army of blind men **follow** anyone? How does an entire army suddenly inflicted with blindness compose themselves to follow anybody?

Obviously, we are not examining an army of visually blind men, but rather men that were psychologically maneuvered. This detail becomes more credible when we note where Elisha **led** the **following** army of Syria to. The army followed Elisha across the desert right into Samaria. Elisha led them right into the very hands of their enemies. The entire army was totally unaware of where they were going, or even where they where when they got there. The entire incident reeks of mass mental manipulation.

Here again, Yahweh and his craft were in the immediate area at the time of the psychological maneuver. (See II Kings 6:15,-17) This would once again indicate that the craft and their pilots were responsible for the psychological procedure.

This same type of mass mental exploitation could be inflicted upon the human race even today, with no one ever being the wiser. Obviously, this surreptitious psychological technique could be utilized to shape and form mankind and its ultimate psychological ambitions for good or evil. Moreover, this psychological control could be saddled upon the savage animal world for obedient or gruesome deeds, as expressed in I Kings.

The Lion and The Donkey

Clearly, both animals were subjected to a mystifying type of psychological control. Normally lions do not kill just to kill, much less stand in one place for any given length of time unless the deathblow was performed for nourishment.

Note the strange behavior of the donkey. The rider had just been torn apart by a lion right in front of the donkey's eyes. It would have been the donkey's nature to run off in fear for his on life. Yet, both the lion and the donkey appear spell bound while standing **together** by the carcass. Each animal appears to be frozen in its tracks, unable to move. Evidently, both animals were being forcibly controlled to maintain their present position so they could be observed by passing eyewitnesses.

Obviously the lion made its sudden appearance only to kill the prophet and nothing else. This can be recognized by the fact that the lion did nothing to the donkey standing right next to him. Furthermore, it would appear that the animals were not only mentally controlled, but physically guided, as in the case of both Lion attacks.

Here again, this mental exploitation of the savage world may account for Noah's ability to lead the various animals into the Ark. This would imply that Yahweh and his craft helped to select, single out, control and even guide the various animals on board.

Analyzing the UFO enigma, we find the same type of control over human beings. Most close encounters or abduction victims claim that during or just before their confrontation, they were placed in a state of what appears to be suspended animation. Or, more simply put, they were completely immobilized, unable to move, while at the same time well aware of what was going on around them. As if this type of mental tampering was not bad enough, the victim is then purposely inflicted with amnesia of the whole affair, allowing the aliens to maintain their anonymity.

The Den of Lions

Seemingly, Yahweh and his host, were employing a technological device to perform the various mental maneuvers upon the unwitting animals. This speculation may also account for the angel found in the den of lions with Daniel. Obviously the angel (man) was placed inside the den for a significant reason. Or are we to believe that the angel simply showed up to comfort Daniel? Evidently, many particulars are missing in this bizarre episode of Daniel's confrontation with the lions in the den.

If Yahweh and his host were capable of psychologically controlling animals, why was it necessary for the angel to be in the den with Daniel? Why not simply control the lions from above as in the previous events we have already examined? Obviously, the angel (man) was responsible for psychologically and physically controlling the lions while in the den with Daniel, as indicated by the verses themselves. But how?

In order to resolve this issue, we need to ask ourselves, what was the only significant **dissimilarity** between the mentally blinded army, the prophet mangled by the lion while the donkey was frozen in place, the bears killing the children, and Daniel's deadlock in the den of lions.

When thoroughly scrutinizing all of the episodes, there appears to be only <u>**one**</u> major discrepancy as to why the angel **had** to physically be in the den with Daniel to control the lions. That one single detail would be non other than the <u>**den**</u> itself.

Every one of the other psychologically maneuvered incidents took place under the open sky, while Daniel's trial took place in a concealed environment (**den**). The very word "den" is clearly self-explanatory, seeing how a den is a hidden cave or hollow cavity usually located **inside** the ground, or in this case a possibly stone-covered structure, such as a dungeon, or underground stockade.

Evidently as long as the subject was exposed to the open sky the craft could utilize their devices to perform the mental maneuver. Obviously, there would be nothing to interfere with the devices being aimed from above to mentally maneuver the subject. However, in Daniel's case the den itself was a major interference when trying to employ their devices **through** the massive stone-covered den concealing Daniel and the lions.

This would once again suggest a possible hand-held device controlled by the angel. The device would allow the angel complete control over the lions while inside the den with Daniel. This would justify the motive for the angel being **inside** the den to avoid the structural interference between the device and the subject (Lions).

The Bears and the Children

What about the children and the two bears? The verses would have us believe that two bears were mentally controlled to come into town and systematically kill ("tare") **forty-two** children. How was it possible for two bears to kill 42 children all at one time? Did all the children just simply wait in line to be killed instead of running for their lives, or did the bears go door to door killing one or two children at a time(?). Where were the parents of forty-two children while the bears were on their killing rampage?

Obviously, significant details are missing from this incident. Even if forty two children were standing right in front of the two bears, there would be no way for the two bears to kill all forty two children simultaneously. The children would have scattered in all directions, possibly heading straight home for their parents. Moreover, the verses inform us that the bears were directed to kill **only** the children and not the parents.

Are we to believe that the parents of forty-two children just simply stood by and did nothing while two bears tore their children apart right before their eyes? Even if each child only had one parent, forty-two parents would be more that a match for the two bears. By adding two parents per child there would be an uncontrollable mob of eighty-four enraged parents out for blood, even if it meant giving up their own lives to protect their children.

In totally examining the verses, we find that more than just mental tampering of the two bears was involved. It would seem unmistakable that some type of psychological manipulation may have also been inflicted upon the children and parents themselves. In fact, one might get the distinct impression that all the children were playing together when the bears began their rampage of death.

All of the children may have been cerebrally frozen in their tracks, in the same manner as the donkey and the lion were. All of the children were powerless to move as the two bears moved from child to child in their mentally controlled binge of death. This speculation would suggest that the parents were also mentally and physically powerless to do anything about what was transpiring right before their eyes.

This is truly a frightening thought, seeing how these cosmic beings could in all probability physically turn the entire animal world against the human populations of this planet. Animals of every shape and size could be psychologically maneuvered or forced out of their own environment to assault mankind.

There would be no mercy as they moved from house to house, attacking and killing everyone in sight. Not to mention the probability that these same extraterrestrial beings could mentally cripple humans so they could not run or even hide to protect themselves from the horrifying onslaught of a systematically controlled and psychologically enraged animal world.

Ezekiel

Thus far, we have analyzed a large volume of data alluding to Yahweh's mysterious cloud and its sudden appearance when miraculous events occur. (Matter Manipulation/Laser Technology/The **hand** of God) Now, for the first time in these writings, we are prepared to embark upon the detailed description of the object's shroud within this atmospheric distortion.

Ezekiel's remarkable encounter is possibly one of the best UFO reports on record to date. Yet, it's significant to remember that Ezekiel was only competent in interpreting the objects the best way his ancient mentality would allow.

As we are about to discover, the cloud-concealed wheels of Ezekiel was not just a single craft of extraterrestrial origin. The wheels depict five separate craft, <u>Four</u> of which fit quite well into the modern UFO phenomena (flying saucer/flying disk), hence the word **wheel.**

The fifth craft or wheel coupled to the flying formation is lacking considerable detail due to the fact that the craft perpetually generates a fiery glow cloaking a large portion of its true form. We will also discover that like most modern UFO reports, this fiery glow appears to be originating from the craft's power source.

This astonishing source of power not only allows the five craft the ability to link up and fly together as a single unit, but permits independent flight capabilities for each craft. Moreover, we will discover that all five of these craft do in fact accommodate a designated pilot.

The Cloud/Whirlwind

Remarkably, Ezekiel describes the same objects by three dissimilar terms. This continual reclassification of the same objects was due to the fact that

Ezekiel constantly renamed the objects based on his continued closer observation. The craft formation starts out as a whirlwind that converted into a cloud. The cloud transformed into creatures that changed into wheel shaped objects. The wheel shaped objects (craft formation) ultimately reveals its designated title known as "Cherubims".

> **1:1 Now it came to pass in the thirtieth year, in the fourth [month], in the fifth [day] of the month, as I [was] among the captives by the river of Chebar, [that] the heavens were opened, and I saw visions of God.**
> **1:2 In the fifth [day] of the month, which [was] the fifth year of king Jehoiachin's captivity,**
> **1:3 The word of the LORD came expressly unto Ezekiel the priest, the son of Buzi, in the land of the Chaldeans by the river Chebar; and the hand of the LORD was there upon him.**
> **1:4 And I looked, and, behold, a whirlwind came out of the north, a great cloud, and a fire infolding itself, and a brightness [was] about it, and out of the midst thereof as the colour of amber, out of the midst of the fire.**
> EZEKIEL

Here again, the hand-shaped device appears to be a significant detail when identifying Yahweh's unique craft. Moreover, we are about to discover that the hand of God being placed upon Ezekiel can be taken literally. Obviously, the cloud and the whirlwind are one and the same object. As mentioned before, Yahweh's craft formation was often referred to as a cloud, where in other instances the formation was alluded to as a whirlwind.

> **26:9 He holdeth back the face of his throne, [and] spreadeth his cloud upon it.**
> **38:1 Then the LORD answered Job out of the whirlwind, and said…**
> JOB
>
> **66:15 For, behold, the LORD will come with fire, and with his chariots like a whirlwind, to render his anger with fury, and his rebuke with flames of fire.**
> ISAIAH
> **23:19 Behold, a whirlwind of the LORD is gone forth in fury, even a grievous whirlwind: it shall fall grievously upon the head of the wicked.**
> JEREMIAH

The dissimilar classifications appear to reflect the craft heightened or decreased state of operation. The faster the craft propelled or energize themselves, the more agitated the created atmospheric disturbance would become, consequently producing what was described as a "whirlwind". Yet, the slower the craft moved or decreased their energized status, the less turbulent the atmospheric distortion became, thus creating a slower moving cloud.

This energizing condition might justify why Ezekiel saw the whirlwind before he observed the cloud. The craft quickly flew in from the north ("came out of the north") as a whirlwind. Yet, after getting closer to Ezekiel's given location, the craft formation slowed down, thus altering the whirlwind or turbulent atmospheric conditions into a restrained cloud where Ezekiel could now see the fiery interior.

Inside the Cloud

Here again, the word "chariots" is directly associated with the whirlwind or cloud, indicating that solid objects (chariots/craft) were concealing themselves inside (in the midst thereof).

> 24:1…How many chariots has the Holy One, blessed be he? He has the chariots of the cherubim, as it is written, "He mounted a cherub and flew."
>
> 24:2 He has the chariots of wind, as it is written, "He soared on the wings of the wind."
>
> 24:3 He has the chariots of swift cloud, as it is written, "See! The lord comes riding a swift cloud."
>
> 24:4 He has the chariots of clouds, as it is written, "I am coming to you in a dense cloud."
>
> 24:5 He has the chariots of the altar, as it is written, "I saw the lord standing upon the altar."
>
> 24:6 He has the chariots of twice ten thousand, as it is written," The chariots of God are twice ten thousand, thousands of angels."
>
> 24:11 He has the chariots of eagles, as it is written, "I carried you on eagles' wings." They are not eagles but fly like eagles.
>
> 24:14 He has the chariots of clouds, as it is written, "He makes the clouds his chariots."
>
> 24:15 He has the chariots of the creatures, as it is written," The creatures ran and returned"—they run by permission and return by permission for the Sekinah is above their heads.
>
> 24:16 He has the chariots of the wheels, as it is written, "Go in between the wheels."

> **24:17 He has the chariots of the swift cherub, as it is written, "Riding upon a swift cherub." When he rides upon the swift cherub, between placing one foot on its back and placing the other foot on it, he perceives 18,000 worlds at a glance; APPENDIX TO 3 ENOCH (PSEU.)**

Evidently, the chariots/cherubim/craft formation was the creatures or flying wheels that one could actually ride on/in. Obviously, the Chariots had to be "mounted" in order to "ride and fly, indicating two entirely dissimilar objects. The first object was the chariot (wheel/craft) the second object was the individual "mounting" the chariot, hence, justifying the word "riding".

Note the location in which Yahweh's personal craft (Sekinah/chariot) is "riding". The verse would outright suggest that Yahweh's chariot is "riding" on the "back" ("upon") of the other creatures/wheels. This would place Yahweh's personal craft (Sekinah/chariot) just above the heads of the other chariots ("the Sekinah is above their heads"). It's extremely important that the reader remember this detail.

The Cloud/Chariots Prepare to Land

Notably, the whirlwind/cloud had now ventured close enough for Ezekiel to recognize some rather interesting points. Ezekiel can now see an amber colored object located inside the engulfing fire ("out of the midst of the fire"). Yet, the "living Bible" would prefer to completely do away with this symbolic delineation (amber) and come right out and confirm.

> **1:4...a huge cloud glowing with fire, with a mass of fire inside that flashed continually; and in the fire there was something that shone like Polished Brass.**
>
> EZEKIEL

Ezekiel appears to be observing a metallic (Brass) object located inside the luminous (blazing) cloud. Seemingly, Ezekiel is associating the color of the object with something he is familiar with, and indeed the color amber take on the appearance of polished brass (**metal**).

Evidently, the cloud had arrived at Ezekiel's position were it began to slowly relinquish its camouflaging effects (whirlwind/cloud). In doing so, it began to expose the physical forms that were hidden within. In fact, it would appear that the de-cloaking or diminishing effects were due to the fact that the craft formation had now slowed down or de-energized to the point of preparing to land.

1:5 Also out of the midst thereof [came] the likeness of four living creatures. And this [was] their appearance; they had the likeness of a man.
1:6 And every one had four faces, and every one had four wings.
1:7 And their feet [were] straight feet; and the sole of their feet [was] like the sole of a calf's foot: and they sparkled like the colour of burnished brass.
1:8 And [they had] the hands of a man under their wings on their four sides; and they four had their faces and their wings.
1:9 Their wings [were] joined one to another; they turned not when they went; they went every one straight forward.
EZEKIEL

It's essential to remember that the four creatures are in fact the four wheels or chariots (craft). Ezekiel now capable of clearly seeing what lurks within the cloud, identifies the four objects as creatures, as if the objects were alive. Yet, Ezekiel did not imply that the objects were living creatures, but rather "the **likeness** of four living creatures." Quite naturally the four wheels/creatures would appear to be alive due to their physical movement required to fly or land.

Each of the four objects possesses "straight feet" leading one to speculate as to just how many feet (landing supports) each of the craft had. Here again, Ezekiel is describing what he observed the best way he knew how.

It would only stand to reason that Ezekiel would associate the metallic (brass) landing gear of these animated objects with feet, seeing how Ezekiel's vocabulary does not contain the words "landing gear". Moreover, the landing gear appears to be underneath the body of the creatures, thereby supporting the living/animated objects, hence feet.

Essentially, Ezekiel referred to the objects as creatures simple because all four of the objects appeared to possess animated appendages (feet) that were in motion corresponding to the movement of the body (craft). Seemingly, the chariots/craft were powering down thus exposing their true physical forms. In doing so, they began lowering their metallic (brass) landing gear (feet), as they prepared to land. Simply put, as far as ancient Ezekiel was concerned, the animated metallic craft/chariots (creatures) were **alive.**

This conjecture is not as bizarre as one might think, considering ancient mankind would have also misinterpreted our modern heavy equipment, cars, trucks, or air craft as noisy creatures that move and fly. Yet, our modern machinery is nothing more than manufactured animated devices that require other animated components such as operators, drivers or pilots (**man**) to function. This might explain why Ezekiel saw the resemblance of a man (pilot) in the craft.

Evidently, Ezekiel was able of distinguish the man (pilot) and the landing gear (feet) of the craft before he was able of fully detail the shape of the craft. This factor would suggest that the pilots of these flying machines control the craft from the **head** or top of the craft. ("Riding upon") A detail that will be confirmed later in this chapter.

Seemingly, the craft powered down to land, at which point the cloaking cloud dissipated from the top of the craft downward. Hence, the pilot at the top of the craft, as well as the protruding landing gear, were seen before the entire body of the craft was.

Clearly, we are no longer analyzing just one cloud-obscured object (creature), but rather **four** metallic (brass) wheels/chariots/craft with flight capability. Each of the metallic creatures appears to be seating the likeness of a man, (pilot) as well as a few other faces. We will go into greater detail about the other faces later in this chapter.

It would seem that Ezekiel is looking up at the four craft as they descend to the ground. This speculation becomes more evident when we consider the fact that Ezekiel not only saw the landing gear, but also the **hand** shaped devices located underneath each of the craft. ("**Under** their wings on their four sides").

Evidently, each of the four creatures accommodates four hand shaped devices protruding out from the undercarriage of each craft. All four of the hand shaped devices appear to be positioned on four dissimilar sides of each craft ("on their four sides").

Here again, Ezekiel is depicting the hand shaped objects the only way he knew how. In this particular case, Ezekiel is gazing at what looks like a man's hand. This might suggest that the hand shaped devices possesses finger like appendages protruding out of the solid part of the telescopic device (arm). As we move deeper into the book of Ezekiel, we will further elaborate upon these remarkable hand shaped device as the data presents itself.

The Wings

Verses 1:8 and 1:9, would lead one to believe that each of the four craft/wheels possesses wings. Yet, the wings did not turn or move when the creature's flew ("went"). This crucial detail would suggest that the wings were fixed or stationary. Furthermore, the wings were joined or connected to each other ("Their wings were joined one to another"), suggesting that all four craft (wheels) were joined together in a tight formation.

Essentially, all four of the creatures (craft) flew together as a single craft that did not make circular turns ("they turned not when they went"). Yet, how does a metallic craft formation of this magnitude move from place to place without physically turning?

It's important for the reader to keep in mind that the very concept of the word "wings" would actually imply that there is a center substructure or **body** that the wings were attached to.

> **1:11 Thus [were] their faces: and their wings [were] stretched upward; two [wings] of every one [were] joined one to another, and two covered their bodies.**
>
> **1:12 And they went every one straight forward: whither the spirit was to go, they went; [and] they turned not when they went.**
>
> EZEKIEL

It's significant to remember that in this particular first time sighting, Ezekiel is observing all four craft (creatures) through an obscured dissipating atmospheric distortion, as well as from a **side** view. This limited observation would naturally obstruct Ezekiel's visual perception of the total shape or design of the entire craft formation.

We also need to keep in mind that Ezekiel was describing what each separate craft (chariot) looks like ("of every one"), and not the entire object/formation as a whole. This would imply that all four craft look alike. Yet, by fully examining a single craft we can better narrow down the actual shape and design of the entire formation.

Utilizing this single craft method, we find that each craft contains two fixed wings that appear to be the undercarriage or **bottom** of the craft itself. This opinion is derived from the verse implying that each craft possessed stationary wings that "stretched" or bowed "upward". This would imply that the bottom wings were curving upward possibly identifying the very upward curve of the undercarriage of the craft itself.

This speculation can be further corroborated by the fact that the verse uses the word "**covered**" to identify the fixed wings located on **top** of each craft. In essence, the "stretched upward" wings were located at the bottom, hence the word "upward". Where the word "covered" would imply that two wings covered the top of the craft.

If you will closely inspect the verses, you will discover that Ezekiel gives one the expression that the wings covered the upper and lower parts of the body. This would indicate that the wings were covering or concealing something larger than the wings themselves. In fact, it took four wings of each craft to cover each of the four **"bodies"**.

However, how did Ezekiel know that the wings were covering a "body" if he had never even seen the **body**? Evidently, the upper and lower fixed wings of each craft appear to be covering another undefined sandwiched structure or body part not defined by Ezekiel at this time. Obviously, we have a missing sub-substructure ("body") that the upper and lower stationary wings are not only covering, but are affixed to.

In essence, we have two stationary structures (wings) on **top** of each craft that connect to a top center section. Likewise, we have two "stretched" upward structures (wings/undercarriage), connected to a center section located at the bottom of the craft.

If in fact the wings were solid parts of the whole body, each of the craft would be joined together at the outer edge of each fixed wing. This would imply that each craft possesses a center substructure containing an upper and lower fixed wing on each side.

Or, in other words, each of the four craft are solid objects with tapered upper and lower sections (wings) covering or sandwiching an undefined inter body that contains a center core to support the "Wings". All four craft were joined together at the outer edge of the body which is covered by the stationary wings.

> **1:13 As for the likeness of the living creatures, their appearance [was] like burning coals of fire, [and] like the appearance of lamps: it went up and down among the living creatures; and the fire was bright, and out of the fire went forth lightning.**
> **1:14 And the living creatures ran and returned as the appearance of a flash of lightning.**
> EZEKIEL

UFO Connection

Ezekiel had now become mentally focused on the fiery characteristic of the four craft. This fiery detail along with the other obvious factors would compel us to enter the modern UFO enigma. Essentially, Ezekiel had now come face to face with a genuine **unidentified flying object** (UFO).

Most of the inhabitants of this planet are totally unaware of the library of documented accounts and consistent patterns found within the typical UFO reports of our modern time. Yet, the Ufologist will quickly recognize the classical UFO profile found in verse 1:13. That consistent outline would entail phenomenal glowing saucer (**wheel**) shaped craft frequenting our planet.

Propulsion System

Most of the reported saucers are engulfed in what is described to be a bright fluctuating glow or colorful fiery flux that surrounds the entire craft. In some cases the craft exhibits a split color profile. Many times the mysterious craft perform an extreme color conversion prior to making a sudden change in direction, or quickly leaving the area. This fiery detail would once again return us to the probability that these exceptional craft are powered by some type of electromagnetic force that produces a colorful spectrum of energy.

It would appear that the craft are capable of generating and controlling massive quantities of electromagnetic power or static electricity, which they utilize to create an outer flux or shield of magnetic energy around the craft. This may be much like a giant electrostatic generator, Synchrotron, or Van de Graff generator, capable of producing massive quantities of raw electrical power.

The electromagnetic shield is manipulated around the outer perimeter of the craft to utilize the magnetic poles of the planet in contrast to the electrically magnified craft. This conjecture may not only account for the dissimilar color variations produced by the glowing craft, but also resolve the issue as to how all four craft are magnetically coupled together as a single unit. In essence, each craft is joined to the others by the very electromagnetic influences allowing the craft flight capability to begin with.

Obviously, the generated electromagnetic fields would have to be manipulated around the outer perimeter of the craft on a continuous basis to compensate for the diverse magnetic variations around the planet. The outer electromagnetic flux or shield changes color due to the variations in the spectrum of electromagnetic energy being engaged around the craft. Essentially, the craft would appear to be alive, possibly accounting for Ezekiel's belief that these four craft were living creatures.

This same speculation may also account for the fact that the four craft were producing what Ezekiel discribed as lightning. This is not an uncommon repercussion seeing how this same type of electrical arcing has been reported in numerous UFO incidents.

If in fact the four craft are generating massive quantities of static electricity and/or electromagnetic energy, it would only stand to reason that the fluctuating electromagnetic fields would produce vigorous repercussions of electrical energy, such as sparks, or electrical arcing. If the reader will recall, Yahweh and his craft formation utilized this energy source as a powerful weapon.

Lighting Facilities

Notably, Ezekiel detected other luminous objects having nothing to do with the glowing attributes of the craft themselves. This additional detail can be easily distinguished by the fact that Ezekiel uses the word "**and**" to differentiate between the two separate glowing objects.

Obviously the craft (creatures), appear to glow or radiate like coals of fire, yet the other luminous objects are identified as "**lamps**". This would suggest that the lamps were located on, or perhaps attached to the craft themselves.

Looking at the word "lamps" from Ezekiel's vintage point of view, lamps were indeed attached to objects as a source of light or heat. Observing the lamps from our modern point of view, the same factor would not only hold true, but could be greatly elaborated upon.

Modern man could not do without lamps (light), to light our homes, industry, and business. Let's not forget modern mankind also possesses cars, trucks, ships and aircraft, all unquestionably requiring lamps of every shape and size in order to safely function in our automated society. Possibly the very same type of lights (lamps) were required by these four craft. In fact, craft capable of traveling the night skies and/or the darkness of outer space would require lighting facilities we may know absolutely nothing about.

Craft Maneuverability

Note Verse (1:14). Ezekiel once again describes an amazing sight not uncommon within the chronicles of UFOlogy. In fact, it would appear that the four craft put on an air show for Ezekiel to demonstrate their lightening fast flight capabilities.

The present UFO phenomena abound with mysterious craft entering our air space and performing lightning speed maneuvers beyond belief, some reaching reported velocities of up to 7000+ mph. These incredible speeds become even more enigmatic when we realize that without warning they can come to an instant dead stop in midair.

These elusive craft are even capable of making right angle turns at lightning speeds without stopping. Furthermore, the craft are skillful in performing what is described as a **zig zag** maneuvers at high speeds. Many times these evasive craft have been reported to ascend straight up, or descend straight down at unbelievable speeds. In fact, it would appear as if the UFO phenomena consist of flying machines that are not fully capable of making rapid **turns** as we know them. But rather wide sweeping turns, or no turns at all, possibly explaining Ezekiel's astonished statement "**they turned not when they went.**"

If in fact these phantom craft are utilizing electromagnetic energy to navigate, it's no wonder they don't always perform wide turns, seeing how the energy source powering the craft may not allow for such maneuvers. Craft utilizing this type of energy would possibly be restricted to only straight up or down maneuvers, or right angle turns, due to the manipulated electromagnetic fields engulfing the craft.

If they are employing surrounding electromagnetic fields to exploit the magnetic fields of the planet, then quite naturally the craft would be forced to conform to the magnetic rules of nature. Natural magnetic rules would entail only right angle maneuvers, or direct contrasting and/or attracting polarization to implement mobility for the craft.

The location of the craft in reference to the planet and its dissimilar magnetic poles would greatly determine the controlling electromagnetic flux encompassing the craft. Essentially, the opposing or attracting magnetic variations would be astronomical.

If it happened that the craft was located in the Southern hemisphere of the planet and decided to maneuver in a Northern direction, the outer electromagnetic flux around the craft would need to generate a southern polarization.

This would instantly thrust and draw the craft toward the North pole. Furthermore, the outer color spectrum of the glowing flux that surrounds the craft would change colors to match the color spectrum of the southern electromagnetic polarization.

Likewise, if the craft was located in the Northern hemisphere and wished to trek South, the electromagnetic flux would have to be altered once again into a Northern polarization. This would naturally repel and attract the craft in a Southern direction, as well as altering the colorful electromagnetic spectrum around the craft. The possibilities would be endless, seeing how the multiple variations within the controlled electromagnetic fields to counter or exploit the Earth's magnetic fields would equal that of the grains of sand on a beach.

If the craft wished to maintain a stabilized position in midair (**hover**) between the two planetary poles, the craft would need to alter its electromagnetic fields to simultaneously counter both the North and South poles. Furthermore, if the craft wished to shoot straight up into the upper atmosphere of the planet, it could create opposing polarizations on both sides, instantaneously hurling the craft straight up into outer space away from both poles.

This lightning fast ascension could also be magnetically reversed into a speedy descent. Quite naturally, all the given maneuvers would greatly depend on the given location of the craft in reference to the polar regions of the planet.

As mentioned before, these unique craft have been observed with split electromagnetic profiles. Simply put, the craft displays two completely dissimilar colored fluxes on two diverse sides of the craft, consequently stabilizing the craft between the two magnetic poles of the planet. Moreover, these remarkable craft have been seen **wobbling** or **staggering** in midair, before or after coming to an abrupt stop or sudden change in direction.

This would suggest that prior to the craft taking off and/or terminating a navigated maneuver such as stopping in midair, they undergo a radical change, or alteration of their encompassing electromagnetic fields, to compensate for the diverse magnetic fields of the planet.

In essence, the craft is momentarily destabilized in midair, until it is capable of fully countering the diverse magnetic fields of the planet in contrast to the altered electromagnetic flux engulfing the craft. Hence, the craft performs a wobble or stager in its efforts to magnetically stabilize itself after its abrupt stop, or before its sudden acceleration.

This same perception would further imply that the craft would never need to make wide turns of any kind. The manipulated electromagnetic field or shield surrounding the craft would instantly change the direction of the craft without ever having to physically turn the craft around in the direction required to travel, regardless of the pilot's position.

This magnetic concept may also justify the wheel shaped design of the craft. The circular/spherical or wheel shaped design of the craft may have something to do with controlling and/or bending the magnetic fields encircling the planet in contrast to the electromagnetic fields encircling the craft.

The circular design may be for more than aerodynamic stability. The circular design may allow the craft to become electromagnetically balanced to travel in any given direction around this spherical world without ever having to physically turn the craft around. Accordingly "**they turned not when they went.**"

The Craft Land

> **1:15 Now as I beheld the living creatures, behold one wheel upon the earth by the living creatures, with his four faces.**
> **1:16 The appearance of the wheels and their work [was] like unto the colour of a beryl: and they four had one likeness: and their appearance and their work [was] as it were a wheel in the middle of a wheel.**
> **1:17 When they went, they went upon their four sides: [and] they turned not when they went.**
> **EZEKIEL**

Evidently a dramatic change had taken place right before Ezekiel's eyes ("as I beheld"). This revealing transformation can easily be recognized by the fact that astonished Ezekiel states "**behold**". Ezekiel, now capable of obtaining a better look at the craft formation, had now reclassified the objects from creatures to wheels.

Creatures to Wheels

Essentially, the verses establish the fact that the creatures and the wheels were in fact one and the same objects. This reveling detail can be found in verse [1:15]. If the reader will recollect, Ezekiel stated that each of the **creatures** possessed faces. Yet, **one** of the creatures has now been reclassified as a wheel. That wheel displays the very same faces found on each of the creatures. But how?

The solution to this perplexing issue can actually be found in the same verse. The verse would return us to Ezekiel's astonished state of mind "**behold**". Behold what? "**Behold one wheel upon the earth**". This surprised assertion actually establishes two conceivable probabilities. Moreover, we will have to examine **both** possibilities if we are to unravel the maneuver the four craft had now performed.

It's significant to remember that all five craft within the formation do in fact possess the power of independent flight, as well as the ability to connect together as a single unit. This would suggest that all **five** craft as a formation or independently could have performed either maneuver.

The first probability would suggest that the four craft had now broke formation. Not only did the four craft dislodged themselves from their coupled formation, but **one** of the craft had now landed on the ground: "one wheel upon the earth". This would place the landed craft (wheel) with its four faces "**by**" or next to the other three craft (creatures) that had not landed.

Yet, more significantly, we find that the entire formation had now quickly followed suit. The very next verse informs us that all four of the metallic craft had now landed. This obvious detail is confirmed in verse 1:16 notifying us of the word "wheels" not wheel. Evidently, all four of the wheel shaped craft had now landed, each of which takes on the appearance of a metallic (brass/beryl) wheel. ("and **they four** had one likeness").

Seemingly the craft formation had separated, consequently **one** of the four craft landed first, consecutively followed by the other three. In the process of landing, each of the craft powered down their energized propulsion systems, "**one**" at a time, thus exposing their true wheel like forms.

This might justify why Ezekiel saw only one wheel first, followed by the other three. Simply put, while the craft were hovering or slowly moving towards Ezekiel's location, their energized condition initially obscured Ezekiel's observation of the true form of the objects concealed within. Hence, the four objects took on the appearance of living creatures by Ezekiel's archaic standards.

However, by the four creatures powering down and physically landing, their propulsion systems were shut down, hence exposing their true wheel like bodies. Consequently the four living creatures had now been reclassified as four wheels, and rightly so, seeing how Ezekiel was now capable of observing in full detail the actual construction ("**their** work") of each craft (wheel).

Our second possibility would suggest an entirely different set of circumstances. This order of events would propose that the four craft formation never broke formation, but rather landed as a single unit. This would imply that all four craft/wheels landed side by side together.

Yet, how can this be, seeing how the verses would suggest that only a single craft was seen or landed before the other three did ("**Behold one wheel upon the earth**"). How was Ezekiel able to detected this single craft (Wheel) before he recognized the other three? The obvious clue to this dilemma can be found in the word ("by"). ("**behold one wheel upon the earth by the living creatures**").

The single craft was located right **by** the other three craft when it landed. This would suggest that all four craft had landed together at the same time. Furthermore, this would place all four craft in a tight formation right next to or "by" each other as they touch down.

However, the one detail that actually unravels the formation dilemma lies in the understanding that Ezekiel was not capable of identifying **any** of the four creatures as wheel shaped craft as long as they stayed airborne. As long as the craft remained in the air, Ezekiel classified them as creatures. Yet, at the very moment that the four craft landed, Ezekiel reclassified the creatures as wheels.

This would suggest that the very operation of the four craft landing caused Ezekiel to modify his description of what the craft actually looked like. This revealing detail would actually indicate the involvement of the propulsion systems of each individual craft. Each of the four craft maintains their own separate propulsion systems. This fiery electromagnetic system not only generates the craft' flight capabilities, but also allow each craft the ability to unite together as a single unit, hence creating the craft formation.

However, just because all four craft landed together as a combined formation does not imply that all four craft shut down their propulsion systems at the exact same time. Obviously, each of the four craft could have terminated their propulsion systems at different times. By each of the four craft **individually** shutting down their shrouding electromagnetic fields, they would expose their true wheel shaped forms at different intervals, depending on which craft terminated its propulsion system first.

The first craft to terminate its propulsion system would be left standing isolated next to ("by") the other three craft that did not. Therefore, the first exposed wheel shaped craft would be observed **first** standing "by" the other three craft that still took on the appearance of creatures. Ultimately, the other three craft systematically exposed themselves by powering down their propulsion systems, consequently all four craft/creatures now took on the appearance of four "wheels".

Wheel within a Wheel

This observation only complicates matters, seeing how we are now confronted with another wheel located within each of the four wheels. Essentially, each of the wheel shaped craft possesses another wheel shaped object located in the **center** ("**middle**").

This puzzling "wheel within a wheel" exposes a major clue to the true construction of the total craft. As mentioned before, the word "wings" would actually imply a **center section** or "middle" substructure that the wings are attached to. In fact, it would appear that we now have confirmation to the structural attributes of the wings themselves.

If in fact the center ("middle") section of the craft is a wheel, then **the outer** wheel like structure (craft) surrounding the center wheel would be a part of the wings, attached to the center ("middle") wheel. This would imply that the wings covering the body are actually circular or wheel shaped upper and lower parts of the body.

In fact, we are about to discover that this center section or "middle" wheel is only **one** of the center sections located within each craft (wheel). Each of the four metallic craft actually possesses **two center sections** located in the "middle" of each craft, one of which Ezekiel has now identified. That established center (middle wheel) section, or "wheel within a wheel" is actually located **underneath** the craft. This detail is not revealed in the verses at this time.

Nonetheless, we are about to discover that this **first** center section, or "middle" wheel positioned within the wheel/craft, would undoubtedly have to be located underneath the craft, seeing how each of these four craft do in fact embody a **top** center section. Therefore the wheel shaped center section (middle wheel) would **have** to be located underneath the craft.

UFO Connection

Evidently, Ezekiel was quite close to the four craft, considering the metallic details he had now elaborated upon. In fact, Ezekiel may be standing right next to one of them justifying his statement in reference to the actual construction of the craft ("**their work was as it were a wheel in the middle of a wheel**").

For those of you that are not familiar with the UFO phenomena, these words may mean absolutely nothing to you, and I may even have to jangle the UFOlogist's memory. Remarkably, this revealing verse actually depicts the very essence of the known UFO phenomena to date.

Most UFO reports involve wheel/disk or saucer shaped craft possessing center **rotating** sections (wheel), located within the undercarriage of the craft. Or, in more simplified terms, a wheel within a wheel. There have even been reports of craft undercarriages displaying binary center rotating sections that oppose each other. Essentially, the craft display a dual rotating wheel shaped structure located within its underbelly. In this particular case, we could classify this craft as a wheel within a wheel within a wheel.

The dual rotating center sections appear to be spinning against themselves suggesting that the two opposing wheels are producing energy to power the craft by diametric rotation. This speculation may also hold true with the single rotating center section commonly witnessed in most UFO reports.

The spinning center section or wheel appears to be performing a gyrating action to produce static electricity and/or electromagnetic energy to power the craft. Yet, the single spinning wheel or center section may be countering itself against the actual body of the wheel shaped craft to produce energy.

However, this "middle" wheel may not be producing electrical energy, as much as the forced accumulation of electrical power. The center rotating wheel may be nothing more than a collector of static electricity abundantly found within this planet's atmosphere.

The accumulated static electricity could be collected and converted into many dissimilar energy alternatives capable of producing unimaginable electromagnetic energy. In either case, it would seem evident that the spinning "middle" wheel of the craft appears to be the main power source for the craft. The faster the center wheel turns the more power it will produce.

Essentially, it would appear that the circular craft is nothing more than a huge electro-static or electromagnetic generator with a ship built around it.

This enormous power supply could generate endless energy for the craft to venture anywhere within the Earth's statically charged atmosphere, as long as the craft follows the natural laws of magnetism. This restricted magnetic rule may also resolve the issue as to why Ezekiel makes the same statement in reference to the craft flight capabilities twice.

> **1:17 When they went, they went upon their four sides: [and] they turned not when they went.**
> **EZEKIEL**

Four Craft/Four Pilots/Four Directions

Note the words "**four sides**" suggesting that the craft formation navigated ("went") from four dissimilar sides. The verse would even appear to suggest that this four-direction maneuver was the **only** way that the four craft formation could pilot itself. By the four craft being joined or coupled together, they form a tight fitting craft formation with four distinct sides.

Each of the four sides consists of one craft, (wheel) as well as one direction that the craft is turned or aimed. By adding four pilots to the four craft, we have a craft formation capable of physically navigating in four distinct directions, depending on the pilot operating the formation at the time. This would once again greatly elaborate upon the common formation and maneuver found within the annals of UFOlogy.

There have been many different types of craft formations reported throughout the history of the UFO phenomena. Some UFO reports involve strange glowing craft that appear to be riding piggy back. These reports state that the assumed single glowing object simply split up into two separate glowing objects that sped off in two diverse directions.

Other UFO incidents recount balls of light hooked together side by side as they maneuver across the sky. Suddenly the glowing balls of light detach or uncouple themselves and disappear in different directions. There have even been reports of air force jets and commercial airlines observing what was believed to be one large bright UFO, only to discover that the bright UFO split up into three, and sometimes four different UFOs that took off in dissimilar directions.

If we consider that these craft are possibly utilizing electromagnetic energy to propel themselves within our atmosphere, it becomes quite feasible that these remarkable craft could attach themselves to each other by way of the very electromagnetic fields that create their flight capability.

This uniting maneuver might actually be for the purpose of conserving energy. The craft may be coupling or bracketing themselves together to form a single unit capable of operating from the combined energy sources of all the craft involved.

In other words, it may be that four craft can operate as a single unit utilizing less energy than four craft operating independently of each other. This speculation may also project profound overtones of greater weapon superiority.

United craft of this superior design could inflict unbelievable martial violence as a joined single force rather than four separated units. In essence, the formation boasts the ability to not only watch one's back in even the most deadly aerial dog fights, but be highly proficient in destroying one's pursuing enemies while literally chasing the opponent.

The Rings

> **1:18 As for their rings, they were so high that they were dreadful; and their rings [were] full of eyes round about them four.**
> **1:19 And when the living creatures went, the wheels went by them: and when the living creatures were lifted up from the earth, the wheels were lifted up.**
> **1:20 Whithersoever the spirit was to go, they went, thither [was their] spirit to go; and the wheels were lifted up over against them: for the spirit of the living creature [was] in the wheels.**
> **1:21 When those went, [these] went; and when those stood, [these] stood; and when those were lifted up from the earth, the wheels were lifted up over against them: for the spirit of the living creature [was] in the wheels.**
> **EZEKIEL**

Ezekiel has now revealed a major missing part of the puzzle. Or perhaps I should say Ezekiel has now furnished us with the missing **body** that will help us piece together the actual design of each craft.

Ezekiel's time involved animal drawn carts, carriages and chariots possessing large wooden wheels. In some instances, the wheels had wooden spokes, but in most cases the ancient wheel consisted of a solid wooden circular body allowing the solid wheel greater strength for hauling heavier loads.

Yet, more significant would be what was used to reinforce some of the wheels against the tortures of the rocky terrain. The ancient wooden wheel would not have endured for very long without some type of outer shield to protect its wooden core. The outer armor protecting the wheel was in fact a metal "**ring**".

It would appear that Ezekiel was associating the outer ring of the wheel as he knew it with the outer ring of the four **wheel** constructed craft". Essentially, the "Ring" is the missing body or mid-sections that the four wings of each craft covered. Moreover, the encompassing body or sandwiched mid-section ("ring") contained eyes "round about".

This is not an uncommon sight seeing how our modern aircraft, water craft, or space craft, also integrate port holes, as well as numerous lights around the entire craft. In fact, Ezekiel's detailed observation would once again give us the actual shape of the four craft. Obviously, the port holes and possible lights were "**round about**" indicating that the craft were actually circular or wheel shaped.

Evidently, Ezekiel was quite fascinated by the large mid section encompassing each of the four craft, justifying his statement that "**their** rings, they were so high that they were **dreadful**". This might suggest that Ezekiel was physically standing right next to, or perhaps underneath the outer edge (ring) of one of the landed craft.

This speculation would not only warrant Ezekiel's spellbound observation of the port holes or lights ("eyes") encircling the craft, but his astonishment at the magnitude of the rings/mid-section that appears to be noticeably thick ("so high") or tall. Obviously the ring/mid section would have to be thick to contain port holes' outer marker lights ("eyes") and possible compartments within the craft for a man to utilize the port holes.

Wheels in Motion

Ezekiel, now able to closely examine the four wheel shaped craft, appears to have figured out how they actually flew. Obviously their power supply derived from what Ezekiel relates to as the wheel. Yet, how can the wheel be the power supply considering the wheel (creature) is actually the craft itself?

However, let us not forget, these craft are more than just a wheel. They are in fact a "**wheel in the middle of a wheel**". Obviously Ezekiel is not referring to the craft itself as the power supply, but rather the wheel (rotation center section) located in the "middle" of the wheel/craft.

When the living **creatures/Wheels** were lifted up (flew), the middle wheels located within the undercarriage of each craft went with them. Essentially, the middle wheel or center rotating section was actually a significant part of each craft. Not only is the "middle" wheel a part of each craft, but is a moving part of the craft.

This design is easily recognized by the fact that "when the living creatures/wheels were **lifted up** from the earth, the wheels were also **lifted up**". In essence, when the wheel shaped craft took off from the ground the rotating center sections (wheels) were also lifted up, indicating two separate actions, both of which obviously coincide with each other.

Put simply, the power driving the craft was in fact coming from the center wheel, a power that Ezekiel could only relate to as the "**spirit**" (power/force) of the creatures. It was the middle wheel that gave the craft their life (spirit) or energy ("for the spirit of the living creature [was] in the wheels").

The verses not only testify that the "middle" wheel was powering the craft, but **how** the middle wheel was powering the craft. The mechanical function is easily recognized by the fact that when the center rotation section (wheel) was **lifted up,** the wheel shaped craft became airborne ("lifted up").

> **1:21 When those went, [these] went; and when those stood, [these] stood; and when those were lifted up from the earth, the wheels were lifted up over against them: for the spirit of the living creature [was] in the wheels.**
> EZEKIEL

The words "those" and "these" actually outline the four craft, seeing how each of the four craft was a wheel in the middle of a wheel. The word "those" would appear to be identifying the wheel shaped craft itself. In contrast, the word "these" seems to identify the rotating center section or wheel located in the "middle" of each craft. When the ("these") rotating center section turned ("went"), the ("those") four wheel shaped craft were capable of flying ("went").

However, when the ("these") rotation center sections (wheels) "stood" still, the ("those") wheel shaped craft also "stood" still (landed). For the power (spirit) of the living creatures (wheel shaped craft) was in the rotating wheel/center section. When those went, these went. When those stood, these stood.

Moreover, it would appear that the simple spinning of the center wheel was not the only energy factor when it came to powering up these machines. Evidently the living creatures/wheels were only capable of flying ("went") if the spirit (power) of the "middle" wheel was "**lifted** up" against the wheel shaped craft ("them").

Quite naturally, if the center section was "lifted up" to empower the craft, it would also possess the ability to be disengaged or lowered downward. Essentially, the middle wheels empowering the four craft were not only spinning ("went"), but were also being moved up or down within the undercarriage of each machine, consequently powering up or powering down the craft.

Evidently, the rotating center section could be disengaged from its primary energy function by lowering the center section away from the central housing located within the undercarriage of the craft. This would appear to stop the center section from spinning, as well as possibly terminating the main power source to the craft.

Here again, a generator comes to mind, seeing how a generator would require a rotating center core to produce power. Seemingly, the rotating core could be manipulated within its outer housing to produce diverse power levels. This would suggest that the rotating center section (core) controlled the amount of power required for the craft to fly. The faster and more immersed the central rotating wheel was elevated ("lifted up") into the lower housing of the craft, the more energy (spirit) it could produce.

Craft Cockpits

> **1:22 and the likeness of the firmament upon the heads of the living creature [was] as the colour of the terrible crystal, stretched forth over their heads above.**
> **1:23 And under the firmament [were] their wings straight, the one toward the other: every one had two, which covered on this side, and every one had two, which covered on that side, their bodies.**
> EZEKIEL

We now have the final missing body segment yet to be established within the design of each craft. This missing part of the craft will actually complete the **total** shape of all four craft. Up until now, this absent section of the craft would not have been fully understood, much less believed without the previous parts of this enigmatic puzzle being examined. However, at this time, we are ready to analyze what might be considered the controlling sector or command center of each craft.

As with any **creature** or human, the controlling sector of the whole body is the "**head**", a body member customarily located above the feet. This governing segment naturally centered above the total body, allows the towering "head" the ability to prevail over and control the entire body. This is a simple law of nature that these four wheel shaped machines were obviously obliged to follow.

Based on the actual design of the four wheel shaped craft, it would appear that we now have confirmation of the **top** center section. This speculation is derived from the fact that each of the craft were wheel shaped objects possessing "**feet**" (landing gear). In order for the craft to land, each of the four wheel shaped machines would need to be supported by those "feet".

This would imply that the four wheel constructed craft using their feet landed on their undersides, thus leaving the **top** ("head") of the craft exposed. The obvious design of the craft resting upon their feet/landing gears, implies that their head was centered just above the supporting "feet" and body "wheel" of the craft.

Seeing how the dislodging "middle" wheel was positioned between the feet centrally located within the undercarriage, it's highly probable that the "head" of the craft was actually located just above the "middle" wheel. This would indicate that the heads of the four craft were located **above** not only the lower "middle" wheel or center rotating section, but also above the established body or mid section "ring".

Yet, more significant would be what is sited just "**above**" or capping the **heads** of the four craft. Obviously, an undefined object is resting "**upon**" the head of each craft. Considering Ezekiel's ancient analogical interpretation leaves much to be desired, we will have to define the crystal objects ourselves. In examining this undefined object, we are once again confronted with the typical UFO profile.

Quite naturally, Ezekiel is recounting what he observed, the only way his intellectual background would allow. In this particular case, Ezekiel is applying the word "**firmament**" to identify what appears to be spread over "**upon**" the heads of the four craft. Quite naturally, the word "firmament" would suggest the sky/heaven.

However, if Ezekiel was in fact identifying the sky, he would also be informing us that the sky was made out of "crystal". Clearly Ezekiel is identifying something other than the sky, an obvious detail found in the verse itself "and the **likeness** of the firmament". Essentially, this riddle comes completely unraveled, and crystal **clear** when one actually defines the word "Firmament".

> ***Firmament***—*the vault or* ***arch*** *of the sky*—***arch*** *is a typical curved structural member spanning an opening and serving as a support, or something resembling an* ***arch*** *in form or function. A curvature having the form of an* ***arch****. Vault is a space covered by an* ***arched structure****, an arched structure forming a ceiling or roof, or an* ***arched*** *or* ***dome shaped anatomical structure****.*

Considering Ezekiel's vocabulary does not embrace the word "glass", we are obviously left with the understanding that Ezekiel was observing a glass dome which he referred to as crystal. In essence, Ezekiel was actually observing a dome ("firmament") shaped structure positioned upon the heads of the four craft. This large hemispherical crystalline roof can further be identified by Ezekiel declaring that the "crystal **stretched forth over their heads above**".

Yet, more significantly, we find that the words "**firmament**" and "**head**" would outright indicate **two** entirely different objects. This notable detail is established by the fact that the firmament was upon the heads of the craft. Or in other words, the dome shaped structures were capping the heads of each craft. Yet, what was the **head** if not the dome shaped structure (firmament)?

Evidently, the "head" appears to be a protruding section found at the **top** center of each wheel shaped machine. Essentially, Ezekiel was observing the cockpits ("heads") that protruded out of the top of each wheel-shaped craft. Each of the exposed cockpits required a clear (crystal/glass) protective dome (firmament) to allow the pilot clear encompassing observation to maneuver the craft.

Installing the Wings

> **1:23 and under the firmament [were] their wings straight, the one toward the other: every one had two, which covered on this side, and every one had two, which covered on that side, their bodies.**
>
> **EZEKIEL**

In recollection of verse 1:11, Ezekiel asserted that the lower wings were stretched upward, suggesting that the bottom wings or undercarriage of the craft was curved upward. Ezekiel then informed us that two wings covered their **body** (mid-section/ring).

This previous verse can now be greatly expanded upon due to the verse above. This revealing verse actually giving us the design of the wings covering the body or mid-section of the craft. Moreover, the verse actually establishes the fact that all four wings genuinely "covered" the "body/ring.

Seeing how each craft possesses two center sections, (Dome/Head and Middle Wheel) we now have a better understanding as to how the stationary wings covered the main body (wheel/ring). Looking at the craft design from a side view, it becomes quite understandable why Ezekiel may have used the word wings in his efforts to identify the upper and lower covering structures of each craft.

Obviously the upper and lower sections would suggest a wing-like appearance, protruding out from both sides of the center sections. This is an obvious assumption, considering Ezekiel comprehended the upper and lower parts (wings) of the wheel shaped craft before he actually observed the body or mid-section (ring) that the wings were covering.

In examining the verse above, we now possess more detail of the top structure of the craft than we did before. This missing blueprint will help us to fully examine each craft as a total unit. Unlike the undercarriage (wings) that curve upward, the top section (wings) of the craft joined to the main body (ring), appears to possess no curvature at all. The upper structure of the craft being attached to the main body/ring was "**straight**": "**under the firmament** **[were] their wings straight**".

One might get the distinct impression that the dome and cockpit (firmament/head) were positioned right on top of the ring or horizontal mid section of the craft. This would suggest that there were no upper wings or outer structure covering the body. Yet, there is another possible solution. Note the words "**under the firmament**" being the exact location of the **wings** that were **straight**. Evidently, the upper wings reside between the bottom of the firmament/dome and the mid-section or ring of the craft.

This would suggest that the outside edge of the ring (body) began a gradual straight slope as it heads towards the lower section of the upper dome (firmament). In essence, the upper structure of the craft was a raised substructure (wings) on which the domed-covered cockpit rested.

Looking at this probability from a different perspective, the domed, covered cockpit is located on a circular platform that tapers down in a "straight" manner to meet with the main body ("ring") of the craft.

Observing this platform from a side view, it would appear as if straight wings were protruding out from under the firmament (domed cockpit), down towards the main body (ring). Each one of the craft would appear to display one upper wing on both sides of the dome, which were connected to the other craft and their upper wings.

If the four craft were joined together in a tight formation, all of their bodies (rings) containing upper and lower covering segments (wings), would actually be touching each other. The upper and lower wings on one side would touch the upper and lower wings of a completely different craft on two sides. Likewise, all four craft would actually be touching, or connected to two other craft at the outer edge or wings of each craft.

Putting Things Together

We have now fully examined all the crucial parts and structural characteristics of each craft. However, to better understand the total design of each craft, it's essential that we do a little paper work. In doing so, I will elaborate upon <u>two</u> possible designs. Under normal conditions, whether ancient Ezekiel or modern man, the wheel is naturally observed as an **<u>upright</u>** circular or round object, thus giving us our first possible design as proposed by Ezekiel.

We are going to take just **one** of the wheel shaped objects and draw a sketch of what the object might look like with the data we now possess. However, in our first design we will scrutinize the wheel shaped craft from an **<u>upright</u>** position.

Taking a sheet of paper and pencil, draw an <u>upright</u> six inch diameter circle. Keep in mind that during Ezekiel's period of time, most wheels did not possess spokes, nor were spokes mentioned in Ezekiel's description of the wheel shaped craft. Therefore, the wheel you have just sketched would be solid.

Like most wheels of that era, there would naturally be a circular substructure containing a hole in the center of the wheel for the shaft. Therefore, in the "middle" of your large wheel draw a small wheel-shaped circle. (A wheel within a wheel) Essentially, this middle wheel represents the rotating center section <u>or</u> top center section of the wheel shaped craft. However, only one center section would be visible.

We now need to attach the wings to the wheel. This will prove to be quite impossible seeing how we are only able to see one side of the wheel. Ezekiel was able to see a total of four wings covering the wheel. Two wings **covered** the top side, and two wings **covered** the bottom side. Obviously, this would place one in quite a pickle when trying to fit four wings <u>between</u> the two wheel shaped structures. Our best bet would be to draw two wing shaped objects between the "middle" and outer wheels.

Now draw three or four straight vertical lines approximately one to two inches long under the outside **bottom** of your outer wheel. These straight lines represent the landing gear ("feet") of the outer wheel, so space them properly. Due to the fact that your drafted wheel is upright, we cannot install port holes or lights ("eyes") round about the "ring".

Next we need to install the head and dome (firmament) on top of your sketched wheel. This would simply propose that you draw a small protruding object on top of your outer wheel. The protruding object ("head") needs to be capped with a firmament, or dome-shaped object to cover the head.

This would complete the total wheel shaped craft as described by Ezekiel, a wheel-shaped mess which is obviously **ridiculous**. However, this example was necessary to better understand the true form of the wheel-shaped craft. Let's start again.

Turn the same sheet of paper over on the opposite side, but <u>long ways</u>. We are going to draw the <u>same</u> six-inch circle (wheel). However, this time, we are going to **lay the wheel down <u>horizontally</u>**.

Essentially, we will no longer see the round circular form which represents the wheel, but rather the hidden horizontal ring or mid-section located around the wheel. As before, the ring is the same diameter, or in this case the same length as the circular wheel, or approximately six inches long.

Ezekiel led us to believe that the ring was thick ("high") so let's make the ring or mid section roughly three quarters of an inch thick on your drawing. This would require that you sketch a straight line across the paper six inches long. Three quarters of an inch **above** the first line, draw another line equally matching the first line in length.

Now close both ends of the lines by drawing curved or straight lines that connect both the top and bottom lines together. You now possess a **<u>side view</u>** of the wheel, which actually furnishes us with a side view of the **ring** (mid-section/body).

Our next step would require that we draw a two and a half inch long line three quarters of an inch **underneath** the ring or mid-section, make sure the line is **<u>centered</u>** just below the ring. This line represents the rotating center section, within the undercarriage of the wheel constructed craft.(a wheel within a wheel)

Next, draw a dome shaped (firmament/head) line **centered** about half an inch **above** the ring or mid-section. Fashion the dome shaped line two inches long, and three quarters of an inch tall, with a gentle curve.

We now need to install the fixed wings onto the mid-section/ring, thus **covering** the body ("two on this side, and two on that side"). The top wings are straight, so on the left side of your drawing take a ruler and draw a straight line from the bottom left edge of the dome to the top left edge of the ring.

The bottom wings were **stretched** upward, so by hand, draw a gentle curving line from the left bottom edge of the ring to the left edge of the line that represents the rotating center section (two wings on this side). Repeat the same procedure on the right side (two wings on that side). Our next step is to install port holes and/or lights ("eyes") around the ring or mid-section (round about). This detail is easily performed by drawing small circles centered across the entire length of the ring/mid section. Last but not least would be the straight "feet" or landing gear. Evidently, the landing gear was straight. Yet, the "middle" wheel would suggest that they were protruding out of the undercarriage at a straight angle. Therefore, on your drawing, just to the outside edge of the center rotating section or "middle" wheel, you will find more than adequate room to install straight angled landing gear ("feet") from the undercarriage (wings)of the craft. By placing three or four different feet (landing gear) around the undercarriage of the craft the landing gear, would not only prove to be structurally proper, but a superior design. It's quite clear what we are dealing with here. Obviously, the dimensions of the craft may vary greatly. In fact, each wheel-shaped craft may only be designed for a single occupant. This might suggest that the craft could be quite small, perhaps fifteen to twenty feet in diameter.

Then again, the wheel shaped craft could maintain cockpits and quarters large enough to support three or four men. This would imply that **each craft** could be as large as thirty feet in diameter.

With all four craft joined together they could actually span an area as large as sixty to seventy plus feet in diameter. (?) For those of you who were unable to sketch the single craft, I have drafted a drawing of the total five craft formation. Yet, it's significant to keep in mind that the actual formation may vary greatly in design and size.

Loud/Silent Propulsion System

> **1:24 and when they went, I heard the noise of their wings, like the noise of great waters, as the voice of the almighty, the voice of speech, as the noise of an host: when they stood, they let down their wings.**
> **1:25 and there was a voice from the firmament that [was] over their heads, when they stood, [and] had let down their wings. EZEKIEL**

Here again Ezekiel applies the words "when they **went**" and "when they **stood**". Evidently Ezekiel witnessed these craft landing and taking off on more than one occasion. Moreover, the landings and take offs obviously produced ear piercing sounds emanating from the propulsion systems of the craft.

Note that Ezekiel conveys the fact that he "heard the noise of their wings", However, Ezekiel makes no mention of any radical movement by their wings. This would once again suggest that the wings were fixed upper and lower structural parts of the body. Yet, why would Ezekiel imply that their wings were creating a loud sound?

We need to consider the probability that Ezekiel may have been standing directly in front of the craft when they landed or took off. This might suggest that the loud noise Ezekiel heard was created by the deafening sounds of the whirling rotating center section or "middle" wheel within the undercarriage (**wings**) of the craft.

The middle wheel may rapidly accelerate to high speeds and ear piercing sounds prior to taking off, landing, or preparing the craft for its normal operating flight mode. However, Ezekiel made no mention of the craft producing any sound as they approached him to land. The craft produce a deafening sound only in the process of **actually landing** or **taking off** (powering up or powering down).

UFO Connection

Remarkably, this alternation of noise and silence may also be UFO related. In most close UFO encounters the **hovering** craft is totally silent, other than a low hum or hissing sound. Yet, the craft may actually be producing an ear piercing sound not heard by the witness. Here again the outer electromagnetic field encompassing the craft may actually resolve the issue as to how the craft could maintain their silence condition even while creating such horrendous noise.

The powerful encompassing field totally encases the craft within, thus blocking anything from entering the field from outside the craft. However, by the powerful fields encasing the craft and stopping anything from entering from outside, it would also be encasing and stopping anything from escaping from the inside.

In essence, the craft powering up (taking off) creates a deafening sound while at the same time it starts producing an energy barrier that ultimately impedes the sound from leaving the craft beyond its created shield. Yet when the craft begins powering down (landing) it ultimately loses its shield integrity thus allowing the deafening sound of the middle wheel to pass through the dissipating shield to be heard. (?)

Pilots Prepare to Disembark

For the first time in our analysis we now have confirmation of the fact that the wings did actually move. "**when they <u>stood</u>, they <u>let down</u> their <u>wings</u>**" How can this be, considering I proposed that the wings were stationary or fixed segments covering the body of the craft? This issue can actually be resolved by asking a second and more substantial question.

Obviously, we are examining four metallic disk/wheel shaped craft. Each of the craft possesses not only landing gear (feet), but dome shaped cockpits for aerial navigation. Moreover, the craft and their flight capabilities would imply superior **intelligent** life forms. Evidently, these life forms require flying machines to function within the limitations of this planet.

If in fact the craft and the pilots were traveling from place to place, they must ultimately **<u>land</u>**. That landing would entail the pilot's departure from the craft. Essentially, the craft would require egress location built into the craft, thus allowing the pilot the ability to enter or exit. In essence the craft would have to be equipped with hatch cover doors and/or ramps to allow for easy exit and entrance.

This simple concept would suggest that Ezekiel had misconstrued the wings that were "**<u>let down</u>**" as possible hatch cover doors, or lowered ramps that open into the internal compartments of the craft. This conjecture becomes even more credible when we realize that the wings were not let down **<u>until</u>** the craft had actually landed ("when they stood").

As long as the craft maintained their airborne status, the wings remained stationary. This would suggest that the hatch cover doors or ramps were actually a dislodged part of the undercarriage (**Lower Wings**) that was "let down" **only** after the craft landed (stood still).

Furthermore, it would be reasonable to assume that these flying machines possess more than one hatch cover doorway leading in and out of the craft. This obvious detail becomes even more astonishing when we realize what has occurred because the hatch cover doors were lowered down to the ground ("**they** let **down** their wings"). This revealing sequence of events had now exposed the internal compartments of the four craft. In fact this unveiling had now personally involved the occupancy or pilots of each craft.

If you will observe verse 1:25, you will discover that Ezekiel could actually hear voices coming from the crystal/glass domes (firmament) of each craft. This revealing detail only occurred **after** the four craft lowered their hatch cover doors (wings), exposing the internal compartments of the craft ("**when** they **stood** and let **down** their wings").

Once the compartment doors were open, Ezekiel could hear people talking from inside the craft. The vocal dialogue ("voice") was not only coming from the internal compartments of the craft, but the very cockpit (firmament/dome) itself. Essentially, Ezekiel was overhearing the pilots' conversation, which may pertain to final landing and/or disembarking procedures ("and there was a **voice** from the **firmament** that was **over their heads**").

The Fifth Craft

> **1:26 and above the firmament that [was] over their heads [was] the likeness of a throne, as the appearance of a sapphire stone: and upon the likeness of the throne [was] the likeness as the appearance of a man above upon it.**
> **1:27 and I saw as the colour of amber, as the appearance of fire round about within it, from the appearance of his loins even upward, and from the appearance of his loins even downward, I saw as it were the appearance of fire, and it had brightness round about.**
> **1:28 as the appearance of the bow that is in the cloud in the day of rain, so [was] the appearance of the brightness round about. This [was] the appearance of the likeness of the glory of the lord. And when I saw [it], I fell upon my face, and I heard a voice of one that spake.**
> EZEKIEL

For the first time in our examination of the craft formation we now possess evidence of the mysterious fifth craft. Evidently, the fifth craft was totally undetectable by Ezekiel until the craft formation had actually landed. Essentially, the optical disguise cloaking the fifth craft had diminished due to the craft formation landing (stood) and terminating their propulsion systems.

The Throne

At first glance, one might assume that Ezekiel was actually observing an isolated throne hovering above the heads (firmaments) of the other four craft. Yet, upon closer inspection of the verses, we discover evidence of a much larger machine supporting the throne. In fact, the throne may actually be much more than just a throne (seat/chair).

Quite naturally the word "throne", brings to mind an immaculate chair or seat. Yet, when closely scrutinizing the verses, we can see that the sapphire throne may not actually be a throne, but an elaborate chair containing lit up instrumentation.

This conjecture may also resolve the issue as to why the throne appears to be sitting up "**above**" what seems to be a raised structure supporting the throne. Seemingly, the throne/chair was elevated up to allow encompassing visual observation and possible command over the four wheel constructed craft.

This speculation actually originates from Ezekiels's own wavering uncertainty that the believed throne only possesses the **likeness** thereof. Obviously, Ezekiel, comparing the elaborate chair to a throne, was not quite sure what type of chair he was actually observing. In fact, the same ambiguous particulars were applied to the physical man (Yahweh) sitting in the chair. Ezekiel was quite sure a physical man was sitting on the throne, yet reported no details. This might suggest that Ezekiel could only see a silhouette of the man (Yahweh).

One element appears certain, Ezekiel was genuinely looking at a tangible chair as well as a real man. Essentially, Ezekiel has now enlightened us to the fact that Yahweh (the **living God**) was in the physical form of a man.

Evidently, the chair or throne was centered within the formation. In fact, it would appear that the throne itself was positioned **inside** another structure. This speculation derives from the word "amber" suggesting that the entire throne was **surrounded** by "amber" "round about".

If Ezekiel's previous verses follow true to form, the "amber" girding the throne would be made of the same metallic elements as the four wheel-shaped craft surrounding the throne. In essence, the throne was encircled with a glowing brass or bronze (amber) metallic substructure (craft). Not only was the metallic structure encompassing the glowing throne, but the entire area around the throne was also glowing.

The verses would lead one to believe that the brass structure surrounding the throne as well as the interior was radiating/glowing." and it had brightness round about". However, just what does "round about" actually imply? Round about what?

Evidently, the enveloping bright glow took on the form of a **rainbow (arch)**. "as the **appearance** of the **bow**...so [was] the **appearance** of the brightness **round about**." This might suggest that Yahweh's metallic craft also exhibited a huge crystal **dome** (bow/arch) covering the metallic ("amber") structure "round about".

The domed/bow was brightly lit up. This might suggest that a powerful but colorful energy field was enveloping the exposed dome, thus protecting Yahweh's personal craft, as well as causing the outer circumference of the colorful dome to appear like a rainbow.

This assumption might provide an explanation as to why Ezekiel was unable to totally identify the man (Yahweh) sitting on the throne. The bow-shaped energy shield obscured Ezekiel's vision. Ezekiel was only able to see a silhouette version of the man sitting on the throne in the interior of the craft.

Moreover, this would suggest that the dome covering Yahweh's craft must have been massive. So enormous in fact, that Ezekiel was capable of identifying the entire throne as well as the internally raised structure on which the throne rested.

Yahweh's Personal Craft

Obviously, Yahweh was piloting his own personal craft (chariot). Furthermore, Yahweh's private craft seemed to resemble the other four craft, apart from having the massive dome capping the craft. Yet, more significantly we find that Yahweh's private craft was huddled within the protective bounds of the other four craft.

Evidently, the fifth craft was positioned, "**above** the firmament (dome) that was over their **heads**". This would imply that the fifth craft was actually located in the center of the other four craft just above their domed cockpits.

As we have already discovered, there are four wheel-shaped craft coupled together. The four craft being joined at the hip actually leave a huge void located within the center of the formation. Obviously the formation cavity is large enough for another craft to easily position itself not only **inside** the basin area, but also magnetically attaching itself to the other four craft as a means of support.

In essence, Yahweh's personal craft is literally "**riding**" on top of the other four craft/chariots. This would place the dome (firmament) of Yahweh's personal craft just **above** the domes of his four escort craft.

> **7:9…his throne [was like] the fiery flame, [and] his wheels [as] burning fire.**
> **DANIEL**
>
> **3:8…thou didst ride upon thine horses [and] thy chariots of salvation?**
> **HABAKKUK**
>
> **24:1…How many chariots has the Holy One, blessed be he? He has the chariots of the cherubim, as it is written, "He mounted a cherub and flew."**
> **24:3 He has the chariots of swift cloud, as it is written, "See! The lord comes riding a swift cloud."**
> **24:15 He has the chariots of the creatures, as it is written," The creatures ran and returned"-they run by permission and return by permission for the Sekinah is above their heads.**
> **24:16 He has the chariots of the wheels, as it is written, "Go in between the wheels."**
> **24:17 He has the chariots of the swift cherub, as it is written, "Riding upon a swift cherub." When he rides upon the swift cherub, between placing one foot on its back and placing the other foot on it, he perceives 18,000 worlds at a glance;…**
> **22:13…The Sekinah rest upon their backs,…Their hands are under their wings and their feet are cover by their wings,…The brilliance of the Sekinah is on their contenances, and the Sekinah rest upon their backs.**
> **APPENDIX TO 3 ENOCH (PSEU.)**
>
> **The [cheru]bim prostrate themselves before him and bless. As they rise, a whispered divine voice [is heard], and there is a roar of praise. When they drop their wings, there is a [whispere]d divine voice. The cherubim bless the image of the throne-chariot above the firmament, and they praise [the**

majes]ty of the luminous firmament beneath his seat of glory. When the Wheels advance, angels of holiness come and go. From between his glorious wheels there is as it were a fiery vision of most holy spirits. About them, the appearance of rivulets of fire in the likeness of gleaming brass, and a work of...radiance in many-colored glory, marvelous pigments, clearly mingled. The spirits of the living 'gods' move perpetually with the glory of the marvellous chariot(s). The whispered voice of blessing accompanies the roar of their advance, and they praise the Holy One on their way of return. When they ascend, they ascend marvellously, and when they settle they stand still. THE DEAD SEA SCROLLS/SONGS FOR THE HOLOCAUST OF THE SABBATH 4Q405 20 ii 21-22

Here again, we find the word chariots, meaning more than one. Yet, Yahweh's "Brass" chariot/craft is actually "riding" on top of the other four charriots/craft. Note that the chariots ("chariots of wheels/creatures") are refereed to as "**Cherubim**". Essentially, the four craft formation is actually titled or named "Cherubim". The fifth craft "**throne-chariot**" "the **Sekinah**" is centrally positioned within the basin of the Cherubim (four craft) just above their "**luminous**" domes (firmament).

Yahweh's Four Escorting Pilots

For the first time in our analysis of the wheels of Ezekiel, we now possess evidence of a possible elite crew piloting the "cherubim" craft formation. Obviously the four high ranking pilots (Cherubs) were referred to as "angels": "**when the wheels advance, angels of holiness come and go**". In fact, the four escorting angels (Cherubs) were actually identified as "living gods": "**the spirits of the living 'gods' move perpetually with the glory of the marvelous chariot(s)**". Or in simpler terms, the four pilots of these unique craft were physical living beings, four living beings that navigated the "chariots" (Cherubims) on which Yahweh's personal craft (Sekinah) "rides" "**thou didst ride upon thine horses** [and] **thy chariots of salvation?**". Moreover, these four sovereign pilots (**The Four Horsemen**) actually possess designated names.

28:1...Above all these are four great princes called Watchers and holy ones, high honored, terrible, beloved, wonderful, noble, and greater than all the celestials, and among all the ministers there in none equal to them, for each of them singly is a match for all the others together.

28:2 Their abode is opposite the throne of glory, and their station is facing the Holy One, blessed be he, so that the splendor of their abode resembles the splendor of the throne of glory, and the brilliance of their image is as the brilliance of the Sekinah.
28:3 They receive glory from the glory of the Almighty, and are praised with the praise of the Sekinah.
39:1...blessed be he, on the four sides of the abode of his glorious Sekinah.
39:2 The angels of the host, the fiery ministers, the ophanim of power, the cherubim of the Sekinah, the holy creatures,...the cohorts of devouring fire, the ranks of firebrands, the host of flame, the holy princes, crowned with crowns, robed with royalty, covered with glory, girded with beauty, girt with magnificence. 3 ENOCH
(PSEU.)
2. On the four wings likewise of the Lord of spirits, on the four sides, I perceived others, besides those who were standing before him. Their names too, I know; because the angel, who proceeded with me, declared them to me, discovering to me every secret thing.
3. Then I heard the voice of those upon the four sides magnifying the Lord of glory.
4. The first voice blessed the Lord of spirits for ever and for ever.
5. The second voice I heard blessed the elect One, and the elect who suffer on account of the Lord of spirits.
6. The third voice I heard petitioning and praying for those who dwell upon earth, and supplicate the name of the Lord of spirits.
7. The fourth voice I heard expelling the impious angels, and prohibiting them from entering into presence of the Lord of spirits, to prefer accusations against the inhabitants of the earth.
8. After this I besought the angel of peace, who proceeded with me, to explain all that was concealed. I said to him, Who are those whom I have seen on the four sides, and whose word I have heard and written down? He replied, The first is the merciful, the patient, the holy Michael.
9. The second is he who presides over every suffering and every affiction of the sons of men, the holy Raphael. The third, who presides over all that is powerful, is Gabriel. And the fourth, who presides over repentance, and the hope of those who will inherit eternal life, is Phanuel. These are the

> **four angels of the most high God, and their four voices, which at that time I heard.**
>
> CHAP. XL.
>
> **16. The Ancient of days came with Michael and Gabriel, Raphael and Phanuel, with thousands of thousands, and myriads of myriads, which could not be numbered.**
>
> CHAP. LXX.
>
> BOOK OF ENOCH

This is the ultimate security team, to pilot and escort the craft formation (Cherubim) supporting Yahweh's personal craft ("the **Sekinah**"/"throne-c**hariot**"). In fact, these five remarkable craft are actually coupled together to form a powerful flying arsenal of high tech weaponry against anyone or anything endeavoring to inflict aggression against Yahweh.

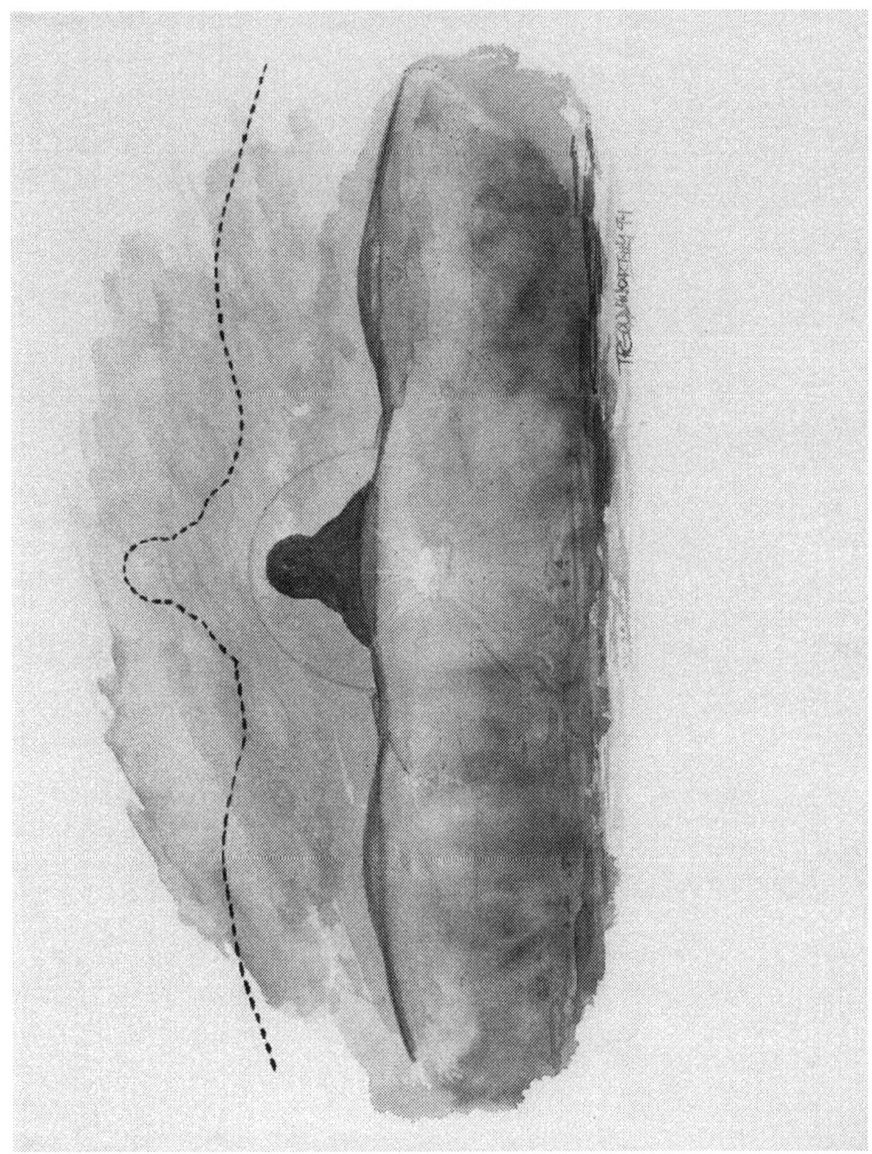

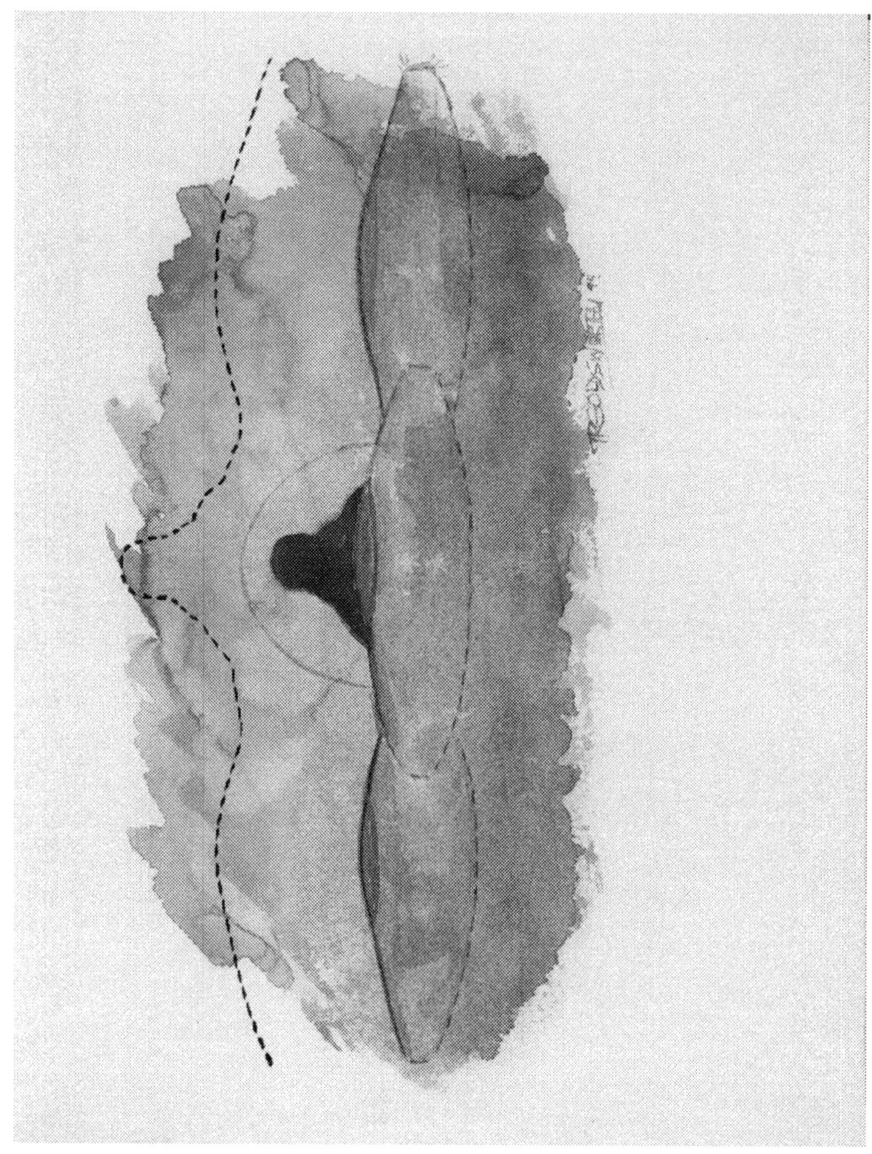

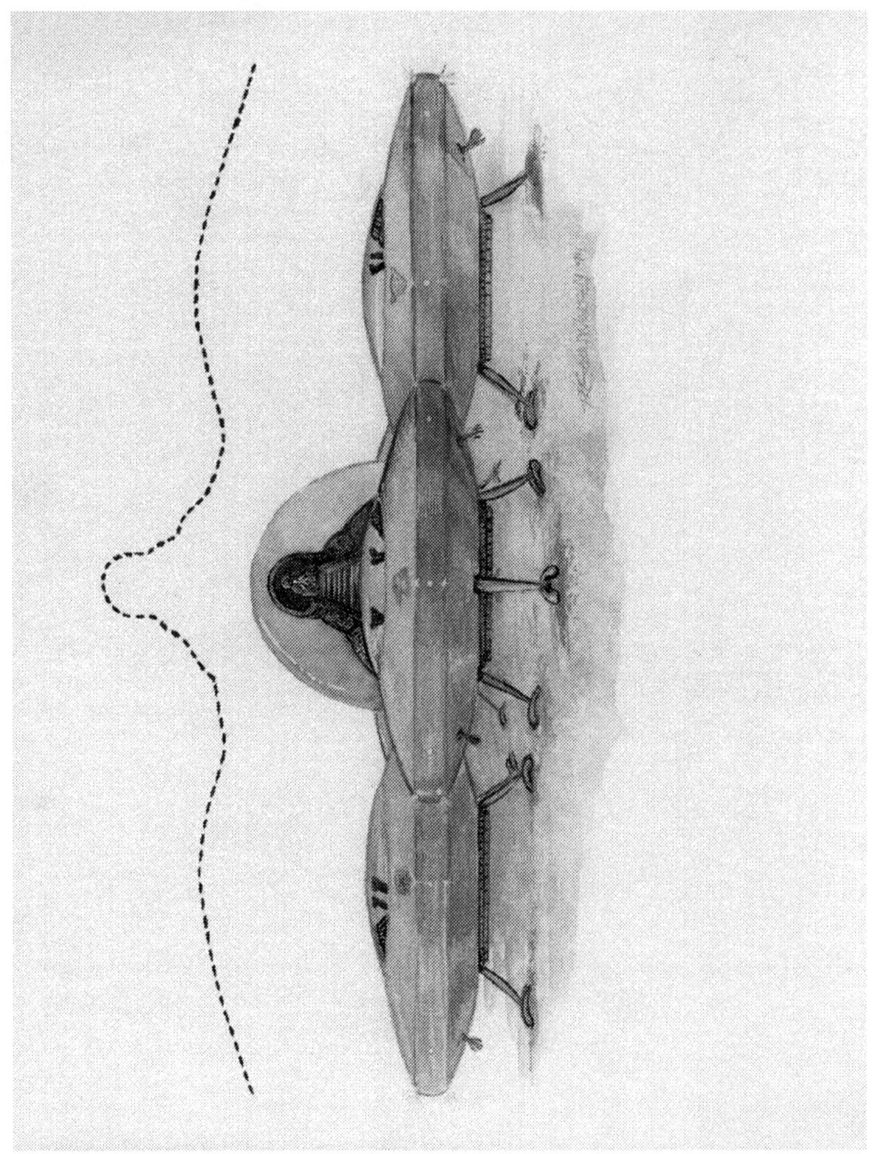

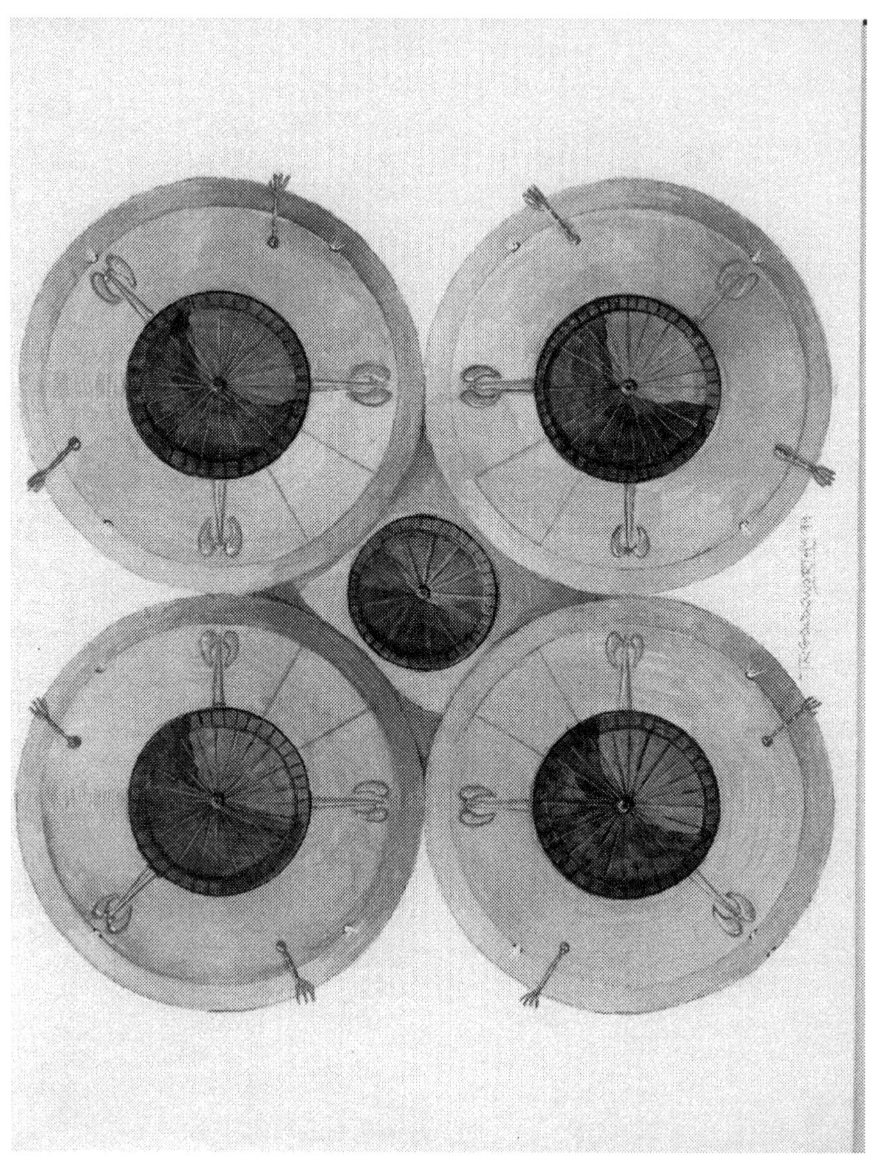

Hand Shaped Devices

"Their hands are under their wings".

As we have already discovered, each of the four craft support "hand" shaped devices or multifaceted weapons mounted within their undercarriage ("under their wings").

> How many winds blow from under the wings of the cherubim? From there the hovering wind blows... "God's wind hovered over the water." From there the strong wind blows,..." From there the east wind blows,... "The east wind brought the locusts." From there the wind of quails blows,... "A wind came from the Lord and it drove quails in."...From there the wind of earthquake blows,...From there the wind of YHWH blows,..."He carried me away by the wind of the Lord and set me down."...Satan stands among these winds, for there is no storm wind that is not sent by Satan. All these winds blow only from beneath the wings of the cherubim...
>
> APPENDIX TO 3 ENOCH 23:1-16
>
> 22:9 On his right hand a flame blazes; on his left hand fire burns;...
>
> 3 ENOCH
>
> 6:14 So will I stretch out my hand upon them, and make the land desolate, yea, more desolate than the wilderness toward Diblath, in all their habitations: and they shall know that I [am] the LORD.
>
> EZEKIEL
>
> 19:16 In that day shall Egypt be like unto women: and it shall be afraid and fear because of the shaking of the hand of the LORD of hosts, which he shaketh over it.
>
> ISAIAH
>
> 3:4 And [his] brightness was as the light; he had horns [coming] out of his hand: and there [was] the hiding of his power.
>
> HABAKKUK

The multifaceted device commands highly advanced laser technology, while at the same time demonstrating astonishing matter maneuvering (force field/Wind) feats, including bodily elevating humans. Moreover, the verses establish the fact that **the same devices and powers are employed by the fallen angels (Satan)**. It's extremely important for the reader to **remember** this revealing detail.

Evidently the "stretched out" device embodies finger ("horns") like appendages protruding out of what appears to be a solid object (hand) secured to a telescopic arm capable of maneuvering in numerous directions. Essentially the "stretched out" device actually resembled, or was anciently equated to as a hand. Clearly, craft, weapons and devices of such superior design would require constant cleaning and maintenance to function properly.

Craft Maintenance

> **15:1…When the Holy One, blessed be he, took me to serve the throne of glory, the wheels of the chariot and all the needs of the Sekinah,…**
> **39:1…blessed be he, on the four sides of the abode of his glorious Sekinah.**
> **39:2 The angels of the host, the fiery ministers, the ophanim of power, the cherubim of the Sekinah, the holy creatures,…**
> **25:5 Why is his name called Opanniel? Because he is appointed to tend the ophanim, and the ophanim are entrusted to his keeping. Every day he stands over them and tends them and beautifies them: he praises and arranges their running; he polishes their platforms; he adorns their compartments; he makes their turnings smooth, and cleans their seats. Early and late, day and night, he tends them, so as to increase their beauty, to magnify their majesty, and to make them swift in the praise of their Creator.**
> 3 ENOCH (PSEU.)

Are we to believe that a ghost or invisible spirit requires a physical seat to sit upon, "seats" that need to be cleaned at regular intervals? Plainly, we are examining the requirements of physical beings, humanoid entities necessitating tangible "platforms" to stand upon, platforms that need to be periodically polished, internal "compartments" that require personal attention and cleaning.

The center rotating sections ("middle wheels"), need to routinely be calibrated ("arrange their running"), lubricated and cleaned to "make their **turnings** smooth". Evidently, the wheel shaped craft need occasional maintenance "to make them swift". The craft needs to be washed occasionally to maintain their "beauty" in the presence of Yahweh and his personal craft ("the **Sekinah**").

Yahweh Enlist Ezekiels' Services

At this point, the supreme question would be, why would Yahweh and his escorts single out terrified Ezekiel, and for what vital purpose.

> 1:28...This [was] the appearance of the likeness of the glory of the lord. And when I saw [it], I fell upon my face, and I heard a voice of one that spake.
>
> 2:1 And he said unto me, Son of man, stand upon thy feet, and I will speak unto thee.
>
> 2:2 And the spirit entered into me when he spake unto me, and set me upon my feet, that I heard him that spake unto me.
>
> 2:3 and he said unto me, son of man, I send thee to the children of Israel, to a rebellious nation that hath rebelled against me: they and their fathers have transgressed against me, [even] unto this very day.
>
> 2:8 but thou, son of man, hear what I say unto thee; be not thou rebellious like that rebellious house: open thy mouth, and eat that I give thee.
>
> 2:9 and when I looked, behold, an hand [was] sent unto me; and, lo, a roll of a book [was] therein;
>
> 2:10 and he spread it before me; and it [was] written within and without: and [there was] written therein lamentations, and mourning, and woe.
>
> 3:1 moreover he said unto me, son of man, eat that thou findest; eat this roll, and go speak unto the house of Israel.
>
> 3:2 so I opened my mouth, and he caused me to eat that roll.
>
> 3:3 and he said unto me, son of man, cause thy belly to eat, and fill thy bowels with this roll that I give thee. Then did I eat [it]; and it was in my mouth as honey for sweetness.
>
> 3:4 and he said unto me, son of man, go, get thee unto the house of Israel, and speak with my words unto them.
>
> EZEKIEL

Yahweh's obvious anger was once again directed towards his own chosen people. We shall continue to discover that the rebellious Israelites consistently transgressed against Yahweh. This was the very motivation behind not only the manuscript that Ezekiel had now been given, but the very enlistment of Ezekiel as a Prophet. Essentially, Yahweh chose Ezekiel to try and reinstate his chosen people now under the covert control of the fallen angels (other gods).

Ezekiel Elevated by the Hand Shaped Device

Before we analyze Yahweh's horrendous reprisal against his own people, it's significant that we once again examine the hand-shaped device. In scrutinizing the verses, one might not easily recognize the fact that the hand-shaped device was utilized twice. Obviously the device handed Ezekiel the book, a puzzling feat, seeing how the device is located underneath the **outside** of the craft, whereas the book itself appears to have originated from **inside** the craft.

Evidently, the device, being mechanical in nature, was operated from inside the craft. This would suggest that the devices could be retracted into the internal compartments of the craft. Seemingly, objects from inside the craft could actually be fastened to the device and transported outside without anyone leaving the craft. Moreover, objects outside the craft could be picked up and taken inside the craft without anyone exiting the craft. The perfect mechanical device for performing a multitude of missions on various planets, as well as outer space.

However, what about the second obscure operation by the device? The second application is not easily recognized due to the fact that the name of the device was changed. If the reader will recall, Ezekiel educated us to the fact that the words power and "spirit" were one and the same when it came to the animated life force or energy of the four craft. The very word "spirit" actually validated this conjecture, seeing how the word "**spirit**" is defined as animation, vigor, or **force** perpetuated by different forms of **power/energy**.

Essentially, Ezekiel having fallen upon the ground was actually bodily lifted up off the ground and "**set**" on his feet by the **power** (**spirit**) of the hand shaped device. This speculation is further confirmed in the following verses.

> **3:12 Then the spirit took me up, and I heard behind me a voice of a great rushing, [saying], Blessed [be] the glory of the LORD from his place.**
>
> **3:13 [I heard] also the noise of the wings of the living creatures that touched one another, and the noise of the wheels over against them, and a noise of a great rushing.**
>
> **3:14 So the spirit lifted me up, and took me away, and I went in bitterness, in the heat of my spirit; but the hand of the LORD was strong upon me.**

> **3:15 Then I came to them of the captivity at Telabib, that dwelt by the river of Chebar, and I sat where they sat, and remained there astonished among them seven days.**
> **EZEKIEL**

Yahweh, having now addressed Ezekiel with the book and his personal mandates, prepared to leave the area. In doing so, Ezekiel could now hear the craft formation powering up their propulsion systems to take off.

For the first time in our survey of the craft formation, we now possess confirmation of the "middle" wheel actually creating a sound. As mentioned before, it would appear that the middle wheel was turning at a high rate of speed, subsequently generating the "**rushing**" power and "noise" required by the craft for flight

You will also note that, for the first time in Ezekiel's description of the formation, they are no longer "joined one to another" but rather "**touching**" one another". This would once again confirm the fact that there were five **separate** craft.

Evidently, the craft formation had now become airborne. However, this time it had taken on a passenger, a passenger who was not allowed inside the craft. Clearly, frightened Ezekiel was being aerially towed along with the formation. Obviously, the "**spirit**" that aerially hoisted Ezekiel off the ground was in fact the hand shaped device. "the **hand** of the Lord was **strong upon me**".

Ezekiel could actually detect the powerful force field ("spirit") exerted upon his body from the device as he was lifted up into midair. Its no wonder Ezekiel "went in bitterness" considering the obvious fear created by the inconceivable feat. The sequence of events ended with Ezekiel being bodily transported to another location where he was gently lowered back down to the ground. However, Yahweh had just begun to engage Ezekiel's services.

> **3:16 And it came to pass at the end of seven days, that the word of the LORD came unto me, saying,**
> **3:17 Son of man, I have made thee a watchman unto the house of Israel: therefore hear the word at my mouth, and give them warning from me.**
> **3:22 And the hand of the LORD was there upon me; and he said unto me, Arise, go forth into the plain, and I will there talk with thee.**
> **3:23 Then I arose, and went forth into the plain: and, behold, the glory of the LORD stood there, as the glory which I saw by the river of Chebar: and I fell on my face. EZEKIEL**

One might envision that an angelic messenger ("the word") was sent to Ezekiel asking him to walk into the plains to meet with Yahweh. However, this assumption may be far from the truth, seeing how the hand-shaped device had once again made its sudden appearance at the same time and place as the messenger: "and the **hand** of the LORD **was there** upon me".

Obviously, the verses conceal a discrepancy in reference to the craft formation. This speculation is based on the fact that Ezekiel was confronted with a single craft possessing a hand-shaped device that transported him to a private location in the "plains" where Yahweh's craft formation "stood". Clearly, Yahweh's craft formation was **already** at the landing site ("stood") in the plains **before** Ezekiel actually got there. This would indicate the presences of a **sixth** unknown craft and pilot that transported Ezekiel to Yahweh's awaiting craft formation.

"the word" that came to Ezekiel was from the individual piloting the craft equipped with the hand-shaped device. The pilot operating the device advised Ezekiel that once again he had to "**arise**" and go forth into the plains, thus preparing fearful Ezekiel for a second bodily ascension.

Evidently, Yahweh's visit was to once again educated Ezekiel about Israel's iniquitous ways. As Yahweh's prophet, he was to "warn" and convey to the people of Israel their unacceptable demeanor, and the repercussions that will follow in the light thereof. Ultimately Israel's disloyalty triggered Yahweh's horrendous retaliation as Ezekiel helplessly stood by and watched. Yet, here again, we are about to discover that Israel's rebellious and traitorous behavior derived from one source, the fallen angels (Satan).

> **8:1 And it came to pass in the sixth year, in the sixth [month], in the fifth [day] of the month, [as] I sat in mine house, and the elders of Judah sat before me, that the hand of the Lord GOD fell there upon me.**
>
> **8:2 Then I beheld, and lo a likeness as the appearance of fire: from the appearance of his loins even downward, fire; and from his loins even upward, as the appearance of brightness, as the colour of amber.**
>
> **8:3 And he put forth the form of an hand, and took me by a lock of mine head; and the spirit lifted me up between the earth and the heaven, and brought me in the visions of God to Jerusalem, to the door of the inner gate that looketh toward the north; where [was] the seat of the image of jealousy, which provoketh to jealousy.**

8:4 And, behold, the glory of the God of Israel [was] there, according to the vision that I saw in the plain.
EZEKIEL

Here again, the hand shaped device aerially transported Ezekiel to another location where Yahweh's craft formation was **already** waiting. This would once again imply that mysterious sixth craft was involved in Ezekiels transportation to Yahweh's given location.

Remarkably, the verses actually elaborate on the energy field (spirit) being utilized to elevate Ezekiel off the ground "between the earth and heaven". Clearly, Ezekiel detected a strong but careful force applied to his "head" ("by a lock of my head"). A logical deduction considering the force originated from overhead.

Obviously, the energy field coming from up above would naturally exert more sudden pressure upon Ezekiel's unsuspecting head than his whole body. Moreover, the energy field would naturally come into contact with Ezekiel's head before his body. Here again, we find a typical levitating maneuver found within the chronicles of UFOlogy.

UFO Connection

As mentioned in the beginning of this book, there are numerous UFO reports involving alien entities, as well as humans that were mysteriously elevated or lowered from hovering craft. Most of these **nocturnal** uplifting incidents are associated with what is described to be beams of light emanating from the mysterious craft. The beams of light are believed to be a type of directional force field, tractor beam, or focused matter maneuvering energy field.

Seemingly, these manipulative beams of energy have been employed during the daylight hours, but were never actually observed by the witnesses. This invisible detail might imply that the rays of the Sun camouflaged or obscure the actual levitating beams during the day, where during the darkness of night the beam becomes noticeably visible.

It's significant to remember that these phenomenal mechanisms could literally be utilized to build or fabricate other mechanisms. In fact the hand fashioned devices are probably quite capable of constructing entire cities as well as destroying them without ever lifting a hand ("**without hands**"). No pun intended! Yet, the limitations of these extraordinary devices would be endless to say the least.

Link to Daniel

Notably, the verses identify a contradiction in reference to the craft formation. Clearly, Ezekiel had been physically picked up by what appeared to be a **single metallic craft**. This factor is easily recognized by not only the description of the craft, but the single pilot identified by the word "his".

Ezekiel recognized that the body of the metallic (amber) craft began at the man's loins or lap. Essentially, the pilot was sitting down inside the craft, suggesting a bright dome was capping the cockpit. This allowed Ezekiel to peer through the dome and actually see the man (pilot). This detailed visitation entails the very same type of visual ("**vision**") observation found in the Book of Daniel.

> 10:4 And in the four and twentieth day of the first month, as I was by the side of the great river, which [is] Hiddekel;
> 10:5 Then I lifted up mine eyes, and looked, and behold a certain man clothed in linen, whose loins [were] girded with fine gold of Uphaz:
> 10:6 His body also [was] like the beryl, and his face as the appearance of lightning, and his eyes as lamps of fire, and his arms and his feet like in colour to polished brass, and the voice of his words like the voice of a multitude.
> 10:7 And I Daniel alone saw the vision: for the men that were with me saw not the vision; but a great quaking fell upon them, so that they fled to hide themselves.
> 10:8 Therefore I was left alone, and saw this great vision, and there remained no strength in me: for my comeliness was turned in me into corruption, and I retained no strength.
> 10:9 Yet heard I the voice of his words: and when I heard the voice of his words, then was I in a deep sleep on my face, and my face toward the ground.
> 10:10 And, behold, an hand touched me, which set me upon my knees and [upon] the palms of my hands.
> 12:5 Then I Daniel looked, and, behold, there stood other two, the one on this side of the bank of the river, and the other on that side of the bank of the river.
> 12:6 And [one] said to the man clothed in linen, which [was] upon the waters of the river, How long [shall it be to] the end of these wonders?

12:7 And I heard the man clothed in linen, which [was] upon the waters of the river, when he held up his right hand and his left hand unto heaven, and sware by him that liveth for ever that [it shall be] for a time, times, and an half; and when he shall have accomplished to scatter the power of the holy people, all these [things] shall be finished.
DANIEL

Daniel's shocking (vision) observation began with only one craft, yet ended with three separate craft in three dissimilar locations. Seemingly, the "**man** clothed in linen" was in a craft hovering "upon the waters of the river". The man was ("**girded**") surrounded by a "body" or metallic structure identified as "polished brass" (metal).

The glowing structure possessed "eyes" suggesting the very same port holes and/or exterior lighting facilities (lamps) as seen by Ezekiel. The metallic craft displayed landing gear ("feet"), as well as mechanical "arms". Were there are "arms" there are "hands".

The craft as well as all the external tools and/or mechanical mechanisms were made out of "brass". The craft even possessed what appears to be a public address system (PA). The external public address system broadcast the internal voice of the pilot outside the craft, "like the **voice** of a multitude".

Evidently, Daniel was observing a **single** craft hovering just above the river. The wheel ("**girded**") shaped craft appeared to be capped with a dome shaped structure, thus allowing Daniel visual observation of the man sitting inside the craft from his "loins" upward. Yet, from his "loins" downward, the brass/beryl craft hid the remaining parts of his body. Notably, the "hand" shaped device was once again employed to pick the body of Daniel up off the ground and gently "**set**" him on his hands and knees.

Obviously, there were three craft positioned in three different locations. All three craft were not joined together or even touching. This would indicate that three separate craft possessed their own individual propulsion systems, thus explaining their diverse locations.

The principal craft appears to be hovering over the river itself, while the other two craft had landed ("there stood") or were possibly hovering just above the bank on opposite sides of the river. This would place one of the hovering or landed craft on the same bank with Daniel.

Evidently, the three isolated craft had come **alone**. In fact, Yahweh, and his four escorting craft were nowhere in sight. Essentially, Yahweh commands many such scout, or surveillance craft, many of which appear to resemble the very same craft found in Yahweh's craft formation, including their weapons and devices.

A Second Craft Formation

Remarkably, we are about to discover that Daniel's detailed sighting will assist us in unraveling the existence of a **second** craft formation. The **two** craft formations consist of ten separate craft accommodating a total of fifteen men, ten of whom are pilots (cherubs). Notably, each of the pilots will be easily recognized by their revealing attire.

Note what the pilot of the craft hovering over the river was wearing: "**man** clothed in linen". This "**man**" was not only the pilot of the craft, but a **cherub.** This significant clue will actually help us to identify all the pilots (cherubs) of the **two** separate craft formations (Cherubim).

> **8:3 And he put forth the form of an hand, and took me by a lock of mine head; and the spirit lifted me up between the earth and the heaven, and brought me in the visions of God to Jerusalem, to the door of the inner gate that looketh toward the north; where [was] the seat of the image of jealousy, which provoketh to jealousy.**
> **8:4 And, behold, the glory of the God of Israel [was] there, according to the vision that I saw in the plain.**
> EZEKIEL

Let's first establish the fact that Ezekiel had been bodily elevated by a single craft and pilot. This detail is easily established by the word "he". However, a wealth of physical activity appears to have taken place from the moment Ezekiel was lifted up off the ground to the time he was actually transported to Yahweh's **awaiting** craft formation. This brief activity would suggest that more than one craft was involved in Ezekiel's transportation to Yahweh's given location.

This revealing detail is confirmed by the fact that Ezekiel was transported to Yahweh **"in visions of God to Jerusalem."** Essentially, Ezekiel was not aerially transported by a single craft but rather many craft ("**visions**").

This conjecture stems from Daniel's own words, seeing how Daniel implied that the single craft hovering over the river was in fact a **single** "**vision**". This would imply that numerous craft could be refereed to as "**visions**".

Evidently, Ezekiel was identifying more than one craft (**visions**), subsequent to his extraction from the surface of the ground by a single craft ("**he**").

In essence, Ezekiel was identifying both events. Ezekiel not only observed the single craft ("he") that aerially elevated him, but he appears to have also distinguished the other craft involved.

Seemingly Ezekiel was observing the entire event unfold from **outside** the craft. Simply put, a single craft elevated Ezekiel up off the ground, a single craft which may have been part of another craft formation ("**visions**") that was already airborne.

Yahweh's Wrath

Before we elaborate on the second company of craft, we need to inquire as to the motivation behind such a complex sighting. Clearly, the motive embraces strong emotions of violent "**jealousy**".

> **Jealousy :** ***suspicious of a rival or of one believed to enjoy an advantage.***

Seeing how Yahweh had the power to liquidate any human opposition, only one powerful opponent would fit this envious analogue. "**Other gods**"/**Satan**/Fallen Angels (rival/adversary). The other gods/fallen angels had not only continued to covertly manipulate the surrounding nations, but in time beguiled the very nation of Israel. The fallen angels ultimately demoralized Israel to the point of worshiping idols that actually "portray", depict and "**image**" the very adversary/rival (Satan/"his imagery"), that Yahweh detested.

Israel Worships the Fallen Angels

> **8:5 Then said he unto me, Son of man, lift up thine eyes now the way toward the north. So I lifted up mine eyes the way toward the north, and behold northward at the gate of the altar this image of jealousy in the entry.**
>
> **8:6 He said furthermore unto me, Son of man, seest thou what they do? [even] the great abominations that the house of Israel committeth here, that I should go far off from my sanctuary? but turn thee yet again, [and] thou shalt see greater abominations.**
>
> **8:7 And he brought me to the door of the court; and when I looked, behold a hole in the wall.**
>
> **8:8 Then said he unto me, Son of man, dig now in the wall: and when I had digged in the wall, behold a door.**

8:9 And he said unto me, Go in, and behold the wicked abominations that they do here.
8:10 So I went in and saw; and behold every form of creeping things, and abominable beasts, and all the idols of the house of Israel, portrayed upon the wall round about.
8:11 And there stood before them seventy men of the ancients of the house of Israel, and in the midst of them stood Jaazaniah the son of Shaphan, with every man his censer in his hand; and a thick cloud of incense went up.
8:12 Then said he unto me, Son of man, hast thou seen what the ancients of the house of Israel do in the dark, every man in the chambers of his imagery? for they say, The LORD seeth us not; the LORD hath forsaken the earth.
8:13 He said also unto me, Turn thee yet again, [and] thou shalt see greater abominations that they do.
8:14 Then he brought me to the door of the gate of the LORD'S house which [was] toward the north; and, behold, there sat women weeping for Tammuz.
8:15 Then said he unto me, Hast thou seen [this], O son of man turn thee yet again, [and] thou shalt see greater abominations than these.
8:16 And he brought me into the inner court of the LORD'S house, and, behold, at the door of the temple of the LORD, between the porch and the altar, [were] about five and twenty men, with their backs toward the temple of the LORD, and their faces toward the east; and they worshipped the sun toward the east.
8:18 Therefore will I also deal in fury: mine eye shall not spare, neither will I have pity: and though they cry in mine ears with a loud voice, [yet] will I not hear them.

EZEKIEL

Satan and his fallen angels were not only very much alive, but still stealthily manipulating the superstitious populace of the ancient world. This mass beguiling of the populations of the planet was once again aimed at debasing everything that the kingdom of heaven has worked so diligently for. At first glance, one may not recognize the deceptive mask worn by the fallen angels. Yet, upon closer scrutiny, Satan and his fallen angels are incapable of cloaking their deceiving identity.

Let's first establish the fact that there was an idolized object ("image') at the very entrance of Yahweh's Temple. Moreover, the image was obviously the root of Yahweh's enraged jealousy. In fact, verse 8:12 would go so far as to suggest a gender relating to the unknown image "**his imagery**".

This could be quite confusing, seeing how the verse could delude one into believing that the image was a direct reference to the seventy men and their private hidden chambers. Yet, the physical "**image**" is exactly what it is defined as.

> **Image:**"*likeness, a representation of, idea, concept, perception, delineation, or reflection of something else in which it portrays*".

Obviously the image and/or idols were identifying something or someone else. In this particular case, that someone else would be the other gods (Satan/fallen angels). Evidently, the idols and unknown image were not only quite real, but allegorically represented other gods that were being secretly idolized to the degree of burning incense. This was the same holy ritual required by Yahweh.

Note verse 8:14, the women were weeping for "Tammuz". Other than being a Mesopotamian fertility god, Tammuz (Dumu-zi) was also known as the brother and lover of Ishtar. Ishtar was the chief Babylonian goddess, boasting a strong relationship to the celebrated Astarte (Queen of the Stars/the **morning star** of heaven/the **Sun**). Simply put, other gods/fallen angels.

However, more notable would be the god allegorically shrouded in verse 8:16. This brightly obscured underworld figure denotes a dark and sinister leader, a rebellious chieftain that instigated the ultimate demise of the new world and its created inhabitancy.

Essentially, twenty-five men were worshiping the Sun towards the **East,** thus turning their back towards Yahweh's temple. In essence, the twenty-five men had turned their backs on Yahweh, substituting their positions and idolization with another god that they were now worshiping towards the **East.**

Quite naturally, one might wonder what type of god could the twenty-five men be idolizing by worshiping the Sun? Yet, this abominable subterranean god is camouflaged by his symbolic reputation. That notoriety actually connects him to the Sun, as well as the East.

> **Lucifer—Satan** *Bearer of light, Son of Morning, Dragon of Dawn, Lord of light, Prince of the power of air, both the Evening and Morning Star (SUN), seen as the dying and reborn light of the air. Dark Prince also named Arsiel/Apollyon (Black Sun), the negative sun of anti-matter which lies within the bottomless pit (The Underworld) better known as the fallen Greek Sun*

God, King of the Demonic Locusts. The bringer of light, the morning Star, the Star which heralds the rising ***Sun*** *in the* ***East.***

In essence, the twenty-five men turned their backs on Yahweh to worship Satan and the fallen angels. This horrendous abomination quickly enraged Yahweh's jealous anger towards his own people. Simply put, Israel's traitorous actions justified and motivated Yahweh's merciless slaughter of numerous men, women and children.

However, before we analyze what might be considered an envious but horrifying rampage of death, we need to reexamine the verses to assemble the needed clues to complete the forth coming chain of events. This will require that the reader closely examine the furnished drawing of the believed Temple of God.

Let's first establish the fact that Ezekiel was brought to Yahweh's **awaiting** craft formation at the temple of Jerusalem by numerous craft (**visions**). This arrival began Ezekiel's observation at the door of the inner gate which faces north. This would indicate that Ezekiel's first location was at the inner court gate on the **South** side of the temple.

> **8:4 And, behold, the glory of the God of Israel [was] there, according to the vision that I saw in the plain.**

Ezekiel was looking towards the **North** when he observed Yahweh's landed ("stood") craft formation on the right side of the Temple "looketh towards the North". This would place Yahweh's craft formation on the **North** side of the temple **inside** the inner court, which can be easily observed from the South side where Ezekiel was standing.

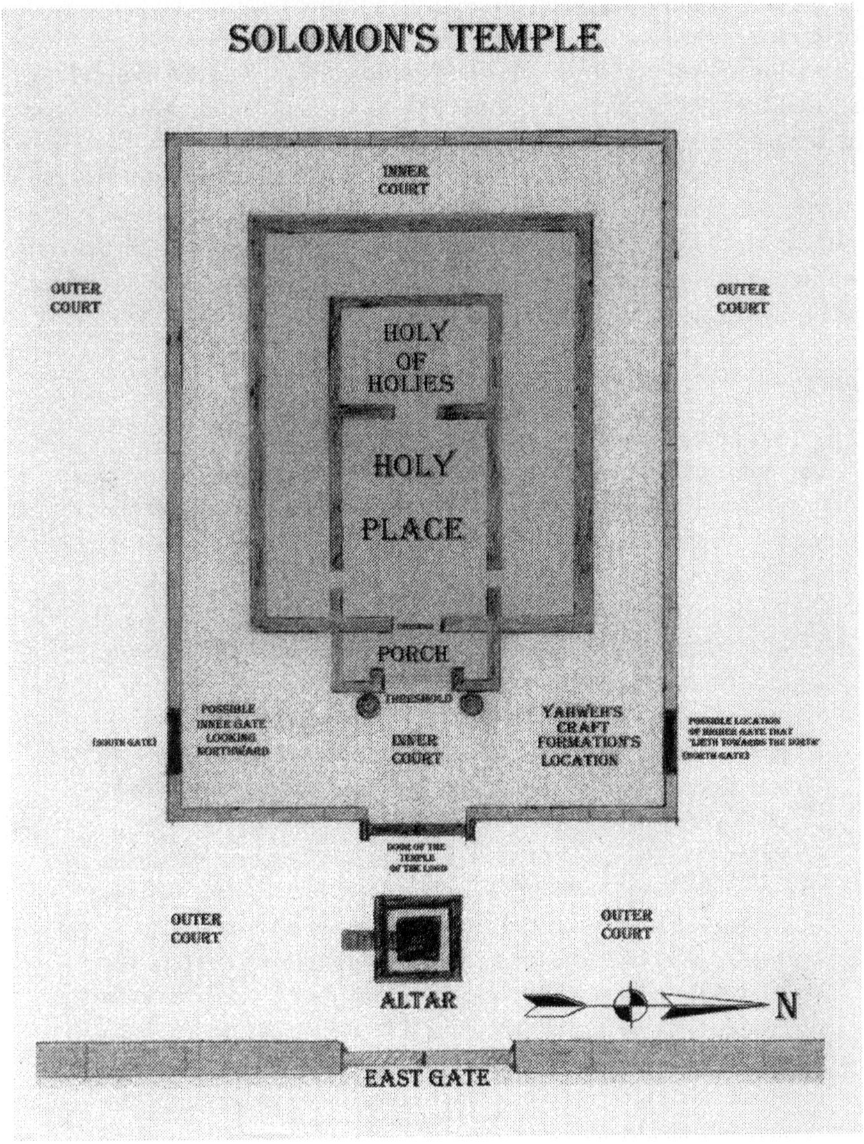

SOLOMON'S TEMPLE

INNER COURT

OUTER COURT

OUTER COURT

HOLY OF HOLIES

HOLY PLACE

PORCH

THRESHOLD

(SOUTH GATE)

POSSIBLE INNER GATE LOOKING NORTHWARD

INNER COURT

YAHWEH'S CRAFT FORMATION'S LOCATION

POSSIBLE LOCATION OF HIGHER GATE THAT "LIETH TOWARD THE NORTH"

(NORTH GATE)

DOOR OF THE TEMPLE OF THE LORD

OUTER COURT

OUTER COURT

ALTAR

N

EAST GATE

Note that each time Ezekiel proceeds to another location, he advances in a **Northward** direction, thus getting closer and closer to Yahweh's craft formation positioned on the North side of the temple. However, keep in mind it was "he" that brought Ezekiel to the inner gate to see Yahweh and his craft formation now landed on the North side of the temple.

Obviously "he" was not Yahweh or his craft formation, but rather an escort that appears to be directing Ezekiel to different locations around the temple grounds. Moreover, ("he") appears to be doing all the talking. Furthermore, keep in mind, we have not yet accounted for the "**visions**" (numerous craft) that brought Ezekiel to the temple in the first place.

Yahweh's S.W.A.T. Team

> **8:16 And he brought me into the inner court of the LORD'S house**

Note that Ezekiel's **last** given location places him **inside** the inner court. Yet, more significantly we discover that Yahweh and his entourage were now positioned and prepared with their own weapons to inflict terrifying retribution against his own people.

> **9:1 He cried also in mine ears with a loud voice, saying, Cause them that have charge over the city to draw near, even every man [with] his destroying weapon in his hand.**
>
> **9:2 And, behold, six men came from the way of the higher gate, which lieth toward the north, and every man a slaughter weapon in his hand; and one man among them [was] clothed with linen, with a writer's inkhorn by his side: and they went in, and stood beside the brazen altar.**
>
> **9:3 And the glory of the God of Israel was gone up from the cherub, whereupon he was, to the threshold of the house. And he called to the man clothed with linen, which [had] the writer's inkhorn by his side;**
>
> **9:4 And the LORD said unto him, Go through the midst of the city, through the midst of Jerusalem, and set a mark upon the foreheads of the men that sigh and that cry for all the abominations that be done in the midst thereof.**
>
> **9:5 And to the others he said in mine hearing, Go ye after him through the city, and smite: let not your eye spare, neither have ye pity:**
>
> **9:6 Slay utterly old [and] young, both maids, and little children, and women: but come not near any man upon whom [is] the mark; and begin**

at my sanctuary. Then they began at the ancient men which [were] before the house.

9:7 And he said unto them, Defile the house, and fill the courts with the slain: go ye forth. And they went forth, and slew in the city.

9:8 And it came to pass, while they were slaying them, and I was left, that I fell upon my face, and cried, and said, Ah Lord GOD! wilt thou destroy all the residue of Israel in thy pouring out of thy fury upon Jerusalem?

9:9 Then said he unto me, The iniquity of the house of Israel and Judah [is] exceeding great, and the land is full of blood, and the city full of perverseness: for they say, The LORD hath forsaken the earth, and the LORD seeth not.

9:10 And as for me also, mine eye shall not spare, neither will I have pity, [but] I will recompense their way upon their head.

EZEKIEL

The escorting angel appears to have been the one to summon the six men, and not Yahweh. "He" or the pilot escorting Ezekiel appears to be positioned somewhere inside the inner court next to the porch. Where Yahweh's craft formation is located on the North side of the temple, quite some distanced from the porch.

Note that the six **mysterious** men came from the way of the higher gate that lies towards the **North**. This was the same location where Yahweh's craft formation had landed ("stood"). This would indicate that the six men either disembarked from Yahweh's landed craft formation, or they entered into the inner court from the outer court by way of an inner court gate (**"higher gate"**) located on the North side of the inner court walls.

Seemingly the six men walked right pass Yahweh's landed craft formation as they came from the outer court and entered into the inner court to get to the altar located back out in the outer court. Essentially, the six men actually walked right through the twenty-five men standing **in** the **open** doorway of Yahweh's temple.

This assumption can further be substantiated by verse 9:2 : "...and they **went in**, and stood beside the altar." Note the words "went **in**". Went in what? They went **in**to the outer court by way of the inner court. You will also note that at the very moment the six men entered the outer court and stood by the altar. **"9:3...the glory of the God of Israel was gone up from the cherub, whereupon he was, to the threshold of the house...."**

This strategically placed the twenty-five men standing at the door of the Lord's house right in the middle of the six men and the craft that had now repositioned itself at the threshold of the temple. This obvious ambush totally entrapped the twenty-five men between the gate. Evidently the six men and the now relocated craft and pilot already knew what they were going to do, and where they were going to position themselves before the incident ever occurred.

Note that the six men entering from the North gate had "**charge**" over the city. Evidently the six men were not just high ranking dignitaries of Israel called upon to kill their own kind, but rather Yahweh's own personal party (angels). Obviously the six men were not of this world, easily identified by not only the **weapons** they were carrying, but by the very word that put them in "charge".

> **Charge**—*give as a task, duty, etc. to make responsible for, to accuse of wrongdoing; censure to put liability on (a person) to make liable for (an error, etc.) to bear down on or set upon with force; attack vigorously, an attack with great force and speed; to bring (a gun or other weapon) to bear on; to attack vigorously or move forward as if attacking.*

The very words "weapon" and "charge" would imply the authority and power to kill. However, in this case, we find a "weapon" boasting the ability to do more than just kill. These weapons are capable of literally "destroying" as well as "slaughtering", two words that readily speak for themselves.

It doesn't take much gray matter deduction to realize that Ezekiel witnessed six men bearing **hand held** weapons capable of startling destructive power. Obviously, Ezekiel could only relate to the powerful weapons by the bodily wreckage they inflict (destroying/slaughtering).

If in fact the weapons were swords, spears, bows and arrows, Ezekiel would have easily recognized and commented on the common killing weapons of that era. Evidently, Ezekiel physically witnessed the gruesome evidence of just what the weapons were capable of doing.

Moreover, the powerful weapons could actually be held and discharged by **one** hand. This detail is easily acknowledged by the fact that each of the six men ("every man") was actually holding a single weapon "in his hand".

If in fact Yahweh's vast stellar arsenal holds true to form, there would be only one type of weapon adept to such destructive power, and yet and still possess hand-held mobility. This had to be the same type of weapon found in the hand shaped devices mounted within each of Yahweh's craft, a miniaturized version of the very same powerful laser (fire) weapon employed by Yahweh time and time again.

There appears to be two different ranks of men manning the six weapons. This obvious technicality is based on the fact that the man clothed in linen was dressed completely different from the other five men standing with him. Ezekiel makes no mention as to what the other five men were wearing, as if the other five men were of a lower rank or position than the man dressed in linen. This might justify why Ezekiel's attention was focused more on the man clothed in linen than the other five men.

This revealing garb would suggest that the man clothed in linen was actually a pilot of one of the craft, while the other five men with him were not. Every time we are confronted with a craft, the pilot sitting inside the craft was always clothed in linen. This consistent detail was found not only in the book of Ezekiel, but in Daniel as well.

This factor might justify why the pilot (cherub) was given the responsibility of marking the innocent populace not involved in Yahweh's horrifying spree of death. A "**charge**" or responsibility given only to a higher-ranking officer.

Fire Verses Metal &Sticks

Seeing how the "cherub/man clothed in linen" also had a hand-held weapon, he obviously took part in the killing. Yet, it doesn't take much gray matter deduction to realize that this killing binge was clearly one sided, seeing how the six men were obviously outnumbered by a hundred to one. However, this one-sided assault was actually in favor of the six men due to the weapons being employed.

In doing the math, we already know that there were seventy men worshiping idols, and twenty-five men worshiping the Sun. This would not include all the men, women, and children within the city to be terminated. In essence, hundreds of people were involved in Yahweh's horrifying temple and city wide reprisal.

For the sake of any argument, let's say that the six men did in fact possess the weapon of choice for that era. This would imply that each of the six men possessed a sword, spear, or bow and arrows. Taking into account the fact that the weapons were hand held, only one such weapon could be held by each man.

To better the odds, let's say that each of the six men possessed all three weapons (sword, spear, bows and arrows). Even with all six men using all three weapons there's **no way** that all six men could have killed the number implied in the verses within the time frame suggested.

Let us be realistic, if all six men began a killing rampage it would be no surprise to most of the victims involved, seeing how the six men could not kill everyone at the **same time.** Obviously, most of the twenty-five or seventy men would have witnessed the six men advancing and killing the other members of their party. More than half of the men would have had plenty of time to quickly run and hide for their lives as the six men were actively engaged in killing the others.

It would have taken days to track down, find and kill all seventy men. Even if the six men were skillful warriors, there's no way six men using swords, spears and bows and arrows could have chased down and killed all ninety-five men in a single day. This would not even include the **alerted** populace of the city of Jerusalem.

If six men wandered into town, killing everyone in sight including women and children, the entire populace of the city would have plenty of time to either mount a counter offensive with the same archaic weapons. Or run for their lives in numerous directions long before the six men could ever get close enough to utilize their vintage weapons. It would have taken six men days to find and kill all of the fleeing unmarked victims. This time frame does not conform to the verses.

The verses would suggest that the entire killing binge only lasted a few hours **or less.** In fact, the verses would lead one to believe that the entire duration of the demise of all victims involved may have only taken two hours or less. Obviously, no sooner did the man clothed in linen leave the temple grounds, than he quickly returned declaring that the lethal deed was done. The same time frame also applied to the five armed men that followed after him.

Obviously, a different weapon was utilized to carry out the slaughter that took place not only on the temple grounds, but within the city of Jerusalem as well. This had to be a weapon capable of killing not only on a massive scale, but on an instantaneous level as well. In essence, by changing the weapon we change the circumstances.

even every man [with] his destroying weapon in his hand.

9:2 And, behold, six men came from the way of the higher gate, which lieth toward the north, and every man a slaughter weapon in his hand;

If in fact the six men employed small hand held weapons reflecting that of the powerful laser weapons mounted on Yahweh's craft, the picture would change intone where the victims had no where to run, no where to hide.

Starting at the temple, the six men and Ezekiel's escorting craft had now positioned themselves in front of the threshold of the house and at the altar, thus surrounding the twenty five men standing in the open doorway. This sudden ambush would only require that the six men open fire with their laser weapons, killing all twenty-five men in moments.

The six men could now quickly proceed to the other seventy men where they once again opened fire, killing all seventy men in just moments of time. Even if the men began to flee for their lives, one does not outrun a laser. Nor would one have to be very close to experience the deadly effects of such a fiery outreaching weapon.

The very same scenario would find the men, women and children of Jerusalem. These weapons had to have been capable of mercilessly killing from possibly a block away. There would be no time to run, much less hide. Seemingly, this killing binge may have left hundreds of half-incinerated corpses lying everywhere (see Leviticus 10:1-6).

The killing spree may have only lasted for a very short length of time due to the proficiency of the weapons being utilized. This human slaughter ended with not only the cherub (man clothed in linen) returning to report the gruesome deed, but an obvious return of the other five men as well.

This unconfirmed return is not illustrated by the verses at this time. Nevertheless, we are about to discover that these same five men did in fact return to the very same site from whence they came: a location that placed them at the North side of the inner court of the temple, being the exact location of Yahweh's craft formation. However, Yahweh in his jealous rage was not through dealing with the city of Jerusalem.

The Second Craft Formation

9:11 And, behold, the man clothed with linen, which [had] the inkhorn by his side, reported the matter, saying, I have done as thou hast commanded me.

> 10:1 Then I looked, and, behold, in the firmament that was above the head of the cherubims there appeared over them as it were a sapphire stone, as the appearance of the likeness of a throne.
>
> 10:2 And he spake unto the man clothed with linen, and said, Go in between the wheels, [even] under the cherub, and fill thine hand with coals of fire from between the cherubims, and scatter [them] over the city. And he went in in my sight.
>
> 10:3 Now the cherubims stood on the right side of the house, when the man went in; and the cloud filled the inner court.
>
> 10:4 Then the glory of the LORD went up from the cherub, [and stood] over the threshold of the house; and the house was filled with the cloud, and the court was full of the brightness of the LORD'S glory.
>
> 10:5 And the sound of the cherubims' wings was heard [even] to the outer court, as the voice of the Almighty God when he speaketh.
>
> 10:6 And it came to pass, [that] when he had commanded the man clothed with linen, saying, Take fire from between the wheels, from between the cherubims; then he went in, and stood beside the wheels.
>
> 10:7 And [one] cherub stretched forth his hand from between the cherubims unto the fire that [was] between the cherubims, and took [thereof], and put [it] into the hands of [him that was] clothed with linen: who took [it], and went out.
>
> 10:8 And there appeared in the cherubims the form of a man's hand under their wings.
>
> EZEKIEL

Clearly, the man clothed in linen reported back to the same person that gave him the orders. "I have done as **thou** hast commanded me." This would imply that the man clothed in linen had reported back to the escort craft located at the threshold of the house.

At that same moment, Ezekiel's attention was suddenly drawn towards Yahweh's craft formation ("then I **looked**"). Evidently, Ezekiel either turned his head, or completely turned towards Yahweh's craft formation standing/landed ("Cherubims **stood**") on the "right side of the house". (the North side of the temple).

It's essential to understand that Yahweh's craft formation was in fact the **Cherubims**, as confirmed in verse 10;1. Or in simpler terms, the four Cherubims were the four wheel shaped craft supporting Yahweh's "throne chariot/craft. It's extremely significant that the reader **remembers** this detail.

10:2 And he spake unto the man clothed with linen, and said, Go in between the wheels, [even] under the cherub, and fill thine hand with coals of fire from between the cherubims,..."

By going in between the wheels, the man clothed in lined would have actually gone in between the Cherubims (wheel shaped craft). This would imply that the man not only went up **under** the landed craft formation (Cherubims), he actually went in **between** the Cherubims/wheels.

The moment the man clothed in linen proceeded "**in**" underneath the landed craft formation, an incredible amount of obscured aerial activity began to take place. In fact, this obscured activity actually establishes a major contradiction within **all** the verses.

10:3...the man went in; and the cloud filled the inner court. 10:4...the house was filled with the **cloud, and the court was full of the brightness** of the Lord's glory. 10:5 And the sound of the **cherubims' wings was heard** [even] **to the** outer court, as the voice of the Almighty God when he speaketh.

What you are observing is the actual description of Ezekiel's first encounter with Yahweh's **flight active** craft formation in the very beginning of the Book of Ezekiel. Yet, this account does not concur with the verses above, seeing how when "the man **went in**", the **cloud** filled the inner court.

How can this be, considering Yahweh's craft formation is not even airborne? How is it that Ezekiel can hear the sound of the energized craft (Cherubims), when Yahweh's craft formation is not even flight active? How could a de-energized and landed craft formation produce enough brightness to fill the **inner court?**

How was the man clothed in linen able of physically walk underneath the craft formation and go in between the craft to retrieve coals of fire from **inside** a highly volatile flight active formation? How can all this activity be taking place when Yahweh's craft formation is stationary, de-energized and in a landed ("stood") condition?

All the details in reference to the **cloud**, the **brightness**, and the **sound** of the **wings** of the Cherubims are not only the exact description of Yahweh's **flight active** craft formation as first seen by Ezekiel in chapter one, they are even in the proper order.

When Ezekiel initially saw the craft formation (wheels) in chapter one, he first observed the "**cloud**", at which point the cloud quickly dissipated into "**brightness**" (see Ezekiel1:4), prior to the formation landing. Later Ezekiel was able to determine that the wings (body/middle wheel) of the Cherubims were producing a "sound" which gave the craft their power **to fly.**(see Ezekiel 1:24).

The solution to this perplexing issue may actually lie in the probability that there was two craft formations instead of one. One of the formations was active while the other was not. This detail informs us of what Ezekiel referred to as "**visions**". Obviously, the numerous craft (**visions**) that brought Ezekiel to the temple grounds were entirely different from that of Yahweh's landed craft formation already at the temple site.

Clearly, the Cherubims could not be producing all this activity standing still in their landed position with their hatch cover doors wide open (let down their wings)? Moreover, Ezekiel was able to observe the man clothed in linen as he "went in". This would indicate that there was no cloud to obscure Ezekiel's vision of Yahweh's entire craft formation as the man clothed in linen "went in".

The man clothed in linen went underneath or partly inside Yahweh's landed craft formation while Ezekiel watched. While at the same time, a bright cloud in the same area of Yahweh's craft formation was also observed by Ezekiel. In fact, the verses actually identify two separate objects in the same location at the same time.

> **10:3 Now the cherubims <u>stood</u> on the right side of the house, when the man went in; <u>and</u> the cloud filled the inner court.**

Obviously Yahweh's craft formation (Cherubims) was located on the right side of the house. Yet, Ezekiel used the word "**<u>and</u>**" to identify another object also located within the same area of the inner court.

Moreover, Ezekiel has actually labeled the cloud that filled the inter court as "Cherubims" due to the familiar sound of the cherubim's wings. Clearly Ezekiel was well aware of the fact that the cloud was concealing another group of Cherubims (wheel shaped craft), just as his first encounter of the cloud (craft formation) did.

We now possess evidence of **two** entirely different craft formations/ Cherubims. One of the formations was obviously Yahweh's personal escort craft already landed on the North side of the house for quite some time. However, the other **flight active** craft formation appears to have just arrived on the scene and is now preparing to land next to Yahweh's touched downed formation. It's no wonder Ezekiel identified a noisy cloud that had now dissipated into brightness as it filled the inner court upon landing. Clearly, Ezekiel was able to visually observe both objects at the same time. This touchdown becomes even more evident when we realize Ezekiel's possible location.

Ezekiel's last given location places him somewhere between, or around the door of the temple and the threshold of the house in the inner court. "Then **I looked**, and behold". By Ezekiel standing somewhere in front of the temple, he would have had to either pivot his head or his whole body Northward, in order to see Yahweh's craft formation situated on the North side of the house. This would place Ezekiel at quite some distance from Yahweh's landed formation. Furthermore it would allow Ezekiel complete encompassing observation of the entire North side of the house and the inner court. This not only allowed Ezekiel a panoramic view of Yahweh's landed craft formation, but also the second noisy formation brightly shrouded within a cloud as it landed in the same proximity.

Go in Between The Wheels

The verses would suggest that curious Ezekiel, endeavoring to gain a better aspect, left his given location to walk over to Yahweh's landed formation and observe the man clothed in linen as he went in between the wheels (Cherubims). This would once again, return us to the bewildering issue as to just what does "go in between the wheels" actually imply?

As mentioned before, the four wheel-shaped craft possess cockpits and transparent domes ("firmament") for the pilots (**cherubs**) at the **top** of each craft. Furthermore, each of the four-wheel shaped craft were supported and standing **up** on landing gear (feet). This would place the four landed craft considerably high up off the ground, thereby allowing easy entrance and exit by the pilot from **below** the craft.

Ezekiel informed us that each craft in the formation displayed lowered hatch cover doors or ramps, ("Wings") leading up into the internal compartments of each craft. This obvious detail was easily recognized by the fact that the formation "let down their wings" (hatch cover doors) only **<u>after</u>** they landed.

When the four craft are positioned in their tight formation, they create a large upper and lower cavity located within the center of the formation. Quite naturally, the **upper** basin is reserved for Yahweh's personal craft to embed itself. This large void not only creates a protective barrier around Yahweh's personal craft, but also establishes a means of support for Yahweh's craft to magnetically attach itself to the upper bodies of the other four craft.

The craft formation also contains a large **lower** cavity located **underneath** Yahweh's personal craft "between the wheels". Naturally, with each craft possessing the ability to turn in any direction, the hatch cover doors or ramps of each craft may actually be facing away from the landed formation. This would allow the pilots to exit their craft facing the open terrain away from the craft formation.

However, the very design of Yahweh's defense oriented formation suggests otherwise. Obviously, Yahweh's craft formation and its high security profile would propose a dissimilar type of landing procedure. Looking at the formation from a security point of view, their landing procedure should not only offer protection for Yahweh, but for Yahweh's protectors as well.

This would suggest that the logical landing procedure would position all the hatch cover doors facing towards the **middle** of the center lower cavity located underneath the landed formation. In doing so, all entrance or exit ramps leading into the craft would actually be facing each other.

This would allow easy entrance or exit from one craft to another while centered within the lower cavity of the formation. With all the ramps or hatch cover doors positioned towards the central lower cavity of the formation, the craft themselves would formulate a defendable stronghold offering excellent protection from anything outside the formation attempting to venture inside.

Obviously this encompassing security team and their powerful craft were designed to safeguard Yahweh's personal craft centrally located in the middle of all four craft ("between the wheels"). Moreover, this huddled design would allow all five pilots the ability to move in and out of all the craft "**in between the wheels**" without ever having to venture outside the outer perimeter of the formation.

The hatch cover doors or ramps lead up into the internal compartments of the craft through their **undercarriage.** This would actually place the ramps or lowered hatch cover doorways **between** the rotating center section ("middle wheel") and the body/Ring ("wheel") of the craft.

In short, each craft is a wheel in a wheel, therefore, the ramps or lowered hatch cover doorways would actually be located "in between the wheels" of each craft. In either case, no matter where the man clothed in linen **"went in"** under the craft formation, he would actually be standing "in between the wheels".

Ezekiel confirmed that the man clothed in lined was instructed to "**go in between the wheels,** [even] **under the cherub**". This would suggest that the man clothed in linen actually walked up **underneath** Yahweh's four craft formation now standing on their landing gear. This placed the man clothed in linen underneath the four craft, as well as **underneath** the pilots (**cherub**) of the craft. **"Then he went in, and stood beside the wheels."** However, there more to this "in between the wheels" than meets the eye.

Ezekiel clearly specified that each craft was as a wheel in a wheel. Obviously the body of the craft was a wheel, while the center rotating section powering the craft was also a wheel. This might suggest that the cherub (pilot) who handed the man clothed in linen the glowing coals was actually positioned partly **inside** the craft. This would place the cherub/pilot of the craft on the ramp or hatch cover doorway **between** the body of the craft and the center rotating section of the craft, or "between the wheels".

Evidently, the man clothed in linen walked up to the hatch cover doorway or ramp located underneath one of the craft. At this point one pilot (cherub) appears to have been standing on the lowered hatch cover doorway or ramp. Seemingly, the pilot was not on the ground, nor totally inside the craft, but rather "between" the brightly lit internal compartment of the craft and the ground on which the hatch cover doors or ramps extend.

It would appear that the cherub standing on the lowered hatch cover doorway or ramp reached ("stretched") into the brightly lite (fire) compartment of the craft and retrieved the glowing orbs of fire from inside the craft and handed them to the man clothed in linen now standing "**under**" the craft and cherub (pilot).

Then again, the pilot (cherub) **seated** in the craft may have "stretched" across the interior of the craft picking up the glowing balls of fire from inside the internal compartment and handed them to the man clothed in linen right from the cockpit via the hatch cover doorways of the craft. This would once again place the man clothed in linen right under the cherub (pilot).

Seemingly, Ezekiel followed behind the man clothed in linen as he walked up to the landed craft formation on the North side of the house. Evidently, Ezekiel was quite close to the formation in order to elaborate on the crucial details we have just examined. However just what were the glowing coals of fire?

One might assume that the fiery orbs were blazing explosives and/or igniting devices used to set fire to the city of Jerusalem. This fiery detail becomes even more apparent when we realize that the man clothed in lined was also a cherub or pilot himself.

In essence, the man clothed in linen was to use his own personal craft to dispense the glowing spheres "**over**" the city. Note the word "**over**" suggesting from above, which would further indicate another craft was utilized to perform the fiery purging of Jerusalem.

> **43:3 And [it was] according to the appearance of the vision which I saw, [even] according to the vision that I saw <u>when I came to destroy the city</u>: and the visions [were] like the vision that I saw by the river Chebar; and I fell upon my face.**
> **EZEKIEL**

Yet, more notably we discover that Ezekiel appears to be standing right next to Yahweh's craft formation as the man clothed in linen was given the spheres of fire. In fact, Ezekiel was so close to the formation that he could now recognize and comment on the hand shaped devices protruding out from underneath each of the four craft.

> **10:8 And there appeared <u>in</u> the <u>cherubims</u> the <u>form of a man's hand under their wings</u>.**

Ezekiel Details the Second Craft Formation

Evidently, Ezekiel's curiosity got the best of him, compelling him to walk around, underneath or perhaps outside the perimeter of the formation in an attempt to observe all the details of the four craft. I bring this substantial clue to the reader's attention simply because Ezekiel was now so close to Yahweh's formation and the hand shaped devices that he actually observed **something** other than Yahweh's personal five craft formation/cherubims.

> **10:9 <u>And when I looked, behold</u> the four wheels <u>by</u> the cherubims, <u>one wheel by one cherub, and another wheel by another cherub</u>: and the appearance of the wheels [was] as the colour of a <u>beryl stone</u>.**
> **10:10 And [as for] their appearances, <u>they four had one likeness</u>, as if a <u>wheel had been in the midst of a wheel</u>.**
> **10:11 When they went, they went upon their four sides; they turned not as they went, but to the place whither the head looked they followed it; they turned not as they went.**

10:12 And their whole body, and their backs, and their hands, and their wings, and the wheels, [were] full of eyes round about, [even] the wheels that they four had.
10:13 As for the wheels, it was cried unto them in my hearing, O wheel.
10:14 And every one had four faces: the first face [was] the face of a cherub, and the second face [was] the face of a man, and the third the face of a lion, and the fourth the face of an eagle.
EZEKIEL

How can this be? Why would Ezekiel repeat his description of the craft formation, unless of course Ezekiel was actually describing an entirely different set of wheels/formation (Cherubim). Note Ezekiel implies that the other set of wheels were located "by" the Cherubims.

The four wheels were not the Cherubims, but rather positioned next to or **by** Yahweh's four craft formation/Cherubims. Ezekiel had now identified the unknown cloud and bright object ("**visions**") that landed next to or "**by**" Yahweh's craft formation (Cherubims) in the inner court.

10:3…the man went in; and the cloud filled the inner court. 10:4…the house was filled with the **cloud,** and the court was full of the brightness of the Lord's glory. 10:5 And the sound of the **cherubims' wings was heard** [even] **to the** outer court, as the voice of the Almighty God when he speaketh.

Ezekiel was actually looking at the other four wheel shaped craft that had previously landed next to ("by") Yahweh's personal craft formation (Cherubims). Obviously, the four wheel-shaped craft look and perform exactly like Yahweh's personal escort craft (Cherubims). The four other craft had not only landed "by" Yahweh's craft formation, but also placed sentries outside each craft.

This detail is easily recognized by the fact that each of the four wheel-shaped craft appears to be guarded by the pilot (cherub). Each of the pilots/cherubs were standing outside next to or "by" the four landed craft: **"one wheel by one cherub, and another wheel by another cherub".**

Why would four additional wheel-shaped craft suddenly shown up at this location? The solution to this issue is actually hidden within the verses. If the reader will recollect, six men came from the way of the higher gate at the Northern inner court walls, being the exact location of Yahweh's landed craft formation. This was the same vicinity in which the brightly lit cloud had also landed.

In recalling this episode, we discovered that all six men, after killing the men in the temple and city return to the temple at approximately the same time the bright cloud made its sudden appearance. Essentially, the second craft formation abruptly appeared on the scene to pick up the five men that had now returned from the city after performing their lethal orders. Naturally one would assume that this speculation is nothing more than that, speculation.

Moving Faces

The verses actually contain confirmation to the fact that the five men not only returned to Yahweh's craft formation, but to four other awaiting craft that landed to recover the five men. This well hidden detail can only be confirmed by reverting back to chapter one of Ezekiel. This chapter will allow us to compare the discrepancy between the two sets of craft formations and their pilots (cherubs).

> **1:10 As for the likeness of their faces, they four had the face of a man, and the face of a lion, on the right side: and they four had the face of an ox on the left side; they four also had the face of an eagle.**
> **10:14 And every one had four faces: the first face [was] the face of a cherub, and the second face [was] the face of a man, and the third the face of a lion, and the fourth the face of an eagle.**
> EZEKIEL

Obviously we have a contradiction when trying to establish the actual faces and their possible locations within the craft. If you will observe the first verse you will discover that Ezekiel saw the **man** on the right side of the craft, placing the face of the **ox** on the left side of the craft.

Yet, in verse 10:14 there is no mention of an ox sited in the craft at all. In fact, the face of a man replaces the face of the ox. Moreover, the face of the man is now replaced with the face of a cherub (pilot). Truly a puzzling game of musical chairs if one has not been closely following the chain of events.

Let's first establish the fact that these two verses actually define two completely different craft formations. Secondly, the defined faces are possible depictions of what lies within the domed cockpits (head/face) and/or insignias or emblems located on the exterior structure of each craft. Yet, if one will observe both sets of verses, it becomes evident that only **two** faces could actually be insignias or outer craft emblems.

This conjecture is based on the fact that the lion and the eagle are the only two faces that **did not** change. Yet, the faces of the man, ox and cherub were displaced. In essence, the faces of the man, ox and cherub (pilot) were movable faces possibly located inside the domed cockpits (Head/Face) of the craft.

The first verse would validate the faces of Yahweh's craft formation as first seen by Ezekiel in chapter one. However, the second verse identifies the faces that Ezekiel saw in the second craft formation that landed next to Yahweh's craft formation to pick up the five men who returned from the city.

The pilots of the craft are identified as cherubs, thus explaining the faces of the cherubs found in the second formation "by" Yahweh's craft formation. The face of the **man** positioned next to the face of the cherub is just that, a man.

Each of the four craft obviously revealed four pilots (cherubs) that navigated their four craft to Yahweh's craft formation to pick up the five men. Therefore, each of the craft now displays faces of not only the pilots (cherubs) navigating the craft, but also the "man" (men) that they picked up.

Essentially, Ezekiel saw the face of a cherub (pilot) and the face of a man inside the domed cockpits of the four craft. Furthermore, this sequence of events did not take place until **after** Ezekiel heard the command: "**10:13 As for the wheels, it was cried unto them in my hearing, O wheel.**"

Quite naturally, this hypothesis would impose an obstacle, considering there were only four retrieving craft but five men to be recovered. Seemingly, the four craft could only carry four men along with their four pilots (cherubs), leaving behind the fifth man. Yet, there is no discrepancy due to the **sixth man.**

If the reader will recall, there were **six men** that entered and returned from the city of Jerusalem. One of those men was referred to as a "man clothed in linen". The man clothed in lined was in fact a "cherub", which would identify him as a pilot. Simply put, the six men returned to Yahweh's craft formation within the inner court. The man clothed in linen, being a pilot, was given the glowing spheres of fire to be scattered "**over**" the city.

The sixth man/pilot retrieved the glowing orbs and "went out". However, he may not have been alone, implying that the cherub also took one of the five men with him. Both men possibly entered another craft to disperse the glowing spheres "over" the city of Jerusalem, leaving behind the four other men and pilots/cherbus that had entered the second craft formation now positioned next to Yahweh's formation (Cherubims).

Ox or Seat?

What was the face of the ox? Obviously the face of the "ox" was a mobile image, seeing how it disappeared in the second craft formation. Yet, the second craft formation actually displays fundamental characteristics identical to the first.

To better comprehend just what we may be examining it's important that I give the reader a reasonable illustration of what Ezekiel may have been observing when he saw the face of the "ox".

To simplify this example, we will use the assistance of a modern automobile. To better establish Ezekiel's possible viewpoint, we will need to elevate the car approximately seven or eight feet up off the ground. This would give us a good example of how far the craft formations may have been standing up off the ground while supported by their landing gear.

Naturally, for a car to be functional it will require a driver (pilot/cherub). We will now place the elevated car and its driver approximately twenty or thirty feet away from us. As the observers down below, standing in front of the car, we will now try to peer inside the car.

Our first observation would allow us to see the transparent windshield (firmament). As we peer through the windshield, we are able to see the driver positioned on the right side of the vehicle. However, we are not concerned with the driver, but rather what resides next to the driver.

By the vehicle maintaining a raised position, we the observers down below would only be able to identify the driver from his shoulders upward (his face). In fact, we would see nothing else inside the car, **except** for one other object located on the opposite side of the driver.

Seeing how a single passenger car is quite rare we would actually be able to see the top section of the empty seat located on the opposite side of the driver. Obviously, cars of our modern era now possess high profile seats and headrest to protect their occupants, headrest which comes in many styles, and forms.

In essence, if one were observing the elevated car, one would naturally see the driver as well as the towering seat and its headrest on the opposite side. This might suggest that the **face** of the "ox" was actually the designed shaped of the **head**rest protruding out of the vacant seat next to the man (cherub) piloting the craft. This probability becomes even more credible when we realize the actual shape of an ox's face.

I personally believe that Ezekiel may have mistaken the headrest of the vacant seat next to the man as the likeness and/or features of an ox. By visualizing the actual shape of an ox's face, it becomes quite understandable why Ezekiel may have misinterpreted the headrest of the vacant seat for the face of an ox. The face of an ox actually sharply tapers upwards and outwards from the nose area of the face to the ears.

Even the ears could be considered a part of the headrest, seeing how headrest of our modern times possess upper outer cushioned areas protruding out from the upper section of the headrest. This would give the headrest the obvious appearance of protruding ears.

This detailed design becomes even more elaborate when we realize that the empty seat and headrest were fabricated for a pilot to navigate a craft. Essentially the pilot's seat and headrest would be greatly modified to support the needs of the pilot.

Evidently, the wheel shaped craft supported **two seats** located within the domed cockpits (heads). This detail is easily acknowledged due to the fact that the **second** craft formation genuinely displayed both the pilot (cherub) and the man sitting next to him in the cockpit. Hence Ezekiel saw the face of a cherub (pilot) and the face of a man.

We also know that Yahweh's four escorting craft are the same type of craft found in the second formation. Hence, all the craft involved in both formations actually maintain **two seats** located within the cockpits (head) of each craft. In essence, Ezekiel saw the face of a cherub (pilot) and the face of a man in the second formation. However, in Yahweh's personal craft formation Ezekiel only saw a single man and empty seat ("ox") positioned next to him.

Obviously, Ezekiel was unaware at the time that the men piloting Yahweh's personal craft were known as cherubs. If Ezekiel knew that the faces of the men sitting inside Yahweh's craft were referred to as cherubs, Ezekiel's **first** observation of Yahweh's craft formation and its faces would have been stated completely differently.

If Yahweh's personal formation was manned by eight pilots, the visible face of the man on the left side would have partly concealed the headrest (ox) that he was using. Hence, Ezekiel would have made no mention of the face of the ox at all, seeing how he would have been unable to observe the empty seat now occupied by the second passenger. Hence there would have been two faces of a man in each craft.

Waylay Craft

Seemingly, the verses harbor another discrepancy in reference to the second formation that landed in the inner court. This missing technicality would beg the question as to just where did the six men that came from the way of the higher gate come from in the first place?

Evidently, the six men arrived on the scene **prior to** the second craft formation landing in the inner court. This speculation is based on the fact that the bright cloud (second formation) did not appear until the man clothed in linen (pilot) reported back to Yahweh. This was approximately the same time when the five men returned from Jerusalem. Yet, where did the six men actually come from, **before** entering the inner court?

In observing the verses, one might assume that perhaps the six men originated from Yahweh's personal formation located inside the inner court. Yet, after closely scrutinizing the verses, we are left with the probability that the six men entered the inner court by way of a higher **gate** located in the North wall of the inner court.

This would indicate that the six men actually came from **inside** the **outer** court as they passed through the North **gate** of the **inner** court wall. Simply put, all six men came from the **outer court** and not the inner court. This would lead one to believe that perhaps numerous unknown craft ("**visions**") had landed **inside** the outer court on the opposite side of the inner court walls. From this location the men disembarked from their craft and walked through the higher gate of the North inner court walls to ambush the twenty-five men.

In fact, one might get the distinct impression that the very motivation behind the unknown craft positioning themselves on the opposite side of the North inner court wall was for the very purpose of hiding their numerous craft to execute the ambush. This might suggest that they concealed their craft so as not to frighten the twenty-five standing in the main gate.

This element of surprise becomes even more credible when we realize that the man clothed in linen was a pilot (cherub). Evidently, this pilot navigated one of the craft located on the opposite side of the North inner court walls, thus explaining why he came into the inner court with the other five men.

This speculation would suggest two probabilities. The first possibility would point to the second formation (**Visions**) landing inside the **outer** court on the opposite side of the North inner court wall. In doing so, the second craft formation dropped off the six men and simply left the area to return at a later time to recover the men from inside the **inner** court next to Yahweh's personal craft formation.

The second probability would suggest that the second formation may have actually landed in the outer court allowing the six men to disembark from the landed craft. Yet, in this case the formation did not leave the area until the six men returned from Jerusalem.

When the six men returned, the second formation powered up their craft and took off, only to land on the opposite side of the wall inside the inner court next to Yahweh's formation to pick the men up. In fact, this second speculation might actually explain this verse: **10:5 And the sound of the cherubims' wings was heard [even] to the outer court, as the voice of the Almighty God when he speaketh.**

The wings (rotating center section) of the second craft formation (Cherubims) could be heard even in the **outer court** simply because that may have been precisely where the formation was located prior to taking off.

However, both probabilities contain a discrepancy in reference to the sixth man/cherub. If in fact the sixth man was a cherub/pilot, where was his personal craft? If in fact the second craft formation consisted of only four craft how could the second formation have departed the area and return at a later time with only three pilots?

How could the second formation move from one side of the wall to the other if one of its pilots (Cherub) was physically engaged in killing the people of Jerusalem, or collecting the orbs of fire from Yahweh? Unless of course there was another unknown **fifth** craft.

This mysterious fifth craft would allow the sixth man/cherub and one of the five men that returned from Jerusalem to not only leave the area, but also distribute the glowing coals of fire "over" the city. In simpler terms, there was not only a fifth craft, but a second four-craft formation located inside the outer court.

The second formation may have actually contained five craft just like Yahweh's formation. This would explain how the man clothed in linen was able to collect the coals of fire "**and went out**". Went out where? He "went out" into the outer court where his own personal craft awaited.

Craft Insignia

As for the two remaining faces of the lion and eagle, we discover an interesting probability. Both faces appear to be a type of insignia or emblem either etched or literally stamped into the metal of the craft. In fact it would appear that the insignia of the "**eagle**" may actually portray the name of the craft itself.

> **48:40 For thus saith the LORD; Behold, he shall fly as an eagle, and shall spread his wings over Moab.**
>
> **49:22 Behold, he shall come up and fly as the eagle. JEREMIAH**
>
> **24:28 For wheresoever the carcase is, there will the eagles be gathered together. MATTHEW**
>
> **17:37 Wheresoever the body [is], thither will the eagles be gathered together. LUKE**
>
> **24:11. He has the chariots of eagles, as it is written, "I carried you on eagles' wings." Appendix to 3 ENOCH**

Most military powers of our modern world perform the very same type of marking techniques. Many such brands or insignias affixed on our modern air craft depict flying insects or birds to reflect their might or flight characteristics.

Two such examples would be the Hornet and Falcon aircraft's, some of which display large colorful replicas of falcons and hornets painted upon their body. This might suggest that Yahweh's stellar arsenal consists of numerous disk shaped craft dubbed the Eagle, a fitting character considering the history behind this distinguished Bird of prey.

The eagle has long been held as the symbol of freedom and power. The Roman warriors also applied the golden figure of an eagle as a sign of strength and bravery. Russian and Austrian emperors also hallowed eagles as symbols of strength. Even the United States chose the bald eagle as its national bird in 1782.

The golden eagle is often referred to as the king of birds, commonly found nesting on high cliffs or in the mountains. This is the very same lofty location where Yahweh prefers to perch himself during his earthly visitations.

Yahweh and his Entourage Leave the Temple

Yahweh and his host, having now purged Jerusalem and its corrupt residents, were now preparing to leave the area. The pilots and their single passengers began to mount their craft to take off. However, this preparation **did not** take place **until** the verbal order was given. In fact, we have already unknowingly examined the broadcasted order.

"10:13 As for the wheels, it was cried unto them in my hearing, O wheel."

The "living Bible" would refer to this affirmation as "**whirl-wheels**". In either case, it would appear as if the order was "cried" out (Public address system) to the pilots to prepare the disk shaped craft for flight. This broadcasted order may have come in the form of "**Roll** Wheels". The same interpretation is found in the "Living Bible"

Seemingly, Ezekiel may have misinterpreted "**O** Wheel" for **Roll/whirl** wheels. Obviously, the **rotating center sections** of all the craft involved would have to **roll** wheel, or "**whirl-wheel**" (power up) in order to take off.

Evidently, the order did not come into play until **after** the man clothed in linen received the coals of fire and "went out". This ended the business at hand, as well as enacting the order for all the men and cherubs to mount up. This revealing detail is confirmed by the fact that Ezekiel was unable to observe the faces of the men and the cherub located inside the craft until **after** the order to mount up was given.

Once the order was given, the guarding cherubs standing outside the wheel shaped craft mounted up their craft and could now be seen inside the cockpits with their passengers (man) as they prepare to take off. (Powered up/roll/whirl wheel)

> **10:15 And the cherubims were lifted up. This [is] the living creature that I saw by the river of Chebar.**
>
> **10:16 And when the cherubims went, the wheels went by them: and when the cherubims lifted up their wings to mount up from the earth, the same wheels also turned not from beside them.**
>
> **10:17 When they stood, [these] stood; and when they were lifted up, [these] lifted up themselves [also]: for the spirit of the living creature [was] in them.**
>
> **10:18 Then the glory of the LORD departed from off the threshold of the house, and stood over the cherubims.**
>
> **10:19 And the cherubims lifted up their wings, and mounted up from the earth in my sight: when they went out, the wheels also [were] beside them, and [every one] stood at the door of the east gate of the LORD'S house; and the glory of the God of Israel [was] over them above.**
>
> **10:20 This [is] the living creature that I saw under the God of Israel by the river of Chebar; and I knew that they [were] the cherubims.**
>
> **10:21 Every one had four faces apiece, and every one four wings; and the likeness of the hands of a man [was] under their wings.**

> **10:22 And the likeness of their faces [was] the same faces which I saw by the river of Chebar, their appearances and themselves: they went every one straight forward.** EZEKIEL

The verses would lead one to believe that Ezekiel kept repeating himself as he recounted the craft lifting up off the ground and becoming airborne. However, by closely observing the verses, we discover that the statement "lifted up" indicates two entirely different set of circumstances.

Evidently, the verses are split up into two parts. Verses 10:15-18, identify Yahweh's personal formation ("Cherubims") taking off from the ground. Yet, verses 10:19&20, refers to the second formation ("Cherubims").

This crucial detail can be confirmed by the fact that Yahweh's craft formation is identified by Ezekiel as the same formation he "saw by the river of Chebar" This would imply that Yahweh's personal formation consist of a total of **five** craft. Yet, the second formation only involved "the living creature that I saw **under** the god of Israel by the river of Chebar." In essence the second formation (Cherubims) only contained four craft, being the same type of creatures/Wheels found **under** Yahweh's craft.

With all the wheels and wings being lifted up, one could become quite confused. Yet, in recollection of all the information we have already assembled, the verse's remain accurate. Obviously **both** formations had to lift/raise their hatch covers or ramps (Wings) in order to take off. Clearly, all the craft had to lift/raise their rotating center wheels to power up (roll wheel) the craft. **for the spirit of the living creature [was] in them**. Hence, the rotating center sections (wheels) went by them.

Evidently, both formations were working as a team. When one set raised their hatch cover doorways, so did the second formation. When Yahweh's personal craft formation (Cherubims) took off from the ground, so did the second formation (wheels). In essence, both craft formations raised their hatch cover doorways (wings), and took off together, as did the unknown craft hovering over "the threshold of the house."

A killing on the Way Out

Seemingly, the craft hovering at the threshold of the house positioned himself over the two craft formations as they "went out' and over to the east gate. In fact, the verses indicate that all the craft "**stood**" at the East gate. This would lead one to believe that perhaps both formations and the unknown craft from the threshold flew over to the East gate of the house, where they just "**stood**" hovering over the top of the gate.

However, this speculation could be quite misleading seeing how the word "stood" would imply that one or both formations may have actually **landed** "at" the East gate of the Lord's house, while the unknown craft hovered overhead as a sentry.

> **11:1 Moreover the spirit lifted me up, and brought me unto the east gate of the LORD'S house, which looketh eastward: and behold at the door of the gate five and twenty men; among whom I saw Jaazaniah the son of Azur, and Pelatiah the son of Benaiah, princes of the people.**
>
> **11:2 Then said he unto me, Son of man, these [are] the men that devise mischief, and give wicked counsel in this city:**
>
> **11:21 But [as for them] whose heart walketh after the heart of their detestable things and their abominations, I will recompense their way upon their own heads, saith the Lord GOD.**
>
> **11:22 Then did the cherubims lift up their wings, and the wheels beside them; and the glory of the God of Israel [was] over them above.**
>
> **11:23 And the glory of the LORD went up from the midst of the city, and stood upon the mountain which [is] on the east side of the city.**
>
> **11:24 Afterwards the spirit took me up, and brought me in a vision by the Spirit of God into Chaldea, to them of the captivity. So the vision that I had seen went up from me.**
>
> **11:25 Then I spake unto them of the captivity all the things that the LORD had showed me.**
>
> EZEKIEL

By the craft formations landing "**at**" the East gate one might assume that both formations landed **outside** of the outer court walls. This might suggest that the gates were open allowing Ezekiel to see through the inner and outer court gates to observe the landing.

At this point, the sentry craft ("he"), hovering just above the landed formations, once again utilized his hand shaped device to bodily pick Ezekiel up off the ground and aerially elevate him from the inner court to the East gate.

This appears to be a deliberate move on Yahweh's part, thus allowing Ezekiel to prophesy against the men standing at the gate that gave evil counsel to the populace of Israel. That prophecy ultimately ended with Yahweh mysteriously killing Pelatiah, son of Benaiah, princess of the people. Yahweh's jealous anger being satisfied, he signaled the landed craft to once again "lift up" their hatch cover doors or ramps ("wings") and depart.

Obviously, the two formations went in one direction, while the unknown craft from the threshold went in another. Note, "the glory of the God of Israel was over them above." Yet, it **was not** the glory of the God of Israel that "went up" from the midst of the city and landed or hovered ("stood") on the mountain East of the city. Rather, it was the glory of the Lord that landed on the East mountain leaving the glory of the God of Israel ("he") behind to aerially elevate Ezekiel and transport him to the captives of Chaldea. In fact, Ezekiel was actually able to see the craft (vision) that transported him to Chaldea as it left the area.

Clearly, all the craft involved left the area, thus leaving their final destination to one's imagination. Then again, the ultimate destination of all the craft involved maybe quite unmistakable considering their small size. Plainly, these small disk shaped craft lacked the ability for interplanetary space travel.

This would suggest that the small craft obviously required a parent ship capable of sustaining the smaller craft as well as intergalactic travel. That mother ship, as we shall soon discover, is so immense in size, that it would not only be capable of harboring thousands of such disk shaped craft, but other mother ships that physically link together to form an enormous starship reaching the massive scale of a small planetoid.

The writings that you have just considered are but a small segment of the celestial data found within the book of Ezekiel. This trivial portion was quite necessary, if the reader is to thoroughly understand the succeeding books of the New Testament and The Revelation.

In leaving Ezekiel, I strongly urge that the reader take the time and thoroughly examine the entire book of Ezekiel. Remarkably Ezekiel's book actually contains many symbolic and hidden clues in reference to our future, as well as establishing numerous chains of events that will take place on this planet **during** and **after** the Revelation.(End of **times**).

Isaiah & Jeremiah

Having shaped Israel into a powerful nation, Yahweh began to lose control and personal authority over his own people. Events changed dramatically when the nation of Israel took command of the surrounding territories and dominating their enslaved remnants. Yet, Yahweh's lost authority of Israel was not due to their increased power as much as it was fathered by the nations Israel subjugated.

Yahweh found he was no longer able of fully maintain their absolute worship for him. This was a horrendous betrayal to Yahweh, seeing how the very nation he forged into a recognized power degenerated back to the doctrines of the other gods and nations he dismantled to create Israel.

This may have been inevitable, seeing how the nation of Israel coexisted with people under the jurisdiction of the fallen angels/other gods. Obviously, the remnants of the enslaved empires maintained a strong reverence towards their gods. Essentially, the subversive nations adoration towards the other gods/fallen angels wreaked a detrimental impact upon the nation of Israel.

Yahweh had strongly cautioned the new nation of Israel not only to be prepared for such treacherous dogma, but the devastating consequences to be inflicted upon Israel if they chose to side with the fallen angels/other gods and their traitorous doctrines towards the kingdom of heaven.

> **8:19 And it shall be, if thou do at all forget the LORD thy God, and walk after <u>other gods</u>, and <u>serve them</u>, and <u>worship them</u>, I testify against you this day that ye shall surely perish.**
>
> **8:20 As the nations which the LORD destroyeth before your face, so shall ye perish; because ye would not be obedient unto the voice of the LORD your God.** DEUTERONOMY

> 11:1 But king Solomon loved many strange women, together with the daughter of Pharaoh, women of the Moabites, Ammonites, Edomites, Zidonians, [and] Hittites;
> 11:2 Of the nations [concerning] which the LORD said unto the children of Israel, Ye shall not go in to them, neither shall they come in unto you: [for] surely they will turn away your heart after their gods: Solomon clave unto these in love.
> 11:4 For it came to pass, when Solomon was old, [that] his wives turned away his heart after other gods: and his heart was not perfect with the LORD his God, as [was] the heart of David his father.
> 11:5 For Solomon went after Ashtoreth the goddess of the Zidonians, and after Milcom the abomination of the Ammonites.
> 11:6 And Solomon did evil in the sight of the LORD, and went not fully after the LORD, as [did] David his father.
> 11:7 Then did Solomon build an high place for Chemosh, the abomination of Moab, in the hill that [is] before Jerusalem, and for Molech, the abomination of the children of Ammon.
> 11:8 And likewise did he for all his strange wives, which burnt incense and sacrificed unto their gods. I KINGS

Yahweh's warning went unheeded by the new generations of Israel, subsequently finding Israel to be the nemesis of the very god that fathered them. Yet, **how** could Israel abandon Yahweh, and venerate other gods in light of all the incredible feats performed by Yahweh and his host of craft?

This puzzling outcome is rooted in the fact that the fallen angels/other gods also possessed some of the same powers as Yahweh. Clearly, the fallen angels had stemmed from the kingdom of heaven, thus mastering many of the same high tech devices capable of easily swaying mankind into believing and/or worshiping almost anything or anyone.

The ancient world was riddled with superstition. High tech demonstrations could therefore easily sway people from one side to another. Ultimately, their tendency to seesaw led to the coming of the prophets.

Yahweh began to cut all ties and communication with his own people due to their pursuit of the fallen angels/other gods. Clearly Yahweh tried time and time again to reinstate his chosen people, only to be met with constant denial due to the powerful grip imposed upon Israel by the fallen angels. Yahweh instituted prophets as a method of persuading his people away from the other gods, while at the same time displaying his intense anger by depriving his people of his physical presence. Eventually, this allowed the other gods/fallen angels even more control over not only their vanquished populations, but the populace of Israel as well.

> 9:6 [But] if ye shall at all turn from following me, ye or your children, and will not keep my commandments [and] my statutes which I have set before you, but go and serve other gods, and worship them:
>
> 9:9...and have taken hold upon other gods, and have worshipped them, and served them: therefore hath the LORD brought upon them all this evil.
>
> I KINGS
>
> 17:35...Ye shall not fear other gods, nor bow yourselves to them, nor serve them, nor sacrifice to them:
>
> 17:36 But the LORD, who brought you up out of the land of Egypt with great power and a stretched out arm, him shall ye fear, and him shall ye worship, and to him shall ye do sacrifice.
>
> II KINGS
>
> 34:25 Because they have forsaken me, and have burned incense unto other gods, that they might provoke me to anger with all the works of their hands; therefore my wrath shall be poured out upon this place, and shall not be quenched.
>
> II CHRONICLE
>
> 44:3 Because of their wickedness which they have committed to provoke me to anger, in that they went to burn incense, [and] to serve other gods, whom they knew not, [neither] they, ye, nor your fathers.
>
> 44:4 Howbeit I sent unto you all my servants the prophets, rising early and sending [them], saying, Oh, do not this abominable thing that I hate.
>
> 44:5 But they hearkened not, nor inclined their ear to turn from their wickedness, to burn no incense unto other gods.
>
> JEREMIAH
>
> 82:1 A Psalm of Asaph. God standeth in the congregation of the mighty; he judgeth among the gods.
>
> 86:8 Among the gods [there is] none like unto thee, O Lord; neither [are there any works] like unto thy works.
>
> 96:4 For the LORD [is] great, and greatly to be praised: he [is] to be feared above all gods.

97:7 Confounded be all they that serve graven images, that boast themselves of idols: worship him, all [ye] gods.
PSALMS

Evidently, a cold war was taking place between the other gods/fallen angels and the kingdom of heaven (Yahweh). Undoubtably, the other gods physically existed, seeing how they could be palpably **served,** sacrificed to, bowed down before, burn incense to, and be physically **feared.** In essence, the other gods/fallen angles were just as real and powerful as Yahweh and his physical host.

Seemingly, the two celestial powers (Yahweh/Satan) were competing to gain control and authority over the incognizant populations. This would once again suggest a global ethnic struggle between the bloodlines of Cain and Seth. Ancient mankind entangled in their superstitious perceptions was wedged between the two dissimilar powers, placing the benighted humans at the mercy of both misconceived technologies.

Each side (Yahweh/Satan), maintained control by technological feats believed to be nothing short of miracles. Each populations was placed in a position of choosing and/or even physically fighting for the side or god that rendered the most miraculous show of power, or primarily supported the population's needs.

However, in this particular case it would appear that the conflict took place on a much larger and more technologically advanced scale. Evidently, the two dissimilar powers/gods (Yahweh/Satan) were clashing with each other at the expense of the ancient civilizations. Each god swayed their populations/servants into believing that he was the only god, while the other gods were imposing the very same ultimatum upon their populations.

Each of the gods was prepared to punish or even kill a multitude of servants if they were persuaded, exploited, or physically engineered to the other side. Each of the concealed gods, whether extraterrestrial (heavenly) or interterrestrial (Underworld) required their populations to worship and perform physical sacrifices in dissimilar ways.

This show of reverence not only substantiated whose side that population was on, but also maintained the hidden control of the ruling gods. In fact, this covert rule gives us clues concerning the identity of these gods.

Idol's, Image's and Altar's

There's a mountain of evidence to suggest that the ancient nations worshiping graven images or idols were actually worshiping physical beings. Put simply, the graven images or idols were nothing more than a bodily likeness or icon of the physical gods being represented.

This should come as no astonishment to anyone seeing how hundreds of thousands of people flock together to worship the statue (image/idol) of the Virgin Mary. Yet, it is not the statue of the Virgin Mary that is being worshiped, but rather the individual that the statue represents. Seemingly, ancient mankind was enacting the same rituals by physical image idolization.

Ancient mankind being easily maneuvered and dominated by these high tech beings/gods joyously reproduced their physical likeness in the form of idols/images, statues, or even altars to venerate the divine being it portrayed.

However, it may not have been the unwitting populace that decided to created the statues or idols to venerate the governing gods. Rather, the controlling gods **required** that a statue, idols or altar be created to maintain their physical godlike presence. This preserved a constant state of reverence for the god. Also, it perpetuated the god's ongoing control over the people, even if the god was not physically seen for long periods of time.

Clearly, idol worshiping, being just a method of choosing sides, ultimately escalated into a very real dilemma for Yahweh. It's no wonder Yahweh became enraged regarding idol worshiping, seeing how the practice allowed the fallen angels significant control over the numerous populations, including Israel

Evidently, the deceptive angels had covertly positioned many different leaders on the surface of the planet, justifying the phrase "other gods". The other gods not only maintained complete control over the various nations through their established idols, but insured that a constant struggle (warfare) would be maintained between the different nations they controlled (War of the gods). In fact, this global battle of religions (other gods) still rages on day.

The ancient nations endless entanglement in war was not the brainchild of the kings controlling the nations, but rather the territorial disputes between the fallen angels/other gods/idols that controlled the kings and their populations. By controlling the kings, the other gods were quite efficient in controlling the unwitting populations into doing almost anything including warfare. Control the king and you control the people.

On the other hand, there may have been an entirely different agenda taking place. This covert timetable appears to be designed to stealthily guide mankind into a habitual state of turmoil, disorder and perpetual warfare. Moreover, this pre-designed program of manipulated corruption originated from one central control factor, their "idols" which translate into other gods/fallen angels. But why?

Organized Order of Disorder

> **7 "But now, O Adam, by reason of thy fall thou art under my rule, and I am king over thee; because thou hast hearkened to me, and has transgressed against thy God. Neither will there be any deliverance from my hands until the day promised thee by thy God."**
> **8 Again he said, "Inasmuch as we do not know the day agreed upon with thee by thy God, nor the hour in which thou shalt be delivered, for that reason will we multiply war and murder upon thee and thy seed after thee.**
> **9 "This is our will and our good pleasure, that we may not leave one of the sons of men to inherit our orders in heaven.**
> CHAP. LVII.
>
> FORGOTTEN BOOKS OF EDEN/ADAM AND EVE

Satan and his host (fallen angels/other gods) are determined to make sure that the lineage of mankind remains in a constant state of disorder and corruption, thus perpetuating continuous death and destruction (war) on a global scale. This preplanned psychological and physical manipulation of the human race is conceivably taking place right under our noses at this very moment.

The hidden plan appears to be aimed at placing humankind in a demoralizing dilemma. This constant state of manipulated corruption, greed, religious wars (Idols/different gods) and failure to globally unite were designed to keep humanity from qualifying for entry into the kingdom of heaven (the Universe).

This plan would allow the fallen angels to reestablish control over their previous **"orders"** in heaven, orders that were lost during their horrendous celestial insurrection. In simpler terms, the fallen angels' "orders" in heaven paraphrases into a third of the stars that followed Satan/the Dragon. The third of the stars identify four constellations (orders) within this Universe: **Draco, (the Dragon)**, **Leo** major/minor (**the Lion**), **Ursa** major/minor (**the Bear**),

Orion (the Leopard), all of which translates into the horrifying beast found in the book of Revelation.

Other Gods/Fallen Angels

It's significant that we take a closer look at the other gods, to **substantiate** just who they are, where they originated from, their hidden bases of operations and the shrouded control they maintained over the ancient nations, as well as our modern civilizations today. Notably, there a variety of gods possessing distinct names and control factors.

Rimmon, Nisroch, Nehushtan, Zoheleth, Adrammelech, Anammelech, Dagon, Nebo, Asherah, Ashtaroth, Ashtoreth, Asheroth, Astarte, Ishtar, Chemosh, Chiun, Sun God, Ra/Re, Amon-Re, Osiris, Melech, Molech, Moloch, Marduk, Baal, Bel, the Queen of Heaven, and Baalzebub.

> 5:26 But ye have borne the tabernacle of your Moloch and Chiun your images, the star of your god, which ye made to yourselves.
> AMOS
> 28:23 For he sacrificed unto the gods of Damascus, which smote him: and he said, Because the gods of the kings of Syria help them, [therefore] will I sacrifice to them, that they may help me. But they were the ruin of him, and of all Israel. II
> CHRONICLES
> 37:38 And it came to pass, as he was worshipping in the house of Nisroch his god,...51:9 Awake, awake, put on strength, O arm of the LORD; awake, as in the ancient days, in the generations of old. [Art] thou not it that hath cut Rahab, [and] wounded the dragon?
> ISAIAH
> 48:1 Against Moab thus saith the LORD of hosts, the God of Israel; Woe unto Nebo!...
> 48:46 Woe be unto thee, O Moab! the people of Chemosh perisheth:...
> 48:7 For because thou hast trusted in thy works and in thy treasures, thou shalt also be taken: and Chemosh shall go forth into captivity [with] his priests and his princes together.
> 48:13 And Moab shall be ashamed of Chemosh,...
> 5:7 And when the men of Ashdod saw that [it was] so, they said, The ark of the God of Israel shall not abide with us: for his hand is sore upon us, and upon Dagon our god. I SAMUEL

> **43:12 And I will kindle a fire in the houses of the gods of Egypt; and he shall burn them, and carry them away captives:...**
> **43:13 He shall break also the images of Bethshemesh, that [is] in the land of Egypt; and the houses of the gods of the Egyptians shall he burn with fire.**
> **7:18 The children gather wood, and the fathers kindle the fire, and the women knead [their] dough, to make cakes to the queen of heaven, and to pour out drink offerings unto other gods, that they may provoke me to anger.**
> **44:17 But we will certainly do whatsoever thing goeth forth out of our own mouth, to burn incense unto the queen of heaven, and to pour out drink offerings unto her, as we have done, we, and our fathers, our kings, and our princes, in the cities of Judah, and in the streets of Jerusalem: for [then] had we plenty of victuals, and were well, and saw no evil.**
> **44:19 And when we burned incense to the queen of heaven, and poured out drink offerings unto her, did we make her cakes to worship her, and pour out drink offerings unto her, without our men?**
> **JEREMIAH**

Amos draws notable significance to the gods Moloch and Chiun, gods so profound they required a tabernacle to be worshiped. Although, more striking would be the "**star**" that these gods seemingly represent, suggesting that Moloch and Chiun were of extraterrestrial origin.

Where did this ancient populace get the idea that these two gods decipher into any type of star at all? Or is it possible that this allegorical representation further illustrates the third of the **stars** from which the fallen angels/other gods originated?

Obviously, the Damascus gods personally assisted the Syrians ("**help them**"), justifying the Syrians' physical worship and "**sacrificed to them**". Damascus venerated the gods/idols of Ashtaroth/Sun God. The Sun God, or bearer of the morning light, also paraphrases into Satan and his fallen angels. Ashtaroth/Astarte was distinguished as the male Duke of Hell (the **Underworld**), also celebrated as Ishtar the Babylonian goddess, the same subterranean gods worshiped by the empire of Tyre.

The kings of the many benighted nations assimilated the names of their believed gods into their own name. This immortalized not only the kings' name and kingship, but also the divine being that assisted in empowering the king and his supervised control. Damascus was no exception to the rule seeing how the King of Damascus was surnamed Benhadad (Ben-hadad), or son of Hadad.

> **49:27 And I will kindle a fire in the wall of Damascus, and it shall consume the palaces of Benhadad.**
> **JEREMIAH**

The last segment of Ben's name would manifest great significance not only in his kingship, but the very supreme being (god), that he and the entire population of Syria idolized. Hadad was well known as a storm god in Southwestern Asia.

This glorified storm god "Hadad" did not acquire his powerful status without reason. Seemingly, this elusive storm god was capable of producing potent atmospheric disturbances, just as Yahweh and his host were. In fact this was a common dogma of faith when referring to **demons**.

Demons/The Gray's

It was commonly believed that **demons** actually existed, belief to the contrary was even considered heresy. Demons were believed to be capable of producing powerful wind storms as well as possessing the power to rain down fire from heaven, mirroring that of Yahweh's greatly feared laser technology. Yet, this is just another symbolic representation of other gods and their high-tech laser weapons and devices at work.

We've all been exposed to the expression "**Satan and his demons**". Remarkably, this would actually imply two entirely dissimilar species. Seemingly, **Satan** and his fallen angels still maintain their humanlike appearance. If so, **who**, or **what** are the **demons**?

Evidently, demons were physically observed in their diabolic intervention and manipulation of humans. Yet, why were demons encountered during humanity's ancient era and not today? The solution to this mystery may actually be available today, even though we are unwilling to accept or even believe the possible demonic intervention now being inflicted upon the oblivious human race.

In simpler terms, the demonic intervention of mankind may be found in the modern UFO enigma. The standard for UFO occupants today are little Gray **demon** like entities whose physical anatomy genuinely indicates their concealed origin.

The very anatomy of these chalk-colored beings would suggest that they exist in a dark environment, possibly explaining their large black eyes. These types of eyes would be needed to see within their subterranean residence. Their albino Gray skin would suggest that these Gray entities are not exposed to bright sunlight. In fact, this lack of light would suggest that these elusive gray beings are residing **inside** this planet. This concealed world within a world may be harboring not only Satan and his fallen angels, but Satan's demons (Grays) as well.

Essentially, the Grays may actually be the underworld demonic forces of Satan and his fallen angels. Yet, where did the Grays genuinely originate from, if not from the subterranean domains of this planet? How, and/or where do these lilliputian Gray beings fit into the modification of this pre-existing world? Were they here **before** the creation, or **after** the creation? These substantial questions will be extensively probed later in these writings.

Underworld Implication

"**Nisroch**" was frequently perceived as an eagle headed deity. This significant deity had presumably returned to the rebel forces (fallen angels) of the Underworld after the demeaning slaughter of the Assyrian armies by Yahweh and his host of craft (see 19:35 II KINGS).

Nisroch is now said to have been placed in a debasing rank as the chief cook for all the dominant rulers of Hell, or lord of the flies. The lord of the flies denote Underworld leaders such as Baal-ze-bub, Satan, Lucifer, Molech, Astarte, along with many other sinister notables (other gods/fallen angels).

Nisroch being one of the winged guardians of the body modifiers/fruit of the tree of life, is now said to season the fallen angels' food with its immortal fruit. Being physical entities the fallen angels require food, as well as the body modifiers to maintain their own longevity within their subterranean hell.

"**Nebo**" was ascribed as a god of wisdom in Babylonian mythology. He was said to have invented the art of writing. Nebo being the son of **Marduk** and controlling the fate of mankind, was also distinguished as a god of the sun, and **water**. This is a notable detail seeing how Satan and his evil brood have many times been cited as a Sun God, or bearer of the morning light. Yet, how could an entire population establish this god as a god of **water**?

Naturally, one might assume that the relationship with water is a direct implication to the rainfall possibly created by the god Nebo. This would once again mirror the ability of Yahweh and his craft to manipulate global weather conditions. However, to better surmise how Nebo possibly became identified with **water**, we must first establish just who Nebo was.

Nebo was the son of the almighty **Marduk**. The deity Marduk was also alluded to as Bel-Marduk, or just Bel. Bel is just another name out of the multitude of distinct titles given for Satan. In essence, Nebo, Marduk, Bel-Marduk was nothing more than a reference to the fallen angels and their Underworld empire.

As we shall soon discover, this hidden underworld empires reside well below the major rivers, seas, and ocean floors of this planet. Moreover, this revealing detail will ultimately expose the horrifying Revelation beast "Dragon" that comes rising up out of the **sea/water.**

In fact, this aquatic implication will unmask the terrifying "leviathan", another horrifying sea monster residing below the oceans and sea floors of this world. These two allegorical sea monsters will ultimately reveal two entirely different species (**Satan and his Demons**).

> **27:1 In that day the LORD with his sore and great and strong sword shall punish leviathan the piercing serpent, even leviathan that crooked serpent; and he shall slay the dragon that [is] in the sea.**
> ISAIAH

Seemingly, Nebo was just another fallen angel masquerading as an all-powerful god in the eyes of the beguiled Babylonian populace. Its quite possible Nebo made his physical presence known by actually descending in or rising from large bodies of water, such as large lakes, rivers, seas or oceans. Hence, Nebo was a god of **water**.

In simpler terms, Nebo was a god of the Underworld that lies below the lakes, rivers, seas and oceans of this world. Nebo was also reverenced as a god of the sun. This might suggest that the mighty Nebo was visually observed as he navigated across the night skies in a brightly glowing craft resembling the radiating attributes of the sun.

Remarkably, there's a library of books detailing bright glowing UFOs entering or departing from large bodies of **water**. Some reports even entail brightly radiated craft seen traveling underwater. These types of aquatic sightings have not only been reported by ships and planes, but witnessed from shore by people who observed these unexplainable glowing craft enter or withdraw from large lakes, rivers, seas and oceans.

It's extremely significant to **remember** the data we are now compiling, seeing how we are about to discover a significant connection between the UFO phenomenon, the fallen angels (other gods), their demonic forces (the Grays) and **water.** This consistent link will ultimately expose the gateways to Hell (**the Underworld**).

Those geographical gateways will help us to establish the numerous locations on the surface of this planet that these elusive craft are entering and/or exiting from their underworld dominion. Moreover, most of these subterranean gateways reside under rivers, seas and ocean floors. In fact we are about to discover that most of the primary gateways leading in and out of this hidden world within a world (Underworld) are located over the major **fault lines** of this planet.

"Chemosh" was considered the national god of Moab. The population of Moab even considered themselves "the people of Chemosh" (see Numbers 22:29/25:1,-3). The women of Moab seducing the tribes of Israel, ultimately lured them into worshiping their god Chemosh. However, as with the other physical deities we have already examined, the god Chemosh also maintains an alias title that once again ties Chemosh to the fallen angels and their subterranean empires.

Chemosh also assumed the title **Baal**-Peor ("lord of Mount Peor") and in some cases just "Balaam." Yet, it is the terms Baal and Balaam we are most concerned with seeing how the word Baal or Balaam is directly associated to Satan and his fallen angels (Baal-Baalzebub). Essentially, Chemosh was just another member of the lord of the flies residing within the underworld domains of this Planet.

"Dagon", this name should sound quite familiar, seeing how the word "Dagon" is only missing the letter 'r' in informing us of this deity's **Dragon** (Satan) like powers. Dagon was the venerated god of the Philistines, a deity that once again reflects strong connotations of a supreme being connected to **water**, as well as land. The word "Dagon" is quite similar to the word "dag" found in the Hebrew language when alluding to the word "fish."

The Philistines worshiped an image/idol depicting half man, half fish, or a merman. The statue or idol portrayed the image of a man above the waist, possessing fish like attributes below the waist. Quite an appropriate image for a supreme being capable of existing in the seas and oceans only to surface later to inflict his deceptive control over the benighted surface dwellers. Essentially,

(**Dragon/Draco**), was just another God/fallen angel residing below the rivers, seas and ocean floors of this world.

It has been suggested that the Philistines' merman may have been a representation of their way of life, seeing how the Philistines were coastal people, living off of the bountiful harvest of the sea. However, this would not explain Yahweh's abhorrent wrath towards a simple idol which may have only portrayed a fisherman's way of surviving (fishing). It quite possible that this merman statue symbolically portrayed Satan and his demons.

As mentioned before, the term "Satan and his demons" would appear to identify two entirely dissimilar species embodying two diverse genetic forms. The genetic differences would single out the fallen angels as the image of man, where the demons take on the appearance of a hideous dwarf like scaly creature residing in an aquatic or dark subterranean environment.

Gray Link?

The Grays have often been described as chalky miniature beings with large piercing black eyes. These same lilliputian beings have also been seen with scaly or reptilian type skin, as well as exhibiting web like hands and feet.

The Grays may in fact be aquatic in nature, possibly explaining the large eyes needed to see in not only a darkened subterranean environment, but murky water as well. This is the same type of eyes used by many species of fish and amphibious creatures.

Essentially, the Grays appear to be a type of amphibious creature capable of living in, as well as out of water, much like frogs, salamanders, turtles, tortoises, snakes, lizards, crocodiles and alligators (**Leviathan**). In essence, the idolized merman (Dagon) of the Philistines may be the allegorical statue of an aquatic demon. Then again, the amphibious humanlike idol may depict both Satan and his aquatic demons of the underworld. [half man, half fish] (?)

Egyptian gods. The gods of Egypt were many times illustrated as physical humanlike beings, possessing human characteristics and behavior patterns, including flying across the sky in fiery boats (craft). The Egyptian gods were said to have frequently had wives, as well as substantial offspring. Egyptian deities even mirrored Yahweh's desire for the consumption of food and wine on a regular basis.

The Egyptian culture, much like the Mesopotamian civilization, proclaimed that their dominating humanlike gods were of extraterrestrial (heavenly) ancestry. Essentially, these extraterrestrial gods were flesh and blood beings requiring the same mortal essentials of sustenance and sheltering as mankind. Remarkably, some of the same correlations can be found in the ancient Mayan culture.

The ancient Mayans and Egyptian culture constructed amazing pyramid structures, presumably in honor of their humanlike extraterrestrial gods. Interestingly, both ancient civilizations idolized the snake or serpent. The Egyptians even went so far as to display the head of the serpent or snake (**Dragon**) on many of the crowns and headdresses worn by the upper class Egyptians. The uraeus or cobra was said to rear up on the forehead of the sun god's (Re/Ra) and spit **fire** (laser technology) at its adversaries.

The Mayans incorporated the snake or serpent into the actual design of their colossal pyramids. Both civilizations idolized the **spotted cat**. The Egyptians venerated the leopard, while the Mayans paid homage to the jaguar, possibly being one and the same spotted cat. Yet, what would snakes (serpents) and spotted felines have to do with fallen angels/other gods?

It was the snake/serpent that altered mankind's true destiny upon the surface of this modified world. Yet, the snake is nothing more than a symbolic delineation of the **Dragon**. The "dragon" translates into the constellation Draco, being the location of the home worlds of the leader of the fallen angels, **Satan** (the Dragon).

The leopard and/or Jaguar (spotted cat) is the symbolic embodiment of Osiris, or god (fallen angel) of the **Underworld**. The high priests of Osiris are many times characterized by wearing leopard skins. The leopard is closely identified with Greek mythology connecting the underworld god Osiris with the constellation of Orion. In fact, the great pyramids of Egypt were at one time cosmically aligned in the same formation as the stars in the belt of the constellation of Orion.

The leopard is Osiris's traditional mount, sometimes seen as a leopard drawn chariot or Osiris's playmates. The leopard, being the trade mark of the underworld god Osiris and the constellation of Orion, brands him as one of the leaders of the third of the star systems (constellations) that chose to rebel against Yahweh and the kingdom of heaven.

Moreover, the **Leopard/Osiris** actually identifies one of the four animals (**leaders**) found in the beast of the Revelation. This horrifying beast symbolically depicts a massive war machine that will come rising up out of the sea

(**Underworld**) to devour mankind during the days of the great Judgment (The Revelation).

Notably, Osiris was not the only masquerading Egyptian god to reveal his fallen angel identity. When searching for the ultimate Egyptian god of the Underworld, one stumbles over **Ra/Re** time and time again. This powerful deity was believed to have originated from the primal oceans of this planet (the Creation).

The Egyptians believed that every day their **sun god Ra** would sail across the sky **in** a sun **boat** that took him to the Underworld. After reaching the Underworld, it was believed that another Nile river existed, on which Ra would continue his journey **in** another boat pulled by the Underworld ruler Osiris. Completing the journey, Ra would reach the horizon where he and his sun boat would begin to rise again.

The very myth would suggest that something other than the sun sailed across the sky/heavens. If Ra was the sun god (sun), what was the boat? If the boat was the sun, what was Ra? Why would one have to be "**in**" the other if they were both one and the same? Why would the physical deity Re even be connected with the sun, much less a boat?

Here again, we have workable testimony alluding to a physical god stemming from a subterranean environment. You will also note that both elements of fire and water appear once again to identify the sun deity Ra. As with the other gods we have already examined, this god of the sun may be the symbolic representation of the misconstrued fiery craft (sun), that Ra sailed across the skies **in** before descending into large bodies of water to enter the underworld.

This conjecture becomes even more convincing when one realizes that Ra was given the attributes of the solar disc (**disk**), which may indeed identify the solar sun. Yet, these same characteristics also identify a fiery flying saucer (flying **disk/UFO**). This would once again mimic the UFO enigma, seeing how these fiery glowing disks (UFOs) have been reported time and time again, to enter and exit large bodies of water, including major rivers.

Evidently, the symbolic characterization of all these gods was nothing more than a twofold depiction of Satan and his fallen angels, along with their demonic disciples, as they travel the open skies in their fiery flying craft (disk/sun).

Ra/Re was no exception to the rule, seeing how "Ra" also translates into the Egyptian serpent (**dragon**) god "Sata" (Satan?). "Sata" was the father of lighting who fell to earth along with all the other seditious angels from a third of the stars.

Essentially, the Egyptian god Ra was one of the commanders of the fallen angels now dwelling within the **underworld** domains of this planet. This conjecture can further be substantiated by the very animal that identifies the god Ra. The Egyptians believed the **lion** to be sacred and the embodiment of Ra. Moreover, the Lion was regarded as part **fire** and part **water**.

Yet, more significantly, we discover that the **lion** believed to symbolize the sun god Ra is also one of the four animals that make up the terrifying beast of the Revelation that will come rising up out of the sea during the days of the great judgment. In essence Ra (the lion) is also one of the four leaders of a third of the star systems (Constellations) that chose to rebel against Yahweh and his universal host. Leo the **Lion (Ra)**, Orion the **Leopard (Osiris),** Draco the **Dragon (Satan).**

> 51:9 Awake, awake, put on strength, O arm of the LORD; awake, as in the ancient days, in the generations of old. [Art] thou not it that hath cut Rahab, [and] wounded the dragon? ISAIAH
>
> 89: 10 Thou hast broken Rahab in pieces, as one that is slain…
>
> 74: 13, Thou didst divide the sea by thy strength: thou brakest the heads of the Dragons in the waters.
>
> 74: 14, Thou brakest the heads of Leviathan in pieces… PSALMS

As we shall soon discover, there is a big difference between "Leviathan/Rahab and the "Dragon". Leviathan/Rahab is a direct reference to the chaotic seas tamed by the forces of order. Leviathan/Rahab being the howling elements of chaos, had to be subdued by the forces of order before **they** subverted the Universe. Yet, how could a storm or the chaotic seas of this planet subvert an entire Universe. (?)

It was Yahweh and his host that brought about the lunar creation of this world by destroying or crippling the Leviathan monster that represents the chaotic seas. However, if the Dragon is the symbolic representation of Satan and his fallen angels, what is "Leviathan"? If the Dragon identifies the monster (fallen angels) that comes rising up out of the sea (underworld), what is the mysterious "Leviathan", the monster that lives in the sea?

Heads of the Dragon

This issue would actually return us to the creation, seeing how the chaotic seas were tamed or altered by the inauguration of a moon around this pre-existing world. Obviously, this modification (creation) did not come easily, seeing how the global manipulation incited a cosmic riot. This universal insurrection instigated a third of the inhabited constellations to rebel against Yahweh and the very creation itself. "and there was **war** in heaven" (outer space).

Clearly, Yahweh and his universal forces were able to subdue the horrendous onslaught of the revolting fallen angels and their cosmic war machine. In fact, the verses elaborate on the certainty that Yahweh "slew the Dragon", "**cut** Rahab, <u>**and**</u> **wounded** the Dragon", "**broken** Rahab in **pieces**", "brakest the **heads** of the Dragon <u>**and**</u> Leviathan in pieces".

Remarkably, the verses inform us that the **war machine** of the fallen angels (the Dragon) was **not** destroyed, but only cut, wounded, and/or broken in pieces. Essentially, the verses indicate the massive damage inflicted upon the physical machines and devices (craft and weapons) used by the fallen angels in their celestial war campaign.

The Dragon symbolizes the physical beings from a third of the inhabited stars systems that took part in this massive cosmic war. Yet, what was the **heads** of the dragon that were "cut, wounded, and broken in pieces"? Notably, the verses use the word heads, and not head, indicating more than one.

The heads of the Dragon may represent the numerous celestial leaders (heads) that orchestrated the universal warfare in heaven. If true, the verses would suggest that the leaders (heads) of the fallen angels were mortally wounded, thus rendering the leaders physically and mentally impaired, subsequently ending their celestial campaign.

However, there appears to be a considerable amount of data missing. Obviously, the "**heads**" of the Dragon were much more than just physical leaders of the nonconformist star systems and their physical inhabitants. This conjecture is based on the fact that these cosmic populations and their leaders would possess no universal power at all without their physical devices and machines (craft and weapons).

By examining this data from an extraterrestrial point of view, we discover that the **heads** of the Dragon may have nothing to do with the controlling leaders of the rebelling star systems, and everything to do with the war machine itself.

Clearly, leaders and their governed populations are useless without their weapons of War. In fact, weapons dictate the true physical power of the leaders and their benefactors. A battle of any significance cannot be waged if one possesses nothing to fight with. We also need to take into consideration that a battle cannot be waged without a battlefield, which in most cases requires **transportation** of the war machines (craft and weapons) to the battlefield.

> **1:6 And the angels which kept not their first estate, but left their own habitation, he hath reserved in everlasting chains under darkness unto the judgment of the great day.** JUDE

It was a third of the stars that chose to rebel against Yahweh and his universal host. Leaving their own estate (**constellations**) in heaven (the Universe), the fallen angels **traveled** to this star system in massive craft ("**heads/Starships**"), to mount their horrendous insurrection against Yahweh and his forces. And there was war in heaven (outer space), thus identifying the heads (**firepower**) of the Dragon, heads that depict the craft and weapons (**power**) of the fallen angels.

The enormous craft, crews and weapons gave the fallen angels (Dragon) their substantial power to not only travel within this Universe, but also incite a universal confrontation. Yet, the craft (**heads**) were ultimately destroyed and/or damaged (cut, wounded, broken in pieces) during the clash of the confrontation, thus concluding the fallen angels' war campaign.

Obviously the immense craft were not totally destroyed, but only crippled (cut, wounded, broken), as well as possibly boarded and seized. In fact it would appear that Yahweh deliberately commandeered the surviving craft as a means to house and sustain what remained of the surviving renounced angels while in their dark subterranean prison of this planet.

In essence, these enormous surviving craft may actually depict the **seven heads** (**seven** Starships) of the Dragon that will coming rising up out of the sea (Underworld) during the Revelation. Here again, the holy number **seven** is repeatedly used to plague the surviving fallen angels with the undeviating reminder of the number of constellations within the Universe that did not chose to rebel against Yahweh. This would suggest that Yahweh intentionally allowed only seven heads/craft/Starships to survive the battle, **seven craft** that are now concealed inside this planet.

Taking Aim at Mankind

Unmistakably, the fallen angels/other gods had not only beguiled but motivated mankind into worshiping and physically serving erroneous gods. This psychological control and obscure manipulation of mankind (**religions**) is still raging on today.

Moreover, this relentless exploitation of humans appears to be aimed at keeping supervised control of this planet from the kingdom of heaven. This would allow the fallen angels the ability to maintain an endless cold war condition within the confines of the kingdom of heaven.

Essentially, the cosmic war of Genesis is far from over, a cold war that will continue until the days of the great Judgment, or final battle between **good** (the kingdom of heaven) and **evil** (fallen angels). Until that time, the fallen angels will do everything in their power to impose their unrelenting anguish upon mankind.

The shrouded demoralization of humankind may be taking place at this very moment. Yet, the contemporary debasing of mankind must now be more subtle, timely, ambiguous and inconspicuous, overshadowed with mankind's own wants and desires (**greed**). Moreover, this hidden demoralization of humanity is conceivably using mankind's own technology against itself.

Two technological marvels, believed to have been created by man, would be the modern radio and television/movies. These mentally manipulative tools have possibly been engineered into the civilizations of humanity by the fallen angels, unknown to the humans utilizing them. These tools are in fact the ultimate debasing and desensitizing devices for psychologically manipulating and brainwashing/programming the masses.

This prolonged scheme appears to be aimed at destroying any good that may come of man. The well-thought out plan seems to be directed towards a covert indoctrination designed to lead the easily mislead populations along the path of corruption spawned by mankind's greed, lust and arrogant pride. And we don't even know it.

In Search of the Underworld

Thus far, we have examined extensive data alluding to the possibility of a genuinely underworld domain existing **within** the very foundations of this planet. Scripture would even have us believe that this underworld region was actually honed out, or physically formed at different levels **inside** this planet. Essentially, this subterranean creation was artificially fabricated by these stellar beings, sometime before, during or perhaps after the Lunar conversion (Creation) of this world.

> **...then I made firm the waters, that is to say the bottomless, and I made foundation of light around the water, and created seven circles from inside, and Imaged it (sc. the water) like crystal wet and dry, that is to say like glass,... XXVII.**
>
> FORGOTTEN BOOKS OF EDEN/SECRETS OF ENOCH
>
> **5 And when I looked in the vision, behold, one of those four angels who came forth, hurled from heaven, collected together, and took all the great stars, whose form partly resembled that of horses; and binding them all hand and foot, cast them into the cavities of the earth.**
>
> CHAP. LXXXVII. THE BOOK OF ENOCH

The subterranean **cavities** (caverns) of this planet are not only quite authentic, but appear to reside within seven subterranean levels that were "imaged" like crystal or glass. This would lead one to believe that these seven different underworld layers along with their cavernous walls and floors look like crystal or glass. In fact, nature itself is quite skillful in forming underground caverns displaying beautiful crystal walls, floors, stalagmites, and stalactites' that take on the appearance of different color glass (crystal).

However, laser technology could have performed the very same task in less than a fraction of the time, while simultaneously producing a glass or crystal like surface in the process. One detail is certain, whether artificial (laser technology) or mother nature, Scripture confirms that this Underworld kingdom and the entities living therein do in fact exist.

> **1:6 Now there was a day when the sons of God came to present themselves before the LORD, and Satan came also among them.**
>
> **1:7 And the LORD said unto Satan, Whence comest thou? Then Satan answered the LORD, and said, From going to and fro in the earth, and from walking up and down in it.** JOB
>
> **1 Then Satan and ten from his hosts, transformed themselves into maidens, unlike any others in the whole world for grace.**
>
> **2 they came up out of the river in the presence of Adam and Eve, and they said among themselves, "Come, we will look at the faces of Adam and Eve, who are of the men upon earth. How beautiful they are, and how different is their look from our own faces."...**

3 Adam and Eve looked at them also and wondered at their beauty, and said, "Is there, then, under us, another world, with such beautiful creatures as these in it?"
4 And those maidens said to Adam and Eve, "Yes, indeed, we are an abundant creation."
5 Then Adam said to them, "But how do you multiply?"
6 And they answered him,"We have husbands who wedded us, and we bear them children,...and thus we increase.
7 Then they shouted over the river as if to call their husbands and their children, who came up from the river, men and children; and every one came to his wife, his children being with him.
14 Then Adam and Eve arose, and prayed to God, while Satan and his hosts went down into the river, in presence of Adam and Eve; to let them see that they were going back to their own regions.
CHAP. LXXII. FORGOTTEN BOOK OF EDEN/ADAM AND EVE

In reading this chapter of Job, one might ask the perplexing question as to who was around to physically **see**, **hear** and record what transpired at this unique meeting between Yahweh, the sons of God and Satan.

Here again, I would like to point out that thus far we have not encountered anything written in Scripture to indicate that we are examining invisible spirits or ghosts, but rather physical beings.

Yet, more significant would be the revealing words spoken by Satan, words that once again draw great significance towards "**water**" Obviously, Satan's and his host not only reside in the Underworld below water, but possess the freedom to interact between the two different worlds.

The fallen angels appear to have complete run of this world, inside or out ("up and down"), even though chained to the planet. This might suggest that Yahweh and Satan are bound by a possible cold war contract. That contract would explain why Yahweh and his host did not immediately seize Satan when he made his appearance at this meeting. This cosmic contract will later be scrutinized in full detail when we examine the New Testament.

Evidently, this mystifying subterranean world may conceal massive populations fathered by the fallen angels. This would once again indicate that the fallen angels are human in nature. If so, what are Satan's Demons (**Leviathan**)?

The verses quietly give us a clue to the Underworld and its possible location. Moreover, this lead contains a common bond that will help us narrow down the geographical locations on the surface of this planet **not** associated with the Underworld. This will help to confine our search to specific regions' on the planet corresponding to the common bond. This common denominator would once again indicate large bodies of "**water**".

In this particular case, Satan and his host were arising and descending out of a river that appears to lead down into their underworld domain. Yet, how could a genuine underworld exist, considering the tremendous pressure and volumes of water threatening the front doors of this hollow empire? Remarkably, this enigmatic issue would compel us to examine what is commonly known as the **"hollow Earth"** theory.

Hollow Earth Theory

There are numerous legends associated with the hollow Earth theory, as well as reports alluding to encounters with inter-terrestrial beings and their highly advanced underground civilizations. I personally don't believe the Earth is hollow. The assertion "**hollow Earth**" is obviously misleading, seeing how the phraseology leads one to conclude that there is no center core located within this planet, hence the word "hollow".

It's believed that the earth contains a solid spinning inner core. Outside the inner core exist the outer core and "inner mantle" consisting of magma/molten rock. Outside the inner mantle rest the "outer mantle" and crust of the planet. The rocky outer mantle is believed to be quite ridged or solid and about 1,800 miles thick.

Quite naturally the thickness of the outer crust and mantle would vary at different locations around the planet. Therefore, the conclusive question should not be what resides in the inner (hollow) core of this planet, but rather what is actually **living inside** the outer crust and mantle of this world?

Underworld Clues/Fallen Angel Connection

There have been many strange and outright bizarre stories of average people stumbling across doorways leading down into the subterranean regions of this planet One such narrative depicts Scandinavian fishermen, who by accident sailed into what they believed to be a great hole at the North Pole. The fishermen reportedly came across a lush and green land **inside** the Earth, inhabited by what the fishermen claim to be towering giants twelve feet or more in height.

It was alleged that these humanlike giants were able to live to be 400 to 800 years of age, populating what was described as a highly advanced metropolis, operating spacecraft that were powered by electromagnetism that they collected from the atmosphere of the planet.

It was even submitted that these giants controlled a material sun inside their subterranean world. The artificial sun appeared to have smoke coming from it, suggesting that this powerful glowing orb was regulated volcanic magma.

This remarkable account reeks of fallen angels and their Genesis lineage. The fallen angels mated with the women of mankind and procreated **giants.** It was the fallen angels, and their goliath descendants, who were allowed to partake of the fruit of the tree of life enabling them to live an immortal existence for hundreds or perhaps thousands of years.

The fallen angels possess glowing craft capable of manipulating the magnetic fields of this planet via electromagnetism. The fallen angels possess devices capable of manipulating physical matter, including volcanic magma capable of producing a massive powerhouse of perpetual energy (Sun?). It was the fallen angels and their mighty issue who were incarcerated inside this planet, and forced to seek refuge within the huge underground caverns to escape the lunar deluge of Noah.

The South Pole has just as many hollow Earth believers. Seemingly, both poles secretly conceal substantial UFO activity well hidden from the prying eyes of mankind, possibly accounting for their frigid geographical locations. Then again, these two polar regions may have nothing to do with the fallen angels' desire to remain hidden from the meddling eyes of mankind. Rather, these two polar regions were at one time lush green land masses **before** the lunar conversion was performed.

Another subterranean mystery can be found in the legend surrounding Mt. Shasta, in the mountain range of Northern California. According to the legend, a race of highly advanced, tall, fair complexion people possessing Siamese blue eyes are said to live deep within the lava caves that honeycomb both Mt. Shasta and Shastina. These People are said to be what is left of a super civilization that existed twenty-six thousand years ago on a continent identified as Lemuria. This vast continent was said to have been destroyed and sank into the Pacific Ocean.

The lava caves were reported to lead down into the subterranean cities of Lletheleme and Yaktayvia, of the Lemurian's highly advanced civilization. It was believed that this mysterious empire had reached such technological heights that our assumed high tech civilization of today would pale in comparison.

This technologically superior civilization appears to have been based on the belief that the only real purpose of civilization was to cultivate the development of advanced narcissism. Yet, this prideful people and their continent ultimately succumbed to destruction by earthquakes and subterranean upheavals. The entire continent sank into the Pacific Ocean, leaving only a handful of survivors. The few survivors ended up in the sanctuary of the huge lava caves in the towering mountain range of Northern California.

This legend mirrors the myth of the lost continent of Atlantis, also believed to have sunk into the ocean. Did both fabled continents exist at the same time, or were they one and the same? In either case, the continent or continents are likely contenders for the first earthly home of the fallen angels and their goliath descendants. Notably, the continents existed **before** the deluge of Noah.

If the reader will recollect, it was the great flood of Noah that was designed to destroy the **arrogant** and **prideful** (narcissistic) fallen angels, along with their titan heirs. Yet, the legendary narrative behind these inundated continents has nothing to do with them sinking into the oceans, but rather, their submersion by rising waters.

In essence, the two mysterious lost continents (now polar caps?) did not sink into the oceans at all. Rather, the oceans of the world covered, displaced and literally relocated them in a global upheaval of earthquakes and tidal waves imposed by a possible pole shift created by the second lunar conversion of Noah.

Many survivors were forced to seek refuge underground (the Underworld), or cling to possible floating debris long enough (one hundred and fifty days) to land on the newly founded continents created by the Moon's new location.

The most detrimental and influential believer of the hollow Earth theory was Hitler. Hitler not only believed in the existence of a genuine Underworld, but it became an obsession that many of his henchmen may have paid for with their lives. Hitler spared no expense in funding an elaborate expedition to the island of Rugen in an effort to find the entrance to what he surmised to be an authentic subterranean empire.

Hitler actually believed that this super race of beings living underground would judge him and his people to be brilliant, simply because they not only believed in the existence of this secret underworld race, but were able to actually find them. By that, Hitler and his people would be allowed to interbreed with these superior beings, thus spawning mutations that would create a new race of mankind.

The Third Reich and it's very birth contained numerous occult overtones that many historical records are unwilling to acknowledge. Nazi mysticism maintained that its true administration derived from extraterrestrial sources, openly declaring that an extraterrestrial society was the significant origin of their ideology, power, warlike organization and devices.

The Nazis cited their hidden extraterrestrial mentors as underground supermen, being nothing short of supervising demigods. This master race was believed to live deep beneath the Earth's surface, as well as fathering the Aryan race believed to be Nazism's true inception.

The Nazis theorized that their underground demigods would ultimately return to the surface of the planet as supreme rulers once the Nazis began their racial purification program to establish the Thousand Year Reich.

The Nazis held the conviction that physical beings of this secret underground race were actually walking among mankind today. Hitler and his high-ranking members of the Third Reich even claimed to have actually come in contact with this race of subterranean supermen. Hitler boldly professed as he shouted, "The new man is living amongst us now! He is here! I will tell you a secret. I have seen the new man. He is intrepid and cruel. I was afraid of him."

It was even alleged that Hitler often awoke in the middle of the night screaming, gripped by convulsions of fear and panic, shouting that "he" has come for him, declaring that "he" was standing in the corner of his bedroom, as "he" emerged from his **underworld kingdom.**

Here again, we have substantial clues pointing to the true probability that Hitler's demigods were actually the fallen angels, technological supermen deriving from an extraterrestrial origin. This might justify why the fallen angels sought out and enticed Hitler, psychologically employing Hitler to performing their covert dirty work, as well as reaching out and indirectly inflicting horrendous atrocities towards Yahweh. Clearly, Hitler's most horrifying deed was deliberately aimed at destroying the one thing that ties this planet to the kingdom of heaven, being none other than Yahweh's chosen peoples, the **Jews.**

It's quite possible Hitler didn't mark the Jews for death, but rather the fallen angels did. As mentioned before, if you control the King (Hitler), you control the people (Germany). The fallen angels, psychologically controlling Hitler and his entire nation, could have selected any ethnic target to cleanse.

Yet, the coincidental order of events targeting the Jewish world, and the alliance between Hitler and these extraterrestrial supermen of the underworld speaks for itself. Hitler being the pawn could have been mentally maneuvered for the sole function of Jewish annihilation without ever knowing the true objective of the fallen angels that he venerated.

Everything Hitler attested to may be factual. Hitler and his ruthless followers may have actually been involved with the Underworld, and its fallen angels' residence, as well as performing the merciless bidding of Satan, including the extermination of Yahweh's chosen people.

This would compel one to question the genuine motives behind the historical leaders who provoked entire populations to go to war. Hitler may have been only one out of hundreds of historical leaders and their populations that were psychologically seduced into bloody warfare by these evasive underworld entities.

Moreover, this may have been the same type of mental tampering that took place during the Biblical war campaigns. It is quite possible that the different nations were constantly fighting among themselves, due to the other gods/fallen angels they venerated. Once again this would establish the fallen angels as organized rulers of disorder.

UFO Connection

Other than legends, lost continents and Hitler's master race, we need to inquire as to what other evidence is there to substantiate the existence of a genuine Underworld. As we have already discovered, scripture contains numerous accounts of highly advanced flying machines under intelligent control by extraterrestrial/heavenly entities. This would include Satan and his fallen angels, seeing how they also derived from the same extraterrestrial origin. Essentially, Yahweh and his host along with Satan and his fallen angels were observed traveling the open skies in glowing craft, which today could only be described as UFOs.

Understandably, most of the world today possesses no knowledge of the UFO phenomena, nor could care less. I could quote from many UFO publications, or list many UFO reports. However, this book is not designed to waste time trying to convince the reader that UFOs exist. This book was created to pick up where the Ufologist left off, knowing full well that the UFO enigma is in fact a **reality**.

Unmistakably, Scripture denotes only **two** locations from which these elusive flying machines (UFOs) could have originated from. The **first** would naturally be outer space, thus identifying Yahweh and his host of the kingdom of heaven (the Universe).

The **second** location would be what is defined as an underworld domain hidden **inside** this planet. As we are discovering, this Underworld dominion conceals high tech devices and populations (Satan, fallen angels, demons/grays) just waiting for the day and hour to be totally released upon the surface of this planet.

Essentially, the kingdom of heaven (the Universe) and the hidden subterranean domains of this world are the primary sources of UFOs. Put simply, this planet and its populations are under constant observation by Yahweh's host, Satan and his fallen angels and their demonic counterparts, the Grays. This surreptitious reconnaissance of the human race would naturally require a bird's eye view of this entire planet, outwardly justifying the UFO activity taking place around the world.

UFOs and the MOON

Our moon may also play a major role in the observation and manipulation of humanity. The Moon would offer a prime location far from the prying eyes of humans as well as allowing an eagle eye on the populations of this planet. It's quite possible that the moon may be concealing technology far beyond the scope of human comprehension. It could be utilized as a base of operations. If true, why haven't we seen these bases on the surface of the Moon with our powerful telescopes?

Half of the answer may lie in the fact that mankind is only able to observe one side of the moon, leaving the far side of the moon a complete mystery. The other half of the equation may be that the super technology utilized by these celestial entities would not only allow them to fabricate a hidden base of operation on the surface of the moon, but construct an entire complex of operations **inside** the moon.

The hollow moon hypothesis is by no means new, and would compel one to question the true origin of our moon. If indeed the moon is hollow, we would be confronted with a new creation thesis. In essence, the moon may be a space station, which could have powered itself into orbit around this planet eons ago. Naturally this would be an absurd conjecture for the simple minds of humans with no concept of super technology.

There have been scientists who suggested that the moon could possibly be hollow. Michel Vasin and Alexander Shcherbakov, senior scientists at the Soviet Academy of Sciences, published a theory in the Sputnik magazine (July, 1990), an official Soviet Government Publication. These two scientists have reason to believe that our moon is not a completely natural planetoid, but rather a hollowed-out world.

Their reasoning behind such a bizarre theory was based on the fact that the Soviets did a density study of the moon, indicating that our lunar satellite was hollow. They surmised that if in fact the moon is hollow, then it must have been **artificially** hollowed out (laser technology?). This lead them to conclude that our hollow moon was possibly fabricated by an unknown alien race that steered it into orbit around this planet eons ago.

Our NASA scientists had sensitive seismographic devices placed on the surface of the moon, attempting to learn more about the internal makeup of the satellite. They then allowed spent stages of rocket boosters and lunar landing modules to crash onto the surface of the moon. Each time this was performed, the NASA scientists detected a hollow reverberation indicating that the Moon rang out like a huge gong or bell.

The vibrations traveled only about 20 to 30 miles down into the surface of the moon, where a different material was detected. That unknown substance was not rock, seeing how the vibrations of the crashed objects travel a great distance **around** the moon, and not into the interior of the moon, indicating a possible internal metal lining.

Observatories around the world have reported numerous strange lights on the surface of the moon. In fact, our own astronauts have reported egg-shaped UFOs and strange lights on the moon, as well as witnessing unknown UFOs as they voyaged back and forth from the earth. One can only speculate as to which of the two stellar parties, the kingdom of heaven or the fallen angels, are in command of Earth's only observational satellite?

UFOs and Water

In searching for evidence to substantiate the existence of a genuine underworld, we discover that the residences of this subterranean empire actually go out of their way to ensure that their hidden origin stays just that, **hidden**.

This would be a logical move for a highly advanced underworld civilization, seeing how mankind would go to elaborate lengths to find them. This might explain why reports deriving from most UFO close encounters are full of information designed to confuse.

However, the UFO phenomenon actually betrays itself by inadvertently exposing its hidden underwater network of operations. In fact this network of operations will resolve the issue as to how so many UFO reports could occur in just a two or three-year period of time. This obvious time table will reveal that there are no light years involved with extraterrestrial craft that reside right under our very noses.

One such case involves police officer Herbert Schirmer, who on the night of December 3, 1967 stated that he had contact with a spacecraft and its occupants in Ashland, Nebraska. Officer Schirmer claimed that at about 2:30 am, his police cruiser lights lit up an object on the road that he thought was a broken down semi (tractor-trailer). However, when Schirmer filed his report he also made comment of a UFO sighting. There was also missing time in patrolman Schirmer's log book that same night.

Schirmer was placed under hypnosis where he stated that he sat in his patrol car that night trying to determine what was on the road in front of him. At about that time, his radio, car engine and head lights all went dead. Schirmer described the object to be shaped like a football with encompassing pulsating lights, and a glowing undercarriage supported by tripod legs.

Schirmer stated that one of the occupants came out of the craft and walked over to his cruiser where he pointed something at him that generated a bright light, causing Schirmer to become paralyzed before he passed out. Awakening, Schirmer found himself on board the craft, where he claims he was able to communicate with the beings through a type of telepathy that caused his head to hurt.

Officer Schirmer was asked questions about power plants and water reservoirs. He was told they landed there to collect electricity from the power lines in the area. Schirmer was also informed that their 102 foot diameter craft worked by inverted electromagnetism that permitted the craft to operate against gravity.

Schirmer's description of the occupants of the craft closely fits the description of the infamous Gray entities often associated with the UFO enigma. They were about four and a half to five feet tall, with large chests, and wore tight fitting suits with silver gray boots.

Schirmer remarked that he was only able to see their faces, seeing how that was the only part of their body not clothed. He stated that their skin was a dough color, their eyes were shaped like large cat eyes, and their mouth was no more than a slit in the face.

Schirmer claimed that he was told they have UFO **bases** located underground and underwater, one of which is located off the coast of Florida in the direction of Bermuda. Schirmer was also informed that these beings were using humans in breeding experiments. Schirmer was then returned to his car, at which point the Grays returned to their craft. The craft produced a reddish orange glow and a high-pitched whine just before it shot straight up into the sky.

Schirmer's remarkable encounter reveals many hidden details. Officer Schirmer was informed that these beings have bases underground and **underwater**. However, Schirmer may have only been told half the truth. This conjecture is based on the fact that the Gray entities used the word **"base"** to describe their point of origin. The word "base" would outright suggest a **temporary** station leading one to believe that these Gray beings came from a place other than this planet.

This would be an excellent dis-information technique. Obviously, a base of operations could simply be moved at any time. Not to mention that trying to find a simple underwater base located within an entire ocean and/or subterranean cavern would be like looking for a needle in a haystack that no one would burden themselves to find. Furthermore, who's going to believe anything from someone who claims they saw a flying saucer?

The truth be known, these Gray beings could have told Schirmer that they physically lived **inside** this planet, and have inhabited this underworld domain for thousands of years. They could have told Schirmer the exact location of the underworld doorways leading to their underwater/underground dwelling, and its highly advanced civilization.

However, this astonishing revelation would have provoked every scientist in the world to come out of the woodwork with every technological device available to find them. There would have been a massive search, not for just a simple base, but an entire underworld civilization living inside this planet right under our very noses.

The very idea that the craft in Schirmer's abduction had to be recharged using electricity from local power lines would suggest that the craft, along with its Gray occupancy, originated from a very close location. Or are we to believe that these craft are capable of traveling the Cosmos on a single charge?

Obviously, the craft was designed for short runs, possibly accountings for the constant recharging requirement. The craft was either housed by a nearby base, mother ship, or literally manufactured **inside** this planet for employment on the surface of this world. The craft itself may indicate a thriving underworld industrial powerhouse maintained by an entire civilization, and not just a simple base of operations.

Schirmer's report clarified that these elusive beings were quite interested in establishing the whereabouts of power plants and water reservoirs. This might suggest a martial strategy on the part of these evasive Gray entities, seeing how power plants and water reservoirs are the life blood of mankind's very existence.

Without power and drinking water, modern man could effortlessly be brought to its knees. Not to mention the fact that these same Gray entities and their craft have been seen all over the world, around **nuclear** power plants, airports, dams and more military installations than one would be willing to believe.

Clearly, these mysterious Gray entities are maintaining a continuous surveillance of everything that mankind does, and every source of energy empowering the livelihood of the human race. This might suggest that the Grays are systematically logging the locations of mankind's very lifelines on the surface of this planet.

It's quite possible that the Grays are involved in a significant plan for global intervention. This might explain why Schirmer was recklessly informed that these beings were conducting breeding experiments on humans. This information is by no means new to the Ufologist, and may be a timely prelude to covert infiltration, prior to their global incursion.

The location of the base given to Schirmer could for all practical purposes be the entrance to a massive underwater, subterranean civilization. This unknown location is off the coast of Florida in the area of Bermuda. That would place this underworld domain inside the mysterious **Bermuda Triangle.**

This is the same location where numerous ships, planes and people have simply vanished without a trace. Moreover, this aquatic location has been teeming with UFO activity for more years than historical chronology can account for.

One factor is certain, the oceans and **seas** (**waters**) of this planet are the vital benchmarks in exposing this elusive Underworld and its bizarre inhabitancy, as well as the UFO phenomenon itself.

Even our navy is well aware that something strange is going on under the oceans of this planet. In the 1960's, a group of scientists for the Office of Naval Research (ONR) was working on a long-range underwater communication test.

After setting up a mile long antenna on the continental shelf, the ONR ship equipped with unique instruments designed to pick up transmissions underwater moved out into the ocean. The instruments were then lowered to the bottom of the Ocean to pick up the signals being transmitted from the mile long antenna.

The transmission began, but to the scientists' surprise, the signal was repeated, but **not** by the Navy. Not only was the signal repeated, but it was followed by some type of strange code that complex computers are still trying to decipher.

ONR reported later that they believed the experimental signals were picked up and copied by "something unknown". That "unknown" began transmitting signals on its own, as well as the signal that it copied. When the scientists finally traced down the foreign signal, they discovered it originated from one of the deepest areas of the Atlantic Ocean, approximately 29,000 feet deep, in the **Bermuda triangle.**

If in fact these Gray beings and the fallen angels are residing inside enormous caverns under the oceans floors of this world, the only way to truly intervene with humans would be to commute to where the human race dwells.

This might explain not only the great number of worldwide UFO reports given in a single year, but the very connection between UFOs and large bodies of water. Unmistakably, something mysterious is taking place under the waters of this planet. Something or some**one** is using intelligently controlled devices capable of flying in and out of large bodies of water, as well as outer space (heaven).

In probing the mountain of data on UFOs, one finds that almost 50 percent of all UFO sightings have taken place over water, coming out of water, plunging into water, navigating **underwater**, coming from the direction of large bodies of water, or traveling towards large bodies of water.

It's quite possible that these aquatic sightings actually depict the fallen angels and the Grays (Demons) covert activity on the surface of this planet. This would leave Yahweh and his host as the remaining 50% of UFO sighting taking place on the surface of this world.

One would think that, **if** in fact, this highly advanced civilization does exist under the ocean floors of this planet, it should have been discovered long ago. However, this assumption may not necessarily be valid seeing how we humans do not live on, or in the oceans. In fact, mankind today only occupies about twenty plus or minus percent of the actual land mass of this planet.

The chances of someone actually witnessing these craft entering or exiting from the oceans or seas would be almost nil. Essentially, the discovery of a highly advanced underwater, subterranean civilization would never happen, especially if that civilization wanted to remain **hidden**.

In just the last fifty years, mankind has technologically advanced to the point of exploring the heavens (outer space), as well as the oceans floors. Inevitably, mankind is going to find them out, unless of course Yahweh's vowed revealing (Revelation) transpires first, factors that even the underworld and its hidden occupants are well aware of.

Mankind is now photographing and charting the ocean floors. It's just a matter of time before humans stumble across active aquatic gateways that these mysterious craft (UFOs) are using to enter or exit from their underwater underworld. Ultimately, mankind will become aware of the obvious connection between UFOs and **water**.

When that happens, we will organize an aquatic launch pad hellbent on finding out just who or what is living under the oceans and sea floors. In fact, this underworld kingdom and its inhabitants are possibly taking extreme measures to eliminate the chances of their craft being seen as they enter or exist from their subterranean dominion.

These high tech craft are possibly equipped with on board detecting systems far beyond the scope of man's primitive radar or sonar. The craft entering or exiting from their aquatic gateways would undoubtedly know whether or not a manmade vessel or vessels were in the immediate area before they surface or enter into their hidden underwater/underworld.

This would rule out a greater number of actual worldwide UFO reports to date. Yet, we are about to discover that even the intellectual heights of a superior being can err, thus allowing themselves and their craft to be caught at inopportune times.

The oceans and seas are not the only bodies of water that UFOs have been seen emerging from, diving into or just hovering over. Let's not forget that most rivers lead to oceans and seas, offering excellent aquatic freeways for these elusive craft. The actual statistics are completely unknown, seeing how they have not been properly evaluated.

With the theories put forth in this publication, it would take substantial support to properly research, compile, systematically catalogue and computerize all the data associated with UFOs and water. Yet, in evaluating a small portion of sightings we discover evidences pointing at the tectonic plate intersections of this planet.

UFOs, Triangle's and Fault Line's

Many reports connecting UFOs with rivers and lakes would suggest that they are regional, implying that certain lakes and rivers are teeming with UFO activity, while others are not. The Great Lakes of North America is one of many such enigmatic locations.

These lakes harbor what is known as a cryptic triangle mirroring that of the Bermuda Triangle off the coast of Florida, and the Devil's Triangle off the coast of China, Japan and the Philippines. All three triangles possess similar perplexing elements, seeing how ships, planes and people simply disappear under mysterious circumstances while sited within the boundaries of these locations.

All three triangles possess strange magnetic inconsistencies. So much UFO activity has been reported from all of these triangles, that all the known reports would have to be compiled into numerous books. All three triangles are located over **water**. All three triangles are located over earthquake epicenters, active or inactive volcanoes, and/or tectonic plate intersections.

To get a better idea of what may be a worldwide pattern, we need to analyze a few illustrations. The examples you are about to examine will be numbered so you can match the number of the illustrated examples with the locations on the geographical maps provided in this publication. Quite naturally, there are many more sightings that have taken place in the same locations given in each of the illustrations. Regrettably, it would take too much time to examine all the sightings and their consistent patterns.

* * *

(#1) Residents of eleven to thirteen cities from Akron, Ohio to Syracuse, New York stated that on the evening of December 2, 1962, they saw what appeared to be a bright light bulb shaped object moving across the sky in an eastward direction. The object suddenly turned towards the North and then dove into Lake Erie.

Note, Lake Erie is not only located in the Great Lakes Triangle, but the one lake that joins all the other lakes together, as well as allowing an exit to the ocean by way of the St. Lawrence River.

(#2) March 9, 1960 Two truck drivers, in two separate locations about twenty-five miles east of Port Angeles, Washington, reported to the Police that they watched a large glowing object about half the size of a barrel from their location. The object plunged into the Strait of Juan De Fuca; the fiery object was thought to be a plane. However, no plane was found nor were there any reports of missing or downed aircraft in the area.

(#3) On the morning of May 20, 1968, three UFOs were reported to have come up out of Moore Lake in Littleton, New Hampshire.

(#4) 1945, in the Northeast Pacific near Alaska, the U.S. Army Transport (Delarof) was hauling munitions and supplies to Alaska. The crew members saw a large object emerge from out of the sea. They were able to see the darkness of the craft against the setting Sun. The craft was reported to have climbed almost straight up, then leveled off and began to circle the ship. The crew of the Delarof estimated the UFO to be about 150 to 200 feet in diameter. The UFO circled the ship about three times, making no sound, and after several minutes, the object took off towards the South followed by three flashes of light as the craft disappeared.

(#5) April 19, 1957, the crew aboard the Kitsukawa Maru, a Japanese fishing boat, located approximately 31 deg's 15' N. and 143 deg's 30' E. in the North Pacific, reported seeing two metallic silvery colored objects coming down form the sky as they dove into the ocean. The fishermen estimated the objects to be about thirty feet long with no wing of any kind. After the objects entered the water, the fishermen reported that there was water turbulence.

(#6) August 24, The Trawler Eros, passing through the Ahu Passage, near the Island of Ninigo located in the Bismarck Archipelago of New Guinea, reported what they believed to be a large yellow "star" that turned red, then green, then to crimson. The object hovered for about fifteen to twenty minutes, then turned from crimson, back to green, at which point the object entered into the sea.

(#7) June 18, 1845, Malta Times reported that the vessel Brig Victoria, located about 36 deg's 40' 56" N. Lat.: 13 deg's 44' 36" E. Long., or about 900 miles West of Adalia Asia Minor, reported seeing three luminous objects come up out of the sea. They were about half a mile from the ship at the time of the sighting, and could be seen for about ten minutes. The objects were estimated to be about five times the size of the Moon and were connected by glowing streamers and were witnessed as far away as the Syrian Coast.

(#8) 1909, a Danish ship called the Bintang, sailing in the Strait of Malacca off the Coast of Malaysia, reported seeing what the Captain described as a huge revolving wheel of light that was sitting in the sea. The wheel of light displayed what the Captain referred to as long arms that protruded from the center of the object from which the whole system seemed to rotate.

(#9) August 4, 1967, March 9,1960 Dr. Hugo Sierra Yepez was fishing in the gulf North of Arrecife, Venezuela. He reported that he felt the sea vibrate and begin to boil in a circle about eighteen feet in diameter. Suddenly a Gray-blue flat globe came up out of the water and hovered close to the surface. The doctor sat looking at the object with water dripping from it. Then the object took off in a curving manner, before it shot upward into space. The witness described the object as having a revolving section and triangular windows.

(#10) September 18, 1961, Officer G. Gendall, aboard the vessel Queensland Star in the Indian Ocean, reported that he saw a UFO in a cloud formation. The craft was white in color. The UFO disappeared into the clouds, then reappeared. After reappearing the UFO dropped down to the sea, at which time the craft appeared to enter the sea. The location where the UFO entered the sea was said to have made the water intensely bright, unknown white particles were also seen on the surface of the water where the UFO had entered.

(#11) May 1968, Five UFOs were seen diving into the sea off the Coast of Arrecife, Venezuela..

(#12) August 25, Catia La Mar, Venezuela, a man by the name of Ruben Norato, while on the beach, stated that he saw abrupt movement in the water from the shore, after which Ruben Norato stated that three enormous disks came up out of the sea and shot out of sight. Ruben described the UFOs as being plate-shaped.

(#13) October 4, 1967, Shag Harbor, Nova Scotia, many residents saw what they described as a bright reddish-orange light in the sky over Bear point. People in the Woods Harbor area and Woods Harbor R.C.M.P. officers also witnessed the UFO. The object appeared to come down out of the sky and set on top of the water. The lights then changed to a single white light and bobbed up and down in the water about half a mile off-shore. The R.C.M.P. called the Canadian Coast Guard, which came, and was joined by the local fishermen. The area was searched where the object had disappeared. The only thing left was a 80 foot wide patch of bubbling water and foam. A fisherman described the froth as being yellowish in color and that he had never seen anything like it before.

* * * *

These illustrations are but a small fraction of UFO reports involving large bodies of water. If these craft and their occupants are trying to hide themselves from the intrusive eyes of man, concealing themselves underwater would prove to be a reliable technique. However, if the craft came form another world, hiding underwater would not make much sense.

The choice location to hide from the inquisitive masses and still maintain constant surveillance, would be to orbit the planet, or base themselves on the Moon. This would not only maintain their stealthy presence and a high level of security, but allow them to physically survey everything that takes place on the surface of the planet.

The lakes, rivers, seas and oceans of the world would not only impede their ability to globally survey the surface, but greatly increase the chances of them being seen as they enter or exit from their aquatic hideout to assess the surface dwellers of this world. So why water?

Evidently, the great waters of this world **are not** hiding places at all, but rather means by which these stellar beings and their craft enter or exit from their internal **habitation.** This would lead us right back to Scripture, informing us of the existence of an authentic Underworld, and the beings dwelling therein (Satan/Fallen Angels/Demons).

Moreover, this might explain why so many UFO reports occur in a single year. Yet, the bewildering issue would be, just **how** do these elusive beings and their remarkable craft physically commute from their underworld environment to ours? How are they able to pass **through** their huge subterranean caverns below the waters, to reach the surface?

UFO Fault Line Connection

As mentioned before, it would appear that these entities are dwelling inside the outer crust and mantle of this world adjacent to the volcanic magma of its interior. Considering the probability that these beings are physically abiding in approximately the same region as the molten magma of the planet (rivers of fire, Hell fire and brimstone, **sulfur**), perhaps the real question should be: **How** does or did the volcanic magma of this planet get from its subterranean pit to the surface of this planet?

The numerous volcanoes and tectonic plate intersections around the world actually provide us with the clue that reveals scores of concealed underworld gateways cracked within the outer surface of this planet. Those inactive fault lines, massive underground fissures, or volcanic portals are large enough to allow craft of untold magnitudes to transit between the two worlds, most of which are concealed **underwater.**

What better way to commute from the Underworld to the surface world, than by aquatically traveling through the huge cracks, voids, rifts, fractures and ruptures created in the Earth's surface, by mother nature itself.

It was the volcanic magma that formed the outer crust of this world from the beginning. The outer crust ultimately cracked, split, and separated into different sections and locations around the world, thus creating the tectonic plates.

The Plates persist in their colossal movement because they are **not** joined together, but rather independently float on the surface of the internal magma. However, therein lies an empty space or void **between** the massive plates commonly referred to as tectonic plate intersections.

Naturally, not all fault lines and their internal fissures or cavities completely reach the surface. However, existing fault lines or plate fissures can be artificially altered to reach the surface providing one has the technological know how (laser technology/matter manipulation/earthquakes). This might shed some light on the explanation behind many fault line gateways leading into this mysterious underworld being well-hidden under**water**, out of mankind's reach.

Profuse volcanic activity not only accounts for enormous land masses on the surface of this planet, but the birth of whole islands. However, what happens to the empty (**hollow**) space that the internal magma occupied after the magma has poured out onto the surface?

Obviously, the volcanic magma from the interior of the planet left behind a massive void **inside** the planet the size of the island or land mass it created on the surface of the planet. In essence, volcanic activity on the surface actually created huge subterranean caverns.

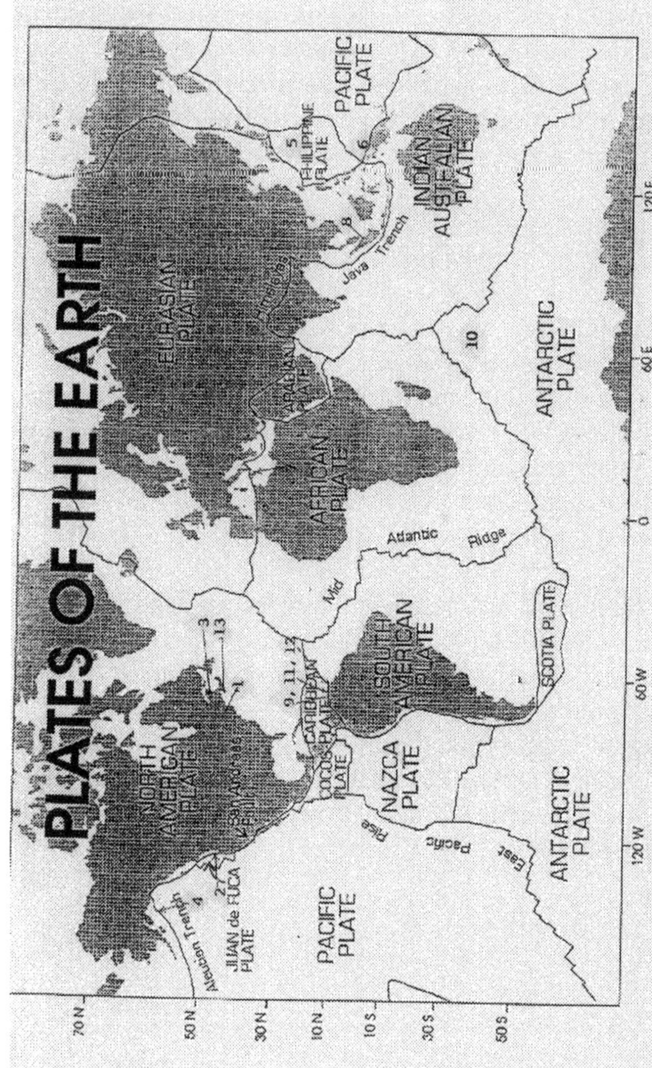

Division of the Earth's surface into a mosaic of moving plates, according to plate tectonic theory. Boundaries between the plates are actively spreading submarine ridges in the middle of the oceans, subduction zones in ocean trenches or mountain ranges on the continents, or margins where the plates slide past one another. Most of the world's earthquakes occur at plate boundaries.

Prepared by the United States Geological Survey National Earthquake Information Center

Courtesy of U. S. Geological Survey National Earthquake Information Center

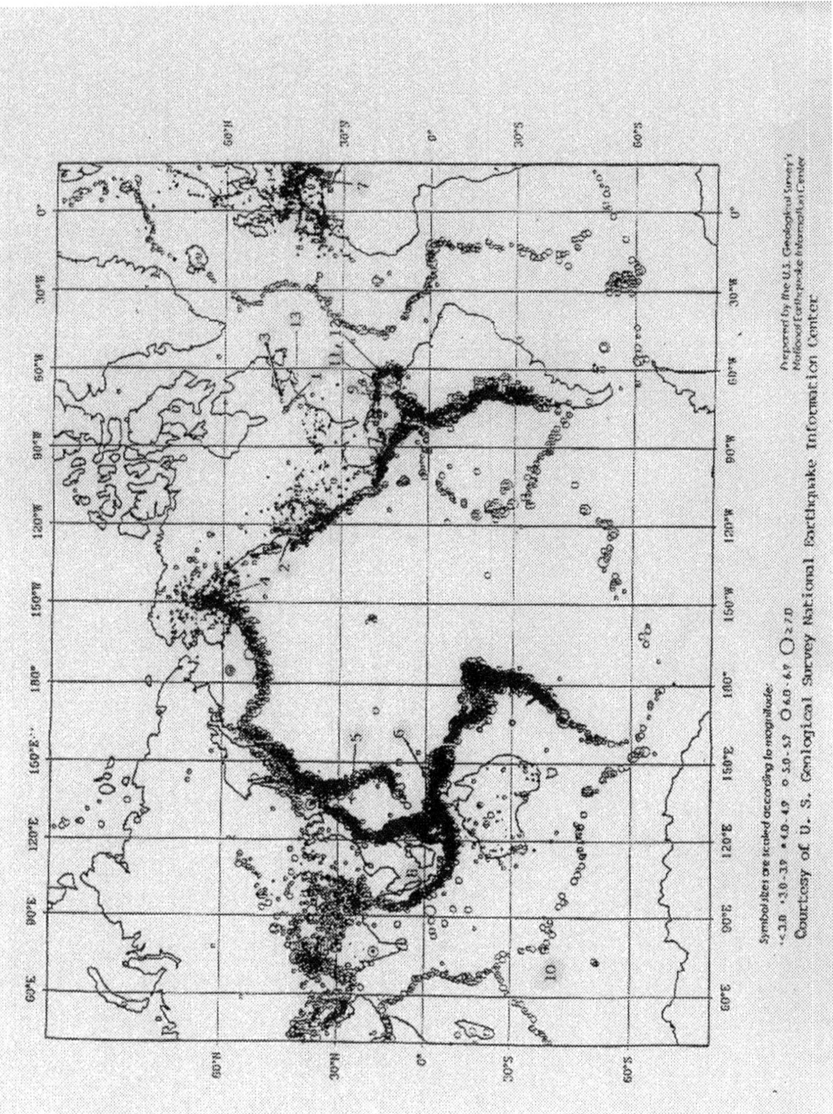
Prepared by the U.S. Geological Survey's National Earthquake Information Center
Symbol sizes are scaled according to magnitude
Courtesy of U. S. Geological Survey National Earthquake Information Center

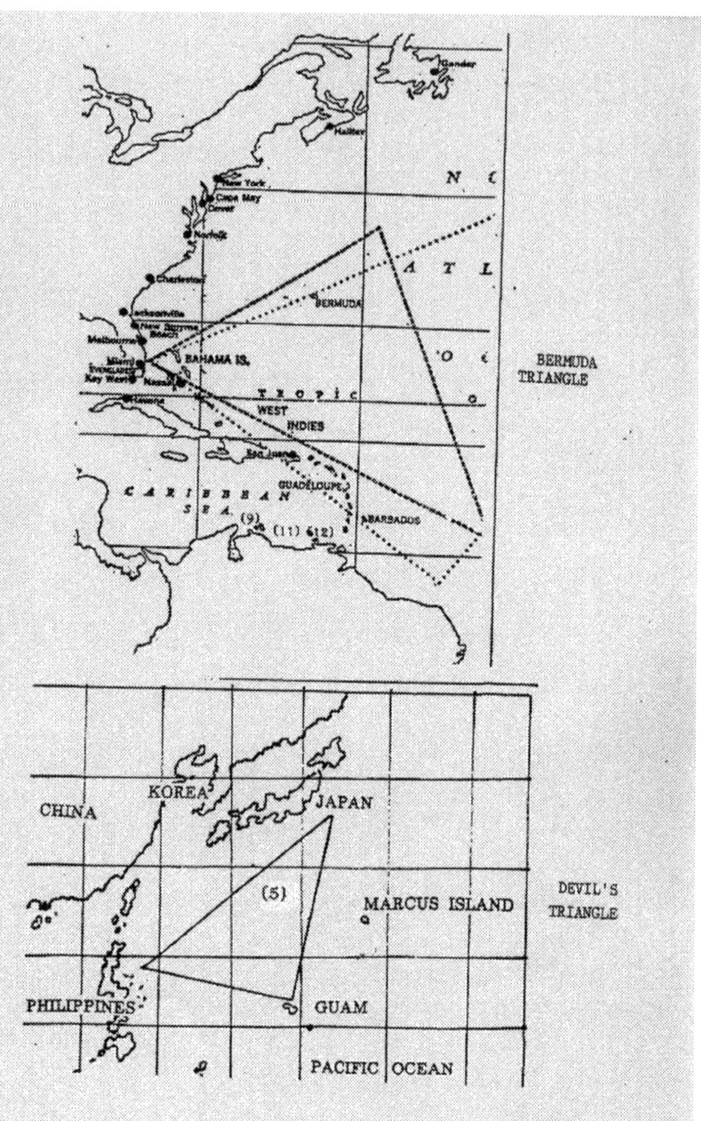
New York
Cape May
Norfolk
Charleston
Melbourne
Miami
Key West
Nassau
BAHAMA IS.
BERMUDA
N
A T L
O
T R O P I C
WEST
INDIES
San Juan
GUADELOUPE
C A R I B B E A N
S E A
(9)
(11)
(12)
BARBADOS
BERMUDA
TRIANGLE
CHINA
KOREA
JAPAN
(5)
MARCUS ISLAND
PHILIPPINES
GUAM
PACIFIC OCEAN
DEVIL'S
TRIANGLE

Surfacing magma only occurs around active or inactive fault lines, and volcanoes. This would indicate that the outer crust of this planet is honeycombed at all the vicinities in the direct path of most fault lines, tectonic plate intersections and volcanoes (seismographic/geothermal activity), including those honeycombed locations (fault lines/volcanoes) **underwater.**

Moreover, those cavernous domains are accessible by way of the solidified and fractured volcanic magma that created them. If one will closely inspect the plate tectonics and volcanic charts provided in this publication, you will discover that most all fault lines and volcanic activity are located **underwater.**

So just how does an underworld environment actually exist, considering the enormous volumes of water and pressure trying to force its way into every nook and cranny of this underwater empire? A simple matter considering the awesome power these cosmic beings harness. Clearly, the fallen angels, and the Grays possess the same powers flaunted by Yahweh and his host.

Even if vast amounts of water were to rush into many of these huge underground caverns, the fallen angels and the Grays are fully capable of maneuvering (matter manipulation) massive amounts of water in a very short length of time, as demonstrated at the Red Sea and the river Jordan. Not to mention all the inherent air-pockets contained in numerous underwater subterranean caverns created by mother nature itself.

These details lead us right back to the (13) UFO illustrations, and their concurrent locations on the maps given in this chapter. **All** thirteen of these UFO sightings took place over large bodies of water, as well as active or inactive tectonic plate intersections, volcanoes or earthquake epicenters.

This is but a small fraction, or tip of the iceberg, when examining UFO reports associated with not only **water**, but plate tectonics, Volcanoes or indirect geothermal activity. The question is, just how many known UFO reports are directly related?

UFO Triangle Connection

Is it also just a coincidence that all three triangles associated with ships, planes, and people that have disappeared under mysterious circumstances, are also located over **water** as well as tectonic plate intersections, volcanoes or earthquake epicenters (underground activity)?

Looking at the map of the earthquake epicenters, only the area of Lake Erie and lake Ontario possesses an epicenter location. In fact, the epicenter is located were the two lakes intersect, known as Niagara Falls.

This termination point runs Northeast along the St. Lawrence river as it empties into the Gulf of St. Lawrence and enters into the Atlantic Ocean. This would suggest that the surface rivers and lakes do not connect to each other, yet the hidden underground fault lines might.

Out of all the lakes in the Great Lakes Triangle, Lake Erie is the only lake that possesses the majority of UFO reports. Moreover, Lake Erie is the shallowest of all the Great Lakes. Yet, we are not concerned with what's in the water, but rather what exists below the **floor** of the water (Underworld).

Lake Erie and Lake Ontario connect all the lakes to the Atlantic Ocean. Any UFOs traveling underwater could enter or exit any of the great lakes by the hidden fault line and epicenter of Lake Erie, or even the Atlantic Ocean. In fact, most Great Lake ports lie over a thousand miles inland. Yet ships can sail from any of these ports to any port in the world, not only by way of the St. Lawrence river connected to Lake Erie and Lake Ontario, but by a unique chain of canals and locks.

The Chicago Sanitary and Ship Canal allows ships to travel from Lake Michigan through the Illinois river and down the Mississippi river to the Gulf of Mexico. Naturally this would lead one to speculate as to just how many UFO reports are involved with not only the Great Lake's area, but all the regions between the areas of the locks, canals, ocean and sea bound rivers leading in or out of the Great Lakes.

And what about the Bermuda Triangle? In examining this area, we discover not only evidence of underground activity and seismic epicenters, but the triangle itself harbors a major fault line intersection known as the Caribbean plate. This location possesses one of the deepest places in the Atlantic Ocean, known as the Puerto Rican Trench.

This location boasts volumes UFO related incidents. Not only have large numbers of ships, planes and people vanished in the Bermuda Triangle, but there have also been strange reports of the waters in the area of the Triangle glowing with a peculiar luminous radiance, as if an enormous light underwater could be seen spanning a massive area within the Triangle.

There have also been reports of fresh water streams running into the salt waters of the Bermuda Triangle, suggesting subterranean fissures under the ocean **floor**. These underground rifts appear to be large enough to allow vast quantities of fresh water to enter the ocean, as well as other large objects (UFOs) unknown to this world. This same mystery haunts the Devil's Triangle.

The Devil's Triangle is located off the coast of Japan and China. This triangle is geometrically shaped in the same pattern as the tectonic plate intersections themselves. The triangle is centered over the Philippine plate. In this aquatic location, hundreds of ships, planes and people have simply vanished without a trace. In addition, the Devil' s triangle is teeming with UFO activity.

To further complicate matters, earthquake epicenters, tectonic plate intersections and significant volcanic regions are also directly connected to Scripture. All the biblical nations and their ruling **underworld gods** were also located in geographical regions subjected to volcanic and tectonic plate activity. In fact, a fault lines runs right up the center of the Red Sea, crosses the River Euphrates, as well as bordering the nation of Israel.

Obviously, the other gods/fallen angels, the Grays, **water** and UFO activity are seismographically **related**. Yet, this is not a new concept seeing how many of the ancient Polynesian gods were also geothermal related. The fire goddess Pele was worshiped in many parts of Polynesia, and abounds with fiery volcanic connotations. The Hawaiians actually believed that their idolized Pele physically lived **inside** the volcano Kilauea.

The people of the Pacific Islands even believed in the existence of Little people, similar to the dwarfs and elves of European folklore. The Hawaiians called these little people the "Menehune" who were believed to be responsible for events that could not be explained. This might indicate a connection between the little people of European and Polynesian folklore, **water,** and the little Gray beings reported in UFO incidents.

> **144:7 Send thine hand from above; rid me, and deliver me out of great waters, from the hand of strange children;**
>
> **PSALMS**

These child-size Gray entities are capable of physical achievements far beyond those of mankind even today. Moreover, the Grays are possibly dwelling in an under**water**, underworld environment close to the volcanic magma of this planet. In essence, these childlike entities may indeed be living **inside** a volcano (gateway to the Underworld).

UFOs, The Underworld, Sulfur and Salt Water

One factor certain, the Underworld and the elusive entities dwelling therein are in some way directly connected with geothermal activity (Volcanic Magma). Scripture greatly elaborates on the rivers of fire, Hell fire and brimstone (**sulfur**), that besieges this hidden subterranean world. In fact, this detail actually reveals a significant clue known as **sulfur**. Sulfur is actually a by-product of volcanic magma, like hydrogen sulfide and sulfur dioxide. Sulfur is not only directly connected with volcanic magma, but literally linked to Satan and his demons (the Grays?).

Satan and his rebel angels were imprisoned in what is ascribed to be the fifth heaven of this planet, an underworld location described as reeking of **sulfur**. Enoch placed this subterranean hell **inside** the **Northern** boundaries of this planet, often referred to as **North** of Eden. In this darkened underworld site volcanic fires burn continuously, polluting the massive cavernous atmosphere with heavy **sulfurous** fumes, as rivers of flame (volcanic magma) flow through a desolate land of cold and **ice** (**North Pole?**).

> **I beheld that the valley in which…arose a strong smell of Sulfur which became mixed with the Waters; and the valley of the angels, who had been guilty of seduction, burned Underneath its soil. through that valley also rivers of Fire were flowing to which the angels shall be condemned, who seduced the inhabitants of the earth.** IXVI. 5-8 BOOK OF ENOCH

If in fact the fallen angels are inhabiting huge subterranean caverns where rivers of volcanic magma are constantly flowing, their cavernous atmosphere would naturally reek of sulfur, considering sulfur is a by-product of volcanic magma.

The verse would suggest that the smell of sulfur became **mixed** with the water, indicating that the smell of **sulfur water** may have been present. However, the verses may be implying two completely dissimilar odors. One of the odors may in fact be sulfur. Yet the word **"mixed"** would suggest a different scent being produced by the water itself.

Let us not forget, this enormous subterranean empire actually resides under the great **saltwater** oceans and seas of this world, and saltwater does in fact possess its own odor. This speculation would hint at the probability that these underworld caverns contain large bodies of fresh/sulfur water or saltwater shores outside their underground cavernous doorways.

This might indicate that these massive caverns maintain aquatic doorways to underground fresh water river's lakes and/or saltwater oceans and seas, as well as volcanic and tectonic plate intersections leading to the surface of the planet.

So how might Satan demons adapt to this environment? If in fact Satan's demons are in reality the gray beings observed in the UFO phenomena, where would "**sulfur**" fit in? Remarkably, the demons/Grays actually expose their earthly lair through their physical anatomy and environment, an environment that actually reeks of "**Sulfur.**"

It would take considerable time to riffle through all the UFO data to properly establish the patterns you are about to observe. What we are about to examine is perhaps one of the largest undefined consistencies found within the UFO phenomena. This enduring pattern is only associated with the close encounters or abduction type cases.

Most UFO close encounters have been carried out by what is referred to as **the Grays.** This is by no means a revelation to the Ufologist, nor is the word **sulfur**, seeing how the smell of sulfur is a predominant odor identified by many victims of UFO abductions or close encounter reports. Many times the victims describe the sulfurous smell in various ways. We also need to keep in mind that ammonia is also a dominant stench associated with UFO abductions or close encounter incidents. Yet, the smell of ammonia is directly related to **sulfur.**

One such example of the sulfurous smells associated UFO abduction was Whitley Strieber's, author of "Transformation". Whitley's abductors were the same lilliputian Gray entities. Whitley asserts that he was taken aboard a UFO, where the interior of the craft smelled like **warm** cheddar cheese with a hint of **sulfur.**

This is quite an interesting statement considering how cheese is actually made. A large amount of **salt** is added in the production of cheese, better known as "**salting** the curd". This might suggest that Whitley may have been smelling a strong form of salt, mixed with sulfur, which would return us to the prior verse of Enoch.

The verse confirmed that a strong smell of sulfur became mixed with the smell of water, suggesting that the water possessed a scent of its own. Whitley may have been subjected to two entirely dissimilar odors, one being that of sulfur, while the other pungency may have consisted of a strong saline (salt) odor that became mixed with the scent of the sulfur. This would lead one to believe that the salty (cheese) odor may have actually been the smell of **saltwater**.

Another such case can be found in the abduction incident of Kathie Davis. Kathie was not only abducted, but reportedly artificially inseminated by these same small Gray entities. This abduction and impregnation found Kathie further imposed upon by the same little Gray beings after they returned at a later time to remove the undeveloped fetus from Kathie's body before term.

Budd Hopkins, author of "Intruders" placed Kathie under various hypnosis sessions, trying to unravel what actually transpired during Kathie's reported abductions. The hypnotic sessions revealed significant information relating to the same details we are now scrutinizing. Essentially, Kathie reported the same odors while on board (**inside**) the craft that abducted her.

Kathie stated that one of the Gray beings touched her left shoulder with what she described as a smooth, cold, moist and clammy hand. Kathie even used the word **reptile** in her efforts to identify the anatomy of the Gray being that physically handled her. Kathie also made the revealing statements that she keep smelling **burning matches**, declaring over and over again that the interior of the craft reeked of burning matches.

Kathie then reported a completely different smell mixed with the odor of the burning matches. She stated that the interior of the craft reeked of **saltwater**, a saltwater odor that was real strong. Kathie even made the remarkable statement that the interior of the craft **smells cold**, which may be a direct implication to the presence of **water**.

This might indicate the presents of a cold moister (**saltwater**) laden atmosphere inside the craft. In essence, the presence of water created the physical feeling of cold, while the odor of salt in the water (**saltwater**) produced the scent, hence the smell of cold. Kathie was then informed by the Gray entities that she had to leave, that if she stayed within the craft much longer she would get sick.

In analyzing Kathie's description of the Grays, it would appear as if these mysterious beings are a form of half man and half reptile, or half man and half fish. Considering that the saltwater oceans and seas of this world may play a major role in the location of this hidden underwater underworld, I would say the latter.

However, that does not rule out the possibly that these demonic looking Gray entities are a highly-developed form of **reptile**, or an amphibious creature resembling the form of a highly evolved fish. Then again, they may be one and the same, considering reptiles primordially originated from fish. Moreover this aquatic anatomy may account for the cold, moist and clammy hands of these beings, as well as the smell of a saltwater environment located inside their craft.

Here again, we have the obvious mix of **sulfur** and **saltwater**. It's common knowledge that burning matches produce a sulfurous odor. In fact, **sulfur** is one of the chemical elements used in the production of matches. Also note that Kathie was informed that if she does not leave soon, she would get sick, a sickness possible due to the atmosphere and environment inside the craft. Obviously, the environment inside the craft was designed to sustain the Gray beings, and not humans. Quite naturally, a celestial craft from another world would duplicate and maintain an atmosphere inside their craft identical or close to the same atmosphere of their own home planet. This logical environmental detail would also apply to the **subterranean** domains of this planet.

If these Gray beings (demons?) have come from the internal caverns of this world where they are subjected to volcanic magma, their normal breathing atmosphere would naturally reek of sulphur (Hell fire and brimstone), as well as saltwater which may be flowing through, or shore lining their underwater, underworld caverns.

It would only stand to reason that these Gray beings would maintain an atmosphere within their craft matching that of their subterranean environment. Essentially, the salty and sulfurous odors inside these elusive craft are normal breathing conditions for these Gray beings.

There have also been many abduction reports involving strong odors of ammonia. However, if we closely analyze ammonia and where it comes from, we find the same scenario as that of sulfur. Ammonia is a by-product in the production of coal and Coke gas.

Bituminous coal when **heated** yields considerable volatile bituminous matter, also known as soft coal. In fact, bituminous matter is the very fuel of volcanic magma, as well as producing a coal gas reeking of odorous **sulfur** compounds.

It's quite understandable why Kathie, or any other human for that matter, might get sick in this type of atmosphere. Yet, how are the falling angels capable of surviving in this type of sulfur laden subterranean environment, seeing how they appear to be human in nature? A puzzling inquiry, which we will go into great detail later in this chapter.

There have also been reports of what is described as a suffocating odor, and the smell of rotten eggs inside these elusive craft. Yet, the rotten egg odor commonly associated with these evasive UFOs and their Grays occupants is quite normal, considering eggs actually contain **sulfur**. Sulfur is brittle and has almost no taste, however when it's rubbed, **heated** or melted, it gives off a rotten egg odor.

As for the suffocating odor often associated with UFO close encounters, we discover the same result. If one will take a little sulfur, place it in a glass cylinder over a flame, the heated sulfur will produce a gas. When this gas is mixed with oxygen (air), it produces a dense colorless (choking) gas, termed **sulfur** dioxide (SO_2). Even ammonia gas (NH_3), a by-product of coal, can also cause suffocation, or even death.

High concentrations of sulfur dioxide (SO_2) are poisonous to humans, as well as a common industrial irritant of mankind's environment today. Sulfur dioxide comes mainly from the burning of **coal** and oil, causing irritation of the nose and throat, as well as respiratory diseases.

Sulfur dioxide can also react with oxygen to form sulfur trioxide (SO_3) which reacts with moisture in the atmosphere or fog to form weak concentrations of an airborne sulfuric acid. Sulfur dioxide gas can also directly unite with water to form sulfurous acid (H_2SO_3), thus creating a very weak liquid acid.

Anatomical Clues

So what is all this data driving at, other than the fact that the atmosphere and environment found within these Gray entities craft is the same type of atmosphere and environment found within the underworld domains of this planet. This is an environment that humans cannot stand for very long. Yet, this environmental detail actually gives us a significant clue to the very anatomy of these dough colored beings and **why** they were given the title, "the Grays".

Seemingly, these small creatures are anatomically Gray due to their underground environment which is not subjected to sunlight, thus causing their skin to appear almost white (albino/light Gray). Yet, it's quite possible that their subterranean atmosphere could have created the same effect.

Obviously, any being or creature not exposed to direct sunlight would take on an albino or light Gray complexion much like subterranean termites that abhor sunlight. However, these Gray entities live in a heated underworld atmosphere possibly loaded with sulfur dioxide (SO 2) due to the volcanic magma sharing the same subterranean regions.

We also need to consider that their underground caverns are under the oceans and sea floors of this planet. There could be vast amounts of fresh water and/or saltwater, in, around or even shore lining these huge underground caverns. Essentially, the subterranean caverns being adjacent to water and **heated** volcanic magma would produce an extremely high humidity factor.

When water (moisture/humidity) is subjected to sulfur dioxide, it produces a weak acid or bleach. The heavy sulfur dioxide gas mixing with the highly moister burdened environment would create an all encompassing airborne acidic atmosphere. This might suggest that the weak acidic atmosphere bleached their complexion to a light Gray color, possibly accounting for the leathery appearance of their skin often identified by UFO abductees.

However, it may be that the two factors—lack of sunlight and weak acidic atmosphere—have combined to produce an albino like appearances. This probability becomes even more credible when we look at Charles Hickman's case.

Mr. Hickman was subjected to a profound close encounter by these small Gray beings. However, in Mr. Hickman's case we discover a significant clue establishing the fact that these evasive Gray beings come from a location where the Sun don't shine (the Underworld).

Mr. Hickman, he made a revealing statement exposing the anatomy of these elusive Gray entities. That statement indicated that these Gray creatures remained within the interior of their landed machine as they called out to Hickman to come inside the craft. Evidently, the door of the craft was open as the Grays coaxed Hickman to enter. Naturally this would lead to question why these Gray beings didn't come out of their craft to escort Hickman inside?

This was a rare daylight close encounter, while most all close encounter or abduction cases occur during the **night/darkness.** This might justify why these Gray entities huddled together in their craft were quite impatient when trying to lure Hickman inside. In fact, they were so intolerant that they actually told Mr. Hickman before entering the craft, **let's go, the Sun burns us.**

Evidently, these Gray creatures physically inhabit an inner-world (underworld) environment where they are not subjected to the burning rays of the sun. This would not only account for their albino or light Gray complexion, but a few other biological features such as their eyes.

In most every case involving the Grays, the eyes are one of the most striking features identified by the abductee. Their eyes are said to be large, protruding, almond-shaped pools of dark matter. Yet their eyes may actually reveal the origin of their anatomy, seeing how their eyes are frequently reported to contain **"no pupil"**.

However, Eyes of a darkened subterranean nature do not require pupils, considering their eyes may be **all pupil.** Naturally, subterranean creatures would need an all-encompassing pupil to physically see in a dark underground and/or underwater environment. Here again, this would suggest that the Grays are highly evolved amphibious or reptilian creatures.

The Grays have many times been reported to possess no obvious protruding mouth, nose or ears, but rather small slits in the same facial sites as humans. Essentially, there are no reflective or collective shields surrounding the hearing or smelling ports of the body. This would seem to suggest that their senses of smell and hearing are impaired due to the lack of protruding body reflectors (ears/nose) required to enhance or amplify scents and sounds within an open area.

However, an amphibious or reptilian creature would not require protruding body features to hear or smell **underwater**. In fact, protruding body attributes would only create a physical drag for a streamlined aquatic being swimming underwater. Moreover, this might explain the scaly skin, webbed hands and feet, or scaly anatomical features often associated with these Gray beings as in the case of Ellen and Laura Ryerson.

Ellen and Laura were working in a bean field in Renton, Washington on August 13, 1965, where they claim that three beings from a flying saucer attempted to chase them down. Laura and Ellen were able to escape by dashing back to their car and driving away.

The women described the three creatures to be about four and a half to five feet tall, with scaly skin and huge protruding eyes. This is the same description of alien entities reported in the Andreasson affair on January 25, 1967, the Lonnie Zamora incident in the area of Socorro, New Mexico, April 24, 1964, and the Kalahari report filed by the South African Air Force, June 1989.

All four reports basically identify the same Gray beings with large heads, large protruding black eyes, facial ports or slits for mouth, nose and ears, scaly skin, along with webbed feet and hands. These reports also suggest a highly-developed form of subterranean amphibious or reptilian creatures

Diverse Underworld Creatures

It's essential to remember that the fallen angels and the Grays are not the only possible underworld inhabitants (demons), of this planet. Many UFO reports contain data indicating that the Grays have been seen in the company of everything from humans (fallen angels?), short stout blue creatures, to bizarre beings which appear to be of an **insect** nature. This might indicate that this concealed subterranean kingdom could be teeming with many dissimilar life forms or creatures (demons), including the elusive Big Foot.

It's no new news to the Ufologist that Big Foot is UFO related. There are many reports of UFOs sightings taking place not only in the same location as Big Foot sightings, but sometimes both sightings occur at the same time. Yet, more significantly, numerous close encounter witnesses have revealed that these large Big Foot creatures reek of a foul smell or odor, often identified as a pungent scent of **sulfur** or **ammonia.**

This would lead one to suspect that these large hairy creatures may be under the supervision of these subterranean beings. In fact, this revealing detail may actually account for their abrupt disappearance, even though a diligent search of the area is conducted the same day of the sighting.

These aloof creatures may actually reside within a geothermal world underground, possibly accounting for their reported ammonia or sulfurous body odor. Remarkably these same details would also apply to the renowned Yeti or Abominable Snowman, said to live on or perhaps **in** Mount Everest and Mt. Makalu in the Himalayan mountain range of Asia.

Is it just a coincidence that most Big Foot or Yeti sightings take place in California, Oregon, Washington, British Columbia Canada and the Himalaya mountain range? All of these sites are global locations of tectonic plate intersections, fault lines, active or inactive volcanoes and earthquake epicenters (see provided maps).

These locations might resolve the issue as to how these mammoth creatures are capable of disappearing as quickly as they appeared. It's quite possible that these elusive creatures come from a subterranean environment by way of fault lines or fissures (**caves**) camouflaged within the mountain ranges, most of which are well hidden in the wilderness far from the inquisitive eyes of humans.

And how might the Loch Ness Monster fit into this equation? This aquatic creature has been seen numerous times as it surfaces to "**breathe air**". If in fact this elusive creature is an aquatic mammal, or an amphibious creature, is should have been seen countless times to breathe air. Yet, this air breathing creature appears as suddenly as it disappears, not to be seen for another number of years.

The mystery behind this aquatic **visitor** might be resolved in the understanding that this amphibious creature is just that, a "**visitor**" from another world. By realizing that the loch itself is actually located over a "**fault line**" we possess evidence to suggest that this amphibious creature may actually be returning to an underworld environment harboring vast caverns and subterranean lakes by way of the fault line within the loch. Essentially, this amphibious creature boasts the ability to breathe on the surface of the planet as well as in an underworld environment within the planet.

Underworld Utopia

The perplexing question would be, how can a diverse anatomical range of beings, whether falling angels (humans), Big Foot or even the Grays (demons) physically coexist together in such a sulfurously polluted subterranean environment?

The solution to this issue may be quite simple when we realize the level of technology being implemented by these underworld entities. Obviously, the fallen angels maintained a high level of technology in order to campaign against Yahweh and his stellar forces.

That underworld technology has possibly been augmented into a massive industrial powerhouse capable of manufacturing everything from flying machines (UFOs), mechanical devices, weapons, power plants, to an entire thriving metropolis we would find amazing. Yet, how could such a massive industrialized underground civilization physically be maintained without a perpetual source of energy?

These subterranean entities not only possess an endless source of power, but an immeasurable power supply deriving from mother nature itself. Moreover, this limitless fountain of energy is actually sharing the same underworld neighborhood. In essence, the underworld commands a never-ending source of volcanic magma. This flowing powerhouse is capable of being harnessed, manipulated and physically engineered into refined power, capable of energy levels far beyond anything we humans' could imagine.

This is not a remarkable premise, considering heat and electrical power are created from power plants run by volcanic induced steam in Italy, Sicily, Iceland, Chile and Bolivia. The most successful of these plants is sited at Larderello Tuscany.

Geothermal hot springs are also used for medical, laundry and bathing purposes. Pumice, which comes from lava, has long been used for grinding, polishing and for building roads. Sulfur, another volcanic product, is used in the production of chemicals.

This timeless fountainhead of power escapes mankind due to his lack of technology which would allow more control and manipulation over the liquid rock. However, when considering the highly advanced level of technology being utilized by these subterranean beings, they may have possessed the technological ability to harness this continuous source of liquid power for thousands of years.

The potentials of this power source is immeasurable. A power supply of this magnitude could run machines for industries to manufacture or produce almost **anything.** They could literally pick up or elevate mass quantities of molten magma with their matter maneuvering devices to form and build solid preformed dams capable of utilizing the massive water supplies within their subterranean regions to create raw energy.

With their ability to physically manipulate matter, they could actually build massive underground cities comprised of enormous buildings, homes, roads, tunnels, airports, all utilizing molten rock (volcanic magma) while still in a liquid state.

They could construct enormous hidden subterranean tunnels leading in and out of their underground environment to the surface world. They could create subterranean lighting facilities on a measureless scale by utilizing flowing magma via matter manipulation. They could extract oxygen form sea water, thus producing an atmosphere allowing them to control the pressures at lower depths for the many dissimilar creatures therein.

They could control the heat and pollution produced by the volcanic magma, by setting up screening force fields (matter manipulation) at any given location within their enormous underground caverns. They could create enormous hydroponic farms capable of feeding mass populations. The possibilities are endless.

This concealed underworld empire may be a technological marvel. In fact this might explain how two dissimilar species—fallen angels/humans and the Grays/demons—are capable of coexisting with each other while confined within the same underworld domain. They can produce different living environments for each species.

Keeping the Underworld a Secret

This remarkable underworld utopia might justify the rash of disinformation techniques, or haunting messages disclosed to UFO abductees. One particular message which keeps turning up time and time again is for mankind to "**stop all atomic testing for warlike reasons, it will upset the balance of the Universe.**"

If this world was involved in a nuclear exchange, even if it destroyed this entire planet, it would have no effect on the Universe. The solar system may suffer, but as far as the Universe is concerned, it would be like a **tiny** firecracker going off on the other side of the world.

However, let us reflect for a moment. Where are nuclear tests performed? Most of the time these atomic tests take place **underground** or **underwater**. If we search the UFO files, we discover that UFO activity picked up ten fold in the late 1940's after the first **underground** atomic test/bomb was detonated.

Naturally, it would seem logical to keep a closer watch on mankind now that he has reached an atomic age, and even more so, if humans are playing with their powerful toys on your front door steps. This might indicate that these threatening universal messages are scare tactics designed to frighten and stop mankind from possibly damaging or destroying the many different levels of the **underwater, underground** municipalities of these diversified beings.

Obviously this subterranean society wants to remain hidden, which might account for the amnesia techniques (mental manipulation) inflicted upon UFO abductees. This psychological exploitation appears to be a method of controlling their victim, as well as preserving the anonymity of the kidnappers.

If the abductees were able to mentally retain everything they saw on board the craft, or what took place during the abduction, they might detect clues that could help identify where these elusive Gray beings originated from. Clearly, it's a chance that these subterranean creatures are not willing to take.

Here again, it becomes apparent that these evasive Gray creatures are coming from a location quite close, seeing how there would be no need to induce amnesia to protect their anonymity if they originated from hundreds of light years away. This distance is so vast that it would be quite insignificant if mankind knew of their cosmic origins, considering we possess no technology or space travel capability to do anything about it, much less live long enough for a second visit.

Obviously the Grays and the fallen angels are taking drastic measures to secure their hidden underworld origin. This would be a logical move on the part of superior beings that may be living right under the very noses of humanity.

The human race would go to extreme measures to find these subterranean beings, if only they knew of their existence. By keeping mankind blind to the actual existence of a genuine subterranean race hidden inside this planet, it allows them more freedom to come and go as they please, without the meddling interference of inferior humans.

Grays Infiltrate the Human Race

It would appear that the Grays are involved in globally implementing a type of smoke screen designed to safeguard their actual purpose or motivation on the surface of this planet. It has been suggested that the Grays are secretly psychologically programming large numbers of people for some unknown purpose.

That obscured mental programming could be activated at a later time to carry out the unknown implanted agenda of these Gray creatures. This surreptitious psychological tactic may be aimed at the Revelation, seeing how the Revelation actually entails the release of the inhabitancy of the underworld by Yahweh and his stellar troops.

This inter-world liberation will not only catch mankind by surprise, but place humanity in an awkward position of choosing a side between Yahweh and Jesus (the kingdom of heaven) or the fallen angels and their Gray associates (the Underworld). This might explain the hidden agenda being implanted within the intellect of the human race.

These underworld entities may need to mentally manipulate all the physical help they can get in order to confront Yahweh and his troops at the time of their visitation. Moreover, this may account for the hybridizing procedures being inflicted upon mankind by these mysterious Gray creatures.

The fallen angels, being human, have no trouble in breathing our air. Nor would they be anatomically detected by the surface dwellers of this world, even if they were talking to each other face to face. However, the Grays could not even show their faces without being discovered. Not to mention the fact that they would immediately be scorched by the sun, as well as become sick breathing our outer world atmosphere, just as we would become ill breathing their inner world atmosphere.

The question is, are the Grays crossbreeding with humans to cultivate hybrids of themselves to better adapt to the atmosphere and environment on the surface of this planet? Or are the Grays crossbreeding with humans to create a hybrid of their own species that would allow massive global infiltration in preparation of a possible approaching agenda?

If the Grays are creating a hybrid crossed between themselves and humans, there is no telling how far they could go. They could possibly end up with a hybridized being that looks almost human, which would allow the hybrid not only the ability to physically endure the rays of the sun and breathe the atmosphere of our outer world, but infiltrate any civilization.

This infiltration procedure would allow possibly thousands of Gray hybrids the ability to covertly enter the government, military and business world of humanity. In doing so, they could manipulate and inconspicuously steer mankind along a path of unknown psychological preparation designed to unwittingly help the Underworld (Satan and his demons) at the time of the Revelation. Yahweh's visitation will herald the ultimate release of the Underworld and its diverse hordes aimed at taking control of the surface of this planet. That forcible global intervention will come much easier when inflicted upon civilizations that may have been timely psychologically maneuvered and beguiled into corrupt doctrines controlled by an infiltrated force unknown to the masses following them.

Obviously, Satan and his demons are quite aware of "the second coming" (the time of our visitation) just as we humans are. It's also common knowledge that the demons (the Grays?) do the bidding of Satan, which might explain the UFO mystery to date. Essentially, the demons (the Grays) are under the command of the fallen angels, thereby performing their directives and allowing them substantial control on the surface of this planet, even though constrained to their subterranean domain.

Fallen Angel and Gray Alliance (Satan and his Demons)

This conjecture gives rise to a monumental question, seeing how we appear to be discussing two entirely dissimilar species. Satan (the Dragon/Draco) and his fallen angels are obviously human in nature, seeing how they copulated with the women of man. However, Satan's demons, (the Grays?) appear to be a repulsive reptilian or amphibious creature.

Quite naturally, this would compel one to question the genuine origin of the Grays (demons). Just **who** or **what** are the Grays? Where did they come from? What is their true evolutionary lineage, and where did it begin? Scripture even labels both species with dissimilar allegorical titles.

> **51:9 Awake, awake, put on strength, O arm of the LORD; awake, as in the ancient days, in the generations of old. [Art] thou not it that hath cut Rahab, [and] wounded the dragon?**
> **27:1 In that day the LORD with his sore and great and strong sword shall punish leviathan the piercing serpent, even leviathan that crooked serpent; and he shall slay the dragon that [is] in the sea.**
> ISAIAH
> **77:16 The waters saw thee, O God, the waters saw thee; they were afraid: the depths also were troubled.**
> **74:13 Thou didst divide the sea by thy strength: thou brakest the heads of the dragons in the waters.**
> **74:14 Thou brakest the heads of leviathan in pieces, [and] gavest him [to be] meat to the people inhabiting the wilderness.**
> **148:7 Praise the LORD from the earth, ye dragons, and all deeps:**
> PSALMS

Naturally, when one thinks of the dragon, the word "serpent" comes to mind. Yet, this may not be the case when individualizing the famed dragon against Leviathan. At first glance one would be inclined to believe that the mythical dragon and Leviathan are one and the same.

However, upon closer examination of the verses, one can easily distinguish that there is a distinct difference between the two. This dissimilarity is clearly identified by the word "**and**". This conjunction implies two entirely dissimilar creatures, which translates into two distinctly different species of beings.

Yahweh cut Rahab **and** wounded the dragon, leading one to believe that the verse repeated itself. Yet, the word Rahab translates into Leviathan, indicating that the dragon is not Leviathan, nor is Leviathan the dragon. The same allegorical information can be found in Isaiah 27:1. In this verse it would appear that Leviathan has been anatomically identified, where the dragon has not.

In observing this revealing verse, it becomes apparent that Yahweh is going to only **punish** Leviathan (the serpent), yet the dragon will be **slain**. In essence, there are two entirely different species being inflicted with two dissimilar castigations. You will also note that Leviathan is referred to as the **serpent,** where the dragon is not. The word "serpent" is just another terminology for **reptile**, an amphibious or **reptilian** creature which resides in or around **water**.

This might explain why the waters **and** their depths were aware of Yahweh's presence, and "were afraid". Or are we to believe that the simple aquatic life forms of the sea (fish) were troubled and frightened at Yahweh's presence? I think not.

The verses seem to establish the fact that two distinctly different species were being forced to coexist together. The verse even reveals the location in which the two species will jointly reside, "**the wilderness**". The word "wilderness" is just a metaphorical term for Underworld, seeing how the Underworld is just that, a wilderness due to its lack of sunlight and geothermal ramifications.

Obviously, Leviathan is to be **meat** for the **people** of the wilderness, suggesting that Leviathan is not human, just as the "**people**" (fallen angels) of the wilderness are not of the Leviathan species. Being referred to as "the **serpent**", not only identifies Leviathans anatomy, but would suggest an entire culture of amphibious or reptilian creatures. In contrast, the **people** (fallen angels) inhabiting the **same** wilderness would appear to be human in nature, hence the word "people".

If in fact Leviathan is the biological equivalent of the Grays/demons, then the **people** would appear to translate into the humanoid fallen angels. If true, the verse would indicate that the species of Leviathan was given to the fallen angels as **meat**, a form of nourishment. Essentially, the Grays will help the fallen angels maintain their physical existence and covert intentions while constrained to the Wilderness/Underworld.

This helping hand appears to have not come by choice, seeing how Yahweh had to **"brake the heads of Leviathan"** to force them into the jurisdiction (nourishment) of the fallen angels. This might indicate that Yahweh and his stellar forces were involved in a war campaign against Leviathan/the Grays/demons, that ultimately crippled or destroyed the leaders (heads) of the demonic forces. That militant campaign subsequently found Leviathan under the control of the incarcerated fallen angels, in which both species now reside within the subterranean realms of this planet.

If true, Leviathan/the Grays maintained a super level of technology all their own. That highly advanced technology allowed Leviathan/the Grays to physically confront Yahweh and his stellar forces. Yet, Leviathan's demonic forces were obviously no-match for Yahweh's cosmic troops, seeing how the demons/Grays lost the stellar campaign. Clearly, Leviathan/the Grays possessed advanced technology **before** they became involved with the fallen angels. Yet, how can this be, unless the Grays/Leviathan existed **before** the lunar creation?

Lineage of the Gray's/Leviathan

If the demons/Grays are in fact **Leviathan** (the Serpent), we possess evidence of their existence on this planet **before** the lunar alteration of this world occurred. **Leviathan** translates into "Rahab", which possesses a dark myth all its own. Rahab was the mythical **monster** destroyed by God/Yahweh at **the beginning of time to create the world.**

Rahab/Leviathan identifies the chaotic seas that were subdued by the forces of order before **they subverted the Universe.** Rahab was also known as the violent one, he was originally perceived as the Prince of the **primordial oceans,** who existed **before** the great oceans of the world were brought under control by the lunar conversion (forces of order/Yahweh). Leviathan also represents the forces of evil in the world (Satan and his demons) to be slain by God at the end of days (the Revelation).

Here again, we return to the oceans as a significant clue to not only the creation of this world, but its underwater inhabitancy as well. Obviously the allegorical Leviathan was considerably more than an unfounded myth of an **aquatic monster.**

Why would anyone worry about a simple myth or large **aquatic** animal subverting an entire Universe? Why would a simple aquatic creature have to be brought under control prior to the actual lunar conversion being performed? Clearly, the myth substantiates the fact that this powerful force had to be reckoned with if the creation was to be rendered at all.

Evidently, it wasn't just the great oceans of this planet that were in a chaotic state, but rather what physically existed in the waters (**Leviathan**). **Before** the creation took place, something or someone already existed in the oceans. That aquatic entity/monster appears to not only be chaotic in nature, but possesses the technological power to advance outward and subvert the Universe. This might suggest that a celestial battle ensued between Yahweh (the forces of order) and **Leviathan** (Prince of the **primordial oceans**/chaotic seas) **before** the lunar conversion was performed.

Seemingly, the lunar transformation took place **before** or during the dawning of fallen angels. In essence, there were **no** fallen angels prior to, or possibly during the actual lunar modification. In fact, it would appear that the lunar creation and the hybridization of mankind touch off the cosmic insurrection (third of the stars) against Yahweh and his stellar host, thus siring the fallen angels.

If true, Satan, along with **all** the constellations (third of the stars) under Yahweh's control, worked **together** to bring about the lunar modification. Yet, the lunar conversion did not take place **until** Leviathan was brought under control ending their ability to subvert the Universe. Put simply, Leviathan was on this planet **long before** the lunar mutation occurred, or the birth of fallen angels. So where did Leviathan's genetic roots spawn from?

The solution to this issue can be found by not only analyzing this planet's existence **before** the creation, but all the data in reference to the Grays/demons that we have examined up to this point. It would seem that a thriving culture may have existed on this planet **before** Yahweh and his forces ever arrived at this unrefined world. Moreover, it would appear that this high tech culture of amphibious or reptilian creatures were known as Leviathan/Rahab (**the serpent/demons/the Grays**).

How can this be, seeing how this planet was mostly under water before the lunar conversion was ever preformed? Yet, this aquatic factor might actually establish the motive behind Yahweh's forceful intervention upon this world to stop Leviathan's subversion of the Universe. Put simply, the lunar alteration may have been the Achilles' heel that destroyed and/or subdued the aquatic forces of Leviathan.

The anatomy of these bizarre aquatic creatures actually identifies their liquid lineage, which literally harmonizes with this planet's previous existence **before** the lunar conversion. The Grays appear to be amphibious or reptilian creatures loathing direct sunlight, as well as possessing scaly skin, webbed hands and feet. Their port hole nose, mouth and ears would justify their amphibious or aquatic streamline anatomy. Their large protruding eyes of only pupil matter would allow better physical sight underwater, and/or in dark subterranean regions. Clearly, these air breathing amphibious creatures were nature's natural design for a darkened or **clouded** aquatic environment.

By understanding the repercussion of the lunar modification we discover the genetic roots of the Grays/Leviathan. Before the lunar transfiguration took place, the surface of this planet consisted mostly of water and possessed insignificant land masses. The atmosphere was radically different from today, due to the highly moisture laden atmosphere created by the massive bodies of water submerging the planet. Essentially, the planet was a cloud engulfed aquatic world blocking out all sunlight.

1:2 …"and darkness [was] upon the face of the deep"…Gen.

The cloud-engulfed planet, perpetuated worldwide rainfall on a continuous basis, thereby producing a rain forest type of environment upon the trivial land masses that may have existed at that time. This would be an excellent dark aquatic environment for the demonic forces of the world (Leviathan/the Grays). This amphibious or reptilian race may have actually occupied the smaller land masses on the surface of the planet long before the lunar installation ever occurred.

Obviously, these webbed hand and footed reptilian creatures abhor direct sunlight and require the direct essentials of water to survive. There would be no need for them to hide themselves from the burning ray of the Sun, seeing how the cloud-engulfed planet would not allow sunlight to penetrate its heavy overcast atmosphere.

These amphibious creatures would love the constant rainfall as a part of their everyday lives. Moreover, they may have actually resided in the underwater, underworld regions of this planet. This might suggest that the concealed underworld domains of this world existed inside this planet **before** the lunar conversion was performed.

Jurassic Implication

In simpler terms, these amphibious creatures may have crawled out of the primordial ooze to spawn evolutionary roots that in time augmented into a technological culture to be reckoned with. These reptilian creatures may have had a 600 million-year head start on mankind, as well as adequate time to evolve into a super technology capable of advancing outward to subvert the Universe. Moreover, this highly advanced amphibious civilization may have timely acquired the technological ability to physically campaign against Yahweh and his stellar forces.

The earliest known subaerial animals came from what is known as the Devonian Strata, which dates back some 300 million years ago. The aquatic life forms of this planet had a 300 million-year head start on us air breathers, and if we consider our mutual aquatic ancestry, it may be possible to add another billion years to that.

The Devonian period, and even as far back as the Cambrian period, being some 600 million years ago, were **aquatic** periods of this planet's history. These primordial time frames confirm that the oceans covered most of the continents of the world. In fact, the Devonian period was referred to as **"the age of fishes"**, thus confirming this planet's watery existence before the lunar metamorphosis was performed. Notably, this aquatic factor would return us to the subject of dinosaurs (reptiles/serpents/Leviathan).

It's believed that the abrupt disappearance of the dinosaurs was due to an asteroid striking the surface of this planet. The massive impact subsequently propelled this planet into total darkness, spawning global repercussions upon an unsuspecting reptilian world.

Yet, in examining Genesis, I argued that the lunar conversion of this preexisting aquatic world may have been solely responsible for the spontaneous disappearance of the prehistoric reptiles. The lunar metamorphosis changed the surface of the planet by exposing enormous land masses, thus altering the atmosphere.

What used to be a cloud-shrouded planet protecting the fragile plant life of the primordial reptiles was altered into a sun-permeated world. The devastating domino effect ultimately found the food chain supporting the reptilian world decimated, taking with it the entire famine stricken reptilian population. So what does all this prehistoric data have to do with **Leviathan?**

The disappearance of the dinosaurs may contain the actual time line for not only the creation of this world, but the extermination of the species of Leviathan (demons) as well. Clearly, this reptilian/dinosaur (Leviathan) civilization had to be eliminated to bring about the creation. Moreover, this Leviathan prince and his primordial civilization had to be subdued before they subverted the Universe.

This might rationalize why Leviathan (The Grays/demons) is referred to as the **serpent/reptile/dinosaur.** Leviathan may actually represent a highly evolved bygone reptilian civilization that existed during the same prehistoric era as dinosaurs, both of which occupied this planet **before** the lunar conversion was implemented.

This speculation is not as bizarre as one might think. There are scientists today who believe that, if the dinosaurs had been allowed to complete their full evolutionary sequence, the final results would be incredible to say the least.

If the dinosaurs were allowed to fully biologically develop, one or more of the species would have ultimately evolved into what is believed to be a **"dinosaur man."** This small tailless manlike creature would be able to stand upright on two feet, supporting two arms and hands with scaly and web like peculiarities.

This reptilian man would possess a larger than normal head bearing large protruding eyes, and would possess no obvious outer nose, ears or mouth, but only port holes or slits around the face and head. Moreover, this dinosaur man could have physically and intellectually evolved into a highly advanced culture capable of complete dominance over this planet.

Considering the many varieties of dinosaurs, it's quite possible that dinosaur genealogy could have produced a genetic strain of reptilian evolution that developed into a highly advanced scaly anthropoid being, otherwise known as **Leviathan/dinosaur man/the Serpent.**

This amphibious anthropoid could have in time developed into an aquatic culture of intellect beings. This advanced reptilian civilization may have bodily shared this planet with prehistoric dinosaurs, up until the time Yahweh and his host made their heavenly appearance. Yahweh's celestial intervention and lunar installment not only mutated the home world of the dinosaurs, but Leviathan (demons/Grays) as well.

Leviathan/The Gray's/Demons Universal Incursion

Clearly, the creation did not come easily, seeing Yahweh and his host had to conduct a major military campaign against the highly evolved Leviathan race before the lunar conversion could be carried out. Seemingly, the Leviathan culture was not willing to stand down and simply give up their aquatic home to what they may have considered to be nothing less than invaders. Ultimately, Yahweh and/or the creation forced the remaining survivors of the species of Leviathan underground (the Underworld).

However, this conjecture may not be the genuine circumstance surrounding this watery campaign, seeing how the Leviathan myth would suggest that this reptilian race was not only evil but determined to inflict their sinister will upon the Universe. This might justify why Yahweh and his stellar forces were compelled to decimate the Leviathan race by altering this planet, thus biologically terminating Leviathan's ability to ever exist on the surface of this world.

Then again, it's quite possible that the Leviathan culture did not spawn from this world alone. The planet Earth may be one out of thousands of primordial planets occupied by not only dinosaurs, but the Leviathan legacy as well. The Leviathan culture and dinosaurs may be a normal biological occurrence found on many naturally formed **Water** planets within the Universe. In fact, this conjecture might resolve the issue as to how a simple race of gray reptilian beings (Leviathan) could subvert a Universe.

Obviously, the only way to truly achieve such a cosmic feat would be to expand one's forces outward. Notably, this assumption would compel one to question the history of the planet Mars. Mars possesses no known life on its surface, although this may not account for the ambiguous inter-workings of this bizarre red world.

Mars was believed to contain vast amounts of **water** on its surface at one time, as well as what was believed to be an enormous underground network of canal systems internally harbored within its outer crust. Naturally this would lead one to reflect on a possible connection between Mars and Earth, seeing how both planets appear to maintain an inner world within an outer world. Not to mention the coincidental aquatic connotations shared between the two different worlds. Both of these considerations suggest a possible aquatic residence deriving from the same source, (gray reptilian creatures/demons).

If Mars was an aquatic world at one time, it's quite possible the Leviathan race inhabited the planet. If true, there's no way the planet could have keep the orbit around the Sun it maintains today. Then again this may have been Leviathan's downfall when trying to dominate two water worlds in the same solar system.

It's quite possible that this solar system contained two water planets in matching or close orbits around the sun. Yahweh determined to keep Leviathan from venturing out and subverting the Universe, may have destroyed one of the aquatic worlds. Since mars is about half the size of the Earth, this could have been done by moving it (Matter Manipulation) closer to the sun. In doing so, the water planet was transformed into a **red** desert wasteland prior to being moved further out into space to ensure that the planet remains a barren world.

Obviously, Leviathan/the Gray's was determined to expand its forces within the Universe, even if it meant the forceful intervention of other worlds. Yet, this notable detail would actually indicate a common denominator, **water**. Water is the main source of all life, not only for humans, but for Leviathan as well. Any planet to be colonized by humans or Leviathan would have to contain a massive quantity of **water**.

This would lead one to consider that the struggle between Leviathan and Yahweh may have been motivated by the aquatic worlds of the Universe. Seemingly, the human components of the Cosmos were determined to keep the demonic forces away from the water bearing planets of this Universe, even if it necessitated celestial hostilities.

Dragon and Leviathan Unite

By altering and colonizing this aquatic world, the human factor caused the Grays/Leviathan race (demons) to lose their natural aquatic home. In doing so, the Leviathan race may harbor intense hatred for the encroaching human race. Yet, how did the human-like fallen angels (the **Dragon**) get involved with the **demons/Grays/Leviathan**?

The solution to this puzzle might be found in the fact that the fallen angels also harbor a furious animosity towards humanity. This intense hatred, like that of Leviathan, is based on the lunar modification of this planet. However, unlike Leviathan, the fallen angels' abhorrence for mankind derives from the human factor physically placed on the creation.

God, genetically creating man, considered him equal or higher than the angels, declaring that the angels should bow before the newly created man.

Satan, the greatest of the Seraphim, refused to bow to Adam when the new man was brought before the presence of the hierarchies of God Satan indignantly professed "How can a Son of Fire bow to a Son of Clay?"

This spiteful declaration not only triggered Satan's war in heaven against Yahweh and his universal host, but ultimately found Satan and the third of the stars that followed him incarcerated within the subterranean caverns of this planet.

Simply put, both the fallen angels (**Satan**) and Leviathan (**demons**/Grays) share a common bond of aversion towards humanity that ultimately formed an underworld alliance focused on debasing the human race at all cost. This underworld alliance is not only hellbent on debauching the human race, but taking direct aim at the kingdom of heaven which created the human factor at the expense of Leviathan and the fallen angels (Satan and his demons).

Evidently, these two subterranean war machines are vindictively waiting for the day (the Revelation) to be unchained. At that time they will abruptly reveal themselves and their highly advanced craft and weapons as they ascend from their underworld **wilderness** to inflict massive destruction upon the surface dwellers of this world.

> **In those days shall the earth deliver up from her womb, and hell deliver up from hers, that which it has received; and destruction shall restore that which it owes.** chapter L.
>
> **In those days shall the mouth of hell be opened, into which they shall be immured; hell shall destroy and swallow up sinners from the face of the elect.** chapter LIV.
>
> **In that day shall be distributed for food two monsters; a female monster, whose name is Leviathan, dwelling in the depths of the springs of waters; And a male monster, whose name is Behemoth; which possesses, moving on his breast, the invisible wilderness.... one being in the depths of the sea, and one in the dry desert.** LVIII. BOOK OF ENOCH

The verses are self-explanatory when one realizes that **Leviathan** defines a reptilian race that requires direct aquatic essentials. Yet, the fallen angels (Behemoth/**the dragon**) being of enormous size and power reflects their **human** nature which requires dry land to survive.

Evidently, one monster (Leviathan) resides in the watery depths of the underground springs or seas of this planet revealing its amphibious genealogy. In contrast, the other monster (Behemoth) dwelling within ("**in**"/inside) the **hidden** ("invisible") wilderness reveals the cavernous Underworld domains of this planet. Essentially, the Underworld could be considered a wasteland or desert due to its lack of sunlight and geothermal ramifications. Yet, the two worlds are neighbors.

In observing the metaphorical verses, it becomes apparent that one of the monsters is identified as a **male** (Behemoth), where the other monster is referred to as a **female** (Leviathan). Why would the verses elaborate upon gender?

Recalling the fallen angels' celestial intervention upon this world, they left their lofty station (space station) in the sky to venture down to the surface of the planet. That intervening endeavor ultimately found the fallen angels gambling with their heavenly status by interbreeding with the hybridized creation (mankind) of the newly altered world. Yet, this proliferating intervention was not to be tolerated by the kingdom of heaven, seeing how the extraterrestrial angels were **immortal male** beings not requiring physical reproduction to maintain their species existence.

> **2. Wherefore have you forsaken the lofty and holy heaven, which endures for ever, and have lain with women; have defiled yourselves with the daughters of men; have taken to yourselves wives; have acted like the sons of the earth, and have begotten an impious offspring?**
>
> **3. You being spiritual, holy, and possessing a life which is eternal, have polluted yourselves with women; have begotten in carnal blood; have lusted in the blood of men; and have done as those who are flesh and blood do.**
>
> **4. These however die and perish.**
>
> **6. But you from the beginning were made spiritual, possessing a life which is eternal, and not subject to death for ever.**
>
> **7. Therefore I made not wives for you, because, being spiritual, you dwelling is in heaven.**
>
> CHAP. XV. BOOK OF ENOCH

Essentially, the fallen angels (Behemoth) are physical **male** beings, which depict the Dragon (Satan) and the third of the inhabited stars systems, or **male behemoth/monster** now residing within the subterranean caverns of this planet.

Leviathan, defines a **female** monster, being nothing less than a baby factory seeded by mankind. Leviathan may be augmenting their own species by self procreation, yet the Grays are also utilizing their female role by producing crossbred hybrids between themselves and mankind.

Seemingly, this hybridization program is aimed at allowing the Grays to biologically become surface bound upon this world. This might explain why many of the occupants of these mysterious UFOs appear to be of conflicting reptilian species, or a bizarre form of Gray creature possessing no reptilian characteristics at all.

The UFO enigma appears to reveal different genetic stages or dissimilar biological evolutions of the hybridization program between mankind and Leviathan. This might suggest that Leviathan/the Grays may have been a raw form of highly evolved reptiles or amphibious beings **before** the hybridization program began.

However, by constantly repeating the hybridizing techniques upon the next generation hybrid, the results would spawn a new generation hybrid to continue the endless genetic manipulation between man and Leviathan. In doing so they would ultimately create a highly evolved hybrid of Leviathan (the Grays) and mankind.

This hybridized creation may even surpass the genetic form and intellectual heights of mankind, thus physically allowing the grays the ability to covertly infiltrate the human race. Moreover, the created hybrid being intellectually superior and strategically placed could be utilized to beguile the masses of man. Control the kings, power and money, and you control the world.

Mankind Caught in the Middle

So where might mankind stand as an end result? In leaving the chapters of Isaiah and Jeremiah, it became evident that Yahweh turned his back on the nation of Israel due to their adoration of the other gods (fallen angels/demons). Yet, Yahweh's rejection of his own people did not come without dire consequences against the nation of Israel.

Yahweh deliberately allowed **Babylon**, "the den of the **dragon**" (fallen angels), an open door to take control of his chosen people. Yahweh not only permitted the incursion, but may have helped to instigate it as a form of chastisement against Israel.

The Babylonian onslaught not only ended Israel's territorial reign in the region, but also heralded Yahweh and his troops' departure from this planet. That departure found the nation of Israel hopelessly waiting for the hidden face of Yahweh to return to this world to bring about Israel's vowed reinstatement.

39:23 And the heathen shall know that the house of Israel went into captivity for their iniquity: because they trespassed against me, therefore hid I my face from them, and gave them into the hand of their enemies: so fell they all by the sword.
EZEKIEL
30:18 And therefore will the LORD wait, that he may be gracious unto you, and therefore will he be exalted, that he may have mercy upon you: for the LORD [is] a God of judgment: blessed [are] all they that wait for him.
8:17 And I will wait upon the LORD, that hideth his face from the house of Jacob, and I will look for him.
ISAIAH

However, Yahweh's earthly departure did not come without a horrifying promise of physical retaliation against **all** the nations under the other gods/fallen angels control. This would beg the question as to how a threat of such horrendous proportions could be carried out upon nations of an ancient bygone era.

6:15 Were they ashamed when they had committed abomination? nay, they were not at all ashamed, neither could they blush: therefore they shall fall among them that fall: at the time [that] I visit them they shall be cast down, saith the LORD.
10:15 They [are] vanity, [and] the work of errors: in the time of their visitation they shall perish.
8:12…in the time of their visitation they shall be cast down, saith the LORD.
50:31 Behold, I [am] against thee, [O thou] most proud, saith the Lord GOD of hosts: for thy day is come, the time [that] I will visit thee.
23:12…for I will bring evil upon them, [even] the year of their visitation, saith the LORD.
JEREMIAH
10:3 And what will ye do in the day of visitation, and in the desolation [which] shall come from far? to whom will ye flee for help? and where will ye leave your glory? ISAIAH "The humble of the flock are those who watch for him they shall be saved at the time of the visitation" "and these are the precepts in which the master shall walk in his commerce with all the living until God shall visit the Earth" (The Damascus Rule) DEAD SEA SCROLLS

Yahweh's vowed visitation to this planet may in fact take aim at the very nations that he promised great vengeance towards. Yet, the nations in question are geographical locations that will never change even though their names and populations have (same location, different time). This futuristic visitation will catch the new populations of the world by complete surprise, a detrimental visitation that will **"come from far"**.

One has to **leave** to **revisit**, hence the word **far**. In essence, Yahweh and his troops left the planet and traveled to a **far** location within the known Universe with the promise of a return **visitation**. Yahweh and his troops will ultimately return to this world to fulfill that promised pledge, a day in which this entire planet will suddenly be awakened to the fact that Yahweh and his troops are not just invisible spirits or ghosts flapping around with invisible wings no one can see, but rather genuine physical entities. Moreover, this shocking reality will come in the horrifying form of incredible craft and powerful weapons of mass destruction to be unleashed upon the heads of the entire world.

> **30:24 The fierce anger of the LORD shall not return, until he have done [it], and until he have performed the intents of his heart: in the latter days ye shall consider it.** JEREMIAH

The entire world will be left with the terrifying assumption that the planet is being invaded by nothing less than aliens from outer space. The populations of the world will not realize that the planet is actually being **reclaimed** by its original creators who have returned at **the time of our Visitation** (the latter days) to harvest this entire world. This horrendous **judgment** will come in the form of many extraterrestrial craft/chariots **"troops"**, fire (laser technology) and massive global destruction beyond human comprehension.

> **96:13...for he cometh, for he cometh to judge the earth: he shall judge the world with righteousness, and the people with his truth.** PSALMS
>
> **3:16...when he cometh up unto the people, he will invade them with his troops.**
>
> HABAKKUK
>
> **1:14 And Enoch also, the seventh from Adam, prophesied of these, saying, Behold, the Lord cometh with ten thousands of his saints,**
>
> **1:15 To execute judgment upon all, and to convince all that are ungodly among them of all their ungodly deeds which they have ungodly commit-**

ted, and of all their hard [speeches] which ungodly sinners have spoken against him.

JUDE

13:5 They come from a far country, from the end of heaven, [even] the LORD, and the weapons of his indignation, to destroy the whole land.

13:6 Howl ye; for the day of the LORD [is] at hand; it shall come as a destruction from the Almighty.

13:7 Therefore shall all hands be faint, and every man's heart shall melt:

13:8 And they shall be afraid: pangs and sorrows shall take hold of them; they shall be in pain as a woman that travaileth: they shall be amazed one at another; their faces [shall be as] flames.

13:9 Behold, the day of the LORD cometh, cruel both with wrath and fierce anger, to lay the land desolate: and he shall destroy the sinners thereof out of it.

13:13 Therefore I will shake the heavens, and the earth shall remove out of her place, in the wrath of the LORD of hosts, and in the day of his fierce anger.

13:10 For the stars of heaven and the constellations thereof shall not give their light: the sun shall be darkened in his going forth, and the moon shall not cause her light to shine.

13:11 And I will punish the world for [their] evil, and the wicked for their iniquity; and I will cause the arrogancy of the proud to cease, and will lay low the haughtiness of the terrible. 50:3 Our God shall come, and shall not keep silence: a fire shall devour before him, and it shall be very tempestuous round about him.

29:6 Thou shalt be visited of the LORD of hosts with thunder, and with earthquake, and great noise, with storm and tempest, and the flame of devouring fire.

ISAIAH

97:3 A fire goeth before him, and burneth up his enemies round about.

PSALMS

64:2 As [when] the melting fire burneth, the fire causeth the waters to boil, to make thy name known to thine adversaries, [that] the nations may tremble at thy presence!

66:15 For, behold, the LORD will come with fire, and with his chariots like a whirlwind, to render his anger with fury, and his rebuke with flames of fire.

66:16 For by fire and by his sword will the LORD plead with all flesh: and the slain of the LORD shall be many.
ISAIAH

Here again, we have confirmation of the location of heaven. It's commonly believed that heaven is an invisible paradise located in an unseen realm where only disembodied souls reside. However, nothing could be further from the truth, as the verses express.

Yahweh and his **palpable troops** will come from a "far country" a location, land or kingdom, found in heaven (the Universe), a heaven that possesses stars and constellations, **"the stars of heaven and the constellations thereof"**. In essence, **heaven** is actually **outer space** (the Universe).

The Universe/Heaven contains many worlds and vast numbers of people (**troops**) and craft (whirlwind/cloud chariots). Yahweh and his troops will return to this planet with legions of craft and "**weapons**" of mass destruction to be used against this world and its unsuspecting populations. As we have already discovered, Yahweh's weapons of fire ("flame of devouring fire) are highly advanced lasers capable of inflicting incredible destructive power, including causing the waters of the world to boil.

This would leave only the imagination to surmise the horrendous firepower and destruction that will be inflicted upon the cities and forest lands of this planet. That worldwide destruction will fill the atmosphere of the planet with so much smoke, soot and ash from the burning cities and forest lands, that no one will be unable to see the Sun, Moon or stars.

This global display of laser technology is but a small part of Yahweh's vowed earthly destruction, considering the inconceivable power of their matter maneuvering devices. The smaller craft possess astonishing matter manipulating force. Yet, what about the enormous parent ships possessing the same matter maneuvering weaponry of massive dimensions and power? Obviously, a titanic mother ship harnessing the same incredible matter maneuvering powers could literally alter this entire planet's rotation or orbit around the Sun ("**and the earth shall remove out of her place**"). In fact, this earth altering detail will help us to unravel the cryptic **666** found within the Revelation.

Their extraterrestrial visitation will catastrophically bring mankind to its knees, as well as the hidden opposition (fallen angels) that perpetuated mankind's evil. The fallen angels will not only pay the price for their disloyalty and evil towards the kingdom of heaven and mankind, but literally help

Yahweh to inflict horrendous destruction upon mankind as a part of their vowed judgment yet to come.

The great day of Judgment (The Revelation/The Time of Our Visitation) heralds the release of the fallen angels from their underworld prison. Their liberation will allow them and their demonic partners to surface upon the unwitting populations of the world. The fallen angels will utilize their awesome craft and weapons to not only try and destroy mankind, but Yahweh and his host as well.

> 1:6 And the angels which kept not their first estate, but left their own habitation, he hath reserved in everlasting chains under darkness unto the judgment of the great day. JUDE
>
> 24:21 And it shall come to pass in that day, [that] the LORD shall punish the host of the high ones [that are] on high, and the kings of the earth upon the earth.
>
> 27:1 In that day the LORD with his sore and great and strong sword shall punish leviathan the piercing serpent, even leviathan that crooked serpent; and he shall slay the dragon that [is] in the sea.
>
> ISAIAH
>
> During all those years Satan shall be unleashed against Israel as He spoke by the hand of Isaiah, son of Amoz, saying, Terror and the pit and the snare are upon you, O inhabitant of the land...
>
> ...They shall be visited for destruction by the hand of Satan. That shall be the day when God will visit. THE DAMASCUS RULE THE DEAD SEA SCROLLS
>
> 34:8 For [it is] the day of the LORD's vengeance, [and] the year of recompenses for the controversy of Zion.
>
> 31:4...[he] will not be afraid of their voice, nor abase himself for the noise of them: so shall the LORD of hosts come down to fight for mount Zion, and for the hill thereof.
>
> 31:5 As birds flying, so will the LORD of hosts defend Jerusalem; defending also he will deliver [it; and] passing over he will preserve it.
>
> ISAIAH
>
> 47:2 For the LORD most high [is] terrible; [he is] a great King over all the earth.
>
> 47:3 He shall subdue the people under us, and the nations under our feet.
>
> PSALMS

Isaiah 24:21 establishes the castigation of two completely dissimilar populations. This obvious difference is confirmed by the word "**and**". Obviously, the kings **upon** the earth are **not** the host of the high ones. In fact, the verse would suggest that the host of the high ones control the kings of the earth, both of which are to be punished. The fallen angels (host of the high ones) will not only take control of the planet, but the kings (mankind) dwelling "upon" the earth.

The Cosmic Controversy

Once released, the fallen angels will strike back at Yahweh and the kingdom of heaven by inflicting horrifying atrocities against Yahweh's chosen people. The fallen angels will not only target the Jewish world, but utilize the city of Jerusalem to operate from, and bolster their incursion on the surface of the planet.("the controversy of Zion")

This global incursion will ultimately force the nations of the world (ten nations/**kings of the earth**) to comply with the fallen angels' doctrines or perish. The fallen angels' invasion will transform the holy city of Jerusalem into a **New Babylon**, ("den of Dragons") being the ultimate **"abomination of desolation"** to Yahweh.

Yahweh, Jesus and their troops will physically fight for **Zion** (Jerusalem), defending the holy city at all costs. "**As birds flying**", Yahweh and his troops will use their extraordinary craft to fly over the holy city of Jerusalem and employ their power weapons to defend the holy city.

It's extremely important that the reader **remembers** this feathered analogy of the craft of the kingdom of heaven ("**as birds fly**"), seeing how it will help us to comprehend the highly symbolic chapters of the Revelation.

Isaiah 31:4 validates what appears to be **two** completely dissimilar locations in reference to the holy city of Jerusalem (**Zion**): "<u>come down</u> to **fight** for mount **Zion**, <u>and</u> the <u>hill</u> thereof". Mount Zion has long been referred to as the Holy City of Jerusalem, but what about the **hill thereof?**

The **hill** of Zion lies in the southeastern district of what is now described as the Old City of Jerusalem. This mountainous site is where King David built his palace, or "city of David", a fortified location or hill that rises some 2440 feet high as it looks out over the modern city of Jerusalem.

During the Christian era it was believed that the hill of Zion was a ridge lying about half a mile to the west. In either case, the hill of Zion depicts a towering fortified location within the boundaries of Jerusalem (Zion). Hence we have the city of Jerusalem (Zion), and the fortified hill thereof. Here again, it's **important** for the reader to **remember** that there is a significant difference between the two.

Entering the Revelation, we will discover that this dissimilarity will establish two separate locations from which the final battle between the kingdom of heaven and the fallen angels will take place, thus "the controversy of Zion" and the hill thereof. Essentially, the fallen angels will take control of Jerusalem, but not the hill thereof (Mt. Zion), hence the controversy.

Yahweh and his troops will set up their base of operation on **top** of the defensible **hill** of Zion, boldly establishing the kingdom of heaven and its troops right in the middle of the den of dragons (fallen angels).

This base of operations will appropriately be under the command of **Jesus** (the Son of **David**), once again authenticating the hill of Zion as the city of David prepared to defending the holy city of Jerusalem from the fallen angels/other gods and the ten nations under their control.

The Fallen Angels Wreak Havoc Upon the World

This horrendous battle will ultimately lead to the final destruction of the fallen angels, the ten beguiled nations, as well as the fallen angels' entire **underworld** base of operations ("subdue the people under us, and the nations **under our feet**"). However, this is not before the fallen angels have had ample time to inflict massive global destruction upon the surface of this world and most of mankind.

> **7:2 Daniel spake and said, I saw in my vision by night, and, behold, the four winds of the heaven strove upon the great sea.**
>
> **7:3 And four great beasts came up from the sea, diverse one from another.**
>
> **7:4 The first [was] like a lion, and had eagle's wings: I beheld till the wings thereof were plucked, and it was lifted up from the earth, and made stand upon the feet as a man, and a man's heart was given to it.**
>
> **7:5 And behold another beast, a second, like to a bear, and it raised up itself on one side, and [it had] three ribs in the mouth of it between the teeth of it: and they said thus unto it, Arise, devour much flesh.**
>
> **7:6 After this I beheld, and lo another, like a leopard, which had upon the back of it four wings of a fowl; the beast had also four heads; and dominion was given to it.**

7:7 After this I saw in the night visions, and behold a fourth beast, dreadful and terrible, and strong exceedingly; and it had great iron teeth: it devoured and brake in pieces, and stamped the residue with the feet of it: and it [was] diverse from all the beasts that [were] before it; and it had ten horns.

DANIEL

Many Biblical scholars or theologians would have us believe that these four animals/beasts depict the ancient Chaldean Empire, the Median Empire, the Persian Empire and the Macedonian Empire. It has also been proposed that these same **four** beasts may represent a revived Roman Empire, or various nations that will ultimately clash together as major war factors on the surface of this planet in our future.

However, these four animals have nothing to do with what is established on the surface of this planet, but rather what is concealed **inside** the planet. As we have already discovered, most of this concealed Underworld and its fallen angel residence lies hidden beneath the rivers, lakes, oceans and sea floors of this planet around major **fault line** locations.

The aquatic origin of these four beasts actually identifies their underworld affiliation, seeing how they "**came up from the sea**", or in simpler terms, up from the Underworld. Notably, all **four** beasts are working together as a team to form a massive war machine. Yet, why were these **four** war machines given the symbolic title of **four** different beasts?

The holy numbers **twelve** and **seven** actually assists us in identifying who and what these **four** assorted animals depict. In the beginning, Yahweh and his celestial host maintained control over **twelve** different constellations within the Universe.

This federation of constellations or star systems existed before the rebellious insurrection by Satan and the **third of the star** systems that chose to follow him. It was this **third** of the star systems and their defiant inhabitancy that elected to take part in a massive war campaign against the remaining **seven** star systems.

12:3 And there appeared another wonder in heaven; and behold a great red dragon, having seven heads and ten horns, and seven crowns upon his heads.

12:4 And his tail drew the third part of the stars of heaven, and did cast them to the earth:...

12:7 <u>And there was war in heaven</u>: Michael and his angels fought against the dragon; and the dragon fought and his angels,
12:8 And prevailed not; neither was their place found any more in heaven.
12:9 And the great dragon was cast out, that old serpent, called the Devil, and Satan, which deceiveth the whole world: he was cast out <u>into the earth</u>, and his angels were cast out with him. REVELATION

Here again, we have confirmation to the location of "heaven". Clearly, outer space or the Universe is were one would find "**the stars**", hence "the stars of heaven"/the Universe. However, the solution we seek can only be found in the "**tail**" of the dragon.

It was the "**tail**" of the Dragon that drew a **third** of the stars (constellations) of heaven (outer space/the Universe). Obviously, the Dragon was located in outer space if it was to prevail upon a third of the inhabited star systems to rebel against Yahweh and the remaining **seven** populated constellations.

If you will observe the given charts of the Universe, you will discover that in the Northern Celestial pole lies the constellation Draco, the **Dragon.** This enormous Dragon (Draco) constellation flaunts a **tail** establishing the location of the inhabited star systems that instigated the universal war campaign against Yahweh and his stellar troops. Under the tail of the Dragon, you will discover **two** of the constellations that the **tail** of the Dragon "drew" to rebel against Yahweh. Ursa Major/Minor (the **Bear**), Leo (the **Lion/Ra**). This would leave only the **leopard** yet to be accounted for in identifying the four beasts that come rising up out of the sea.

However, we have already identified the Leopard. The leopard represents the constellation of Orion, which identifies the Egyptian underworld god Osiris. The leopard is the symbolic embodiment of Osiris, god of the **Underworld**, the third animal/beast.

The **four** beasts that come rising up out of the sea identify four constellations found within the Universe. Together, the four constellations symbolically depict the home star systems of the fallen angels. All four constellations represent the third of the stars that chose to rebel against Yahweh and his celestial troops. However, where is the twelfth constellation?

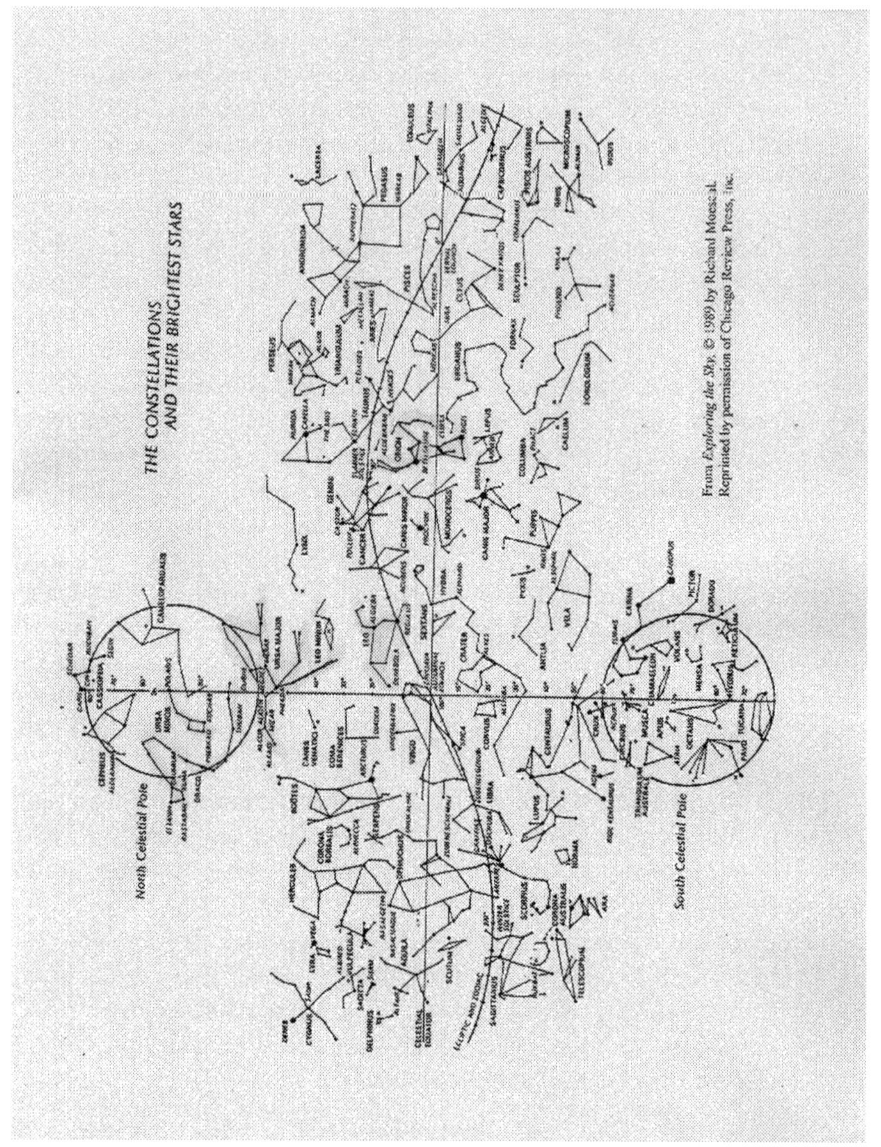

From *Exploring the Sky*, © 1989 by Richard Moeschl.
Reprinted by permission of Chicago Review Press, Inc.

THE CONSTELLATIONS IN OUTLINE

From *Exploring the Sky.* © 1989 by Richard Moeschl.
Reprinted by permission of Chicago Review Press, Inc.

If in fact Yahweh controlled **twelve** constellations **before** the stellar revolt began, we have a missing constellation. A **third** of twelve is only **four**. Yet, seven and four don't add up to twelve. This cosmic puzzle is not as difficult as one might think, considering **we** are the missing twelfth constellation.

By adding the four known constellations (third of the stars) that revolted against Yahweh with the seven (unknown) constellations that did not, we end up with a total of eleven constellations. When we add the constellation Sagittarius, which contains our own Milky Way Galaxy, we end up with a total of twelve constellations.

Seemingly, each of the constellations is governed by a specific leader or dignitary responsible for that individual constellation under Yahweh's leadership. Essentially, the third of the stars which represent the four constellations and animals/beasts, also depict four leaders who were responsible for those constellations and their residence.

> **7:17 <u>These great beasts</u>, which are <u>four, [are] four kings</u>, [which] shall <u>arise out of the earth</u>.**
>
> **7:18 But the saints of the most High shall take the kingdom, and possess the kingdom for ever, even for ever and ever.**
>
> **7:19 Then I would know the truth of the fourth beast, which was diverse from all the others, exceeding dreadful, whose teeth [were of] iron, and his nails [of] brass; [which] devoured, brake in pieces, and stamped <u>the residue</u> with his feet;**
>
> DANIEL

Obviously, the fallen angels will not show up bearing gifts. In fact, Yahweh, Jesus and their universal troops will have to mount a major campaign against these four fallen angel leaders and their underworld hordes.

The verses do not conceal the location from whence these four underworld leaders/kings will originate from ("arise **out** of the Earth"). All four leaders will ascend up from the Underworld/the Sea. Each of the four leaders with their different campaign strategies will work together to form a massive war machine capable of taking control of the surface of this planet.

Yet, it will be the <u>fourth</u> fallen angel leader (the Dragon) that will "**stamp the residue**" thereof. In essence, the leader of the constellation Draco/Dragon (Satan) will come in behind the other three beasts and destroy what is left from the destruction of the first three.

The Bear, or fallen angel leader of the constellation Ursa Minor/Major, appears to be the major killing force behind the future extermination of mankind. This lethal detail is easily identified by the **three** symbolic ribs found within the mouth of the bear. In fact, this same allegorical depiction of the destruction of a **third** of mankind can be found in the Revelation.

> **9:14 Saying to the sixth angel which had the trumpet, Loose the four angels which are bound in the great river Euphrates.**
> **9:15 And the four angels were loosed, which were prepared for an hour, and a day, and a month, and a year, for to slay the third part of men.**
> **9:16 And the number of the army of the horsemen [were] two hundred thousand thousand: and I heard the number of them.**
> **9:17 And thus I saw the horses in the vision, and them that sat on them, having breastplates of fire, and of jacinth, and brimstone: and the heads of the horses [were] as the heads of lions; and out of their mouths issued fire and smoke and brimstone.**
> **9:18 By these three was the third part of men killed, by the fire, and by the smoke, and by the brimstone, which issued out of their mouths.**
> **9:19 For their power is in their mouth, and in their tails: for their tails [were] like unto serpents, and had heads, and with them they do hurt.**
>
> REVELATION

Obviously, these four angels were earthly incarcerated, thus justifying the words "loose", "bound", and the sixth angel that **released** the "**four** angels" from their underworld prison. Note that the four angels were bound and loosed from within the river Euphrates, indicating **down inside** the river itself. The river Euphrates runs through what was known as Mesopotamia or Samaria, as well as what was commonly known as the Babylonian Empire (den of Dragons) **after** the flood of Noah.

The verses indicate that during the Revelation the total release of the fallen angels will occur at the river Euphrates. But why this location? The Euphrates river crosses a major **fault line** (Underworld Gateway) in Iraq. Moreover, this fault line location is teeming with underground activity (See seismographic and fault line maps).

Quite naturally, this would compel one to think twice when assuming that this underground activity is all volcanic in nature. It's quite possible that some of this underground activity is being created by a fallen angel industrial power house, right under our very noses. This buried Mecca of technology is **"preparing"** itself for the day it will be unleashed upon the surface of this world, an oblivious world unable to combat such awesome technology.

The verses are quite specific when establishing the fact that these **four** angels will be "**prepared**" right down to the very month, day and hour to inflict massive global destruction upon their release. Obviously, this underworld empire is well aware of the time frame for them to be released. The very word "**prepared**" would suggest that the fallen angels are currently engaged in mass production of high tech craft, weapons and technological devices in preparation of their contracted release.

This binding agreement will abruptly terminate at the bloodstained expense of a third of mankind, as these underworld hordes forcibly implement their **prepared** plan of action to gain control of the surface of this world. Yet, their technology would be nothing without personnel.

As the verses so amply articulate, this underworld empire will lead a charge of ascending armies two hundred million strong. This inconceivable figure will be equipped with craft and weapons of unthinkable destruction that mankind will be helpless to challenge.

It doesn't take a brain surgeon to realize that horses do not breathe fire out of their head, much less their tail. These symbolic verses are depicting an immense underworld army that commands astonishing flying machines mounted with laser weapons of unbelievable destruction.

These smaller craft are but a trivial drop in the bucket when compared to the enormous craft that may be hidden within the subterranean caverns of this world. Their primary craft may be of such enormous size and power, that one or two of these massive machines would be fully capable of obliterating this entire world and all its populations in just weeks of time.

The Beast of the Revelation

If you will reexamine verses 9:14-19 of the Revelation, you will discover a significant inconsistency in the verses. The verses inform us that **four** fallen angel leaders were released to slay a third part of mankind. The verses then turn right around and state that "by these **three** was the third part of men killed." So what happened to the **fourth** angel?

If you have been studiously observing the verses of Daniel and the Revelation, you should have discovered the same inconsistency found within both books. Clearly, the first three beasts are different from the fourth beast. It was this forth beast that stamped the residue of the other three beasts.

Obviously, all four beasts are working together as a militant team. Yet, the forth beast appears to be the primary power source and leader.

> **7:19 Then I would know the truth of the fourth beast, which was diverse from all the others, exceeding dreadful, whose teeth [were of] iron, and his nails [of] brass; [which] devoured, brake in pieces, and stamped the residue with his feet; DANIEL**
>
> **13:1 And I stood upon the sand of the sea, and saw a beast rise up out of the sea, having seven heads and ten horns, and upon his horns ten crowns, and upon his heads the name of blasphemy.**
>
> **13:2 And the beast which I saw was like unto a leopard, and his feet were as [the feet] of a bear, and his mouth as the mouth of a lion: and the dragon gave him his power, and his seat, and great authority.**
>
> **13:3 And I saw one of his heads as it were wounded to death; and his deadly wound was healed: and all the world wondered after the beast.**
>
> **13:4 And they worshipped the dragon which gave power unto the beast: and they worshipped the beast, saying, Who [is] like unto the beast? who is able to make war with him?**
>
> **REVELATION**

In closely examining the previous verses of the Revelation, **four** angels (fallen angels) came up out of the river Euphrates. These verses also clarified that only **three** of these angels (beasts) were involved in the initial destruction of one third of mankind with their smaller craft. The fourth angel left the other three angels and departed to an undisclosed location to accomplish some unknown task, while the other three angels were busy engaging mankind.

We can only speculate as to what happened to the forth angel, until we search chapter 13 of the book of Revelations. Chapter 13 reveals the same forth beast found in chapter seven of the book of Daniel. These verses actually assist us in resolving the issue as to **where** the forth beast went and **why**.

Evidently, the forth fallen angel leader left the other three and went to a undisclosed location to retrieve something that would not only help the other three angels complete their combined takeover of the surface, but surpass the powers of all three angels put together. In fact, the verses provide us with the location of where the forth angel went, as well as what the forth angel recovered. That location is identified as the sea (the Underworld) in which the forth angel came rising up out of.

In examining both verses of Daniel and the Revelation, we discover the unknown power that the forth angel went to retrieve from below the sea (Underworld). In the book of Daniel, that power is symbolically described as "great iron teeth" and "nails of brass". Yet, it is the book of Revelation that reveals where those iron teeth and nails of brass are kept. Obviously, this iron and brass object identifies the **seven heads** of the dragon in which its iron teeth and brass nails reside.

The Seven Head's of the Beast

It will be the **seven heads** of "the dragon that will give power to the beast." Obviously, the seven **heads** are powerful objects that will be utilized to help the combined armies of the four fallen angels.

Quite naturally, one would assume that the word "**heads**" symbolically translates into the four powerful fallen angel leaders. However, this may not be the case, considering these seven heads are referred to as powerful objects comprised of iron and brass, or metal/mechanical devices. Moreover, these metal objects were literally broken and wounded at one time.

> **74:13 Thou didst divide the sea by thy strength: thou brakest the heads of the dragons in the waters. PSALMS**
>
> **51:9 Awake, awake, put on strength, O arm of the LORD; awake, as in the ancient days, in the generations of old. [Art] thou not it that hath cut Rahab, [and] wounded the dragon?**
>
> **ISAIAH**

One would think that the seven leaders (heads) of the fallen angels were psychologically crippled, or inflicted with physical head injuries that ended their ability to lead their rebellious armies. Or do the verses conceal a more substantial event that took place during the "**generations of old**", "**the ancient days?**"

Evidently, the verses are a direct confirmation of the battle of the third of the stars that choose to rebel against Yahweh in "the ancient days." That horrendous battle ultimately broke and wounded the seven **heads** of the dragon. If so, what were these seven iron heads that were broken and wounded?

The only way to truly resolve this mystery is to travel back in Scripture to the ("generations of old" "the ancient days") a time when the fallen angels intervened upon this lunar creation. This was a time in which Enoch appears to be our only source of knowledge to explain this ancient puzzle.

Enoch being the grandfather of Noah, resided on the planet **before** the inundation of Noah occurred. Enoch was also involved in relaying to the fallen angels their ensuing punishment due to their ruination of the lunar creation and its created inhabitancy. Moreover, Enoch was shown the **underworld** location in which the fallen angels were first incarcerated, as well as the **seven wounded heads** of the dragon that were imprisoned with them.

> **1. Then I made a circuit to a place in which nothing was completed.**
>
> **2. And there I beheld neither the tremendous workmanship of an exalted heaven, nor of an established earth, but a desolate spot, prepared, and terrific.**
>
> **3. There, too, I beheld seven stars of heaven bound in it together, like great mountains, and like a blazing fire. I exclaimed, for what species of crime have they been bound, and why have they been removed to this place? Then Uriel, one of the holly angles who was with me, and who conducted me, answered: Enoch, wherefore dost thou ask; wherefore reason with thyself, and anxiously inquire? These are those of the stars which have transgressed the commandment of the most high God; and are here bound, until the infinite number of the days of their crimes be completed.**
>
> CHAP. XXI BOOK OF ENOCH

Let's first establish the fact that Enoch was not located on the surface of this planet. This detail can be easily confirmed by the fact that Enoch was **not** able to see the "established earth" or surface of the planet. In fact, Enoch can't even see the sky (heaven) or atmosphere of the planet.

Yet, as mentioned before, Enoch is now in the same location where the fallen angels were imprisoned. Enoch was located in the underworld regions of this planet, thus resolving why he was unable to physically see the surface of the planet.

This desolate underworld terrain was obviously perpetuated by its innerworld geothermal ramifications and lack of direct sunlight (hidden wilderness). Moreover, this "prepared" and terrific location appears to have been fabricated to be the underworld prison for the fallen angels.

One would think that the verses have contradicted themselves, seeing how Enoch informs us that he was unable to see the exalted heaven and its vast workmanship, yet, he could see seven stars of heaven. However, there is no contradiction, seeing how these seven stars are not of the planetary variety when gazing up into the heavens (the Universe).

The verses are quite explicit in deciphering just what these seven glowing ("blazing") stars of heaven are. These seven stars are so close that Enoch can actually define their shape, and glowing attributes. Moreover, these seven stars have actually been imprisoned (bound). How does one jail a star?

Clearly, these are not stars of the Universe (heaven), but rather the seven stars of the fallen angels, justifying their incarcerated/bound status. In essence, these seven stars are actually seven physical structures in the bodily shape of glowing mountains.

These huge mountainous structures are not stars, but rather **of** the stars "these are those **of** the stars which have **transgressed**". Essentially, these seven glowing mountainous structures originated from the stars, even though they are now imprisoned within the underworld domains of this planet.

If true, Enoch was observing seven surviving mountainous starships from the star systems or constellations that chose to rebel against Yahweh. These seven mountainous starships were imprisoned inside this planet along with their rebellious crews. Each of the seven starships not only appears to be in the bodily shape of a mountain, but may be just as large. This would suggest that each of the seven mountainous craft could span three to five miles across and reach a towering summit one, to two miles high (or more).

In essence, what we have just analyzed may in fact be the **seven heads** (mountainous craft) of the dragon. These mountainous craft were bound inside the underworld domains of this planet "**until** the infinite number of the days of their crimes be completed."(The Revelation/the time of our visitation). At that time they will be released to come rising up out of the sea.

If true, we now know what happened to the forth angel that left the other three angels. The forth angel proceeded to the sea, (gateway to the underworld) where the seven mountainous heads (starships) were being kept (bound). The forth angel (Satan) made ready the seven massive craft (seven heads) and came rising up out of the sea to join forces with the other three angels, thus destroying the residue thereof

This terrorizing ambush has been "**prepared**" for from the very moment that the seven heads (starships) of the dragon were broken and wounded. Put simply, the seven heads of the dragon, being the seven mountainous starships, were damaged during the stellar insurrection of the third of the star systems against Yahweh. Yahweh bounded the damaged mountainous craft inside the underworld along with the revolting fallen angels, thus allowing them refuge while imprisoned within the underworld.

This extended imprisonment allowed the fallen angels time to "**prepare**" for the day that they would be unleashed upon mankind. This would resolve Enoch's verse informing us that he was taken to a location were "**nothing was completed**" as if major construction was taking place, yet not finished.

That major construction may in fact be the fallen angels preparing themselves for the day they will be released from their underworld incarceration. That preparation entails the reconstruction of their **seven** mountainous starships (**heads**) that were broken or wounded in the celestial battle against Yahweh and his troops.

When the seven mountainous craft are released, they will be fully functional and no one will be "able to make war with him." [Satan the Dragon]. This might explaining the "brass nails." Where are nails located? "The **Hand**."

These seven mountainous craft may possess the same mechanical/brass **hand** shape devices as Yahweh's craft. If so, these seven massive craft possess the fire power (lasers) and matter maneuverability to destroy this entire planet in a matter of days, and mankind will be helpless to do anything about it.

The Last Hope for Mankind

One factor is certain, Yahweh will return to this planet with the horrifying intentions to exterminate most of the inhabitancy of this world. In fact, it would appear that Yahweh and his stellar forces will intentionally release the fallen angels as a method of weeding out the sinners of the world. This will place mankind in a perplexing situation of choosing a side between the fallen angels, or the kingdom of heaven. This might explain why Yahweh arranged a method for mankind to **save** itself from the horrifying castigation yet to come.

Yahweh's salvation objective will help a measure of mankind to make the right choice, thus sparing his eternal soul and physical immortal life yet to be established. Essentially, the salvation of humanity will come in the form of one placid man being the one physical element of power not expected by the fallen angels. The fallen angels will let down their guard and be open to a breach of <u>contract</u> that will ultimately end their worldly control over human kind.

That one subtle man is **Jesus**. This hidden thorn in the side of the fallen angels was not expected to inflict the downfall of an entire underworld empire, much less the salvation of mankind. Through Jesus, Yahweh's pledge will allow mankind to be forgiven of many of their worldly sins.

Jesus will allow the human race to atone (repent) for ignorantly following the dogma of the fallen angels. That atonement will **save** many who recognize and believe the true doctrines (requirements/gospel) of the kingdom of heaven, thus bestowing new meaning to the phraseology "**to be saved**". However, without a powerful but believable teacher to put forth the **requirements** of the kingdom of heaven, the mandatory words (**gospel**) would fall on deaf ears. Hence the promise of the teacher of salvation (**Jesus**) **before** the final days of judgment upon this world.

> 34:22 Therefore will I save my flock, and they shall no more be a prey; and I will judge between cattle and cattle.
>
> 34:23 And I will set up one shepherd over them, and he shall feed them, [even] my servant David; he shall feed them, and he shall be their shepherd.
>
> 34:24 And I the LORD will be their God, and my servant David a prince among them; I the LORD have spoken [it]. EZEKIEL
>
> 42:1 Behold my servant, whom I uphold; mine elect, [in whom] my soul delighteth; I have put my spirit upon him: he shall bring forth judgment to the Gentiles.
>
> 42:2 He shall not cry, nor lift up, nor cause his voice to be heard in the street.
>
> 42:3 A bruised reed shall he not break, and the smoking flax shall he not quench: he shall bring forth judgment unto truth.
>
> 42:4 He shall not fail nor be discouraged, till he have set judgment in the earth: and the isles shall wait for his law.
>
> 42:6 I the LORD have called thee in righteousness, and will hold thine hand, and will keep thee, and give thee for a covenant of the people, for a light of the Gentiles;
>
> 42:7 To open the blind eyes, to bring out the prisoners from the prison, [and] them that sit in darkness out of the prison house.
>
> 42:9 Behold, the former things are come to pass, and new things do I declare: before they spring forth I tell you of them.
>
> 42:16 And I will bring the blind by a way [that] they knew not; I will lead them in paths [that] they have not known: I will make darkness light before them, and crooked things straight. These things will I do unto them, and not forsake them.
>
> 42:18 Hear, ye deaf; and look, ye blind, that ye may see.

42:20 Seeing many things, but thou observest not; opening the ears, but he heareth not.

42:21 The LORD is well pleased for his righteousness' sake; he will magnify the law, and make [it] honorable.

42:23 Who among you will give ear to this? [who] will hearken and hear for the time to come?

43:7 [Even] every one that is called by my name: for I have created him for my glory, I have formed him; yea, I have made him.

43:8 Bring forth the blind people that have eyes, and the deaf that have ears.

43:9 Let all the nations be gathered together, and let the people be assembled: who among them can declare this, and show us former things? let them bring forth their witnesses, that they may be justified: or let them hear, and say, [It is] truth.

43:18 Remember ye not the former things, neither consider the things of old.

43:19 Behold, I will do a new thing; now it shall spring forth; shall ye not know it? I will even make a way in the wilderness, [and] rivers in the desert.

53:3 He is despised and rejected of men; a man of sorrows, and acquainted with grief: and we hid as it were [our] faces from him; he was despised, and we esteemed him not.

53:4 Surely he hath borne our griefs, and carried our sorrows: yet we did esteem him stricken, smitten of God, and afflicted.

53:5 But he [was] wounded for our transgressions, [he was] bruised for our iniquities: the chastisement of our peace [was] upon him; and with his stripes we are healed.

53:6 All we like sheep have gone astray; we have turned every one to his own way; and the LORD hath laid on him the iniquity of us all.

53:7 He was oppressed, and he was afflicted, yet he opened not his mouth: he is brought as a lamb to the slaughter, and as a sheep before her shearers is dumb, so he openeth not his mouth.

53:8 He was taken from prison and from judgment: and who shall declare his generation? for he was cut off out of the land of the living: for the transgression of my people was he stricken.

53:9 And he made his grave with the wicked, and with the rich in his death; because he had done no violence, neither [was any] deceit in his mouth.

53:10 Yet it pleased the LORD to bruise him; he hath put [him] to grief: when thou shalt make his soul an offering for sin, he shall see [his] seed, he shall prolong [his] days, and the pleasure of the LORD shall prosper in his hand.
53:11 He shall see of the travail of his soul, [and] shall be satisfied: by his knowledge shall my righteous servant justify many; for he shall bear their iniquities. ISAIAH